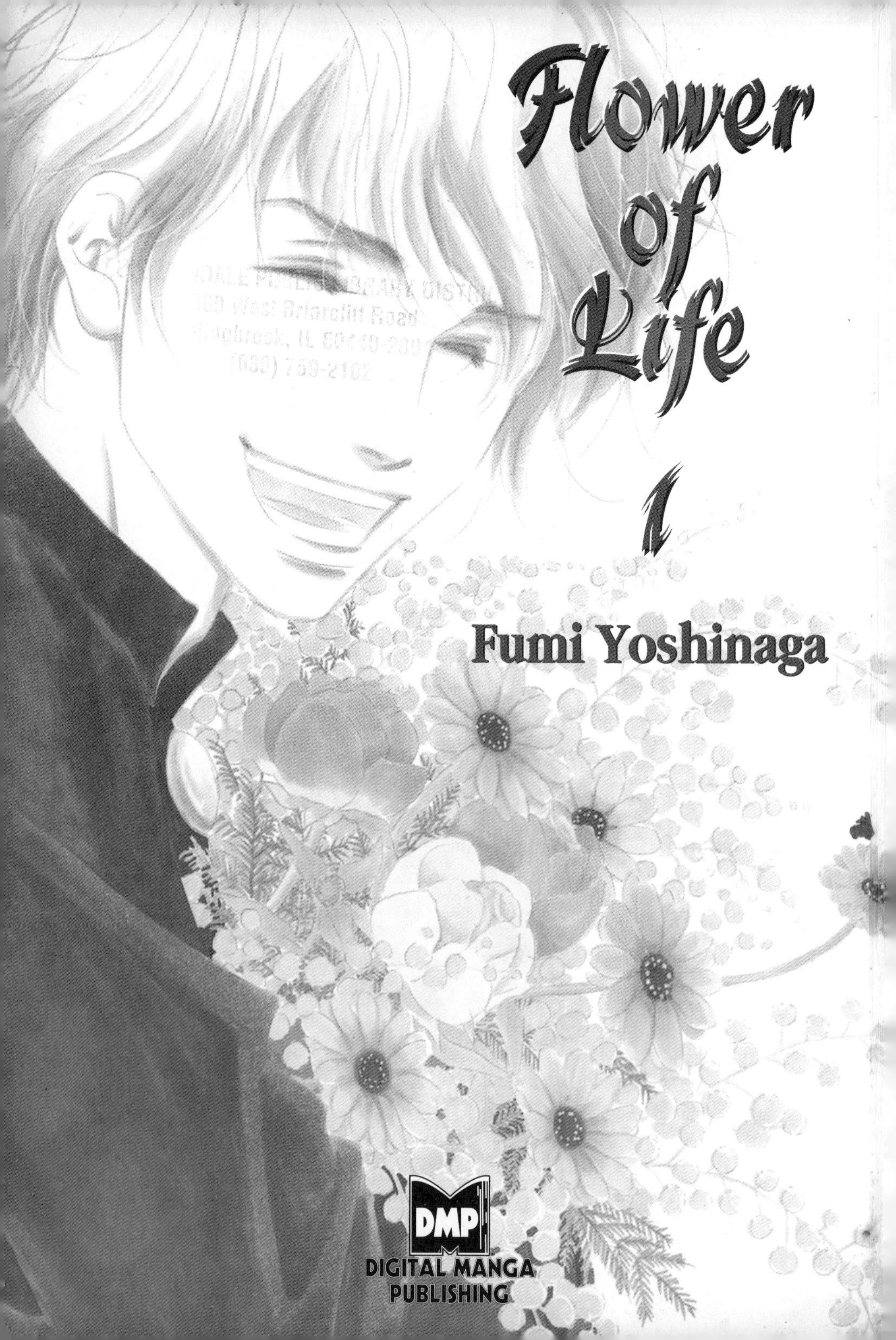
Flower of Life
1
Fumi Yoshinaga
DMP
DIGITAL MANGA PUBLISHING

Flower of Life

#1	003
#2	039
#3	071
#4	103
#5	139
Extra	171

Translation	**Sachiko Sato**
Lettering	**Replibooks**
Graphic Design/Layout	**Daryl Kuxhouse/Fred Lui**
Editing	**Daryl Kuxhouse**
Editor in Chief	**Fred Lui**
Publisher	**Hikaru Sasahara**

English Edition Published by
DIGITAL MANGA PUBLISHING
A division of DIGITAL MANGA, Inc.
1487 W 178th Street, Suite 300
Gardena, CA 90248

www.dmpbooks.com

First Edition: January 2007
ISBN-10: 1-56970-874-6
ISBN-13: 978-1-56970-874-3

1 3 5 7 9 10 8 6 4 2

Printed in China

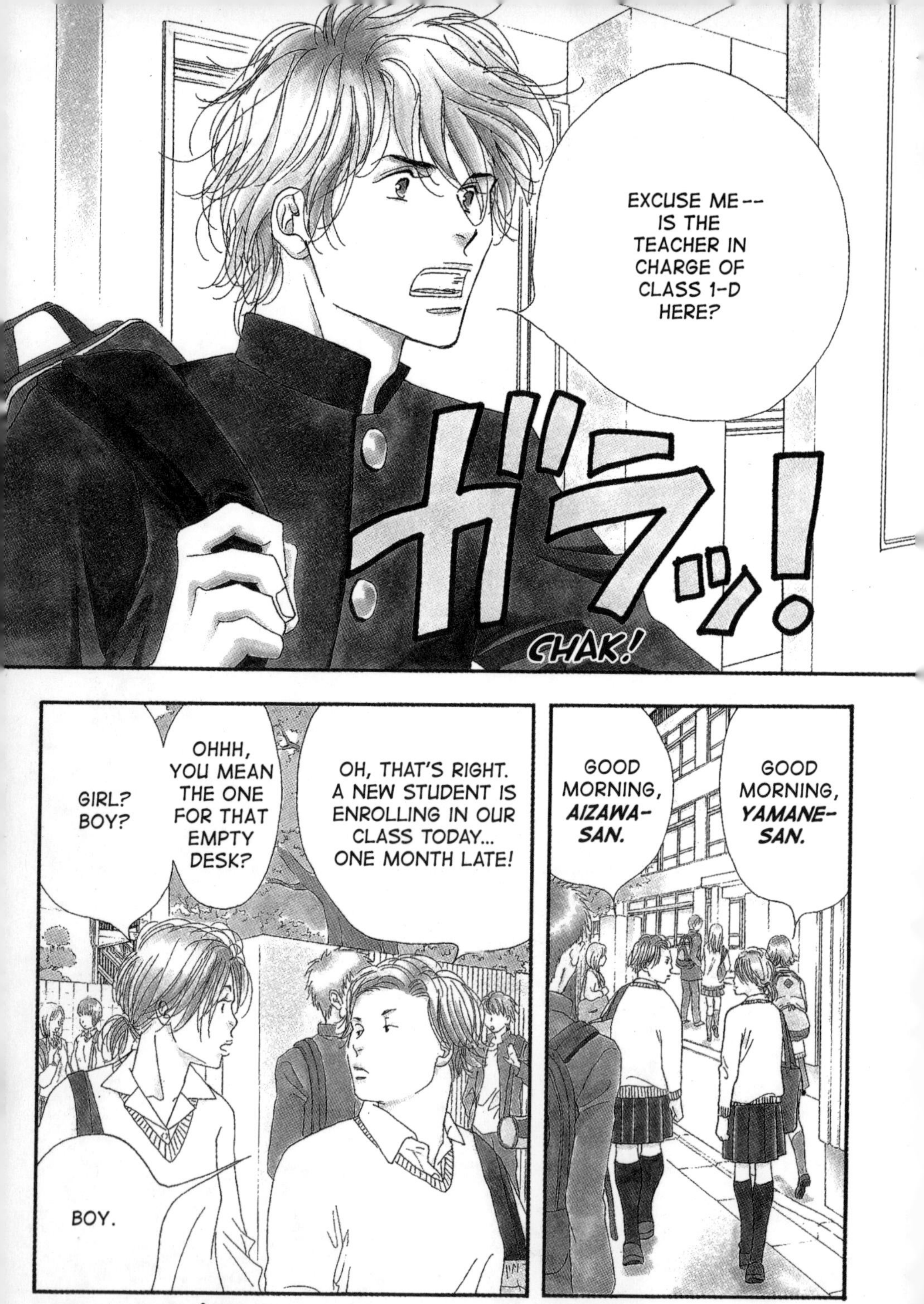
EXCUSE ME-- IS THE TEACHER IN CHARGE OF CLASS 1-D HERE?
ガラッ!
CHAK!
GOOD MORNING, **YAMANE-SAN.**
GOOD MORNING, **AIZAWA-SAN.**
OH, THAT'S RIGHT. A NEW STUDENT IS ENROLLING IN OUR CLASS TODAY... ONE MONTH LATE!
OHHH, YOU MEAN THE ONE FOR THAT EMPTY DESK?
GIRL? BOY?
BOY.

FLOWER OF LIFE ✻ #1

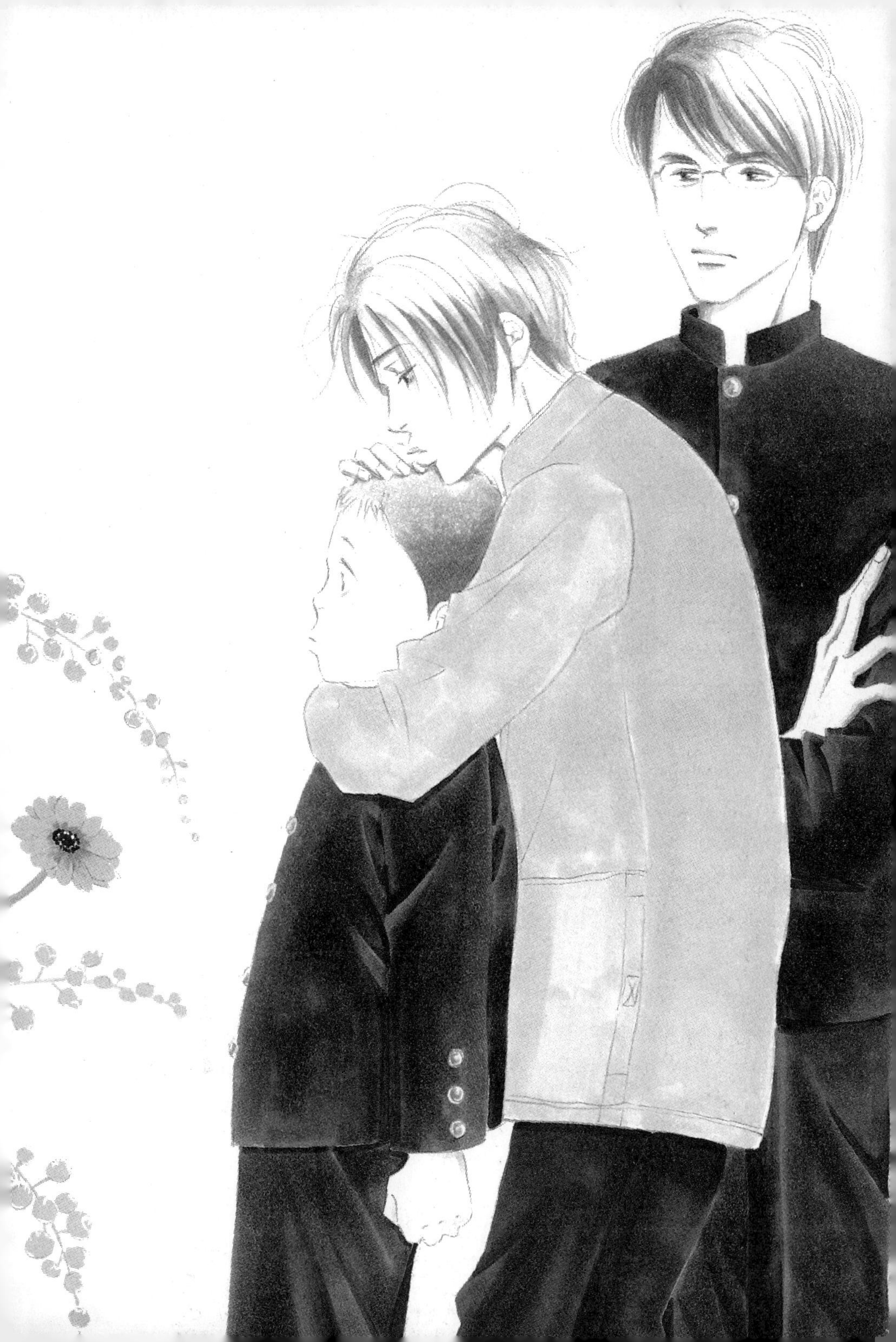

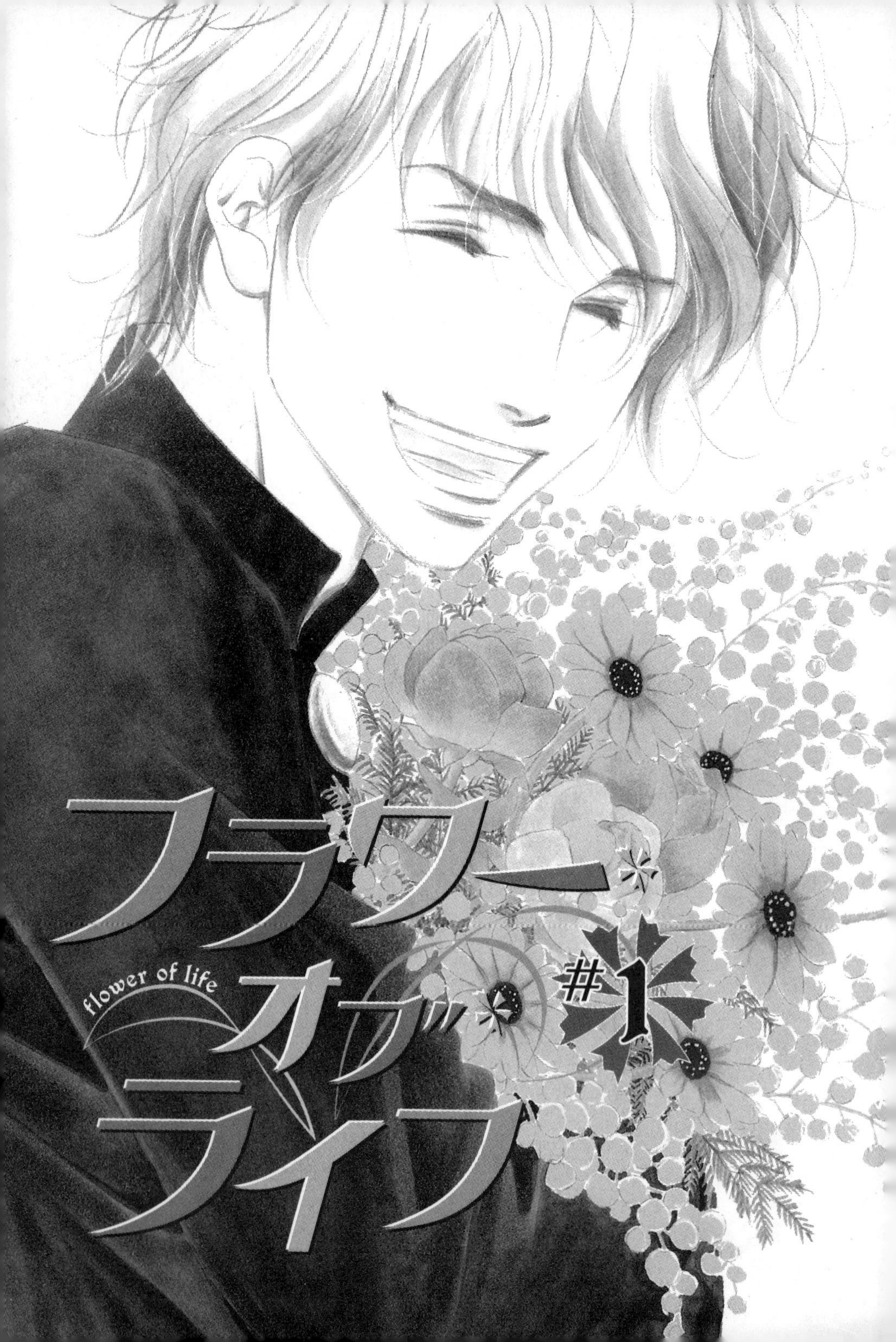
フラワー
オブ
ライフ
flower of life
#1

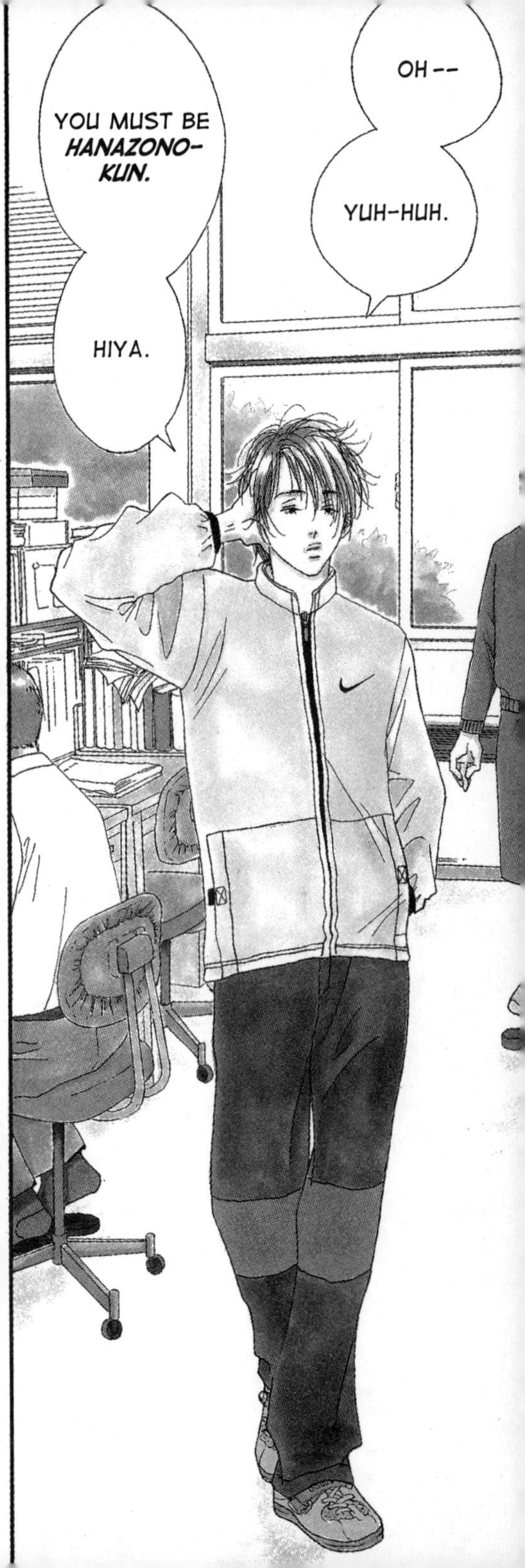
OH --
YUH-HUH.
YOU MUST BE ***HANAZONO-KUN.***
HIYA.

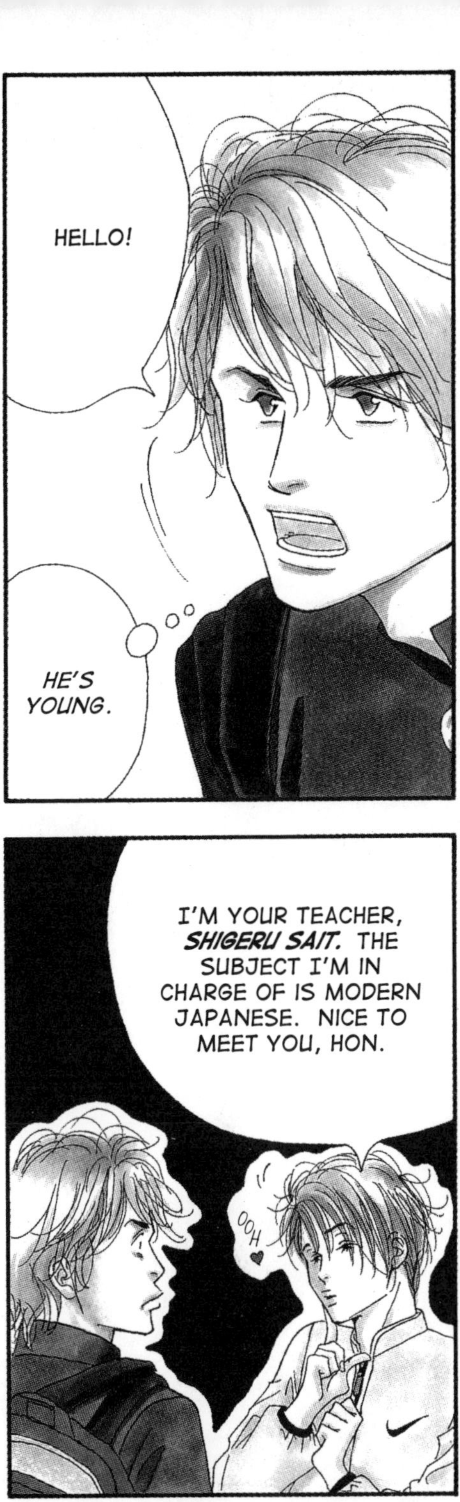
HELLO!
HE'S YOUNG.
I'M YOUR TEACHER, ***SHIGERU SAIT.*** THE SUBJECT I'M IN CHARGE OF IS MODERN JAPANESE. NICE TO MEET YOU, HON.

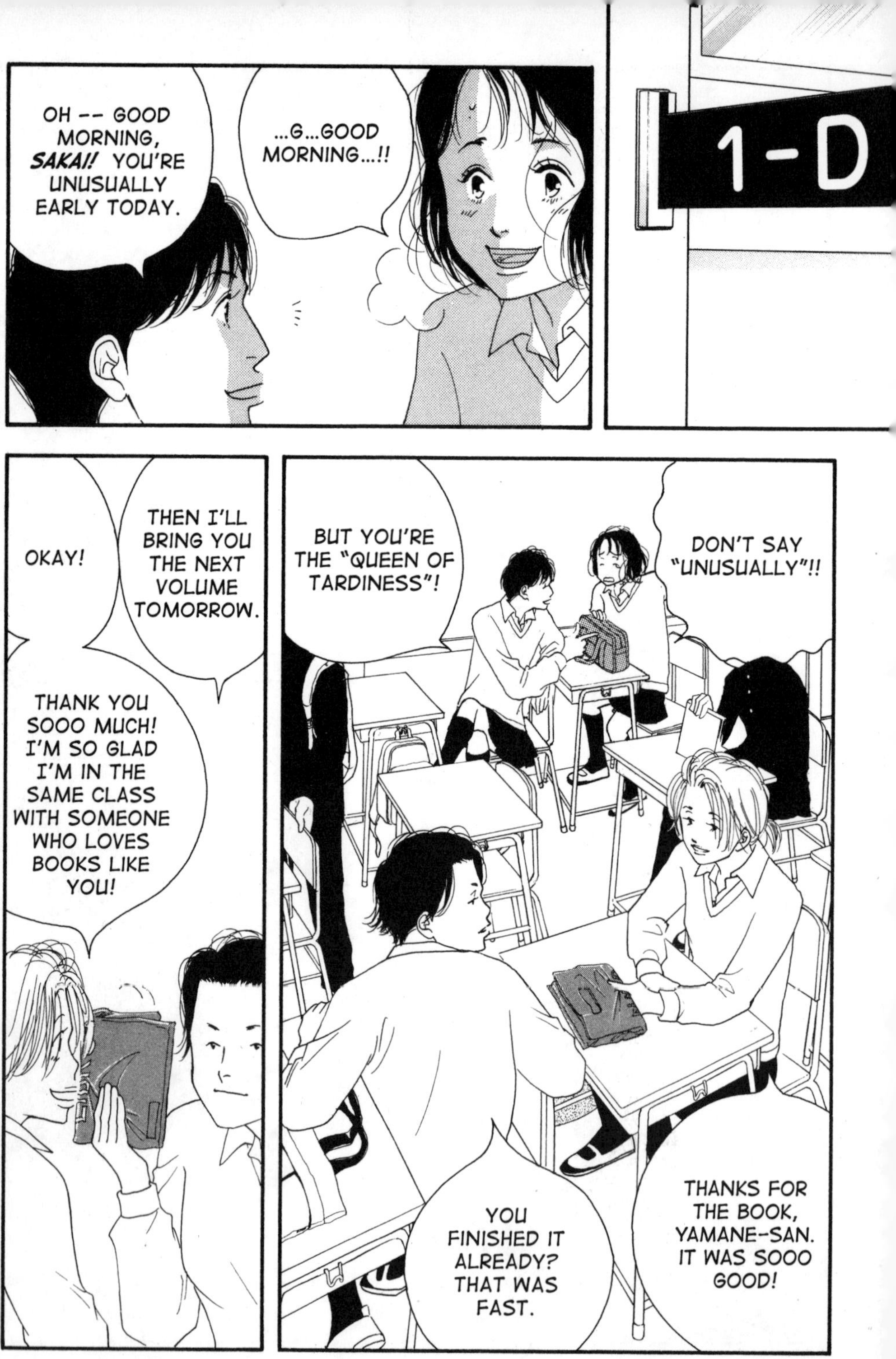
1-D
...G...GOOD MORNING...!!
OH -- GOOD MORNING, **SAKAI!** YOU'RE UNUSUALLY EARLY TODAY.
DON'T SAY "UNUSUALLY"!!
BUT YOU'RE THE "QUEEN OF TARDINESS"!
THANKS FOR THE BOOK, YAMANE-SAN. IT WAS SOOO GOOD!
YOU FINISHED IT ALREADY? THAT WAS FAST.
THEN I'LL BRING YOU THE NEXT VOLUME TOMORROW.
OKAY!
THANK YOU SOOO MUCH! I'M SO GLAD I'M IN THE SAME CLASS WITH SOMEONE WHO LOVES BOOKS LIKE YOU!

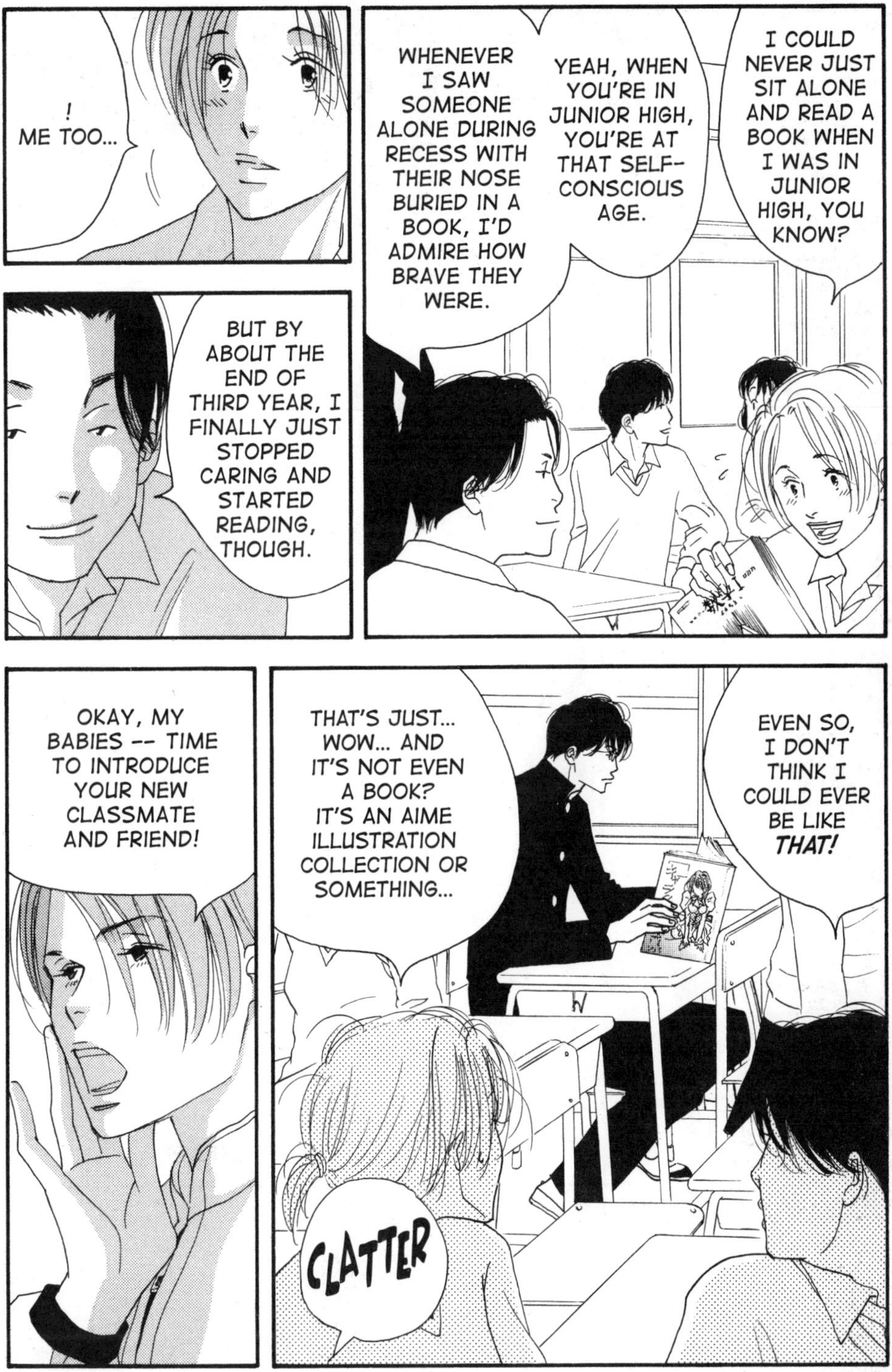
I COULD NEVER JUST SIT ALONE AND READ A BOOK WHEN I WAS IN JUNIOR HIGH, YOU KNOW?
YEAH, WHEN YOU'RE IN JUNIOR HIGH, YOU'RE AT THAT SELF-CONSCIOUS AGE.
WHENEVER I SAW SOMEONE ALONE DURING RECESS WITH THEIR NOSE BURIED IN A BOOK, I'D ADMIRE HOW BRAVE THEY WERE.
! ME TOO...
BUT BY ABOUT THE END OF THIRD YEAR, I FINALLY JUST STOPPED CARING AND STARTED READING, THOUGH.
EVEN SO, I DON'T THINK I COULD EVER BE LIKE ***THAT!***
THAT'S JUST... WOW... AND IT'S NOT EVEN A BOOK? IT'S AN AIME ILLUSTRATION COLLECTION OR SOMETHING...
CLATTER
OKAY, MY BABIES -- TIME TO INTRODUCE YOUR NEW CLASSMATE AND FRIEND!

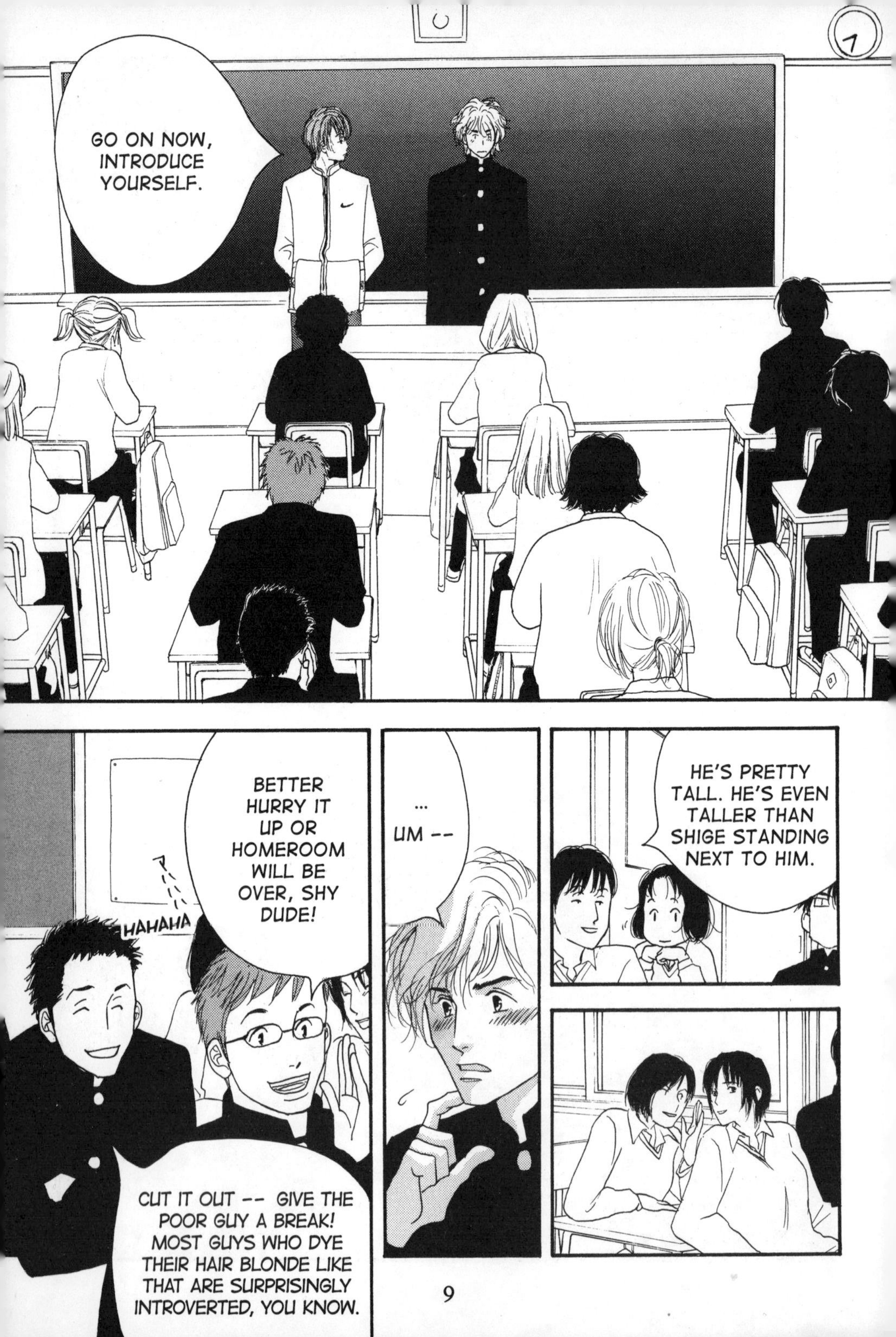
GO ON NOW, INTRODUCE YOURSELF.
HE'S PRETTY TALL. HE'S EVEN TALLER THAN SHIGE STANDING NEXT TO HIM.
... UM --
BETTER HURRY IT UP OR HOMEROOM WILL BE OVER, SHY DUDE!
HAHAHA
CUT IT OUT -- GIVE THE POOR GUY A BREAK! MOST GUYS WHO DYE THEIR HAIR BLONDE LIKE THAT ARE SURPRISINGLY INTROVERTED, YOU KNOW.

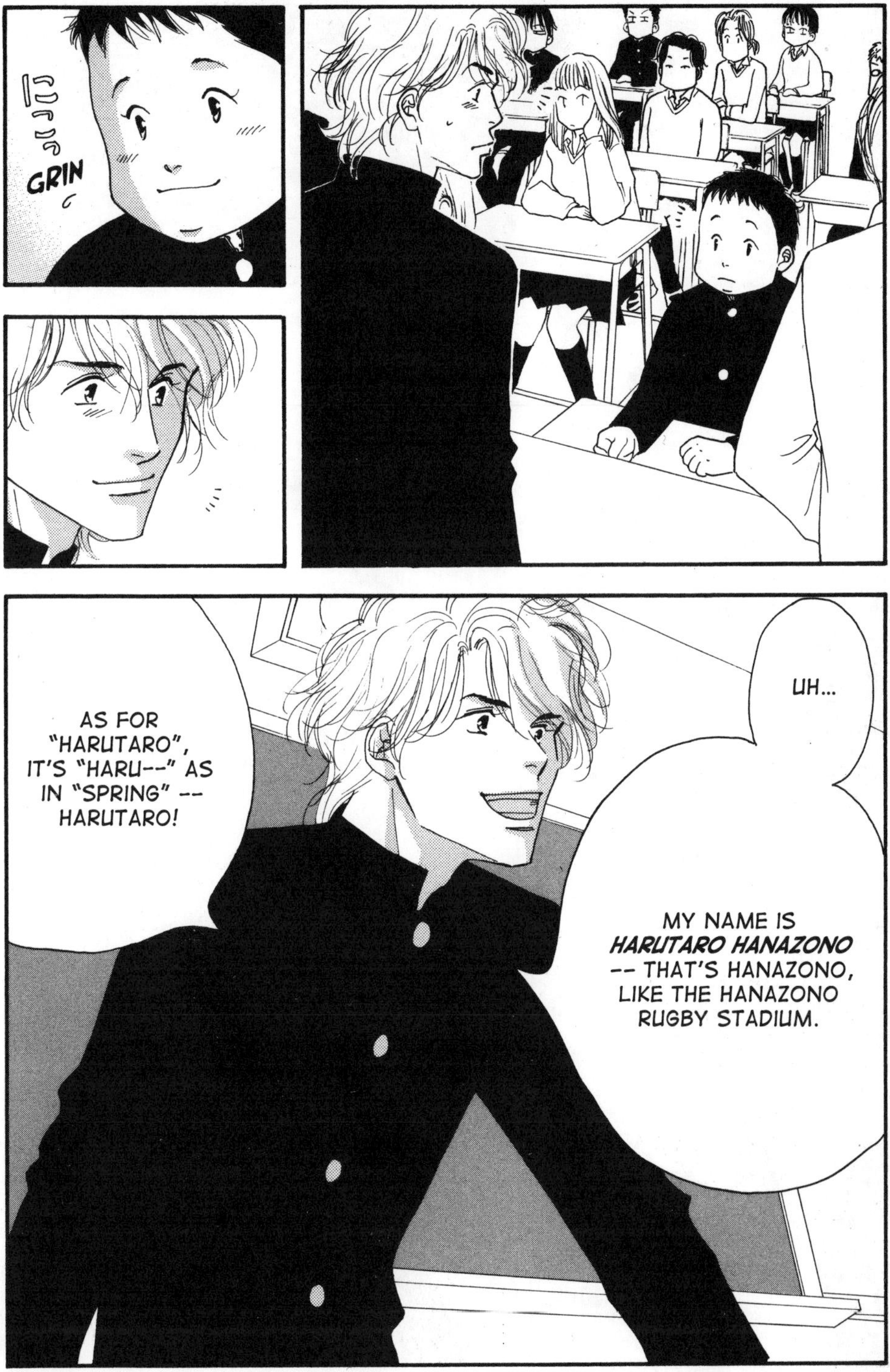
GRIN
UH...
MY NAME IS *HARUTARO HANAZONO* -- THAT'S HANAZONO, LIKE THE HANAZONO RUGBY STADIUM.
AS FOR "HARUTARO", IT'S "HARU--" AS IN "SPRING" -- HARUTARO!

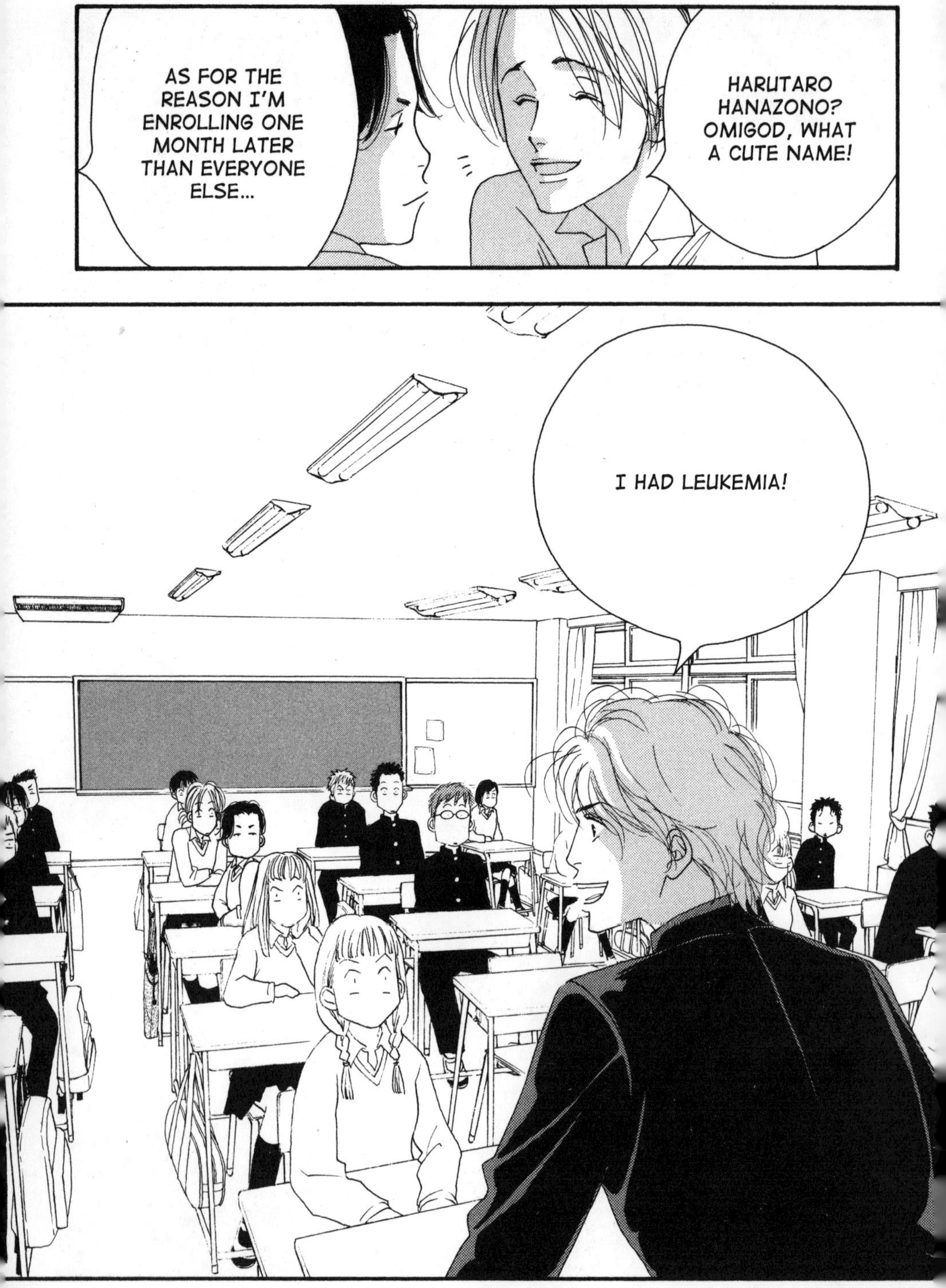
HARUTARO HANAZONO? OMIGOD, WHAT A CUTE NAME!
AS FOR THE REASON I'M ENROLLING ONE MONTH LATER THAN EVERYONE ELSE...
I HAD LEUKEMIA!

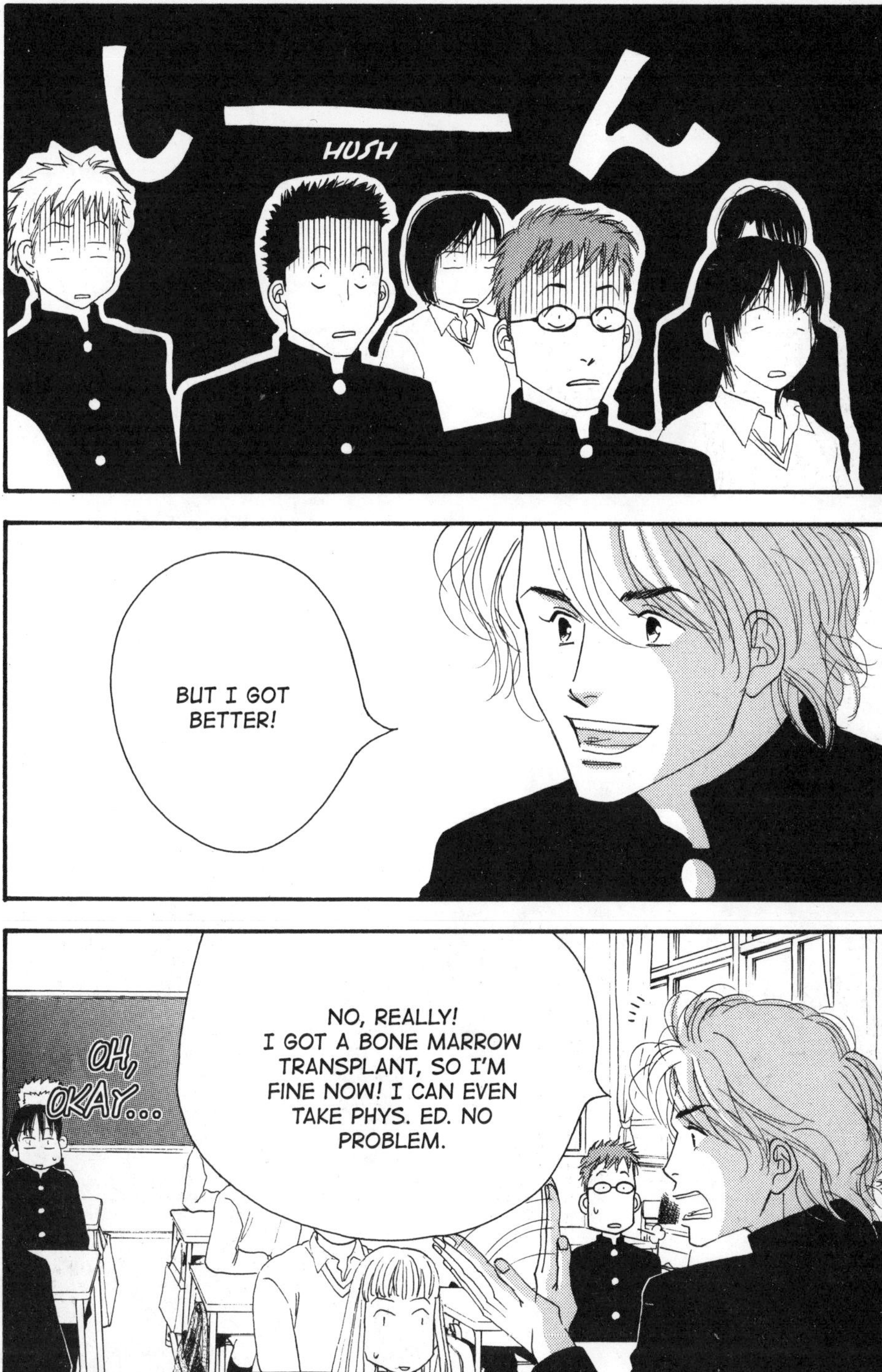
しーん
HUSH
BUT I GOT BETTER!
NO, REALLY! I GOT A BONE MARROW TRANSPLANT, SO I'M FINE NOW! I CAN EVEN TAKE PHYS. ED. NO PROBLEM.
OH, OKAY...

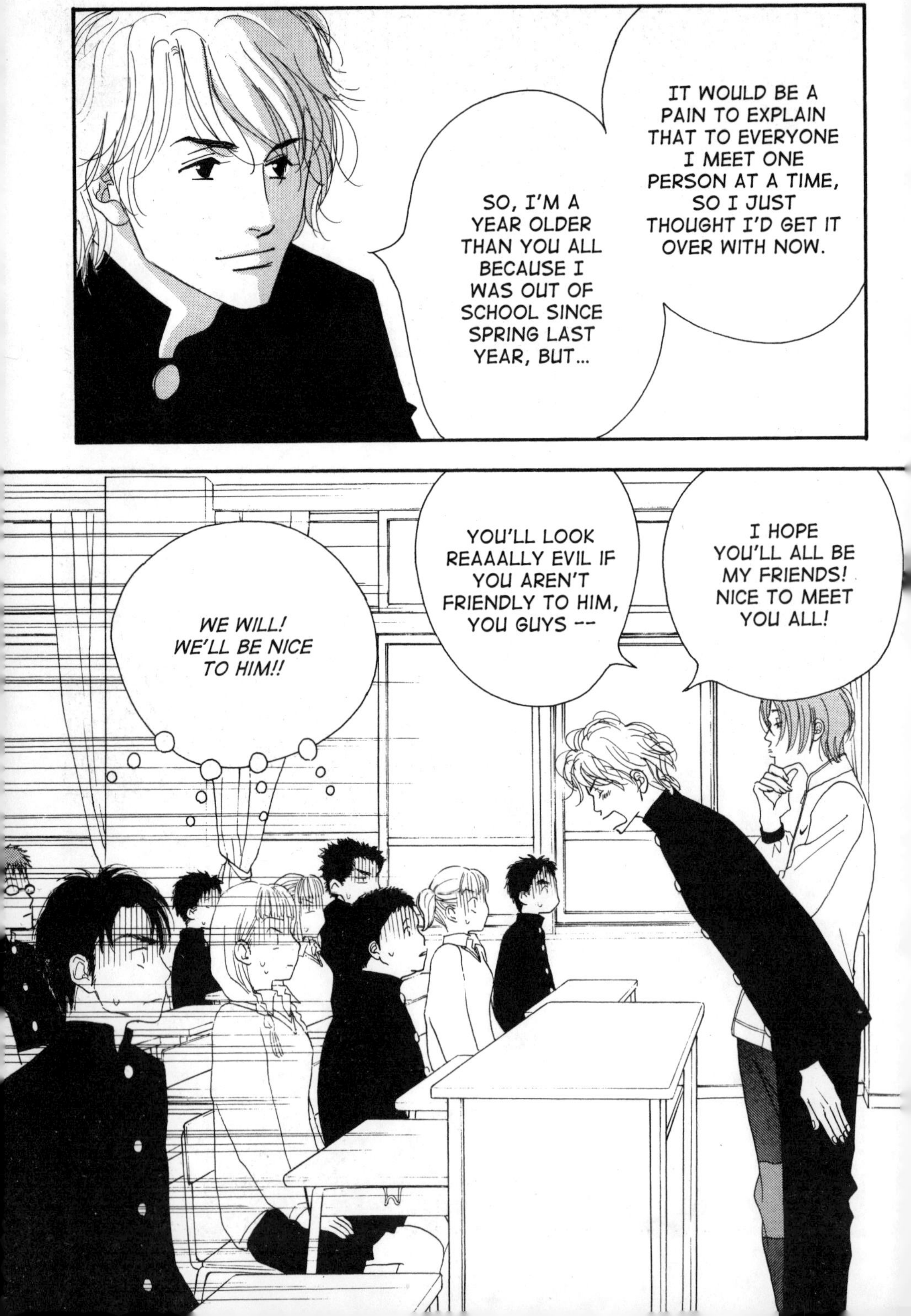
IT WOULD BE A PAIN TO EXPLAIN THAT TO EVERYONE I MEET ONE PERSON AT A TIME, SO I JUST THOUGHT I'D GET IT OVER WITH NOW.
SO, I'M A YEAR OLDER THAN YOU ALL BECAUSE I WAS OUT OF SCHOOL SINCE SPRING LAST YEAR, BUT...
I HOPE YOU'LL ALL BE MY FRIENDS! NICE TO MEET YOU ALL!
YOU'LL LOOK REAAALLY EVIL IF YOU AREN'T FRIENDLY TO HIM, YOU GUYS --
WE WILL! WE'LL BE NICE TO HIM!!

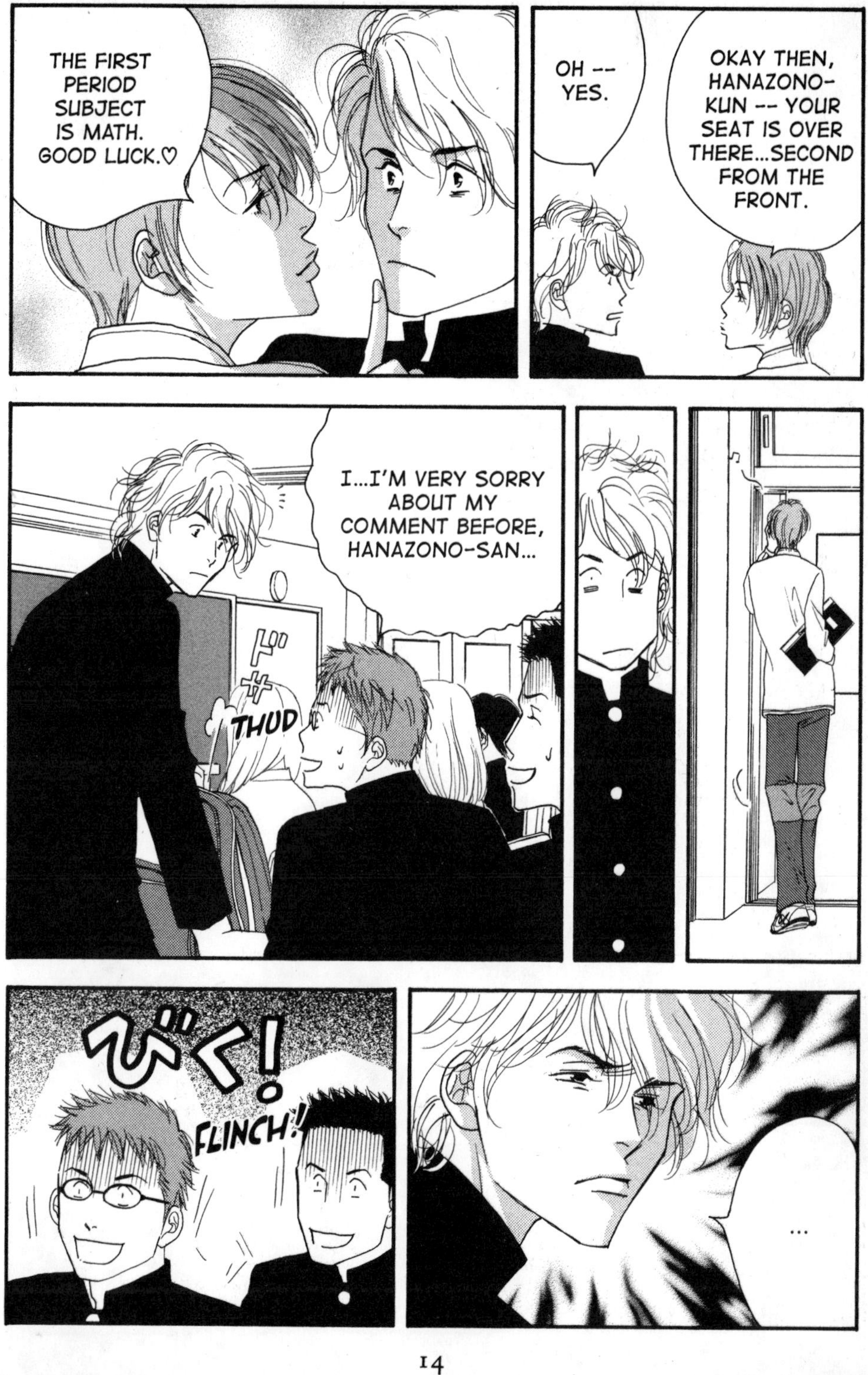
OKAY THEN, HANAZONO-KUN -- YOUR SEAT IS OVER THERE...SECOND FROM THE FRONT.
OH -- YES.
THE FIRST PERIOD SUBJECT IS MATH. GOOD LUCK.♡
I...I'M VERY SORRY ABOUT MY COMMENT BEFORE, HANAZONO-SAN...
ドサ
THUD
...
びく!
FLINCH!

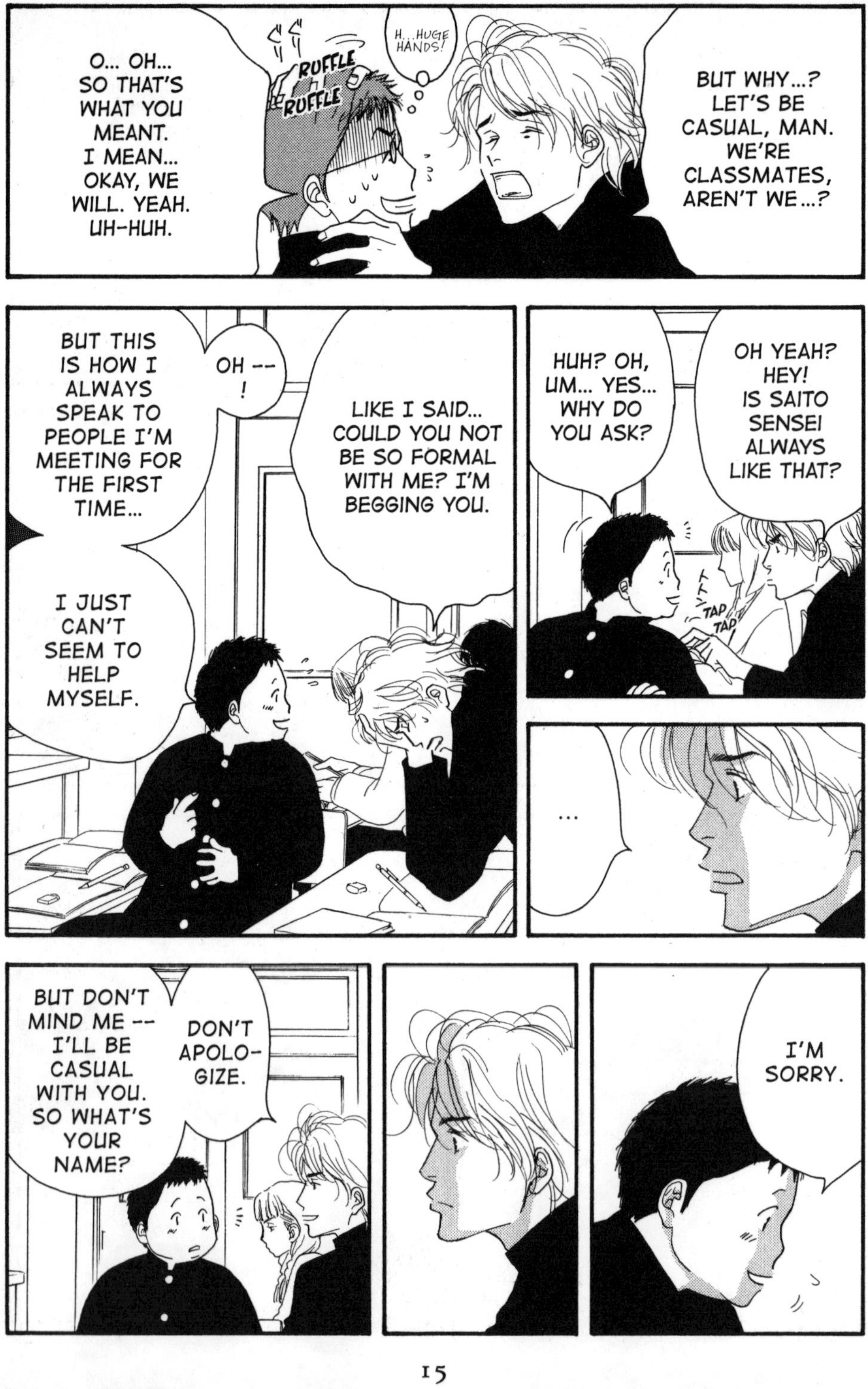
BUT WHY...? LET'S BE CASUAL, MAN. WE'RE CLASSMATES, AREN'T WE...?
H... HUGE HANDS!
RUFFLE RUFFLE
O... OH... SO THAT'S WHAT YOU MEANT. I MEAN... OKAY, WE WILL. YEAH. UH-HUH.
OH YEAH? HEY! IS SAITO SENSEI ALWAYS LIKE THAT?
TAP TAP
HUH? OH, UM... YES... WHY DO YOU ASK?
...
LIKE I SAID... COULD YOU NOT BE SO FORMAL WITH ME? I'M BEGGING YOU.
OH --!
BUT THIS IS HOW I ALWAYS SPEAK TO PEOPLE I'M MEETING FOR THE FIRST TIME...
I JUST CAN'T SEEM TO HELP MYSELF.
I'M SORRY.
DON'T APOLO-GIZE.
BUT DON'T MIND ME -- I'LL BE CASUAL WITH YOU. SO WHAT'S YOUR NAME?

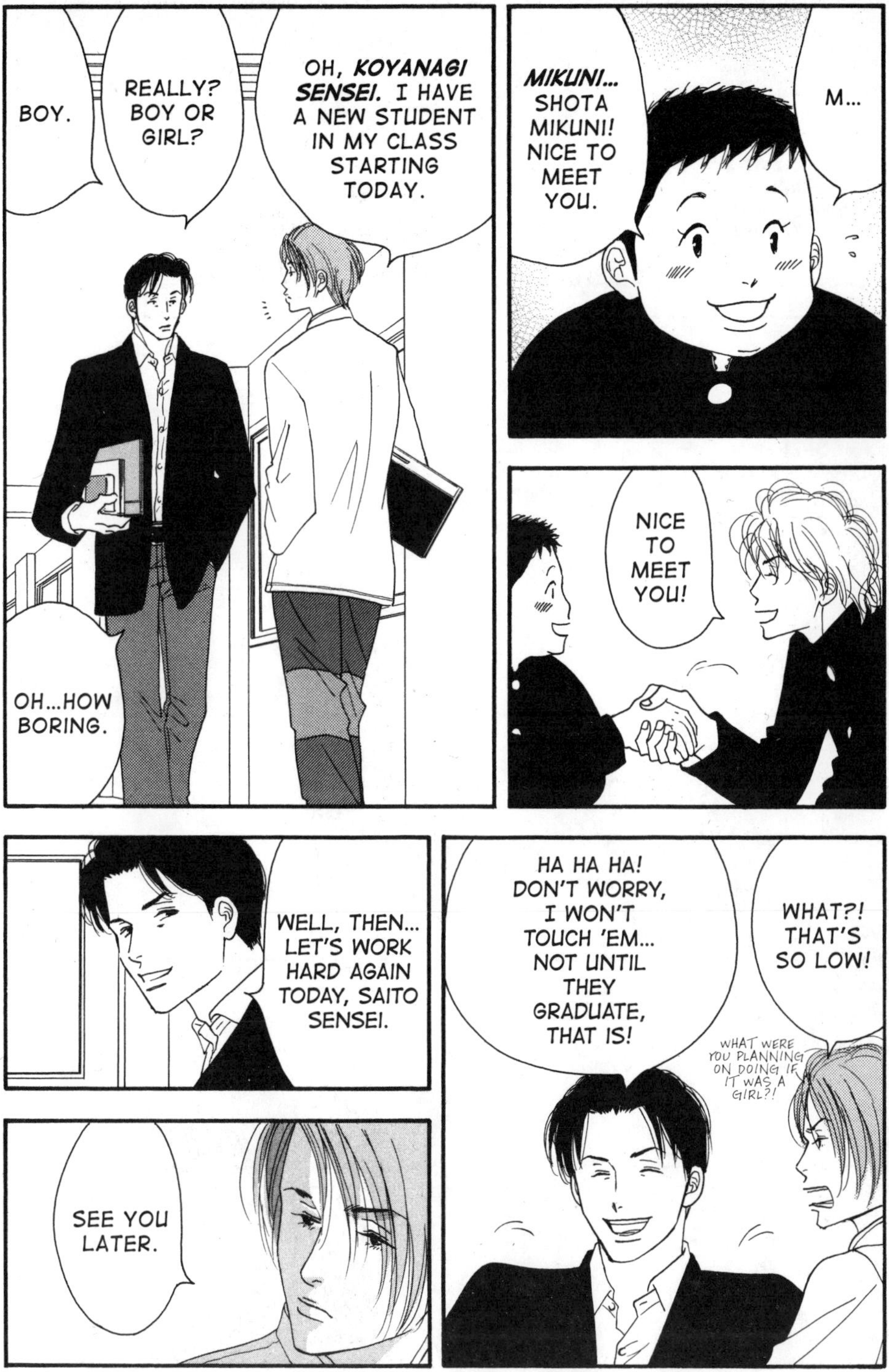
M...
MIKUNI... SHOTA MIKUNI! NICE TO MEET YOU.
NICE TO MEET YOU!
OH, KOYANAGI SENSEI. I HAVE A NEW STUDENT IN MY CLASS STARTING TODAY.
REALLY? BOY OR GIRL?
BOY.
OH...HOW BORING.
WHAT?! THAT'S SO LOW!
HA HA HA! DON'T WORRY, I WON'T TOUCH 'EM... NOT UNTIL THEY GRADUATE, THAT IS!
WHAT WERE YOU PLANNING ON DOING IF IT WAS A GIRL?!
WELL, THEN... LET'S WORK HARD AGAIN TODAY, SAITO SENSEI.
SEE YOU LATER.

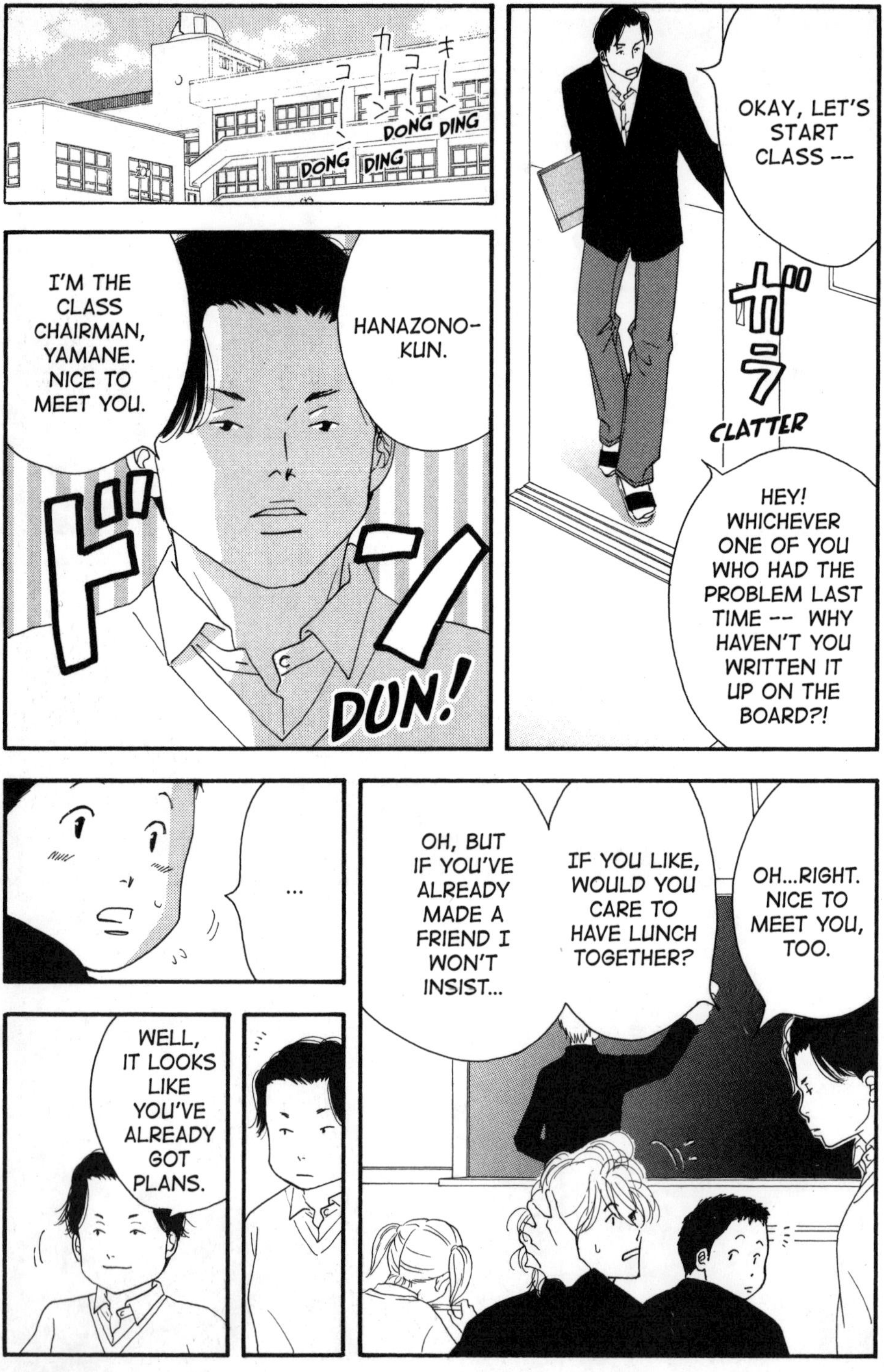
OKAY, LET'S START CLASS --
ガラ
CLATTER
HEY! WHICHEVER ONE OF YOU WHO HAD THE PROBLEM LAST TIME -- WHY HAVEN'T YOU WRITTEN IT UP ON THE BOARD?!
DING
DONG
DING
DONG
HANAZONO-KUN.
I'M THE CLASS CHAIRMAN, YAMANE. NICE TO MEET YOU.
ドーン
DUN!
OH...RIGHT. NICE TO MEET YOU, TOO.
IF YOU LIKE, WOULD YOU CARE TO HAVE LUNCH TOGETHER?
OH, BUT IF YOU'VE ALREADY MADE A FRIEND I WON'T INSIST...
...
WELL, IT LOOKS LIKE YOU'VE ALREADY GOT PLANS.

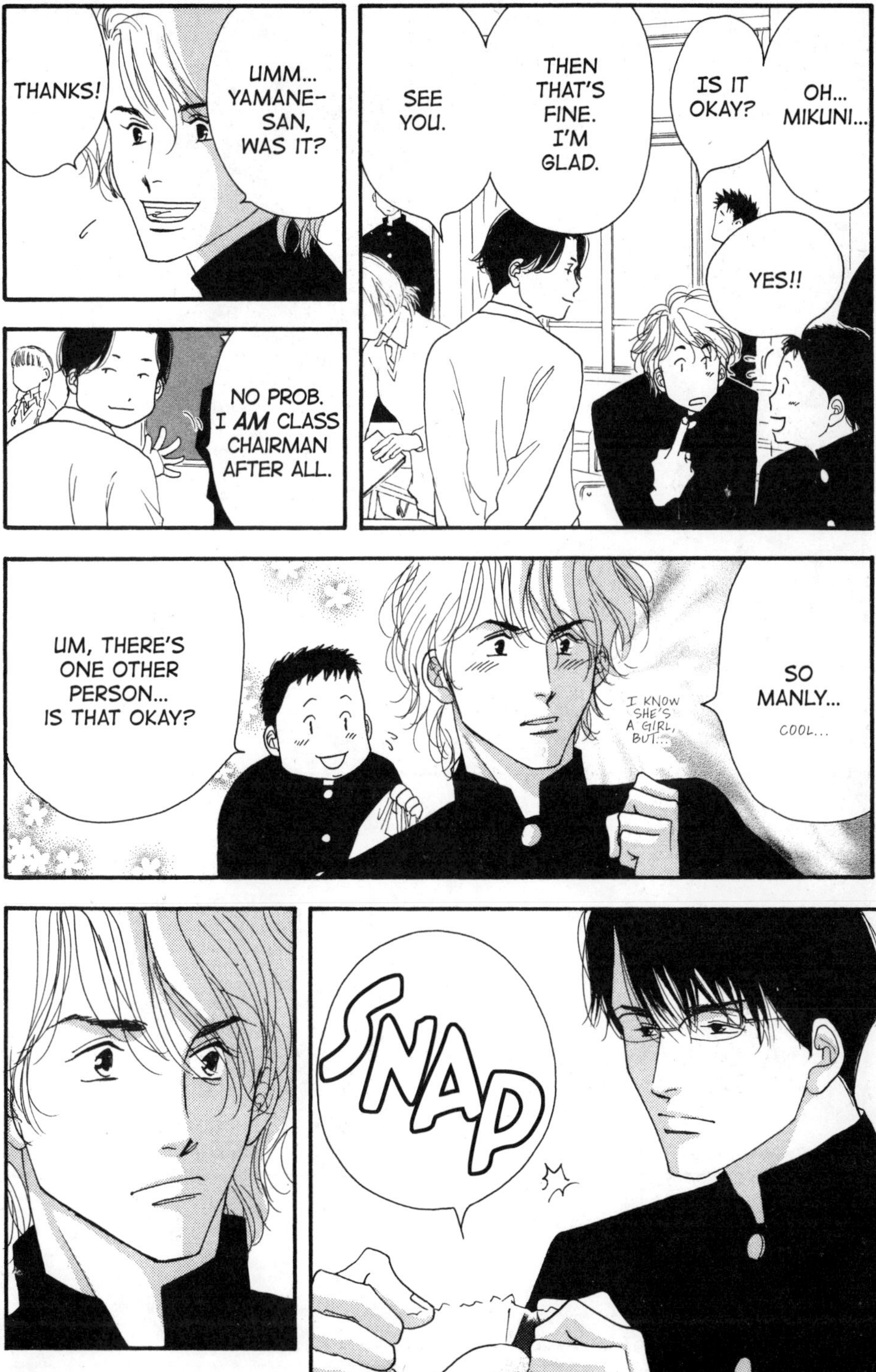
OH... MIKUNI...
IS IT OKAY?
YES!!
THEN THAT'S FINE. I'M GLAD.
SEE YOU.
UMM... YAMANE-SAN, WAS IT?
THANKS!
NO PROB. I *AM* CLASS CHAIRMAN AFTER ALL.
SO MANLY...
COOL...
I KNOW SHE'S A GIRL, BUT...
UM, THERE'S ONE OTHER PERSON... IS THAT OKAY?
SNAP

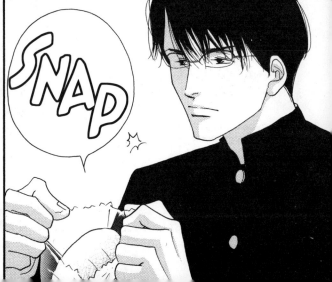

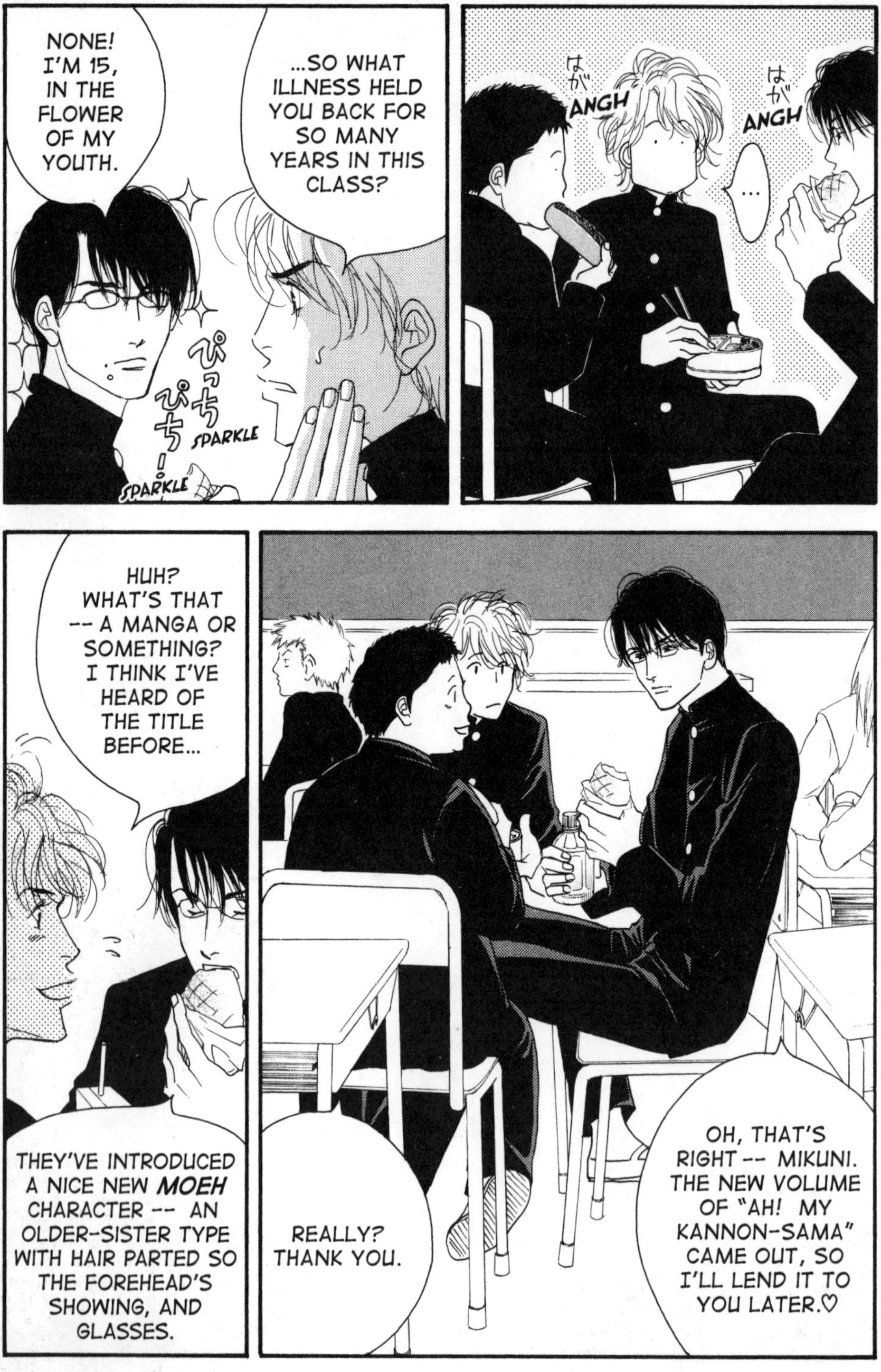
はが
ANGH
はが
ANGH
...
...SO WHAT ILLNESS HELD YOU BACK FOR SO MANY YEARS IN THIS CLASS?
NONE! I'M 15, IN THE FLOWER OF MY YOUTH.
ぴっち
SPARKLE
ぴっち
SPARKLE
OH, THAT'S RIGHT -- MIKUNI. THE NEW VOLUME OF "AH! MY KANNON-SAMA" CAME OUT, SO I'LL LEND IT TO YOU LATER.♡
REALLY? THANK YOU.
HUH? WHAT'S THAT -- A MANGA OR SOMETHING? I THINK I'VE HEARD OF THE TITLE BEFORE...
THEY'VE INTRODUCED A NICE NEW ***MOEH*** CHARACTER -- AN OLDER-SISTER TYPE WITH HAIR PARTED SO THE FOREHEAD'S SHOWING, AND GLASSES.

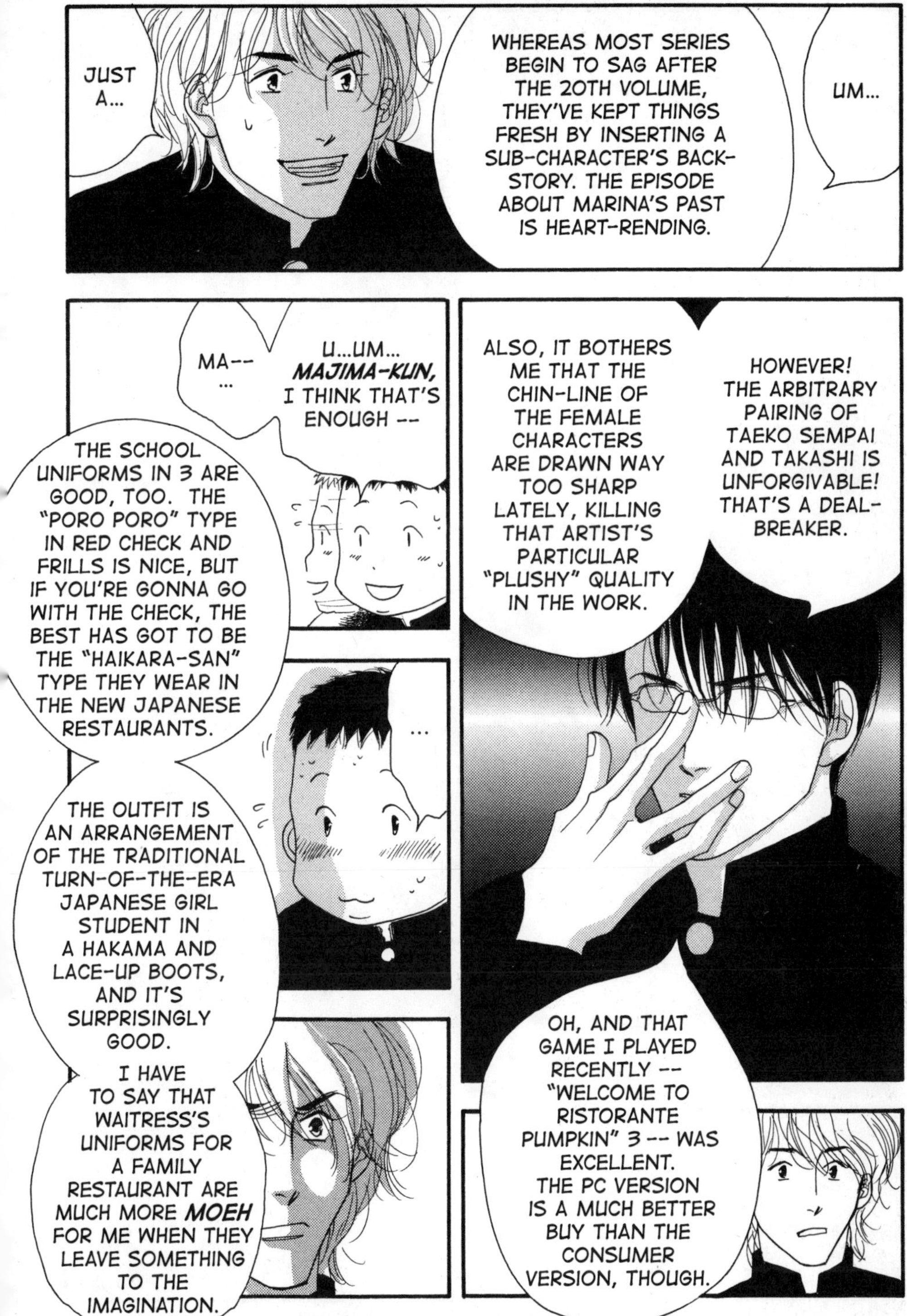

UM...
WHEREAS MOST SERIES BEGIN TO SAG AFTER THE 20TH VOLUME, THEY'VE KEPT THINGS FRESH BY INSERTING A SUB-CHARACTER'S BACK-STORY. THE EPISODE ABOUT MARINA'S PAST IS HEART-RENDING.
JUST A...
HOWEVER! THE ARBITRARY PAIRING OF TAEKO SEMPAI AND TAKASHI IS UNFORGIVABLE! THAT'S A DEAL-BREAKER.
ALSO, IT BOTHERS ME THAT THE CHIN-LINE OF THE FEMALE CHARACTERS ARE DRAWN WAY TOO SHARP LATELY, KILLING THAT ARTIST'S PARTICULAR "PLUSHY" QUALITY IN THE WORK.
OH, AND THAT GAME I PLAYED RECENTLY -- "WELCOME TO RISTORANTE PUMPKIN" 3 -- WAS EXCELLENT. THE PC VERSION IS A MUCH BETTER BUY THAN THE CONSUMER VERSION, THOUGH.
U...UM... ***MAJIMA-KUN,*** I THINK THAT'S ENOUGH --
MA-- ...
THE SCHOOL UNIFORMS IN 3 ARE GOOD, TOO. THE "PORO PORO" TYPE IN RED CHECK AND FRILLS IS NICE, BUT IF YOU'RE GONNA GO WITH THE CHECK, THE BEST HAS GOT TO BE THE "HAIKARA-SAN" TYPE THEY WEAR IN THE NEW JAPANESE RESTAURANTS.
...
THE OUTFIT IS AN ARRANGEMENT OF THE TRADITIONAL TURN-OF-THE-ERA JAPANESE GIRL STUDENT IN A HAKAMA AND LACE-UP BOOTS, AND IT'S SURPRISINGLY GOOD.
I HAVE TO SAY THAT WAITRESS'S UNIFORMS FOR A FAMILY RESTAURANT ARE MUCH MORE ***MOEH*** FOR ME WHEN THEY LEAVE SOMETHING TO THE IMAGINATION.

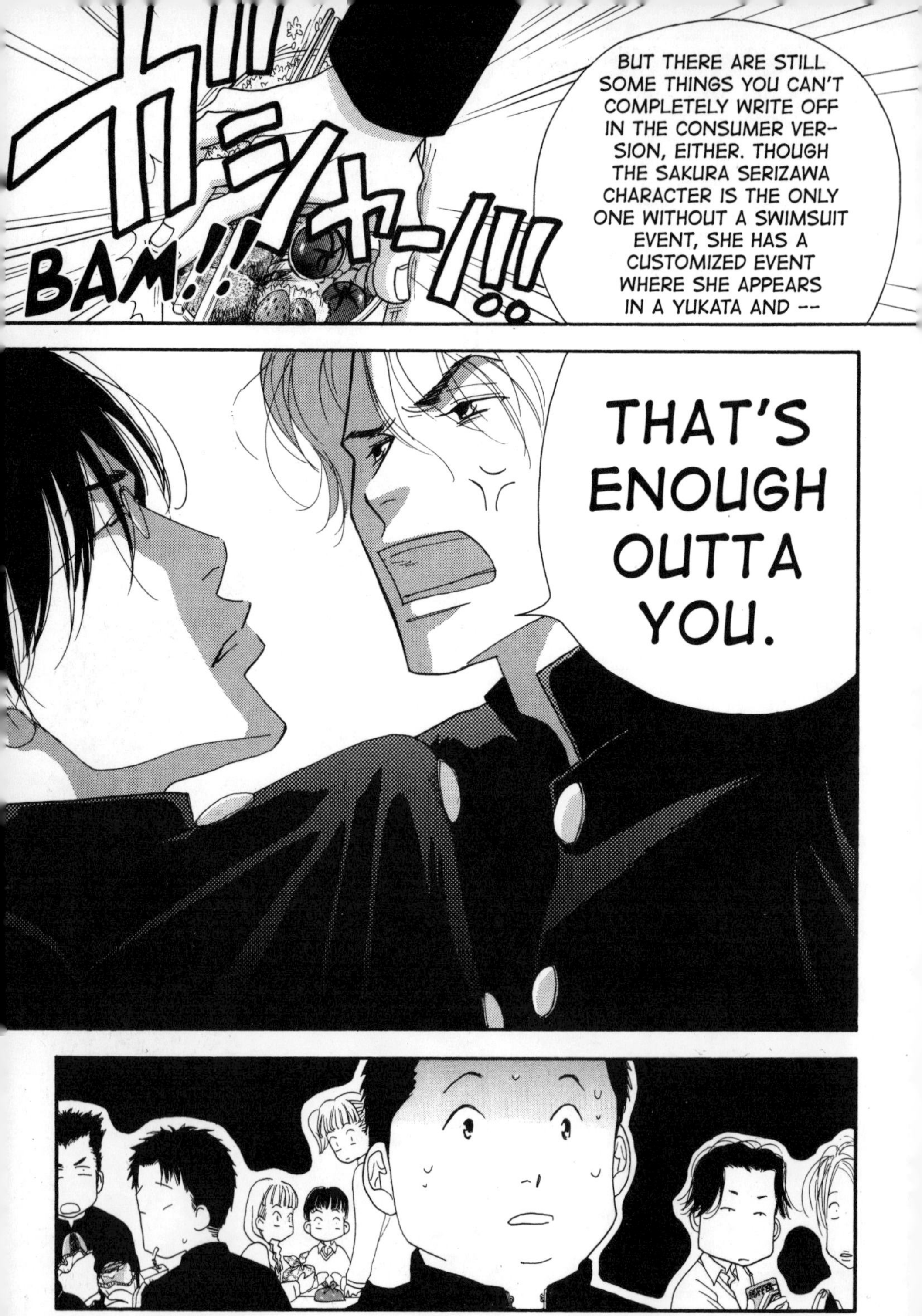
BUT THERE ARE STILL SOME THINGS YOU CAN'T COMPLETELY WRITE OFF IN THE CONSUMER VER-SION, EITHER. THOUGH THE SAKURA SERIZAWA CHARACTER IS THE ONLY ONE WITHOUT A SWIMSUIT EVENT, SHE HAS A CUSTOMIZED EVENT WHERE SHE APPEARS IN A YUKATA AND --
ガシャー!!!
BAM!!
THAT'S ENOUGH OUTTA YOU.

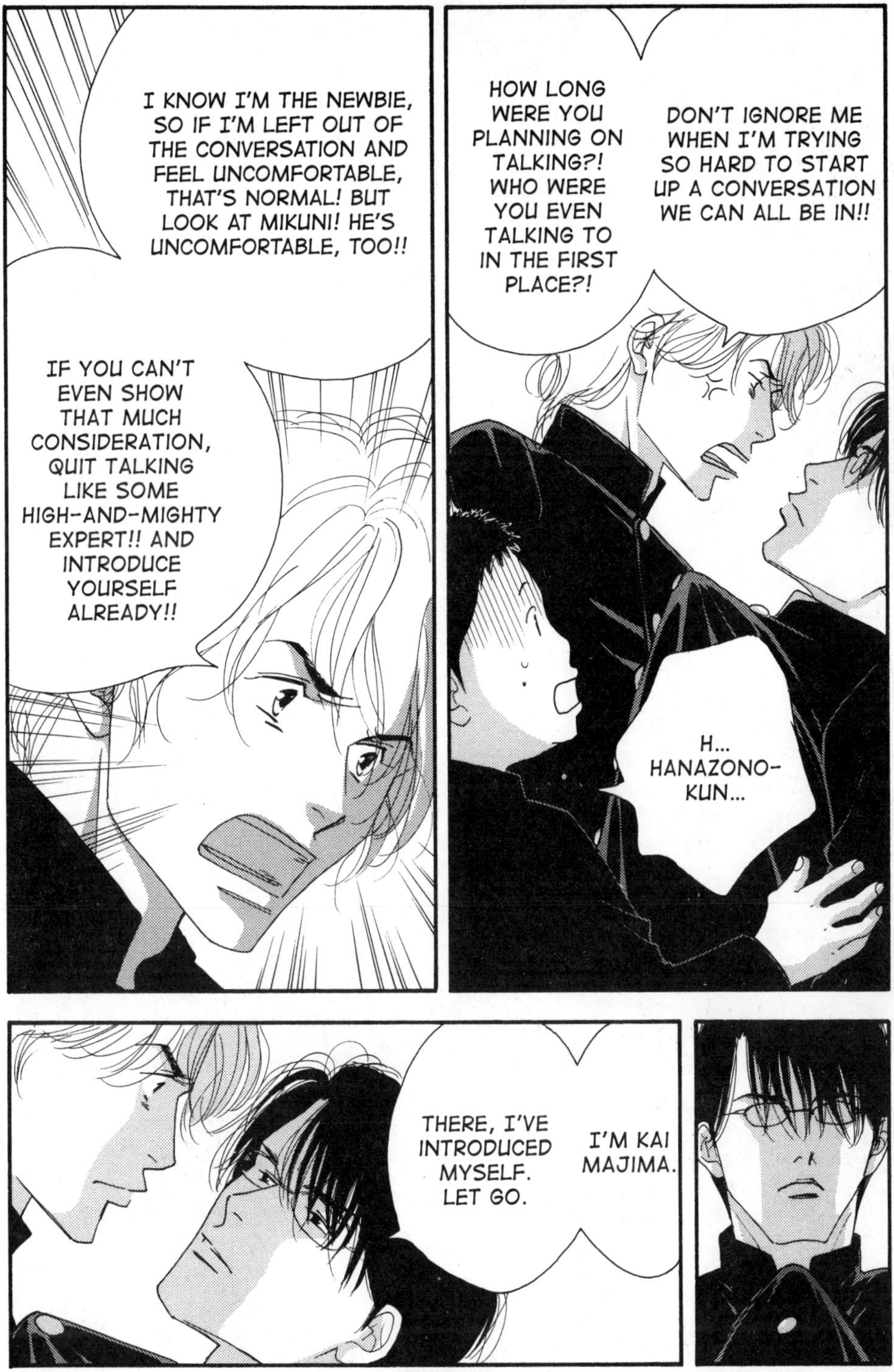

DON'T IGNORE ME WHEN I'M TRYING SO HARD TO START UP A CONVERSATION WE CAN ALL BE IN!!
HOW LONG WERE YOU PLANNING ON TALKING?! WHO WERE YOU EVEN TALKING TO IN THE FIRST PLACE?!
H... HANAZONO-KUN...
I KNOW I'M THE NEWBIE, SO IF I'M LEFT OUT OF THE CONVERSATION AND FEEL UNCOMFORTABLE, THAT'S NORMAL! BUT LOOK AT MIKUNI! HE'S UNCOMFORTABLE, TOO!!
IF YOU CAN'T EVEN SHOW THAT MUCH CONSIDERATION, QUIT TALKING LIKE SOME HIGH-AND-MIGHTY EXPERT!! AND INTRODUCE YOURSELF ALREADY!!
I'M KAI MAJIMA.
THERE, I'VE INTRODUCED MYSELF. LET GO.

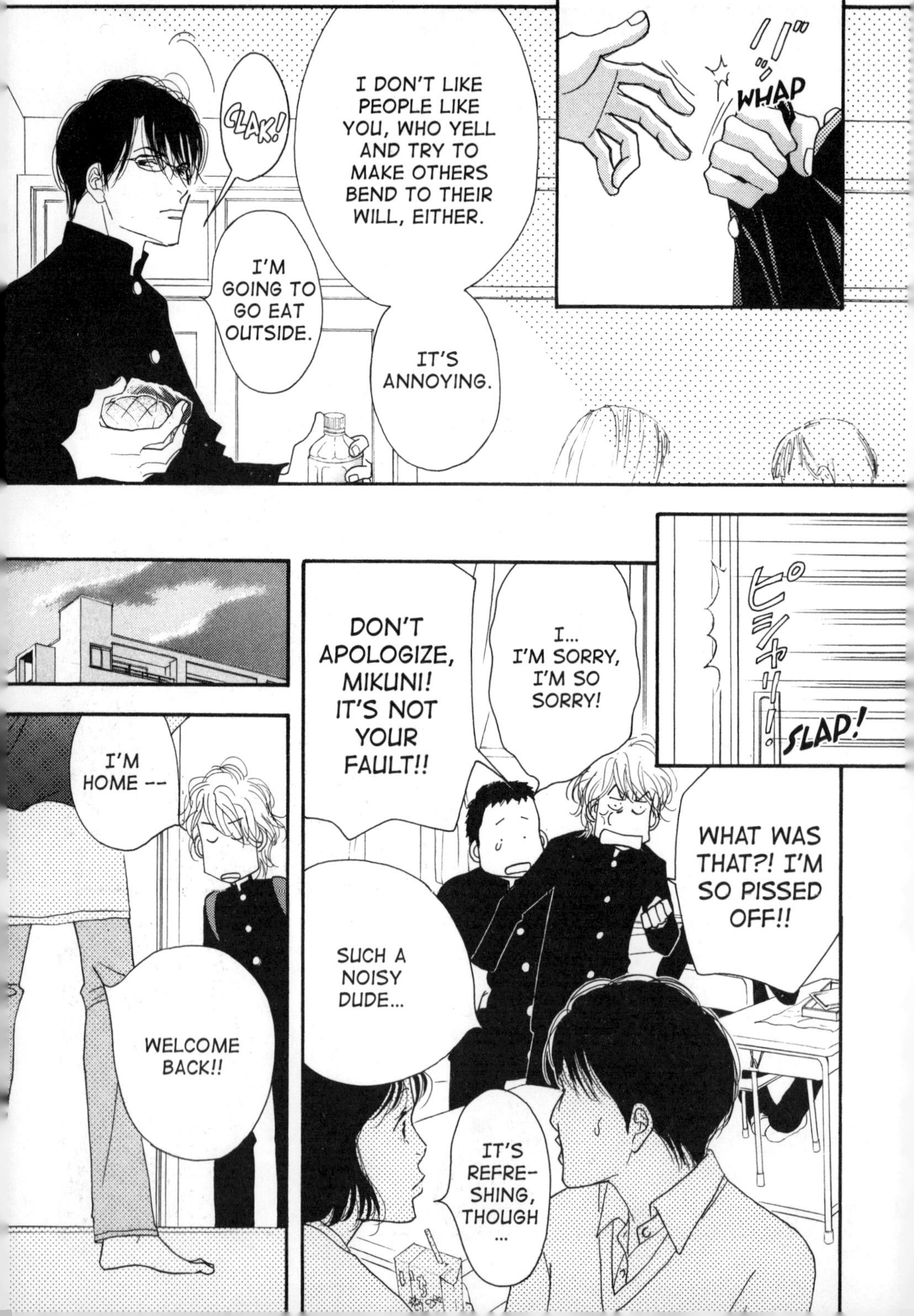
WHAP
I DON'T LIKE PEOPLE LIKE YOU, WHO YELL AND TRY TO MAKE OTHERS BEND TO THEIR WILL, EITHER.
IT'S ANNOYING.
CLAK!
I'M GOING TO GO EAT OUTSIDE.
ピシャ!
SLAP!
WHAT WAS THAT?! I'M SO PISSED OFF!!
I... I'M SORRY, I'M SO SORRY!
DON'T APOLOGIZE, MIKUNI! IT'S NOT YOUR FAULT!!
SUCH A NOISY DUDE...
IT'S REFRESHING, THOUGH ...
I'M HOME --
WELCOME BACK!!

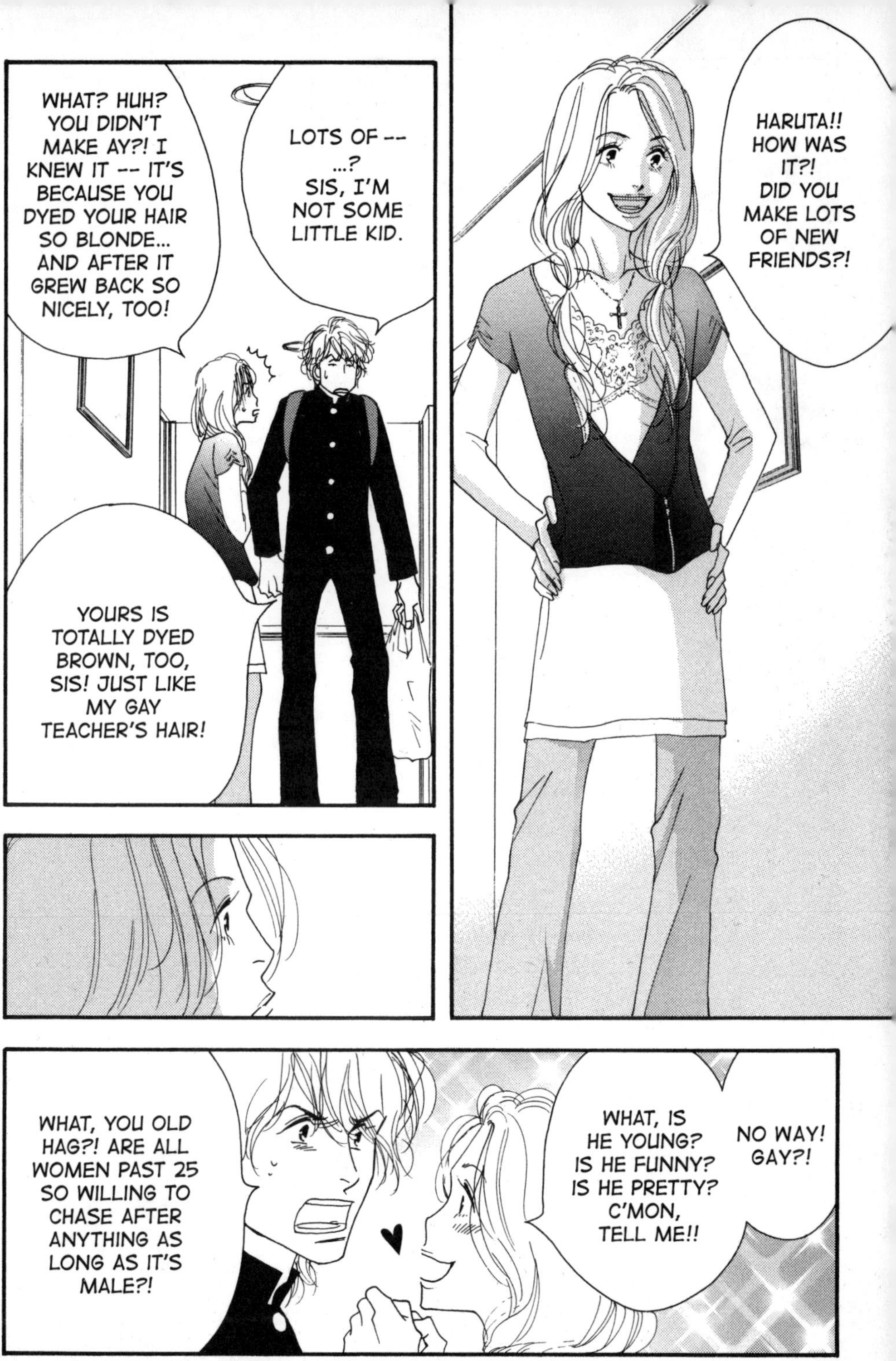
HARUTA!! HOW WAS IT?! DID YOU MAKE LOTS OF NEW FRIENDS?!
LOTS OF -- ...? SIS, I'M NOT SOME LITTLE KID.
WHAT? HUH? YOU DIDN'T MAKE ANY?! I KNEW IT -- IT'S BECAUSE YOU DYED YOUR HAIR SO BLONDE... AND AFTER IT GREW BACK SO NICELY, TOO!
YOURS IS TOTALLY DYED BROWN, TOO, SIS! JUST LIKE MY GAY TEACHER'S HAIR!
NO WAY! GAY?!
WHAT, IS HE YOUNG? IS HE FUNNY? IS HE PRETTY? C'MON, TELL ME!!
WHAT, YOU OLD HAG?! ARE ALL WOMEN PAST 25 SO WILLING TO CHASE AFTER ANYTHING AS LONG AS IT'S MALE?!

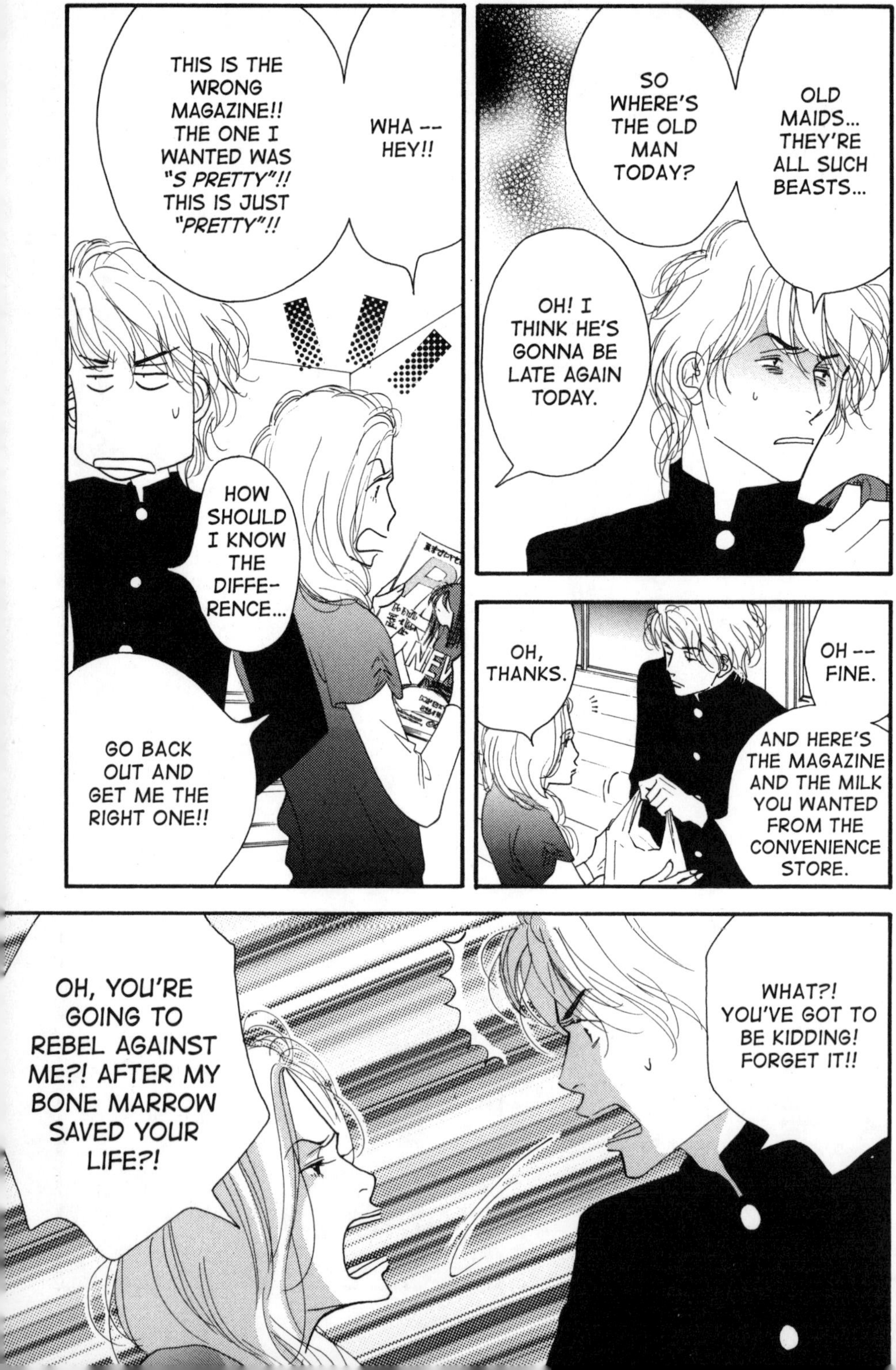
OLD MAIDS... THEY'RE ALL SUCH BEASTS...
SO WHERE'S THE OLD MAN TODAY?
OH! I THINK HE'S GONNA BE LATE AGAIN TODAY.
OH -- FINE.
AND HERE'S THE MAGAZINE AND THE MILK YOU WANTED FROM THE CONVENIENCE STORE.
OH, THANKS.
THIS IS THE WRONG MAGAZINE!! THE ONE I WANTED WAS *"S PRETTY"*!! THIS IS JUST *"PRETTY"*!!
WHA -- HEY!!
HOW SHOULD I KNOW THE DIFFE-RENCE...
GO BACK OUT AND GET ME THE RIGHT ONE!!
WHAT?! YOU'VE GOT TO BE KIDDING! FORGET IT!!
OH, YOU'RE GOING TO REBEL AGAINST ME?! AFTER MY BONE MARROW SAVED YOUR LIFE?!

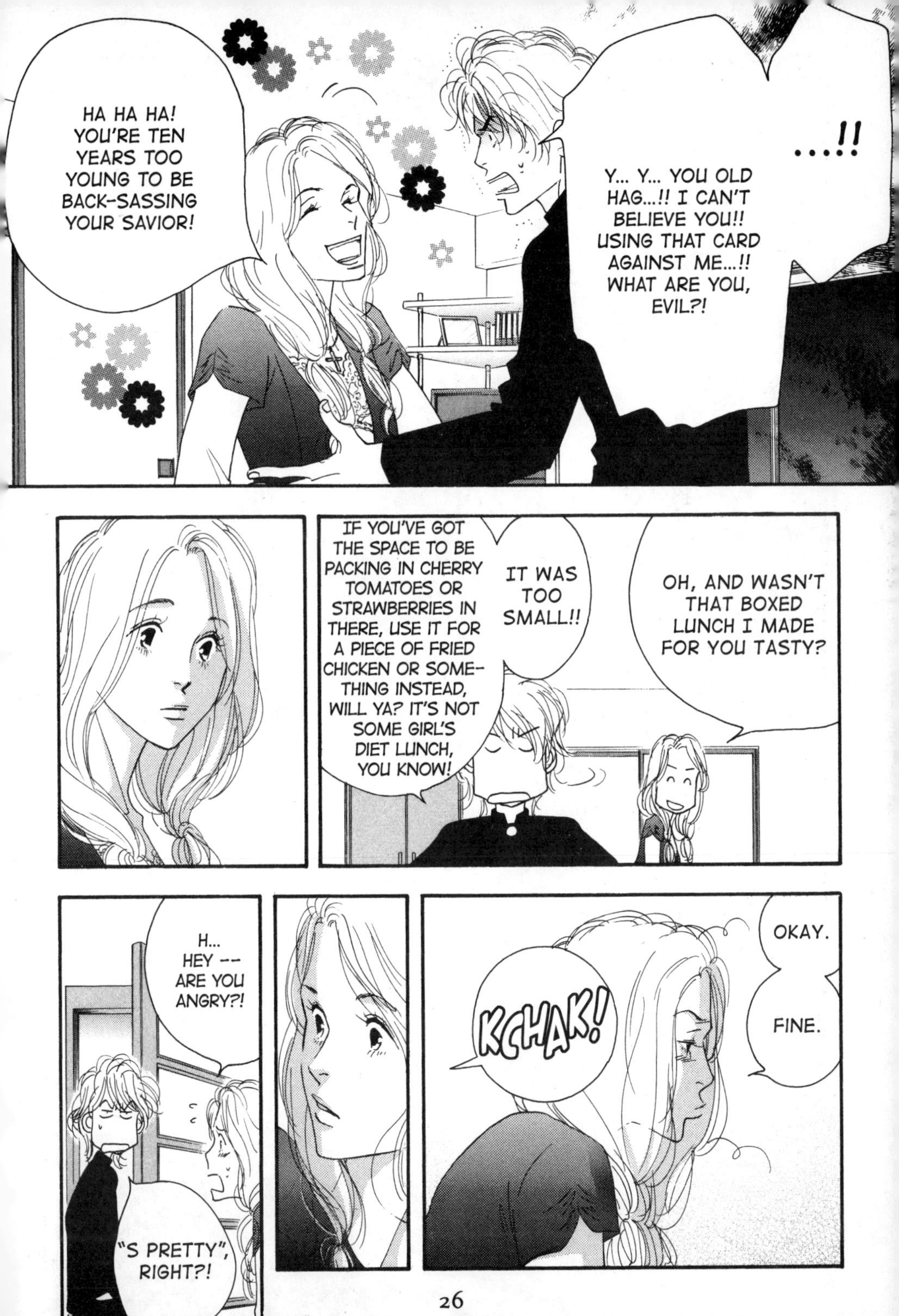
...!!
Y... Y... YOU OLD HAG...!! I CAN'T BELIEVE YOU!! USING THAT CARD AGAINST ME...!! WHAT ARE YOU, EVIL?!
HA HA HA! YOU'RE TEN YEARS TOO YOUNG TO BE BACK-SASSING YOUR SAVIOR!
OH, AND WASN'T THAT BOXED LUNCH I MADE FOR YOU TASTY?
IT WAS TOO SMALL!!
IF YOU'VE GOT THE SPACE TO BE PACKING IN CHERRY TOMATOES OR STRAWBERRIES IN THERE, USE IT FOR A PIECE OF FRIED CHICKEN OR SOME-THING INSTEAD, WILL YA? IT'S NOT SOME GIRL'S DIET LUNCH, YOU KNOW!
OKAY.
FINE.
KCHAK!
H... HEY -- ARE YOU ANGRY?!
"S PRETTY", RIGHT?!

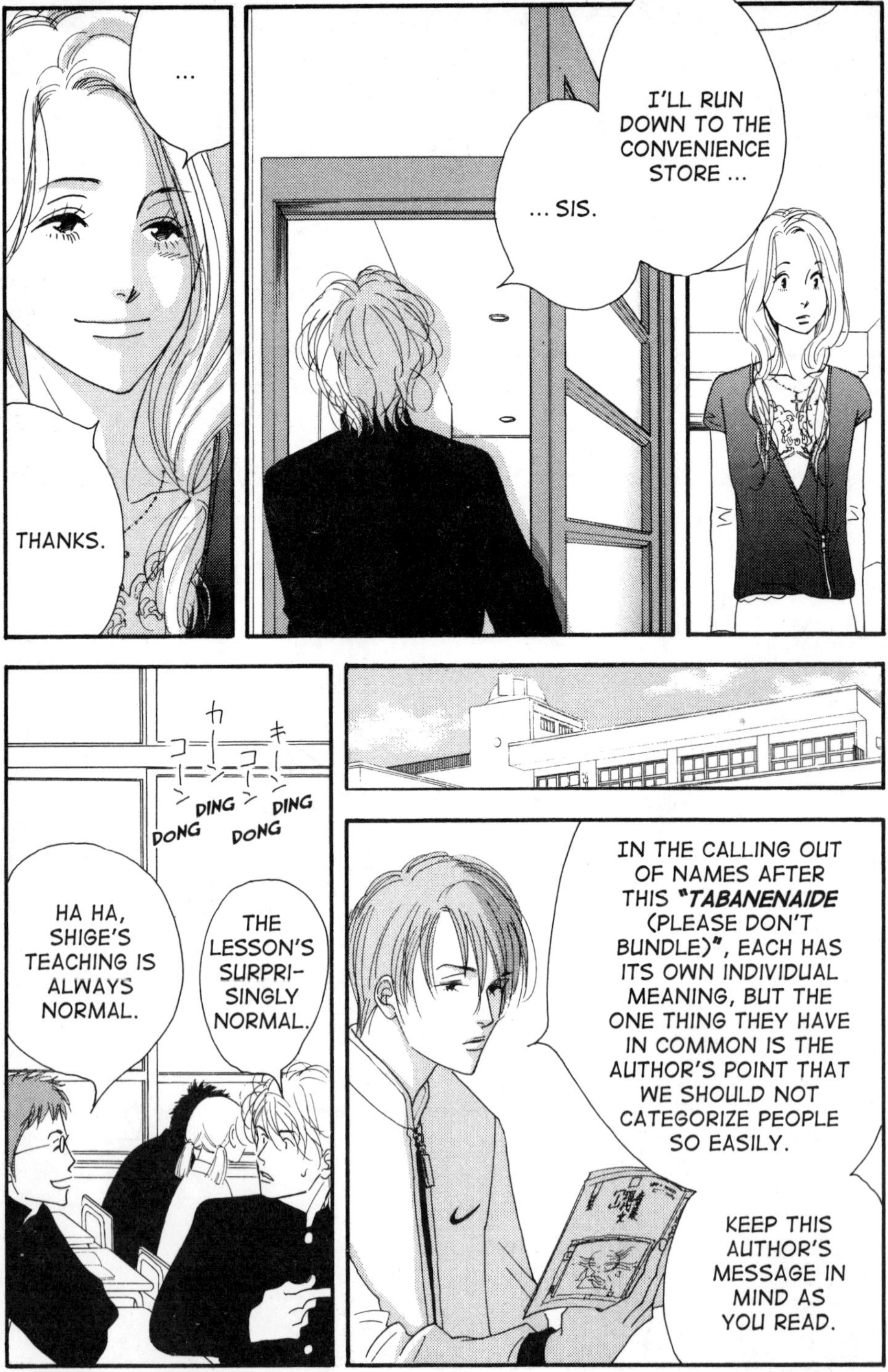
I'LL RUN DOWN TO THE CONVENIENCE STORE ...
... SIS.
...
THANKS.
IN THE CALLING OUT OF NAMES AFTER THIS "TABANENAIDE (PLEASE DON'T BUNDLE)", EACH HAS ITS OWN INDIVIDUAL MEANING, BUT THE ONE THING THEY HAVE IN COMMON IS THE AUTHOR'S POINT THAT WE SHOULD NOT CATEGORIZE PEOPLE SO EASILY.
KEEP THIS AUTHOR'S MESSAGE IN MIND AS YOU READ.
キーンコーンカーンコーン
DING DONG DING DONG
THE LESSON'S SURPRI-SINGLY NORMAL.
HA HA, SHIGE'S TEACHING IS ALWAYS NORMAL.

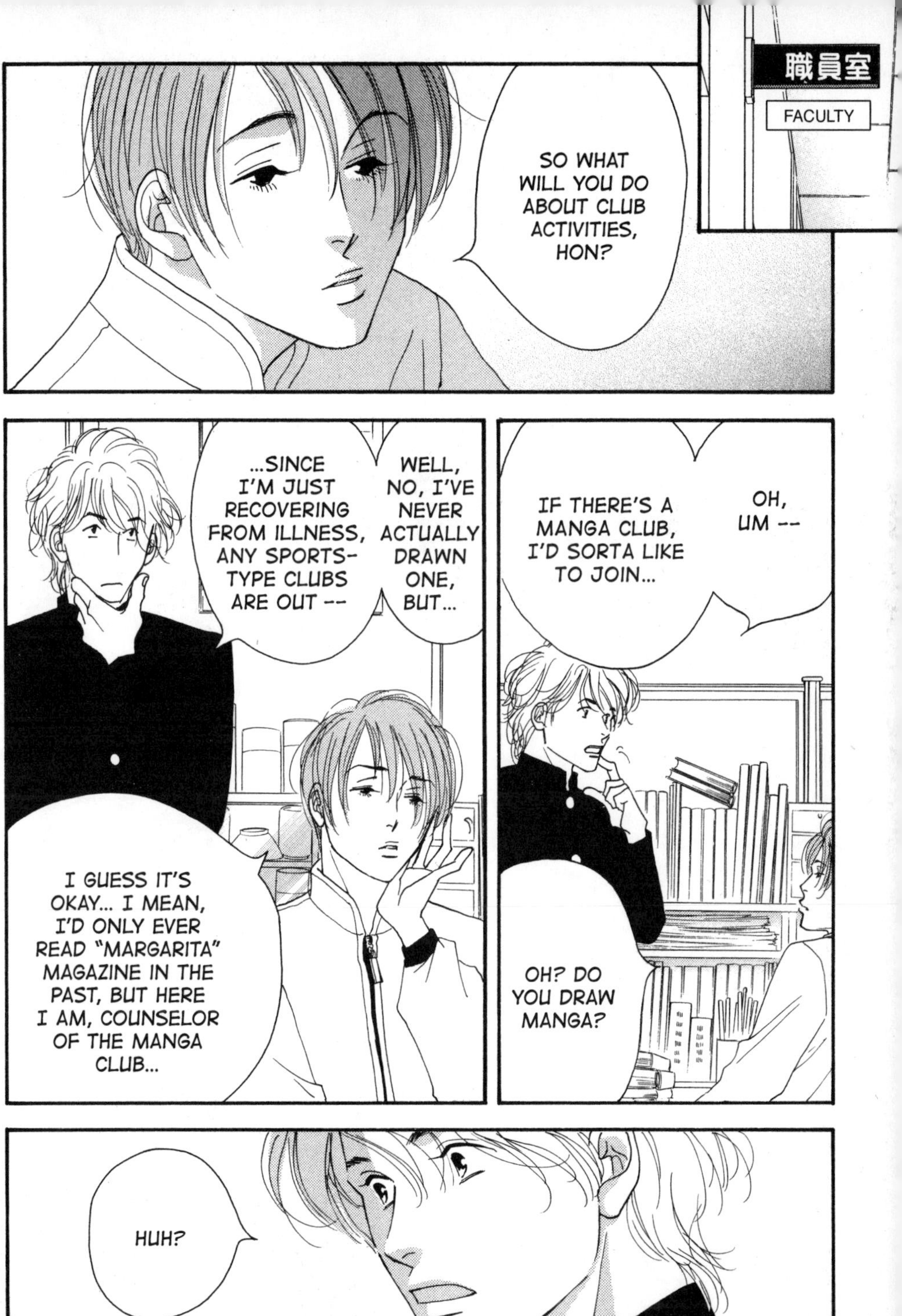
職員室
FACULTY
SO WHAT WILL YOU DO ABOUT CLUB ACTIVITIES, HON?
OH, UM --
IF THERE'S A MANGA CLUB, I'D SORTA LIKE TO JOIN...
OH? DO YOU DRAW MANGA?
WELL, NO, I'VE NEVER ACTUALLY DRAWN ONE, BUT...
...SINCE I'M JUST RECOVERING FROM ILLNESS, ANY SPORTS-TYPE CLUBS ARE OUT --
I GUESS IT'S OKAY... I MEAN, I'D ONLY EVER READ "MARGARITA" MAGAZINE IN THE PAST, BUT HERE I AM, COUNSELOR OF THE MANGA CLUB...
HUH?

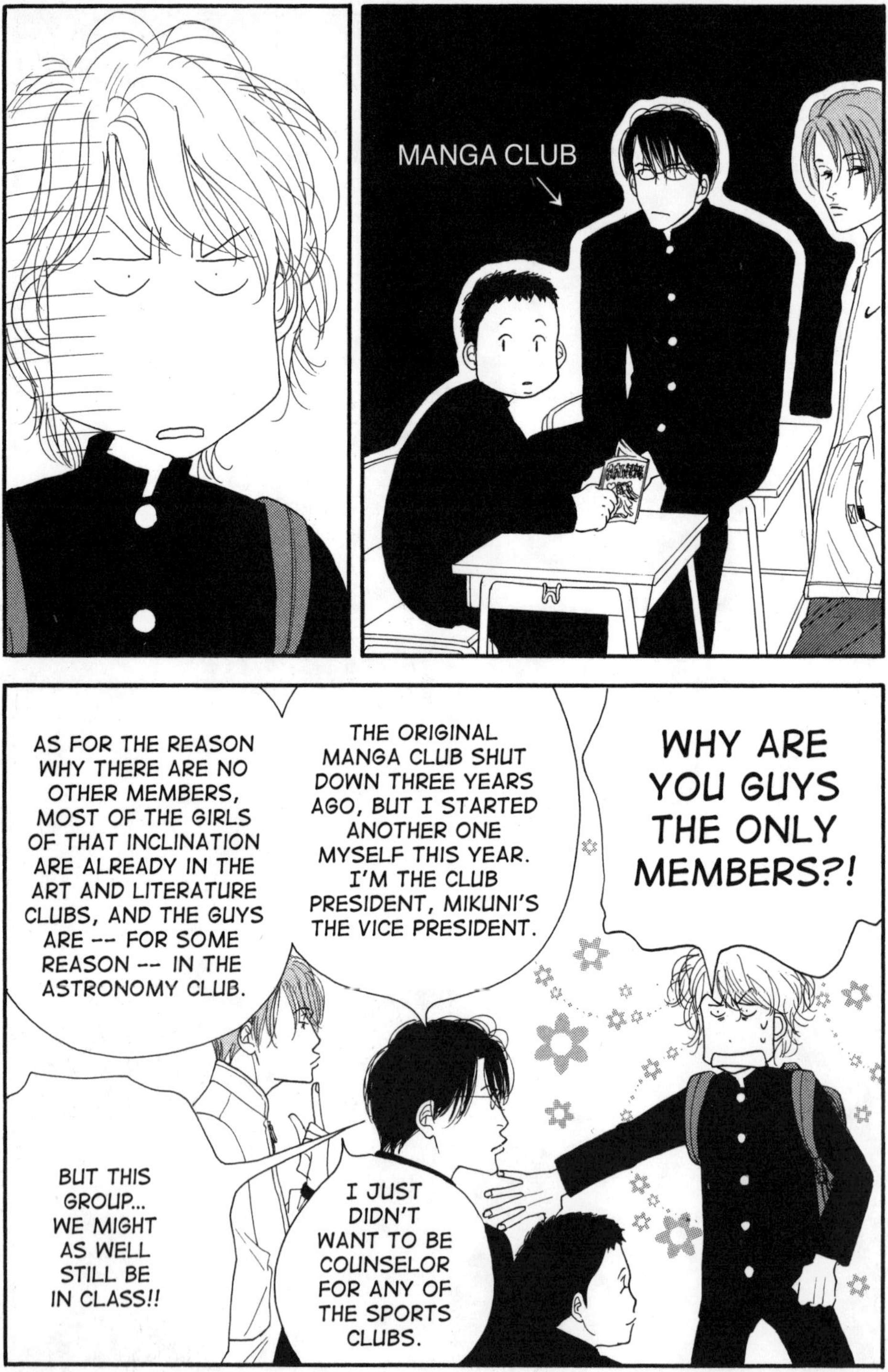
MANGA CLUB
WHY ARE YOU GUYS THE ONLY MEMBERS?!
THE ORIGINAL MANGA CLUB SHUT DOWN THREE YEARS AGO, BUT I STARTED ANOTHER ONE MYSELF THIS YEAR. I'M THE CLUB PRESIDENT, MIKUNI'S THE VICE PRESIDENT.
AS FOR THE REASON WHY THERE ARE NO OTHER MEMBERS, MOST OF THE GIRLS OF THAT INCLINATION ARE ALREADY IN THE ART AND LITERATURE CLUBS, AND THE GUYS ARE -- FOR SOME REASON -- IN THE ASTRONOMY CLUB.
I JUST DIDN'T WANT TO BE COUNSELOR FOR ANY OF THE SPORTS CLUBS.
BUT THIS GROUP... WE MIGHT AS WELL STILL BE IN CLASS!!

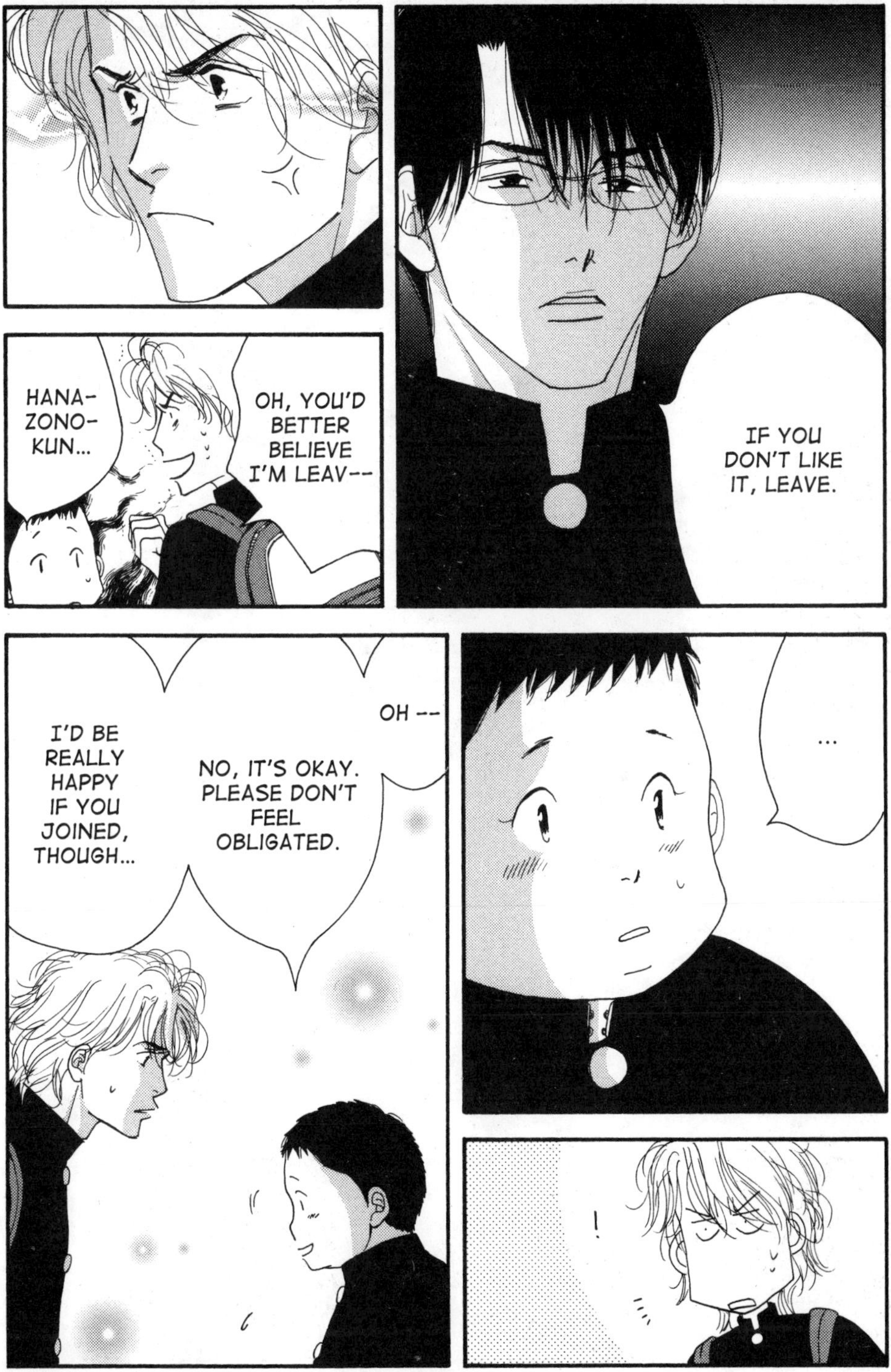
IF YOU DON'T LIKE IT, LEAVE.
OH, YOU'D BETTER BELIEVE I'M LEAV--
HANA-ZONO-KUN...
...
!
OH --
NO, IT'S OKAY. PLEASE DON'T FEEL OBLIGATED.
I'D BE REALLY HAPPY IF YOU JOINED, THOUGH...

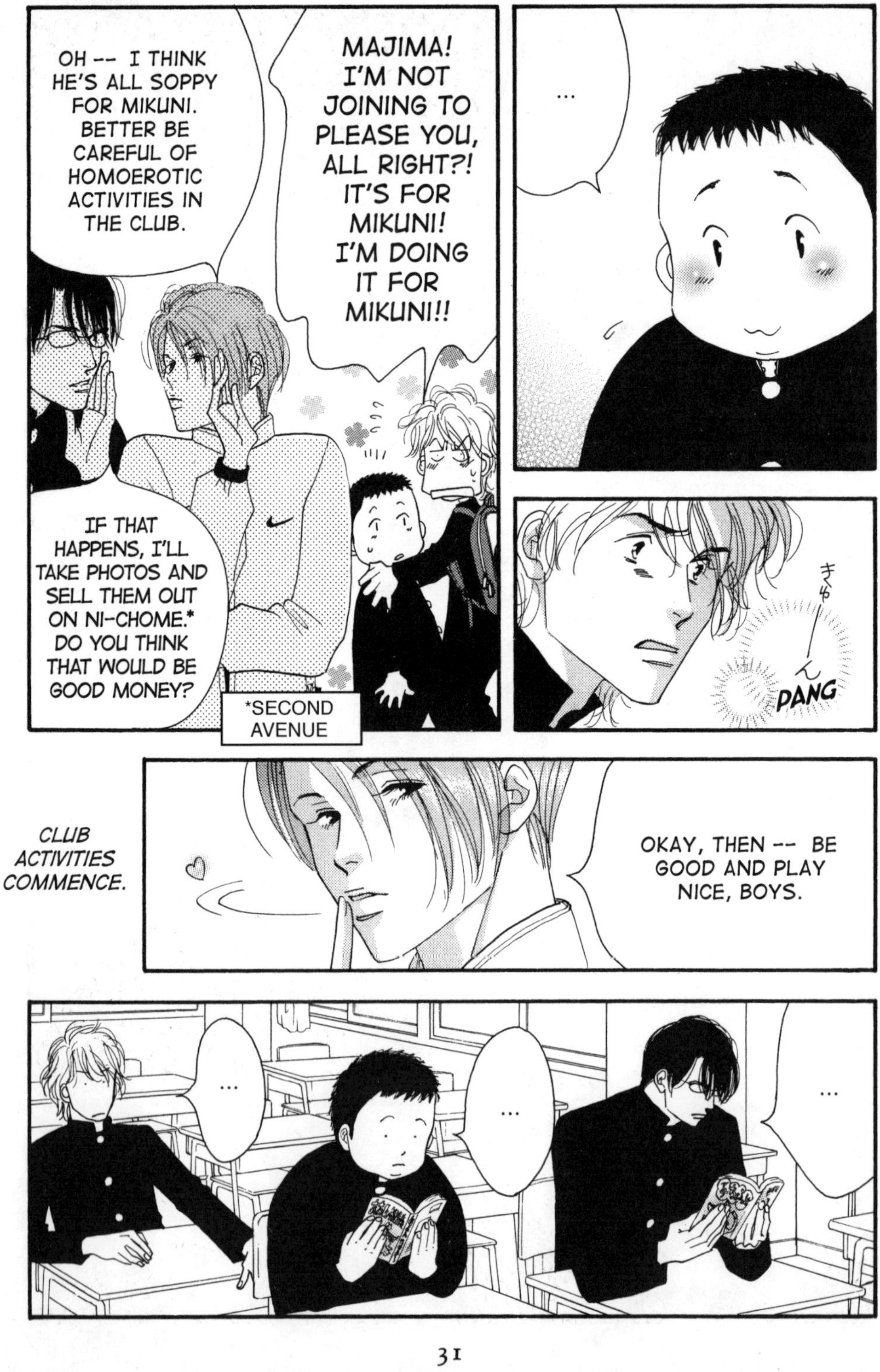
...
きゃーん
PANG
MAJIMA! I'M NOT JOINING TO PLEASE YOU, ALL RIGHT?! IT'S FOR MIKUNI! I'M DOING IT FOR MIKUNI!!
OH -- I THINK HE'S ALL SOPPY FOR MIKUNI. BETTER BE CAREFUL OF HOMOEROTIC ACTIVITIES IN THE CLUB.
IF THAT HAPPENS, I'LL TAKE PHOTOS AND SELL THEM OUT ON NI-CHOME.* DO YOU THINK THAT WOULD BE GOOD MONEY?
*SECOND AVENUE
OKAY, THEN -- BE GOOD AND PLAY NICE, BOYS.
CLUB ACTIVITIES COMMENCE.
...
...
...

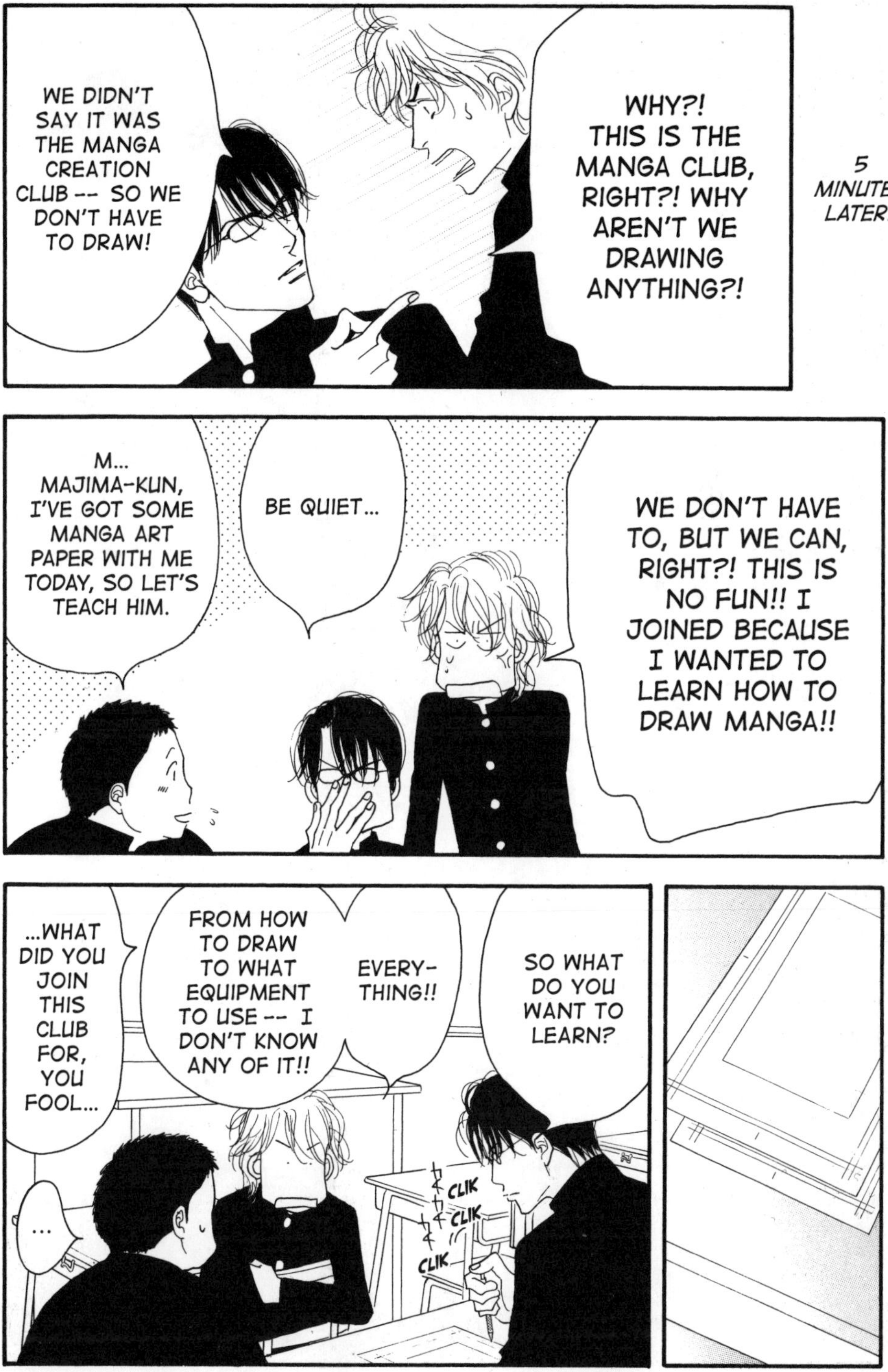
5 MINUTES LATER...
WHY?! THIS IS THE MANGA CLUB, RIGHT?! WHY AREN'T WE DRAWING ANYTHING?!
WE DIDN'T SAY IT WAS THE MANGA CREATION CLUB -- SO WE DON'T HAVE TO DRAW!
WE DON'T HAVE TO, BUT WE CAN, RIGHT?! THIS IS NO FUN!! I JOINED BECAUSE I WANTED TO LEARN HOW TO DRAW MANGA!!
BE QUIET...
M... MAJIMA-KUN, I'VE GOT SOME MANGA ART PAPER WITH ME TODAY, SO LET'S TEACH HIM.
SO WHAT DO YOU WANT TO LEARN?
EVERY-THING!!
FROM HOW TO DRAW TO WHAT EQUIPMENT TO USE -- I DON'T KNOW ANY OF IT!!
...WHAT DID YOU JOIN THIS CLUB FOR, YOU FOOL...
CLIK
CLIK
CLIK
...

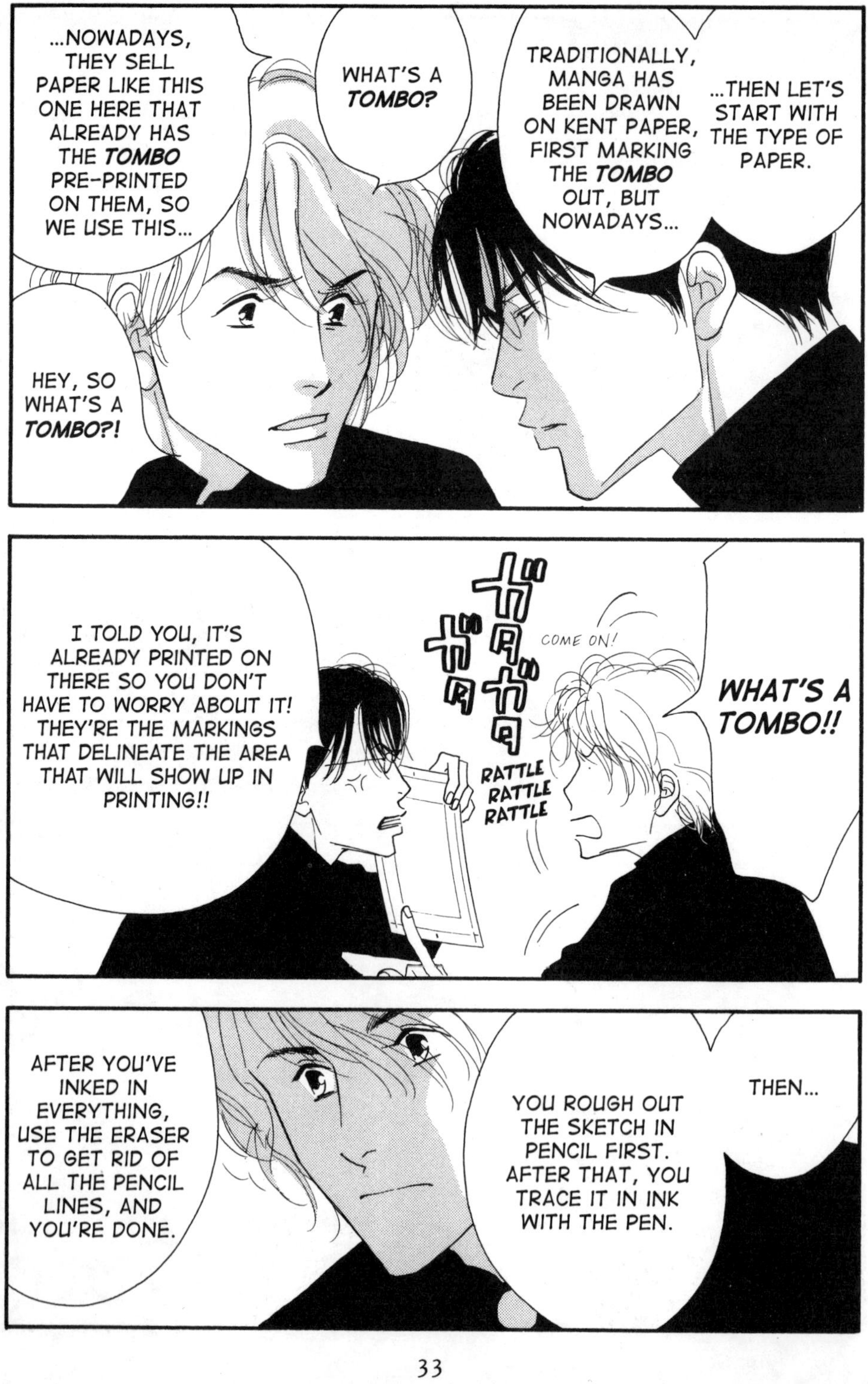
...THEN LET'S START WITH THE TYPE OF PAPER.
TRADITIONALLY, MANGA HAS BEEN DRAWN ON KENT PAPER, FIRST MARKING THE *TOMBO* OUT, BUT NOWADAYS...
WHAT'S A *TOMBO?*
...NOWADAYS, THEY SELL PAPER LIKE THIS ONE HERE THAT ALREADY HAS THE *TOMBO* PRE-PRINTED ON THEM, SO WE USE THIS...
HEY, SO WHAT'S A *TOMBO?!*
WHAT'S A TOMBO!!
COME ON!
RATTLE RATTLE RATTLE
I TOLD YOU, IT'S ALREADY PRINTED ON THERE SO YOU DON'T HAVE TO WORRY ABOUT IT! THEY'RE THE MARKINGS THAT DELINEATE THE AREA THAT WILL SHOW UP IN PRINTING!!
THEN...
YOU ROUGH OUT THE SKETCH IN PENCIL FIRST. AFTER THAT, YOU TRACE IT IN INK WITH THE PEN.
AFTER YOU'VE INKED IN EVERYTHING, USE THE ERASER TO GET RID OF ALL THE PENCIL LINES, AND YOU'RE DONE.

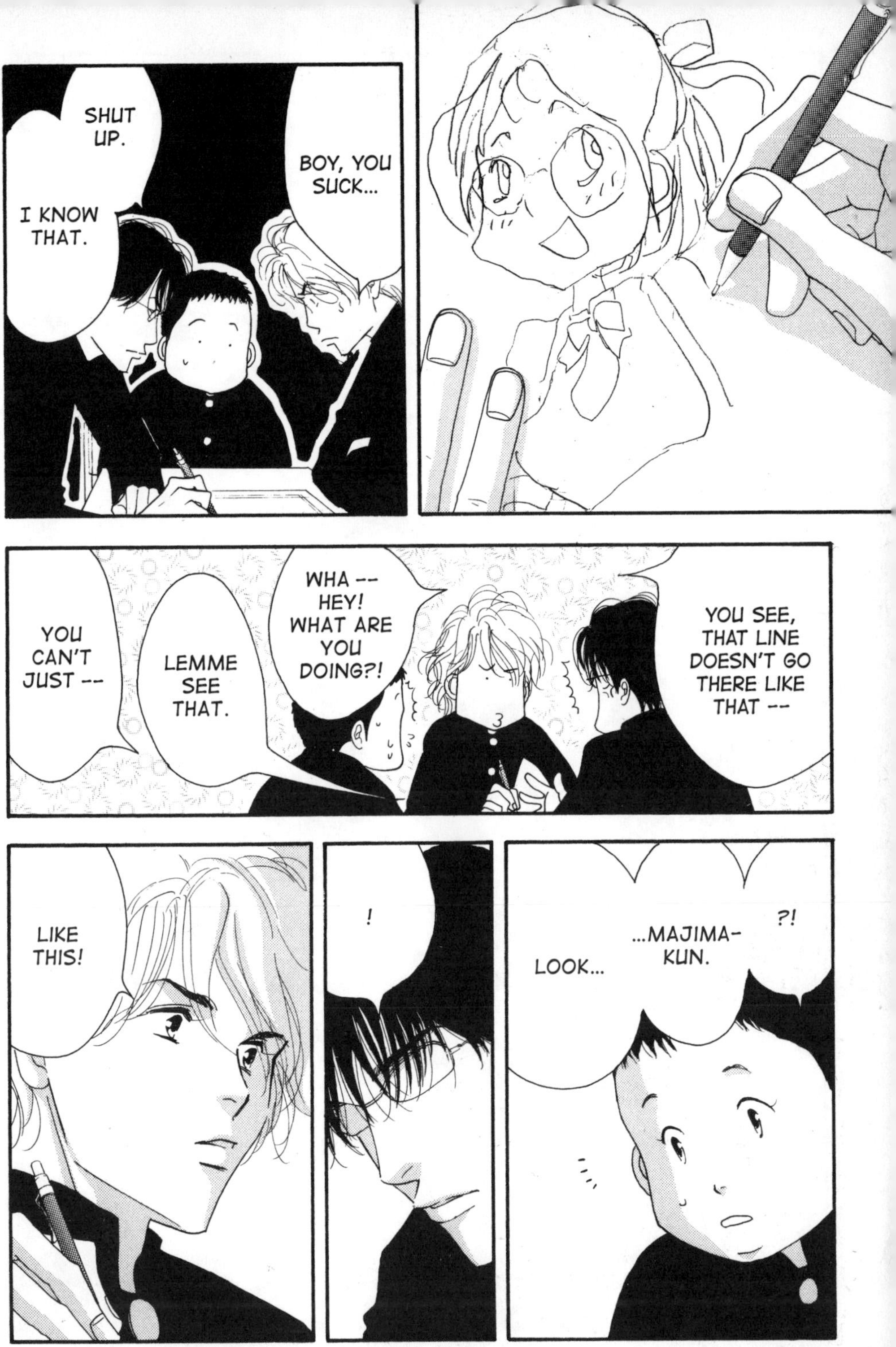
BOY, YOU SUCK...
SHUT UP.
I KNOW THAT.
YOU SEE, THAT LINE DOESN'T GO THERE LIKE THAT --
WHA -- HEY! WHAT ARE YOU DOING?!
LEMME SEE THAT.
YOU CAN'T JUST --
?!
...MAJIMA-KUN.
LOOK...
!
LIKE THIS!

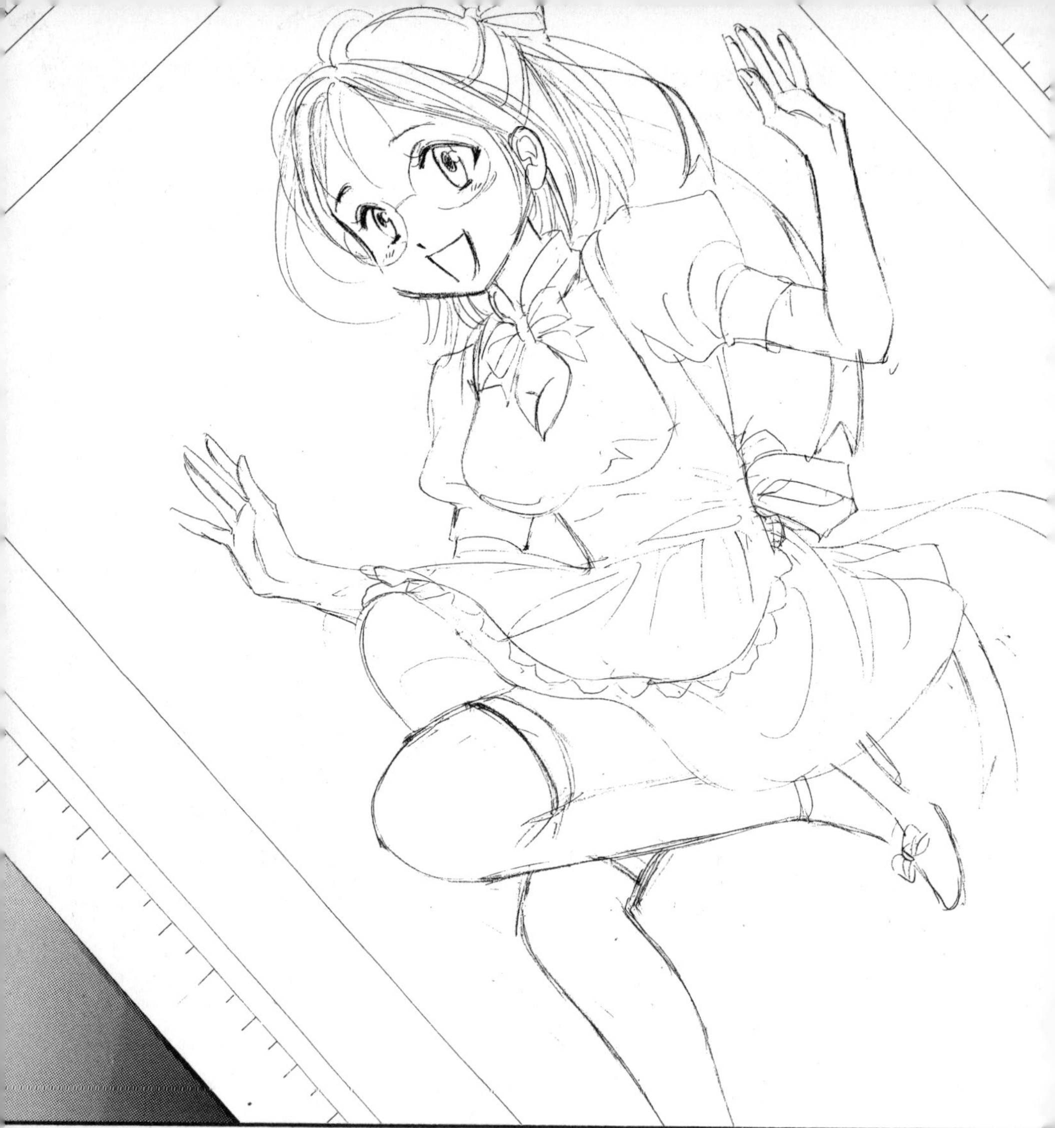

SAMPLE DRAWING ASSISTANCE: AKIRA HOUJOU

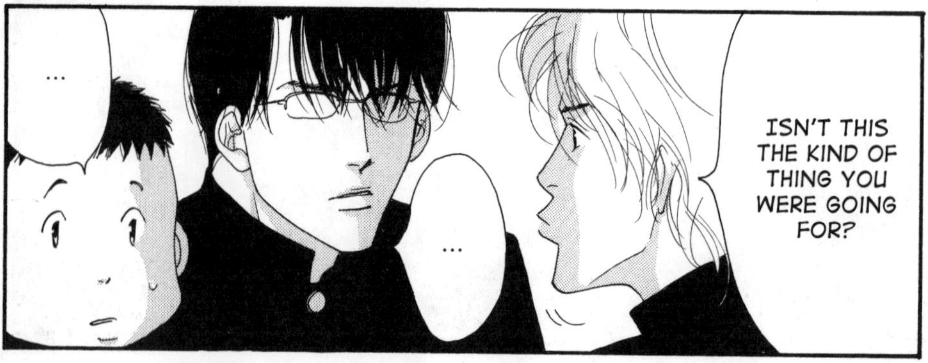
ISN'T THIS THE KIND OF THING YOU WERE GOING FOR?
...
...

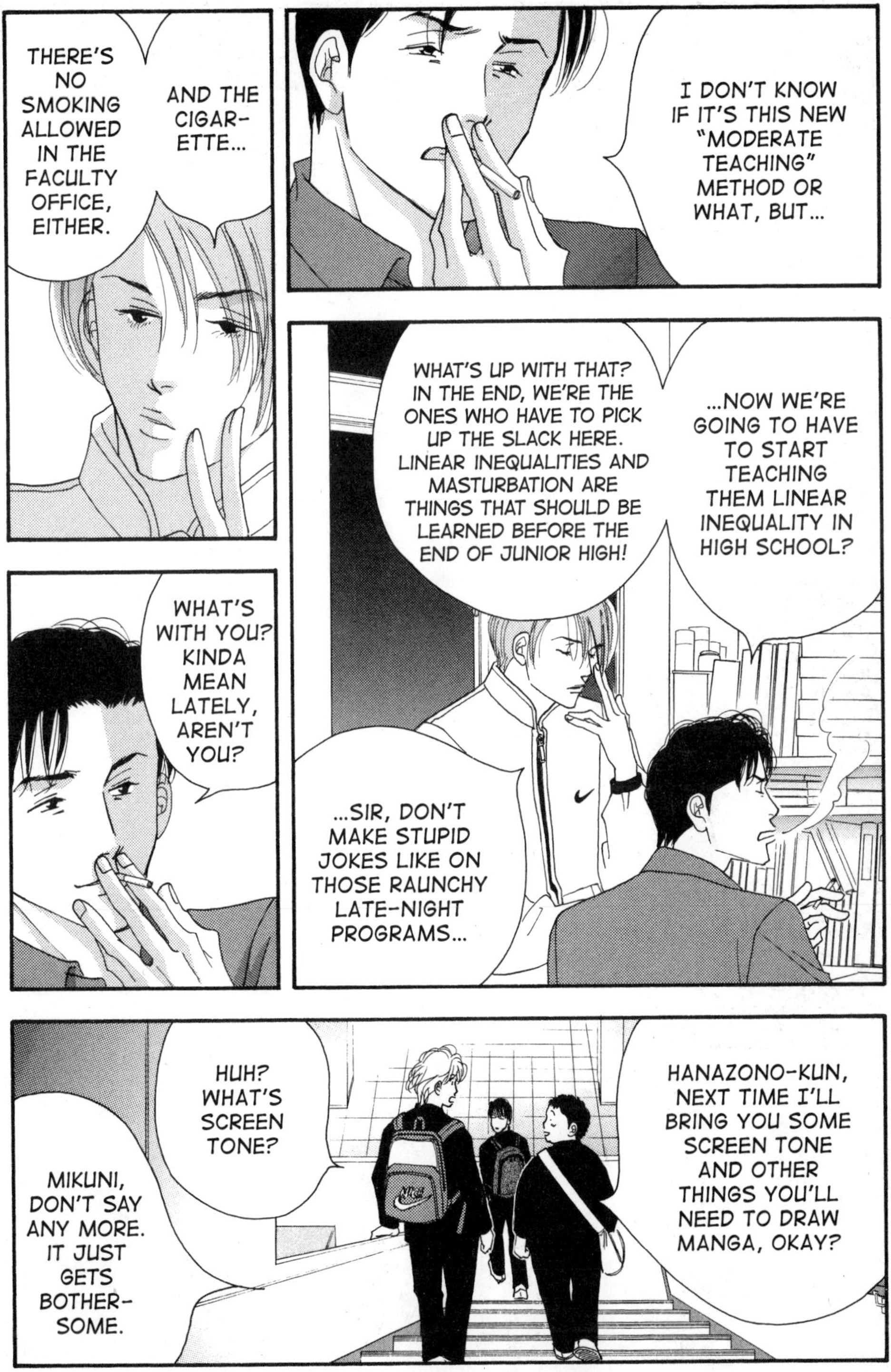
I DON'T KNOW IF IT'S THIS NEW "MODERATE TEACHING" METHOD OR WHAT, BUT...
AND THE CIGARETTE...
THERE'S NO SMOKING ALLOWED IN THE FACULTY OFFICE, EITHER.
...NOW WE'RE GOING TO HAVE TO START TEACHING THEM LINEAR INEQUALITY IN HIGH SCHOOL?
WHAT'S UP WITH THAT? IN THE END, WE'RE THE ONES WHO HAVE TO PICK UP THE SLACK HERE. LINEAR INEQUALITIES AND MASTURBATION ARE THINGS THAT SHOULD BE LEARNED BEFORE THE END OF JUNIOR HIGH!
...SIR, DON'T MAKE STUPID JOKES LIKE ON THOSE RAUNCHY LATE-NIGHT PROGRAMS...
WHAT'S WITH YOU? KINDA MEAN LATELY, AREN'T YOU?
HANAZONO-KUN, NEXT TIME I'LL BRING YOU SOME SCREEN TONE AND OTHER THINGS YOU'LL NEED TO DRAW MANGA, OKAY?
HUH? WHAT'S SCREEN TONE?
MIKUNI, DON'T SAY ANY MORE. IT JUST GETS BOTHERSOME.

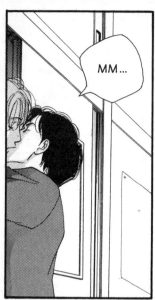

MM...

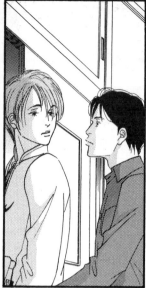

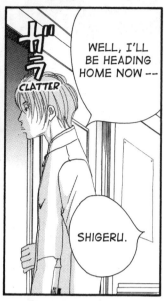

CLATTER

WELL, I'LL BE HEADING HOME NOW --

SHIGERU.

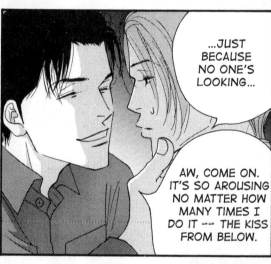

...JUST BECAUSE NO ONE'S LOOKING...

AW, COME ON. IT'S SO AROUSING NO MATTER HOW MANY TIMES I DO IT -- THE KISS FROM BELOW.

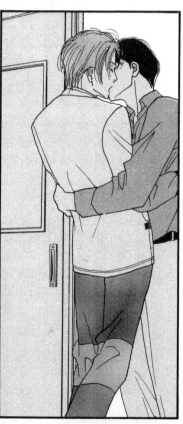

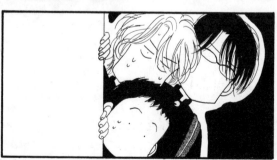

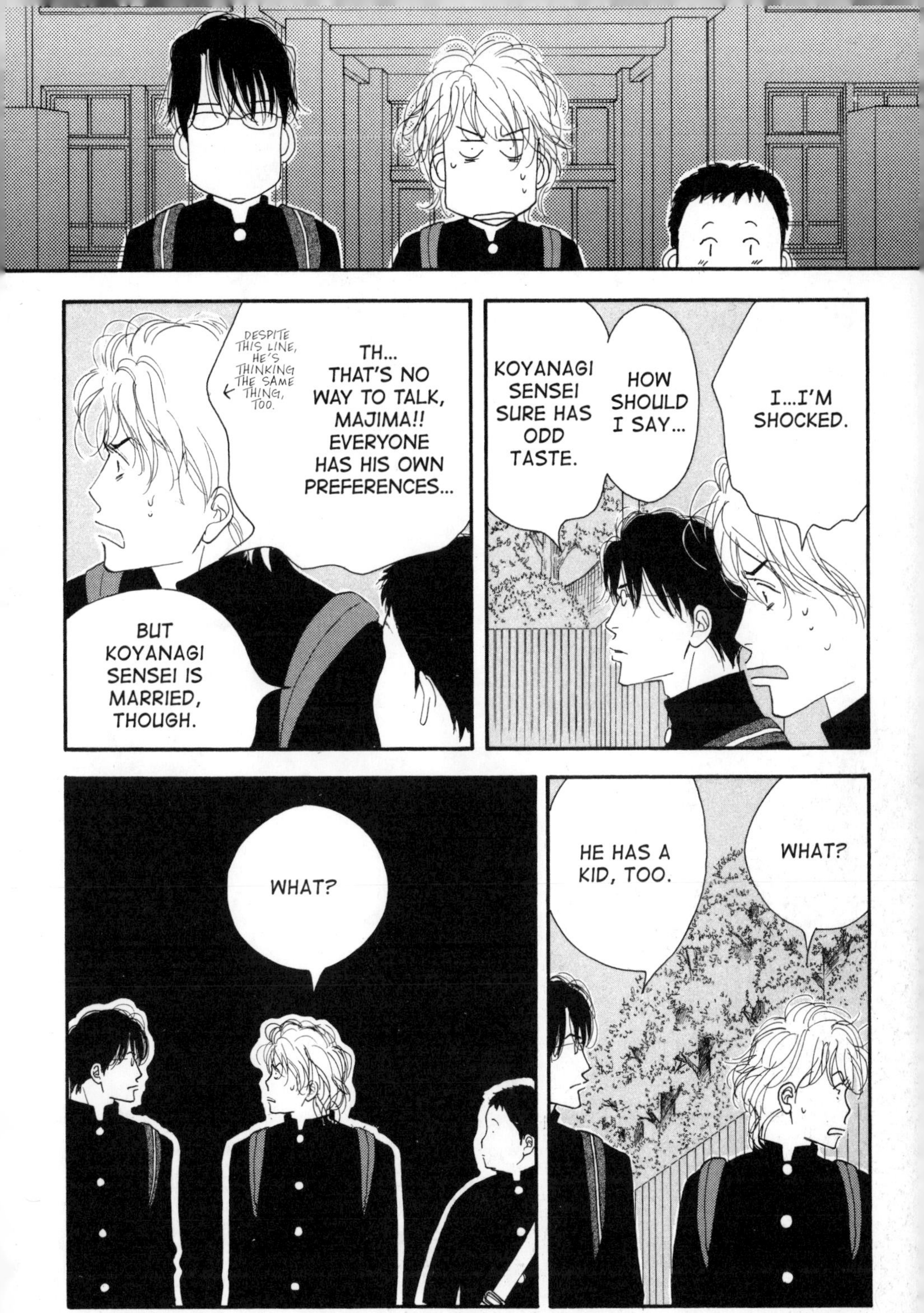
I...I'M SHOCKED.
HOW SHOULD I SAY...
KOYANAGI SENSEI SURE HAS ODD TASTE.
TH... THAT'S NO WAY TO TALK, MAJIMA!! EVERYONE HAS HIS OWN PREFERENCES...
DESPITE THIS LINE, HE'S THINKING THE SAME THING, TOO.
BUT KOYANAGI SENSEI IS MARRIED, THOUGH.
WHAT?
HE HAS A KID, TOO.
WHAT?

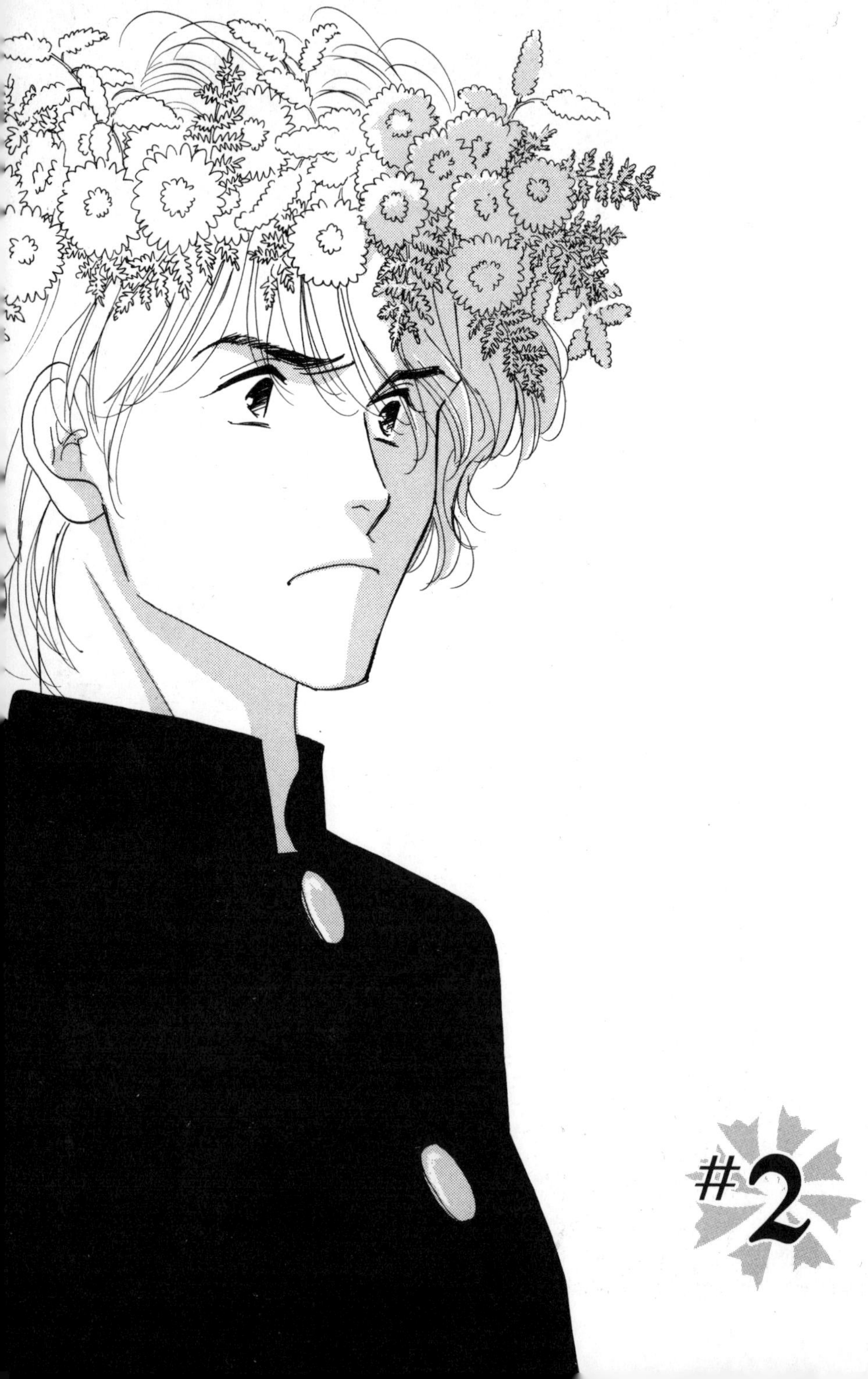
#2

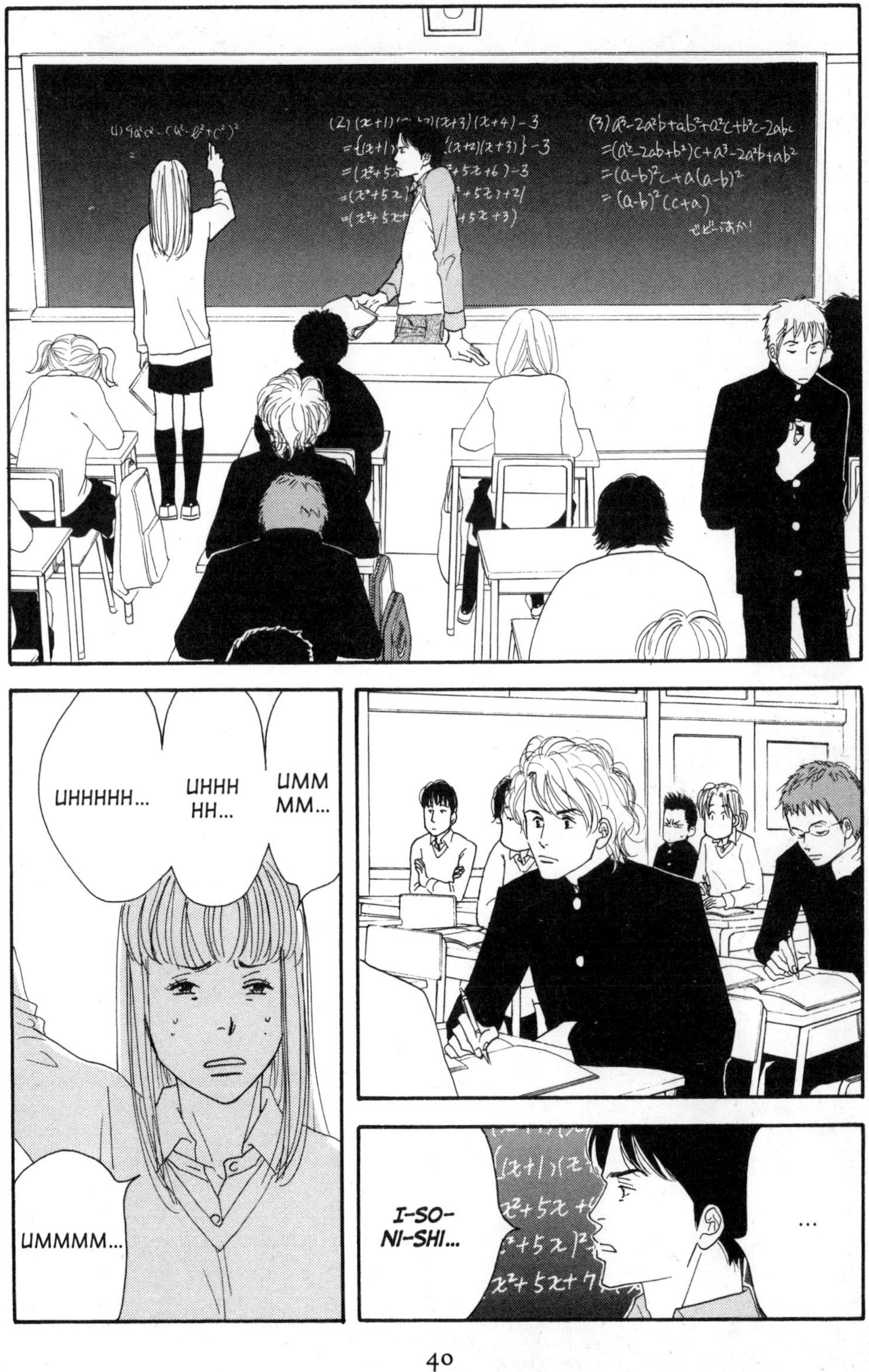
UMM MM...
UHHH HH...
UHHHHH...
UMMMM...
...
I-SO-NI-SHI...

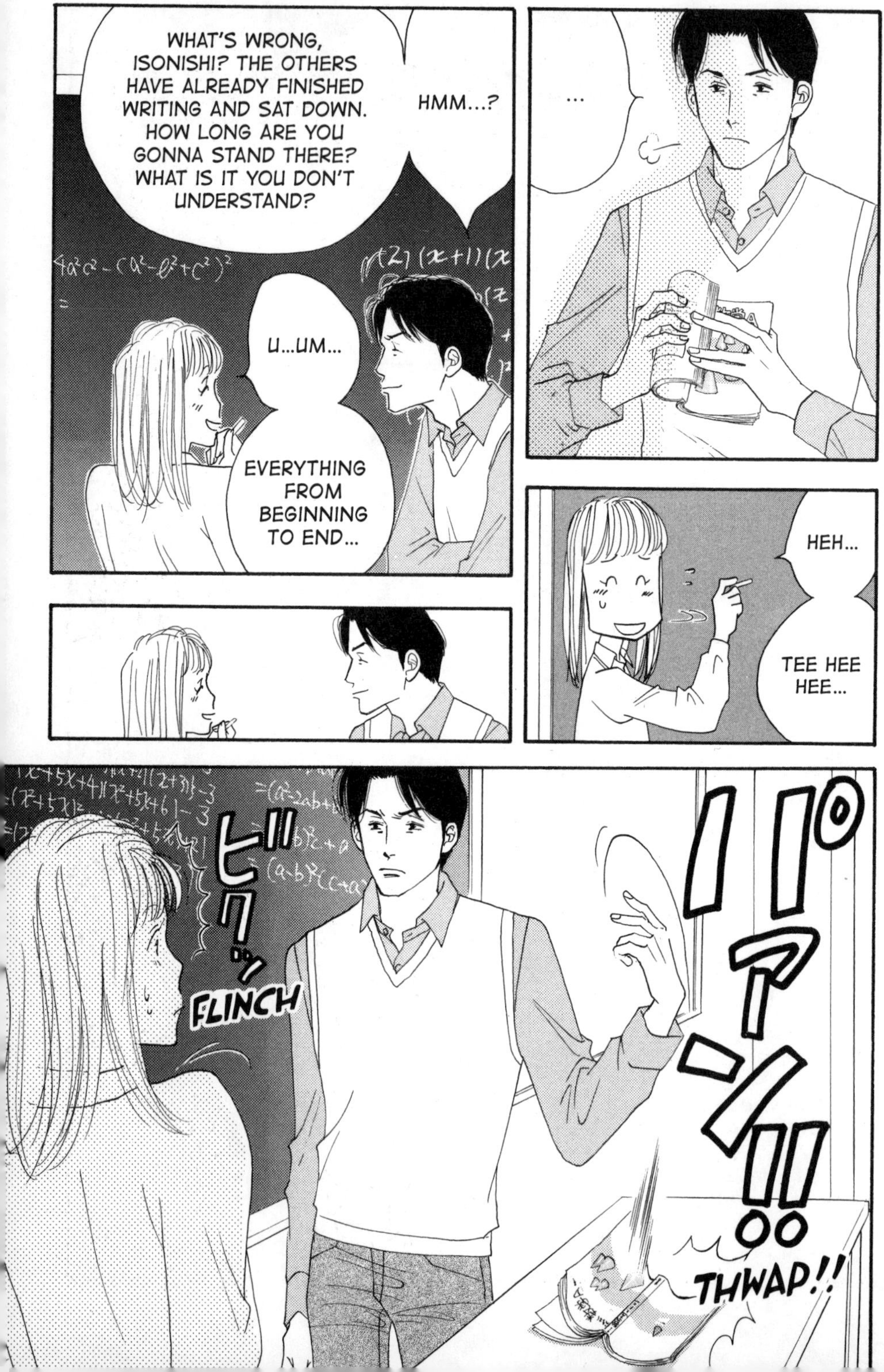
...
HMM...?
WHAT'S WRONG, ISONISHI? THE OTHERS HAVE ALREADY FINISHED WRITING AND SAT DOWN. HOW LONG ARE YOU GONNA STAND THERE? WHAT IS IT YOU DON'T UNDERSTAND?
U...UM...
EVERYTHING FROM BEGINNING TO END...
HEH...
TEE HEE HEE...
パァン!!
THWAP!!
ビクッ
FLINCH

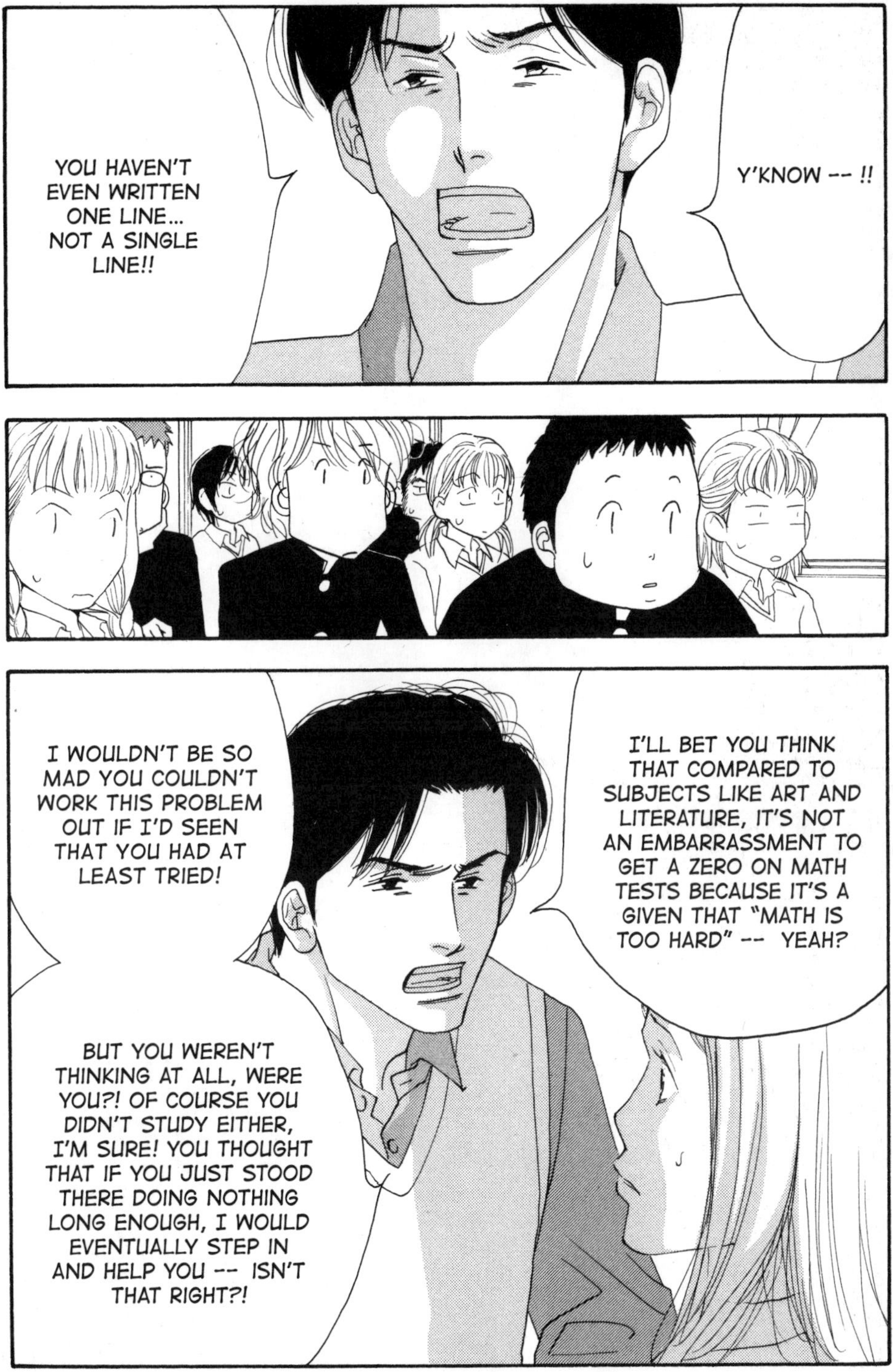
Y'KNOW -- !!
YOU HAVEN'T EVEN WRITTEN ONE LINE... NOT A SINGLE LINE!!
I'LL BET YOU THINK THAT COMPARED TO SUBJECTS LIKE ART AND LITERATURE, IT'S NOT AN EMBARRASSMENT TO GET A ZERO ON MATH TESTS BECAUSE IT'S A GIVEN THAT "MATH IS TOO HARD" -- YEAH?
I WOULDN'T BE SO MAD YOU COULDN'T WORK THIS PROBLEM OUT IF I'D SEEN THAT YOU HAD AT LEAST TRIED!
BUT YOU WEREN'T THINKING AT ALL, WERE YOU?! OF COURSE YOU DIDN'T STUDY EITHER, I'M SURE! YOU THOUGHT THAT IF YOU JUST STOOD THERE DOING NOTHING LONG ENOUGH, I WOULD EVENTUALLY STEP IN AND HELP YOU -- ISN'T THAT RIGHT?!

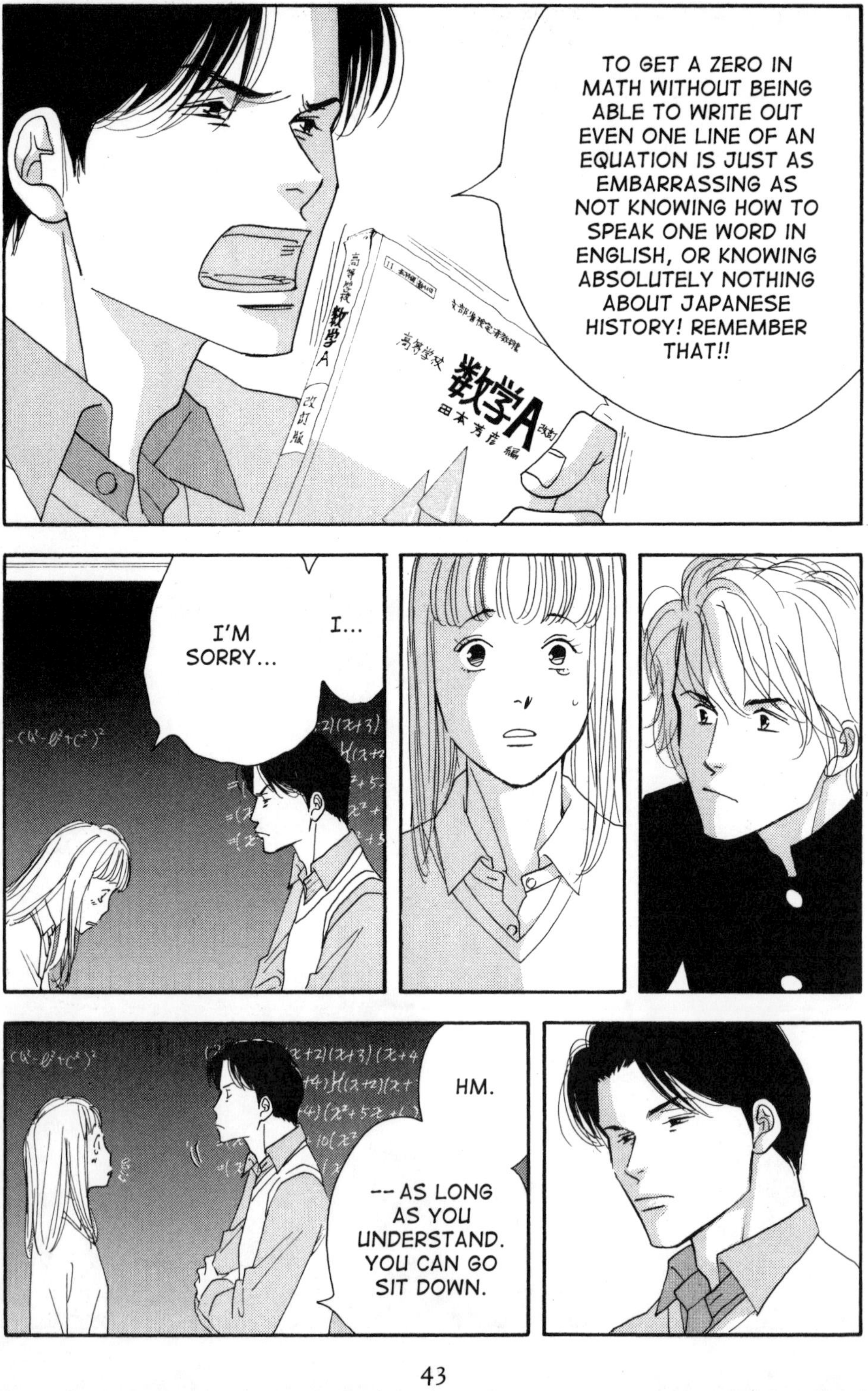
TO GET A ZERO IN MATH WITHOUT BEING ABLE TO WRITE OUT EVEN ONE LINE OF AN EQUATION IS JUST AS EMBARRASSING AS NOT KNOWING HOW TO SPEAK ONE WORD IN ENGLISH, OR KNOWING ABSOLUTELY NOTHING ABOUT JAPANESE HISTORY! REMEMBER THAT!!
数学A
I...
I'M SORRY...
HM.
--AS LONG AS YOU UNDERSTAND. YOU CAN GO SIT DOWN.

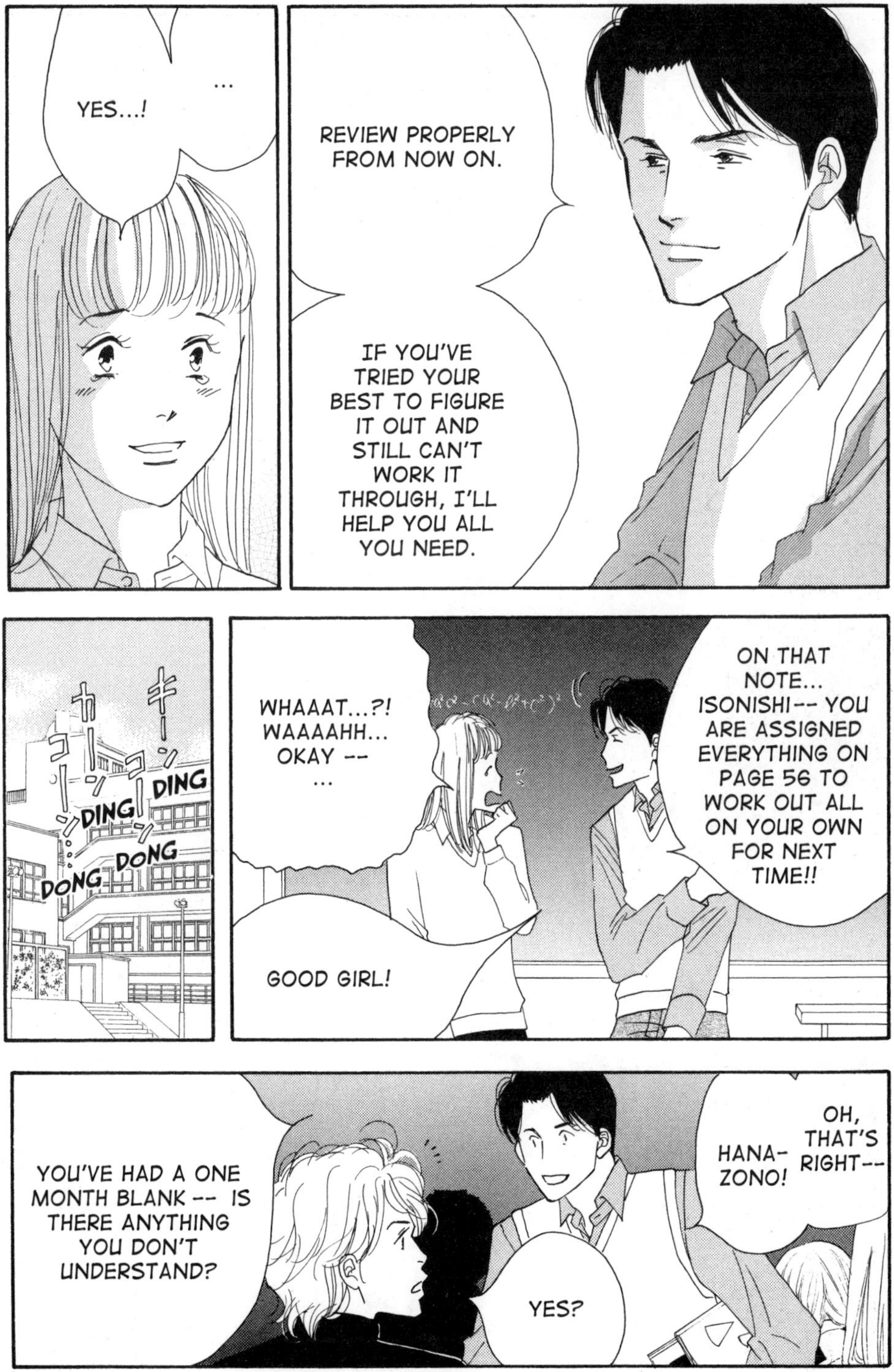
REVIEW PROPERLY FROM NOW ON.
IF YOU'VE TRIED YOUR BEST TO FIGURE IT OUT AND STILL CAN'T WORK IT THROUGH, I'LL HELP YOU ALL YOU NEED.
...
YES...!
ON THAT NOTE... ISONISHI-- YOU ARE ASSIGNED EVERYTHING ON PAGE 56 TO WORK OUT ALL ON YOUR OWN FOR NEXT TIME!!
WHAAAT...?! WAAAAHH... OKAY -- ...
GOOD GIRL!
DING
DING
DONG
DONG
OH, THAT'S RIGHT--
HANA-ZONO!
YOU'VE HAD A ONE MONTH BLANK -- IS THERE ANYTHING YOU DON'T UNDERSTAND?
YES?

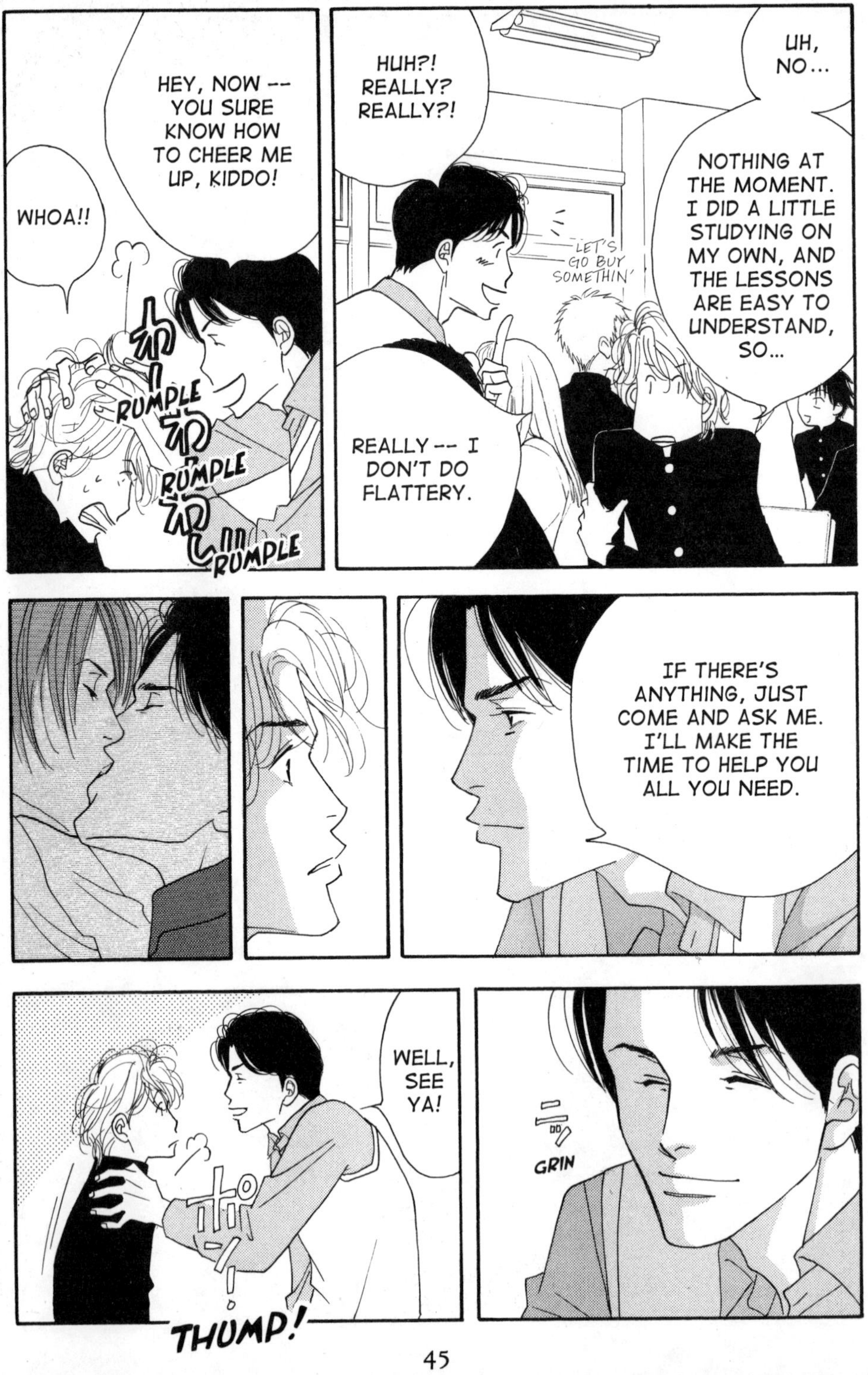
UH, NO...
NOTHING AT THE MOMENT. I DID A LITTLE STUDYING ON MY OWN, AND THE LESSONS ARE EASY TO UNDERSTAND, SO...
HUH?! REALLY? REALLY?!
LET'S GO BUY SOMETHIN'
REALLY -- I DON'T DO FLATTERY.
HEY, NOW -- YOU SURE KNOW HOW TO CHEER ME UP, KIDDO!
WHOA!!
RUMPLE
RUMPLE
RUMPLE
IF THERE'S ANYTHING, JUST COME AND ASK ME. I'LL MAKE THE TIME TO HELP YOU ALL YOU NEED.
GRIN
WELL, SEE YA!
THUMP!

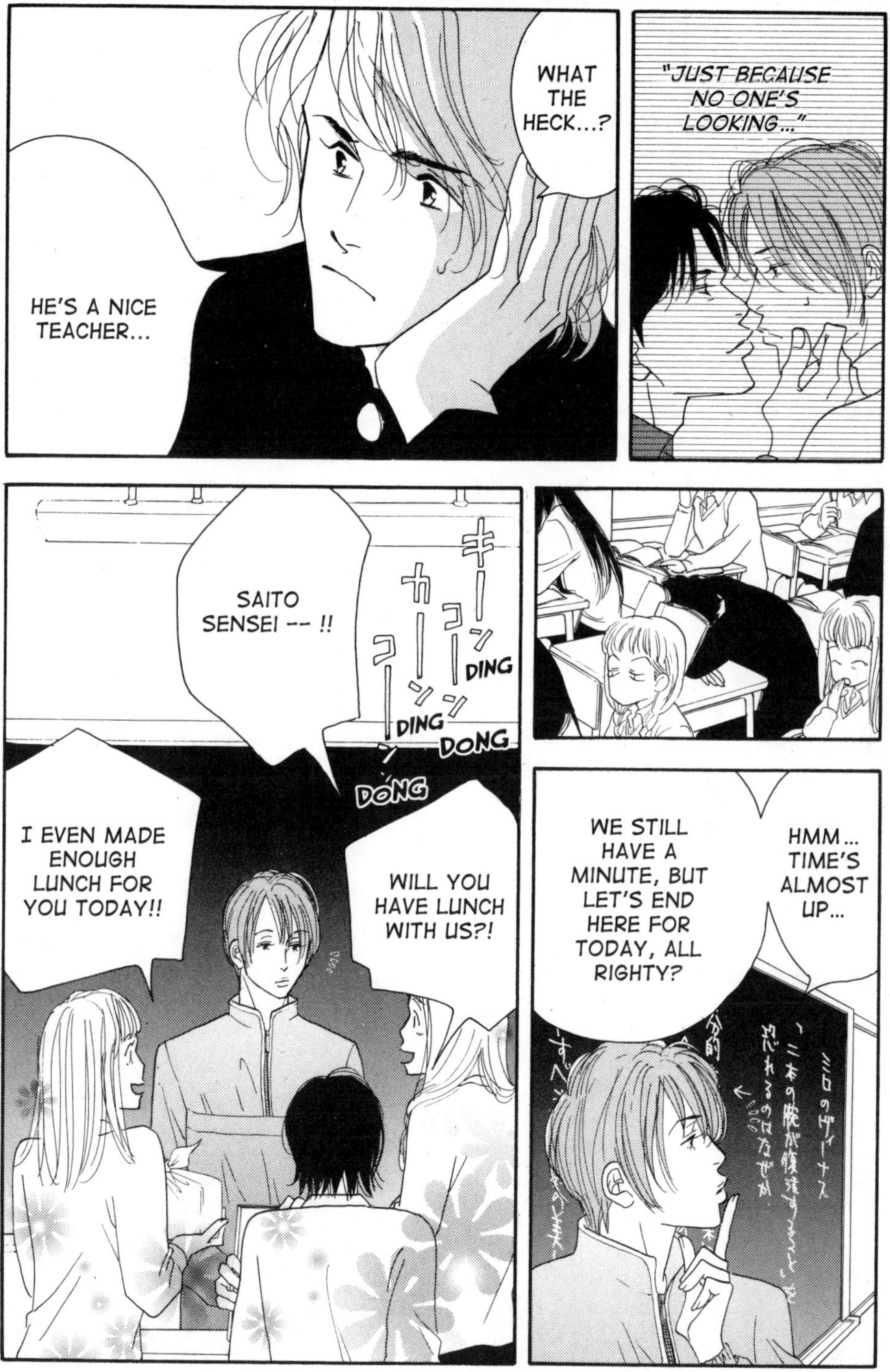
"JUST BECAUSE NO ONE'S LOOKING..."
WHAT THE HECK...?
HE'S A NICE TEACHER...
HMM... TIME'S ALMOST UP...
WE STILL HAVE A MINUTE, BUT LET'S END HERE FOR TODAY, ALL RIGHTY?
SAITO SENSEI -- !!
DING DONG DING DONG
WILL YOU HAVE LUNCH WITH US?!
I EVEN MADE ENOUGH LUNCH FOR YOU TODAY!!

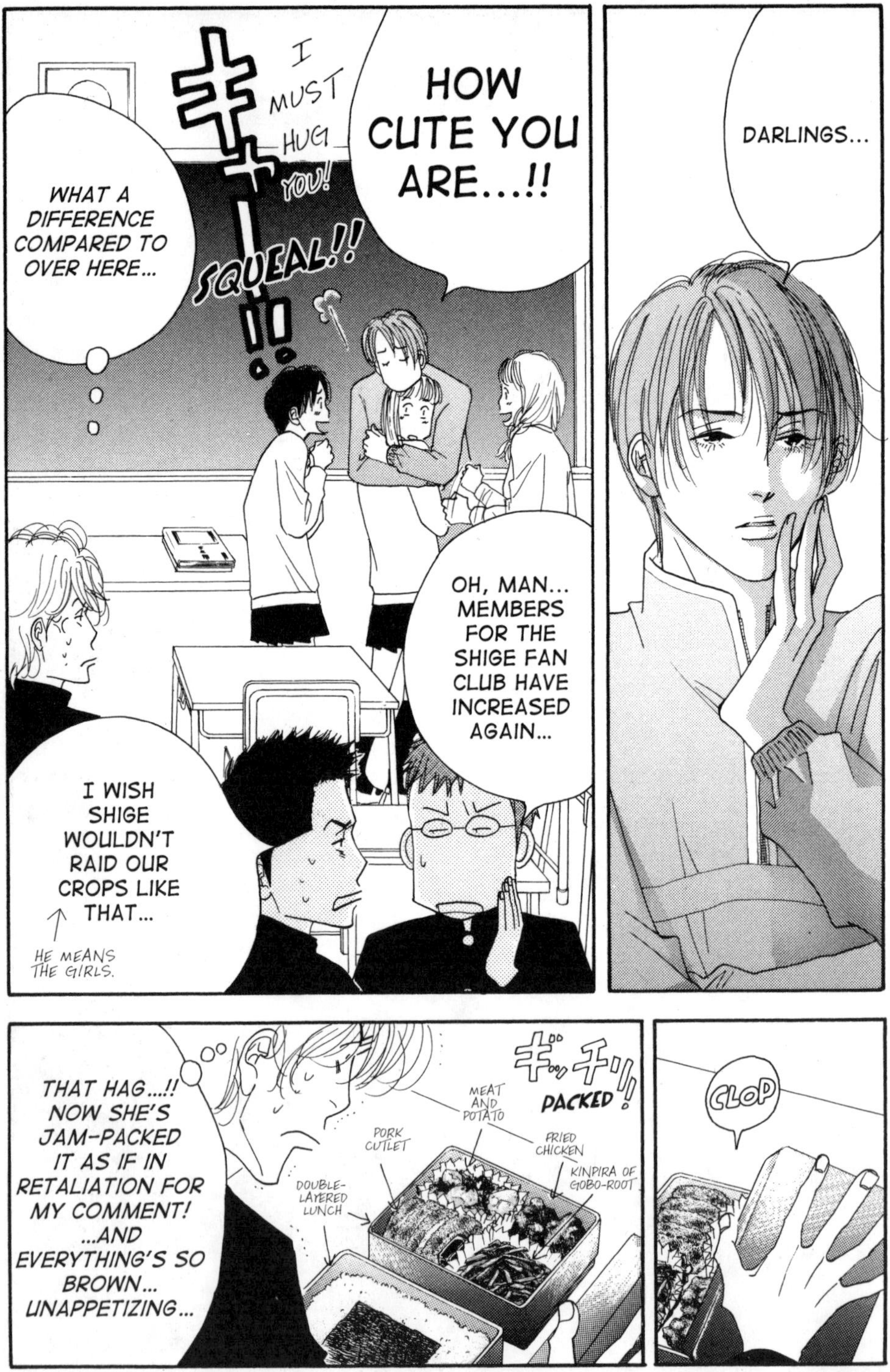
DARLINGS...
HOW CUTE YOU ARE...!!
I MUST HUG YOU!
SQUEAL!!
WHAT A DIFFERENCE COMPARED TO OVER HERE...
OH, MAN... MEMBERS FOR THE SHIGE FAN CLUB HAVE INCREASED AGAIN...
I WISH SHIGE WOULDN'T RAID OUR CROPS LIKE THAT...
HE MEANS THE GIRLS.
CLOP
PACKED!
MEAT AND POTATO
PORK CUTLET
FRIED CHICKEN
KINPIRA OF GOBO-ROOT
DOUBLE-LAYERED LUNCH
THAT HAG...!! NOW SHE'S JAM-PACKED IT AS IF IN RETALIATION FOR MY COMMENT! ...AND EVERYTHING'S SO BROWN... UNAPPETIZING...

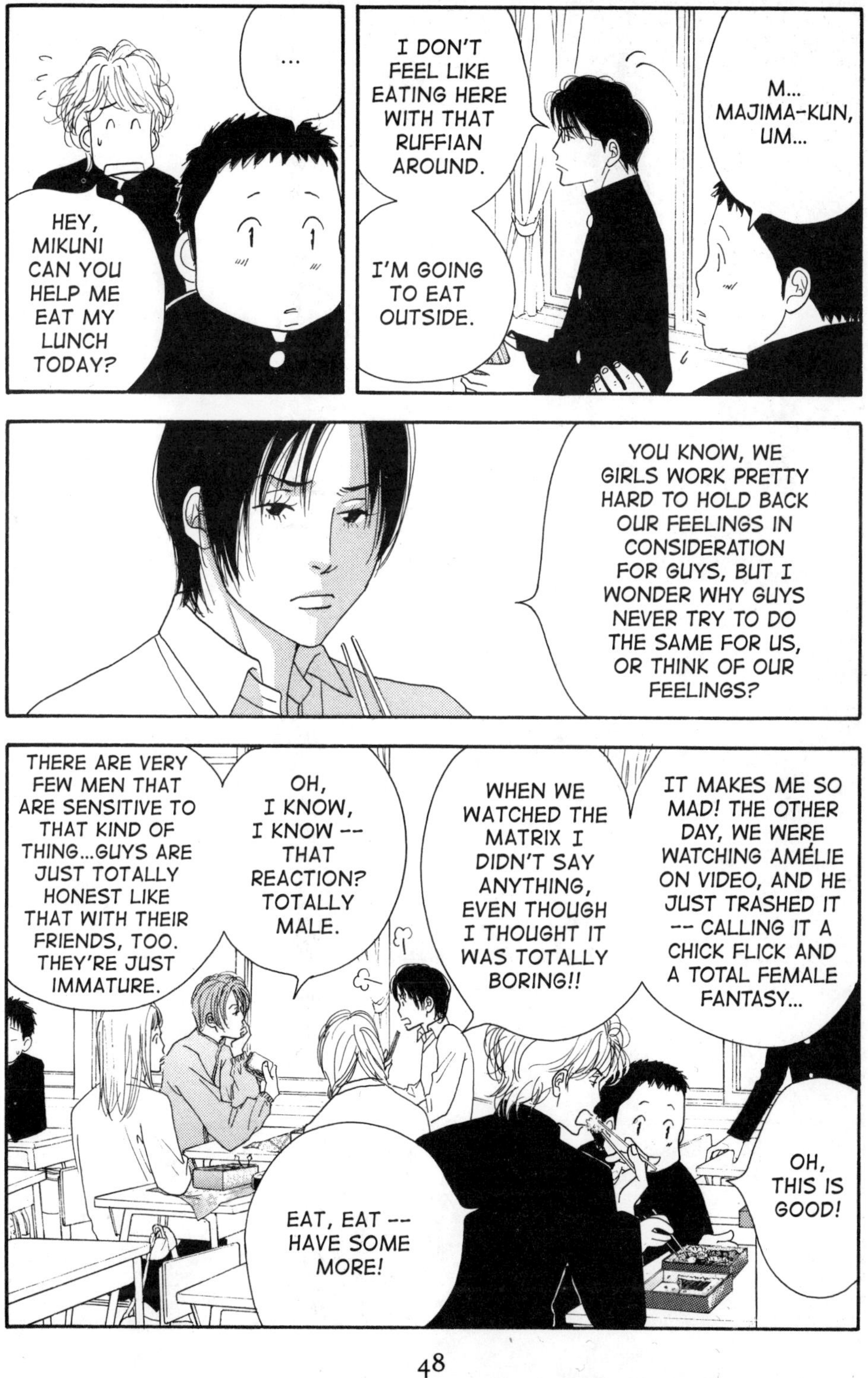
M... MAJIMA-KUN, UM...
I DON'T FEEL LIKE EATING HERE WITH THAT RUFFIAN AROUND.
I'M GOING TO EAT OUTSIDE.
...
HEY, MIKUNI CAN YOU HELP ME EAT MY LUNCH TODAY?
YOU KNOW, WE GIRLS WORK PRETTY HARD TO HOLD BACK OUR FEELINGS IN CONSIDERATION FOR GUYS, BUT I WONDER WHY GUYS NEVER TRY TO DO THE SAME FOR US, OR THINK OF OUR FEELINGS?
IT MAKES ME SO MAD! THE OTHER DAY, WE WERE WATCHING AMÉLIE ON VIDEO, AND HE JUST TRASHED IT -- CALLING IT A CHICK FLICK AND A TOTAL FEMALE FANTASY...
WHEN WE WATCHED THE MATRIX I DIDN'T SAY ANYTHING, EVEN THOUGH I THOUGHT IT WAS TOTALLY BORING!!
OH, I KNOW, I KNOW -- THAT REACTION? TOTALLY MALE.
THERE ARE VERY FEW MEN THAT ARE SENSITIVE TO THAT KIND OF THING...GUYS ARE JUST TOTALLY HONEST LIKE THAT WITH THEIR FRIENDS, TOO. THEY'RE JUST IMMATURE.
OH, THIS IS GOOD!
EAT, EAT -- HAVE SOME MORE!

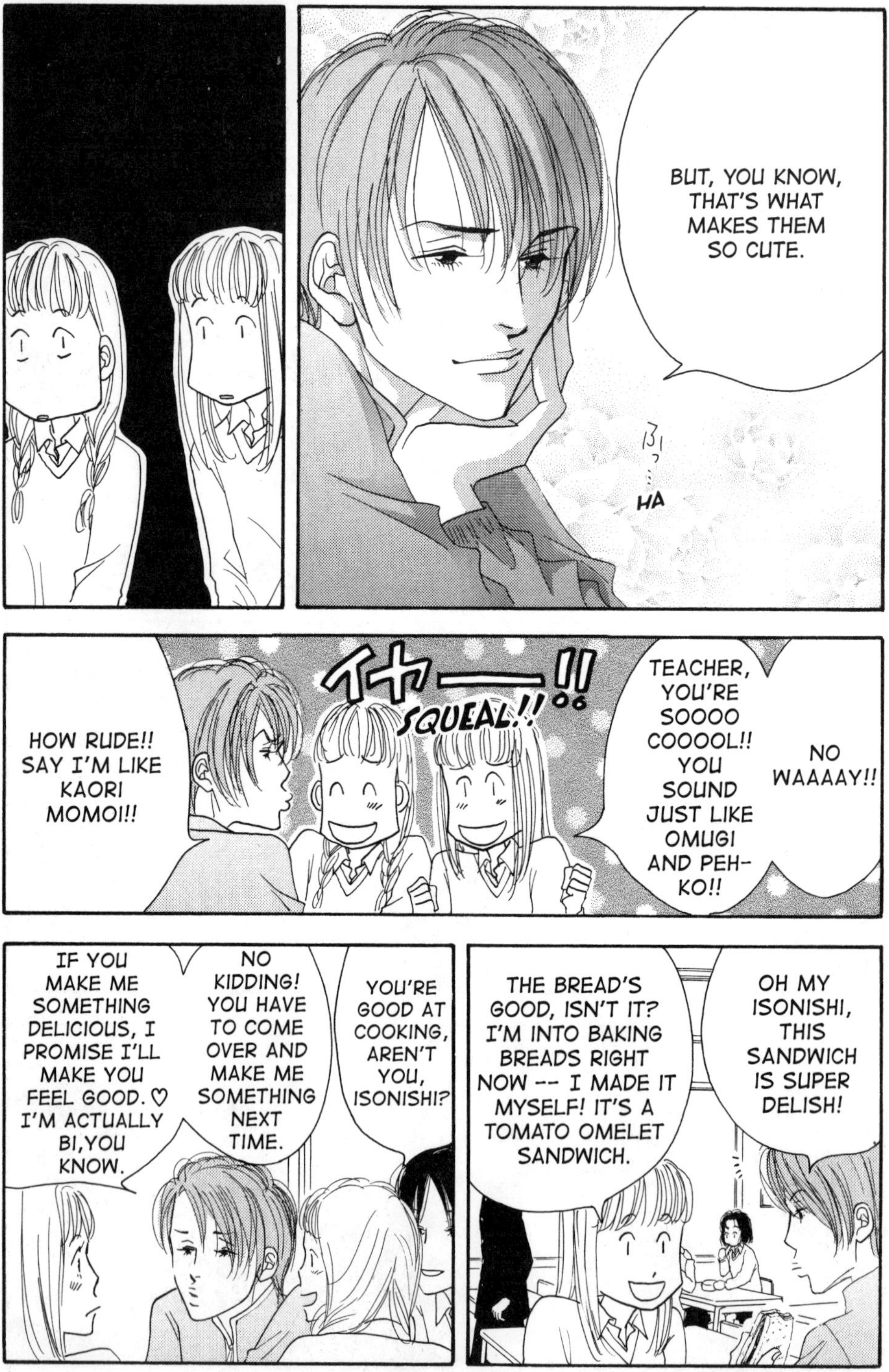
BUT, YOU KNOW, THAT'S WHAT MAKES THEM SO CUTE.
ふっ…
HA
NO WAAAAY!!
TEACHER, YOU'RE SOOOO COOOOL!! YOU SOUND JUST LIKE OMUGI AND PEH-KO!!
イヤー!!
SQUEAL!!
HOW RUDE!! SAY I'M LIKE KAORI MOMOI!!
OH MY ISONISHI, THIS SANDWICH IS SUPER DELISH!
THE BREAD'S GOOD, ISN'T IT? I'M INTO BAKING BREADS RIGHT NOW -- I MADE IT MYSELF! IT'S A TOMATO OMELET SANDWICH.
YOU'RE GOOD AT COOKING, AREN'T YOU, ISONISHI!?
NO KIDDING! YOU HAVE TO COME OVER AND MAKE ME SOMETHING NEXT TIME.
IF YOU MAKE ME SOMETHING DELICIOUS, I PROMISE I'LL MAKE YOU FEEL GOOD. ♡ I'M ACTUALLY BI,YOU KNOW.

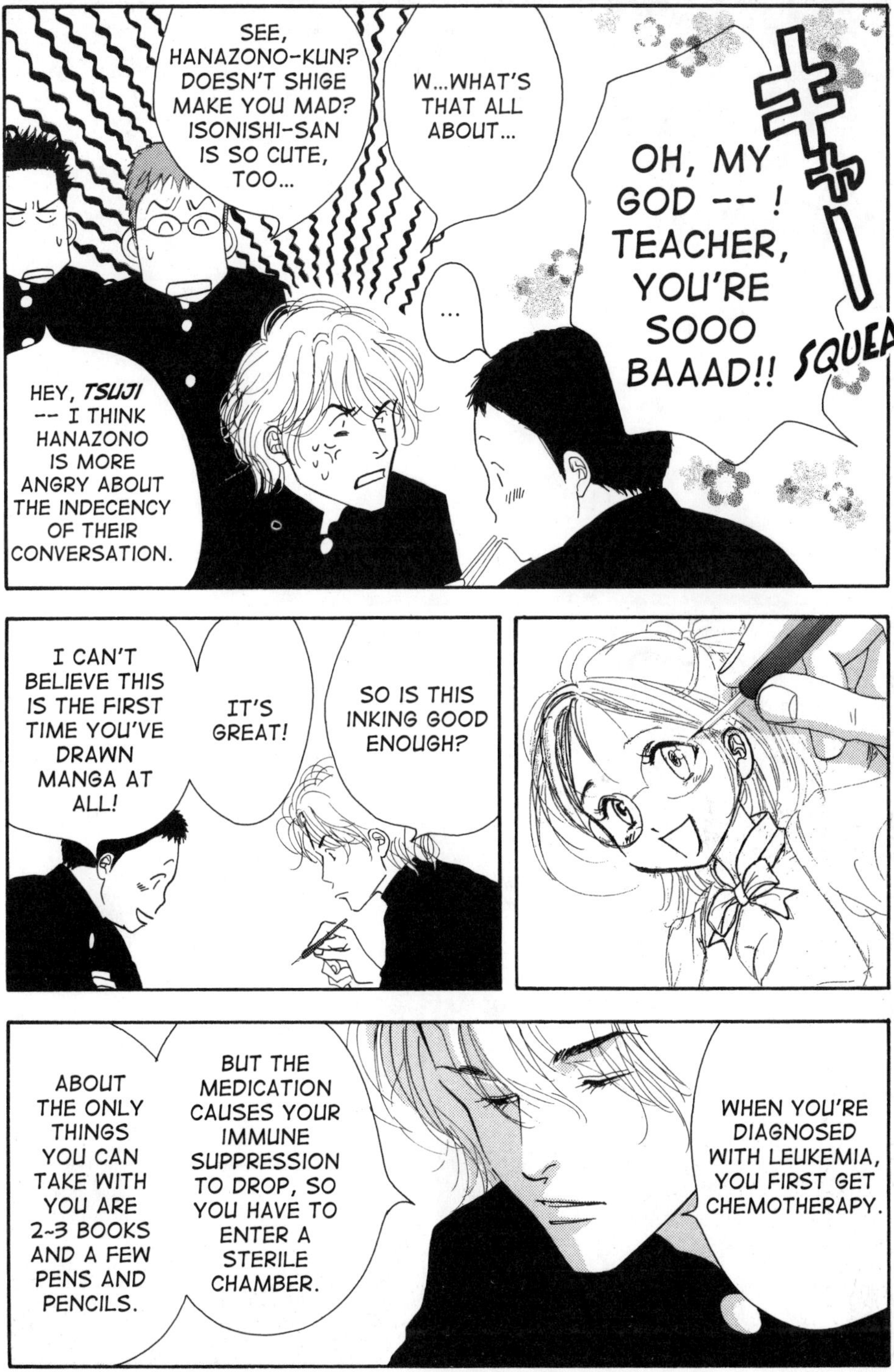

OH, MY GOD -- ! TEACHER, YOU'RE SOOO BAAAD!!
キャー
SQUEAL!
W...WHAT'S THAT ALL ABOUT...
SEE, HANAZONO-KUN? DOESN'T SHIGE MAKE YOU MAD? ISONISHI-SAN IS SO CUTE, TOO...
...
HEY, *TSUJI* -- I THINK HANAZONO IS MORE ANGRY ABOUT THE INDECENCY OF THEIR CONVERSATION.
SO IS THIS INKING GOOD ENOUGH?
IT'S GREAT!
I CAN'T BELIEVE THIS IS THE FIRST TIME YOU'VE DRAWN MANGA AT ALL!
WHEN YOU'RE DIAGNOSED WITH LEUKEMIA, YOU FIRST GET CHEMOTHERAPY.
BUT THE MEDICATION CAUSES YOUR IMMUNE SUPPRESSION TO DROP, SO YOU HAVE TO ENTER A STERILE CHAMBER.
ABOUT THE ONLY THINGS YOU CAN TAKE WITH YOU ARE 2~3 BOOKS AND A FEW PENS AND PENCILS.

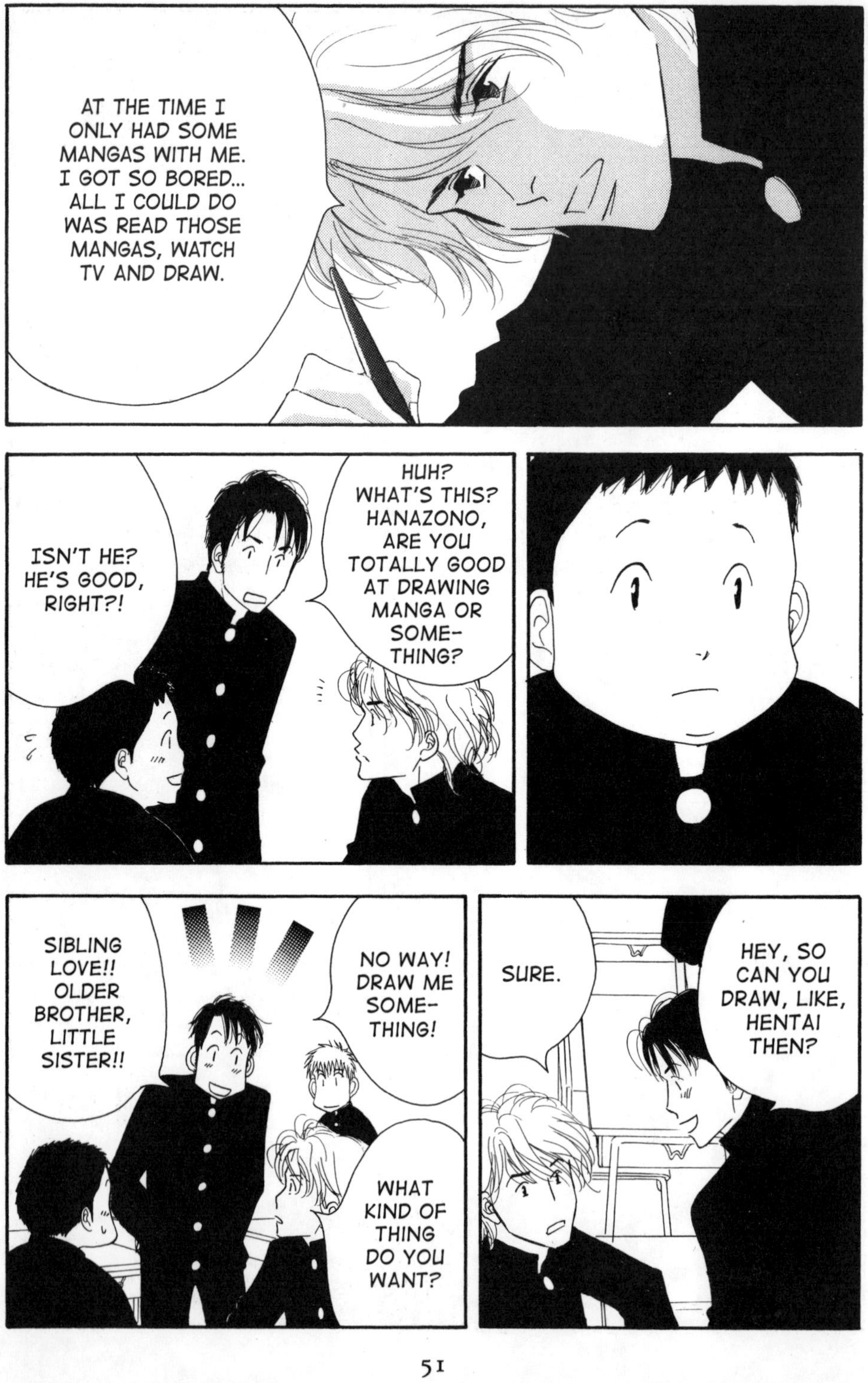
AT THE TIME I ONLY HAD SOME MANGAS WITH ME. I GOT SO BORED... ALL I COULD DO WAS READ THOSE MANGAS, WATCH TV AND DRAW.
HUH? WHAT'S THIS? HANAZONO, ARE YOU TOTALLY GOOD AT DRAWING MANGA OR SOME-THING?
ISN'T HE? HE'S GOOD, RIGHT?!
HEY, SO CAN YOU DRAW, LIKE, HENTAI THEN?
SURE.
NO WAY! DRAW ME SOME-THING!
WHAT KIND OF THING DO YOU WANT?
SIBLING LOVE!! OLDER BROTHER, LITTLE SISTER!!

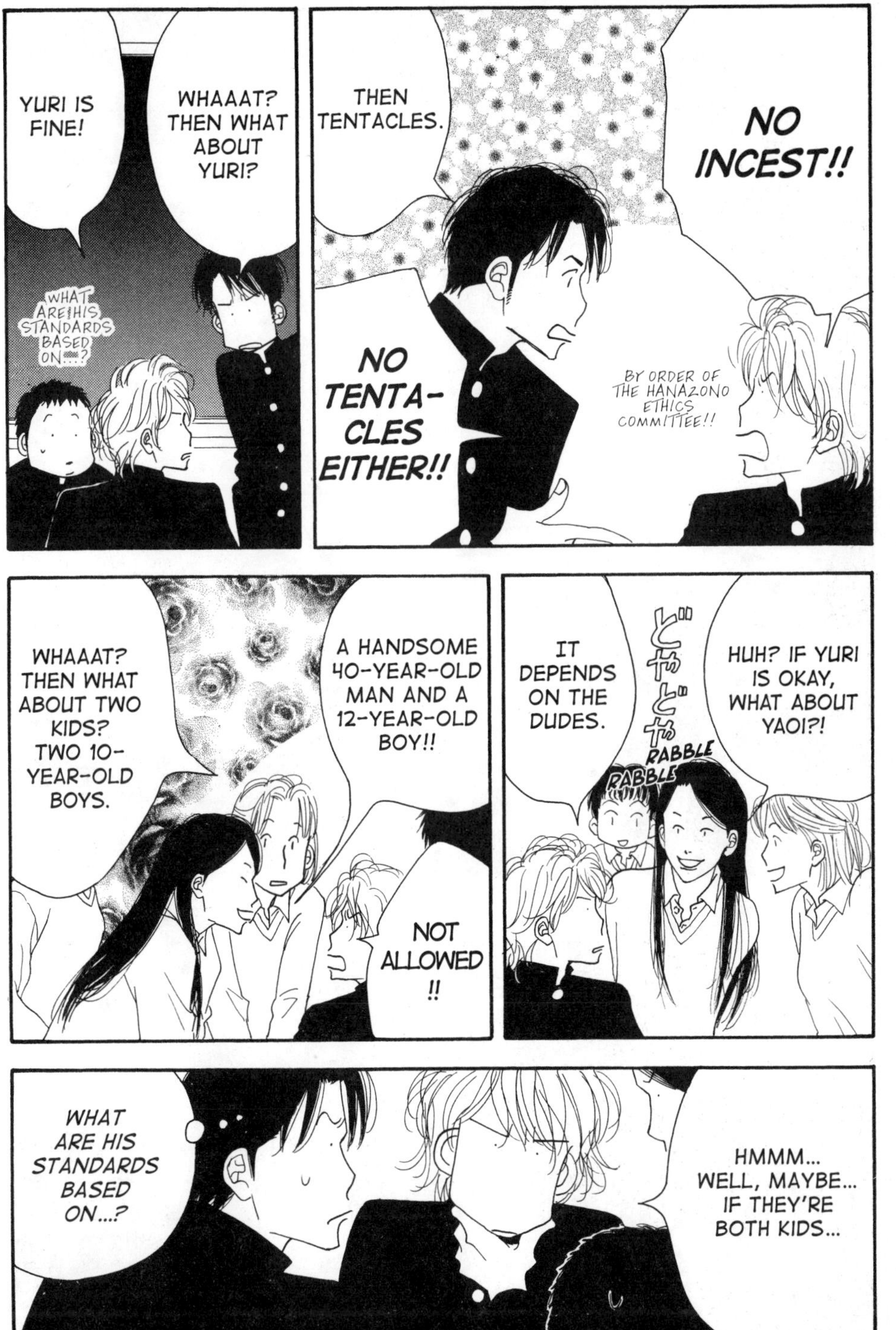
NO INCEST!!
THEN TENTACLES.
BY ORDER OF THE HANAZONO ETHICS COMMITTEE!!
NO TENTACLES EITHER!!
WHAAAT? THEN WHAT ABOUT YURI?
YURI IS FINE!
WHAT ARE HIS STANDARDS BASED ON...?
HUH? IF YURI IS OKAY, WHAT ABOUT YAOI?!
どやどや
RABBLE RABBLE
IT DEPENDS ON THE DUDES.
A HANDSOME 40-YEAR-OLD MAN AND A 12-YEAR-OLD BOY!!
NOT ALLOWED!!
WHAAAT? THEN WHAT ABOUT TWO KIDS? TWO 10-YEAR-OLD BOYS.
HMMM... WELL, MAYBE... IF THEY'RE BOTH KIDS...
WHAT ARE HIS STANDARDS BASED ON...?

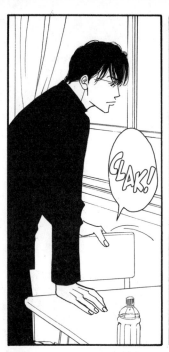

CLAK!

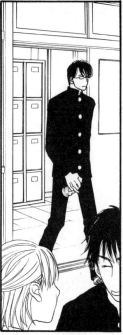

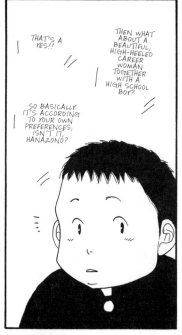

THEN WHAT ABOUT A BEAUTIFUL HIGH-HEELED CAREER WOMAN TOGETHER WITH A HIGH SCHOOL BOY?

THAT'S A YES!!

SO BASICALLY IT'S ACCORDING TO YOUR OWN PREFERENCES, ISN'T IT HANAZONO?

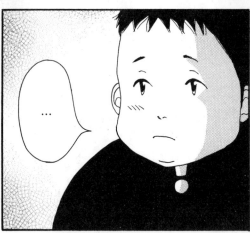

...

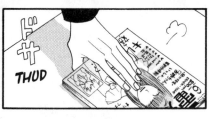

THUD

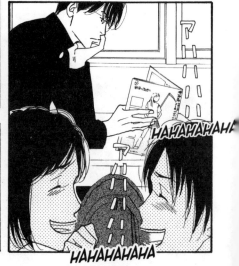

HAHAHAHAHA

HAHAHAHAHA

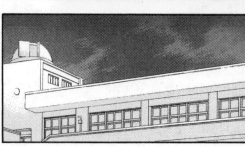

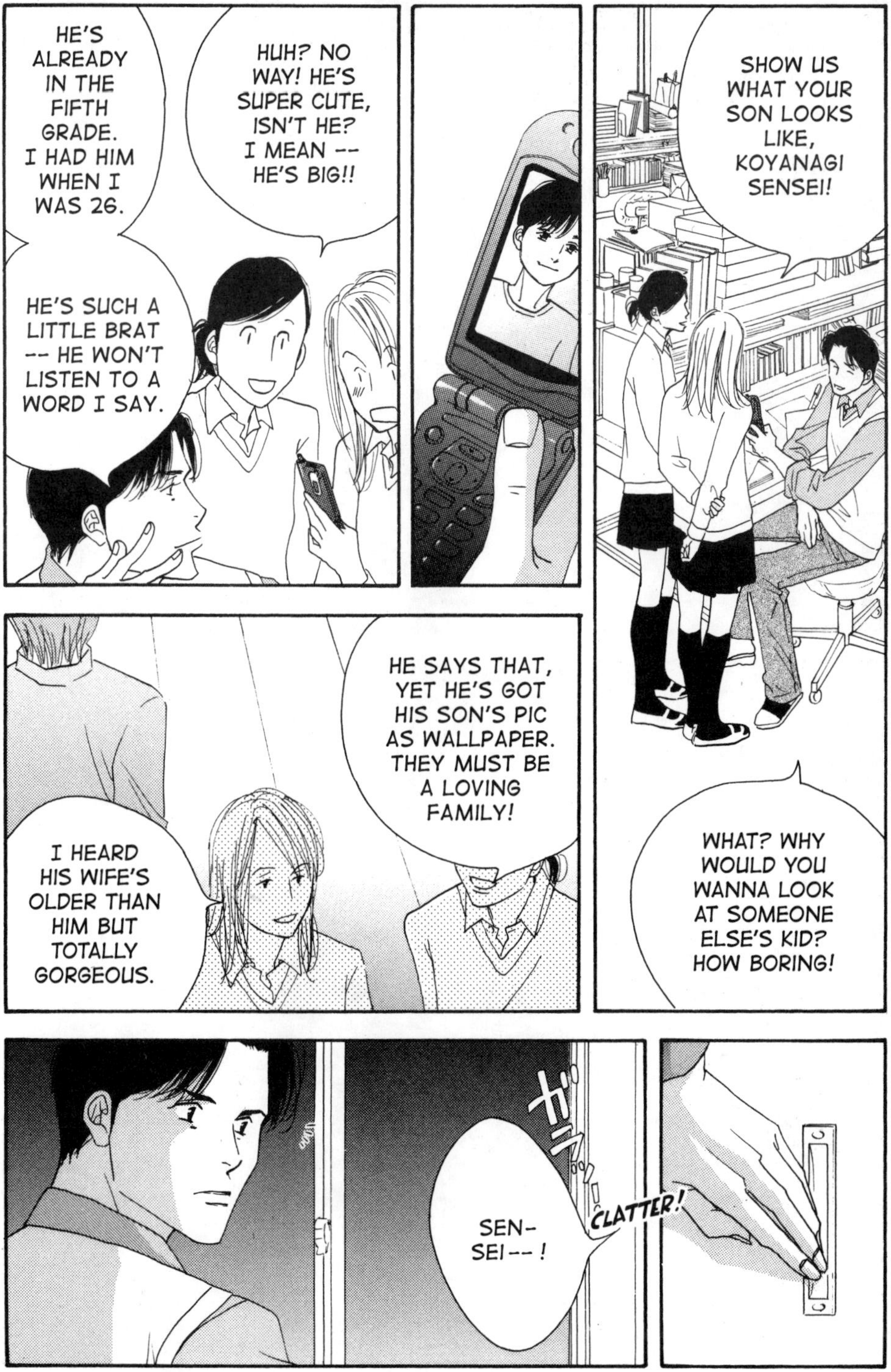
SHOW US WHAT YOUR SON LOOKS LIKE, KOYANAGI SENSEI!
WHAT? WHY WOULD YOU WANNA LOOK AT SOMEONE ELSE'S KID? HOW BORING!
HUH? NO WAY! HE'S SUPER CUTE, ISN'T HE? I MEAN -- HE'S BIG!!
HE'S ALREADY IN THE FIFTH GRADE. I HAD HIM WHEN I WAS 26.
HE'S SUCH A LITTLE BRAT -- HE WON'T LISTEN TO A WORD I SAY.
HE SAYS THAT, YET HE'S GOT HIS SON'S PIC AS WALLPAPER. THEY MUST BE A LOVING FAMILY!
I HEARD HIS WIFE'S OLDER THAN HIM BUT TOTALLY GORGEOUS.
CLATTER!
SEN-SEI-- !

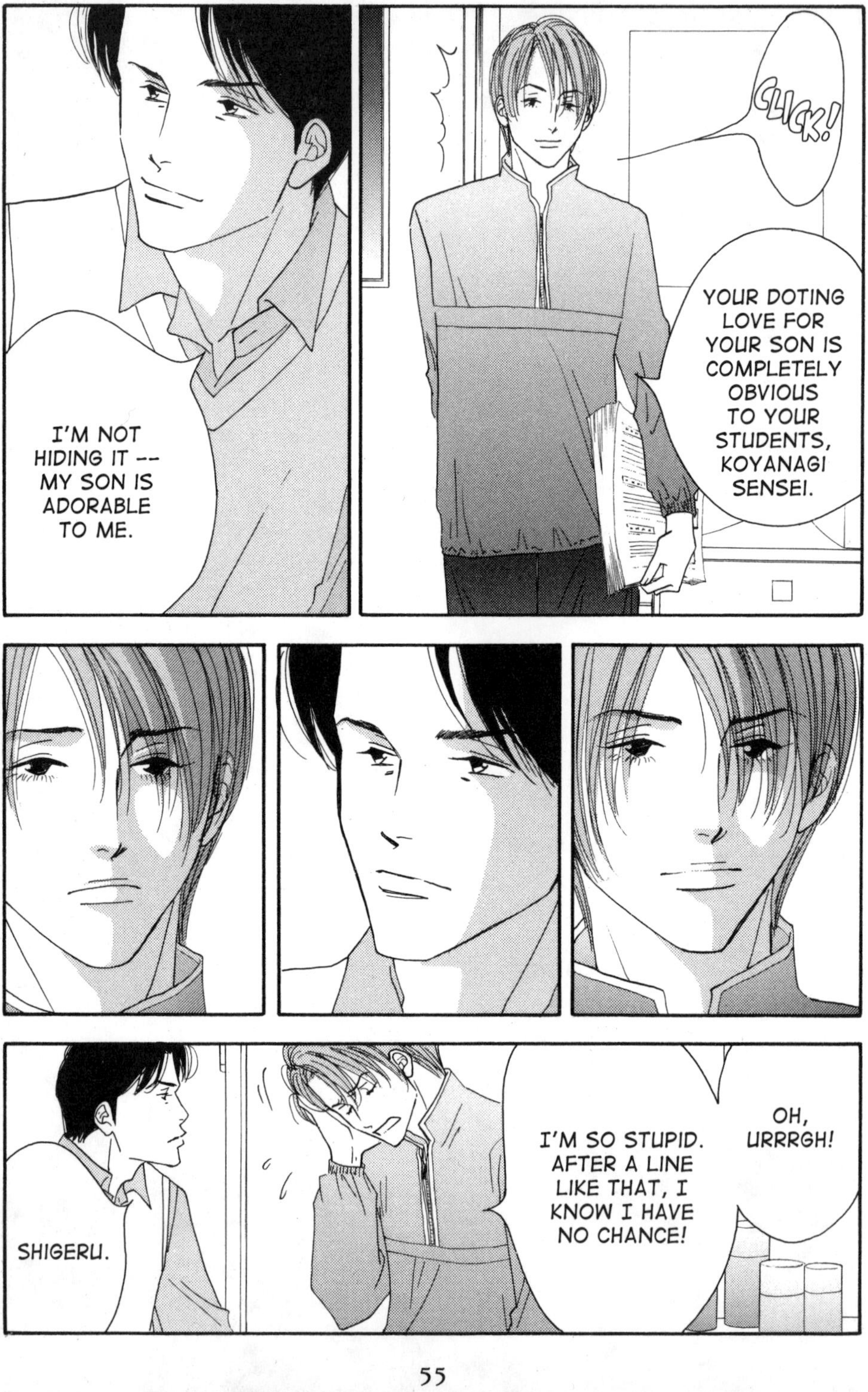
CLICK!
YOUR DOTING LOVE FOR YOUR SON IS COMPLETELY OBVIOUS TO YOUR STUDENTS, KOYANAGI SENSEI.
I'M NOT HIDING IT -- MY SON IS ADORABLE TO ME.
OH, URRRGH!
I'M SO STUPID. AFTER A LINE LIKE THAT, I KNOW I HAVE NO CHANCE!
SHIGERU.

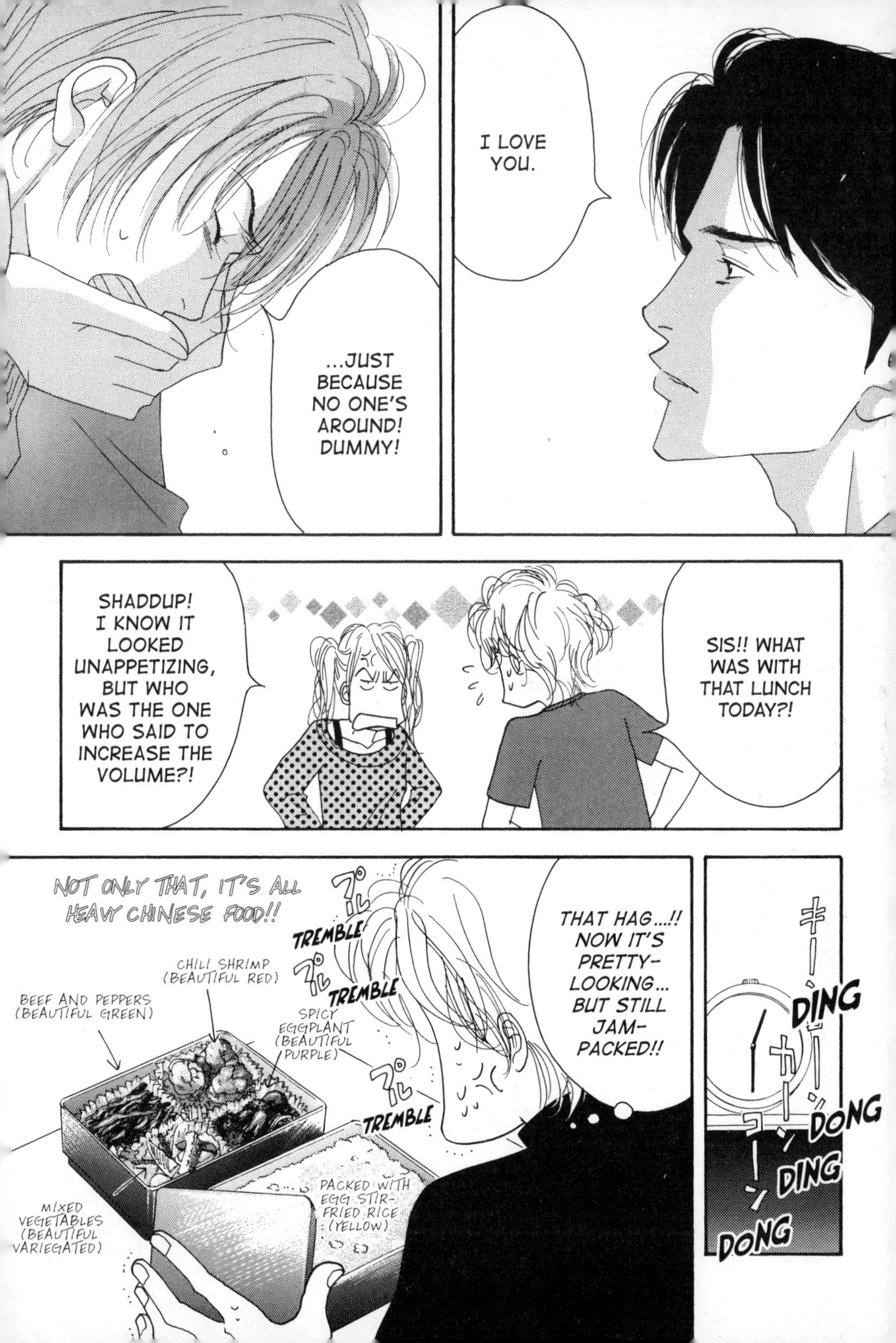
I LOVE YOU.
...JUST BECAUSE NO ONE'S AROUND! DUMMY!
SIS!! WHAT WAS WITH THAT LUNCH TODAY?!
SHADDUP! I KNOW IT LOOKED UNAPPETIZING, BUT WHO WAS THE ONE WHO SAID TO INCREASE THE VOLUME?!
キーン
DING
カーン
DONG
DING
コーン
DONG
THAT HAG...!! NOW IT'S PRETTY-LOOKING... BUT STILL JAM-PACKED!!
プル
TREMBLE
プル
TREMBLE
プル
TREMBLE
NOT ONLY THAT, IT'S ALL HEAVY CHINESE FOOD!!
CHILI SHRIMP (BEAUTIFUL RED)
BEEF AND PEPPERS (BEAUTIFUL GREEN)
SPICY EGGPLANT (BEAUTIFUL PURPLE)
MIXED VEGETABLES (BEAUTIFUL VARIEGATED)
PACKED WITH EGG STIR-FRIED RICE (YELLOW)

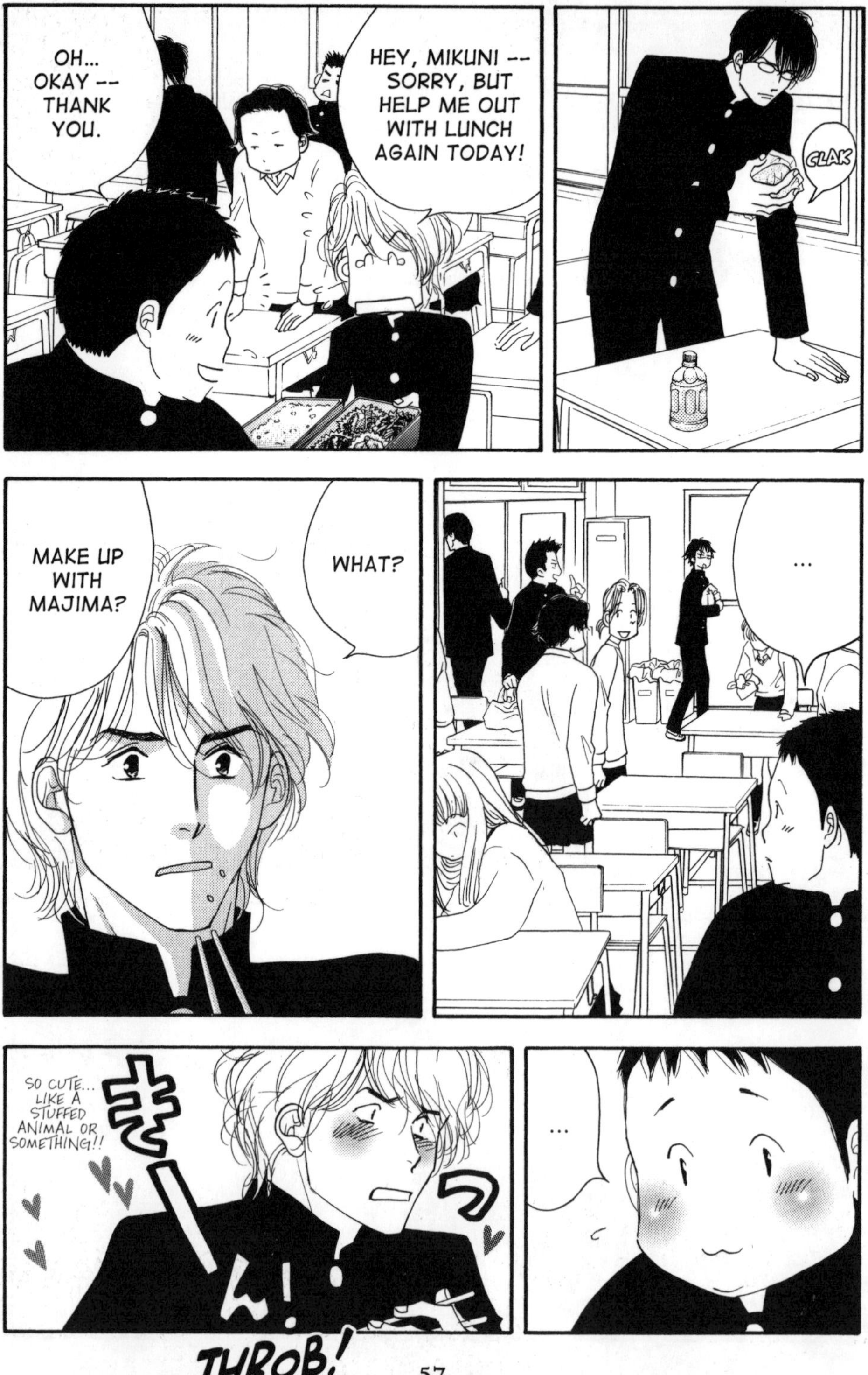
CLAK
HEY, MIKUNI -- SORRY, BUT HELP ME OUT WITH LUNCH AGAIN TODAY!
OH... OKAY -- THANK YOU.
...
WHAT?
MAKE UP WITH MAJIMA?
...
SO CUTE... LIKE A STUFFED ANIMAL OR SOMETHING!!
THROB!

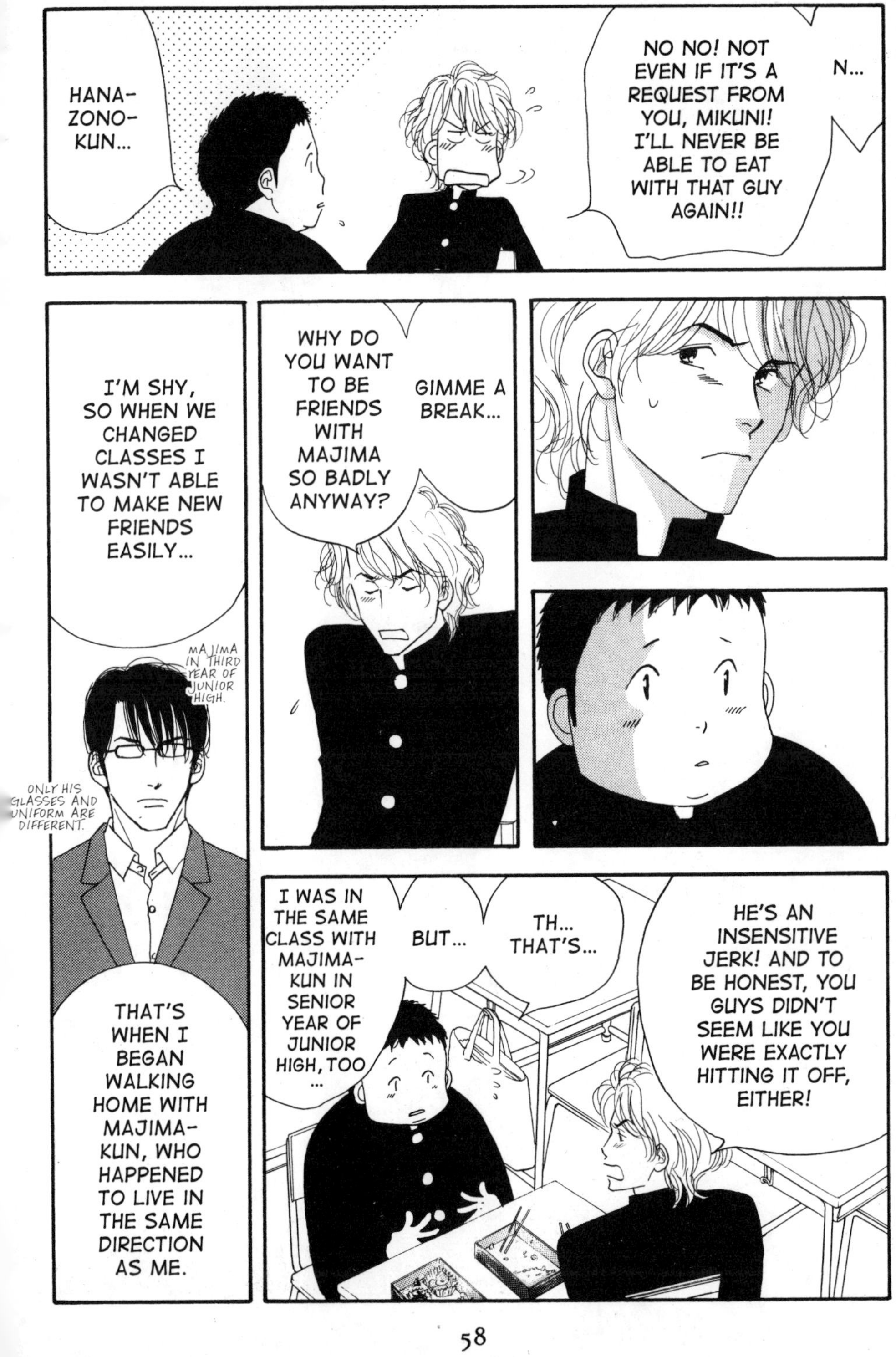
N...
NO NO! NOT EVEN IF IT'S A REQUEST FROM YOU, MIKUNI! I'LL NEVER BE ABLE TO EAT WITH THAT GUY AGAIN!!
HANA-ZONO-KUN...
GIMME A BREAK...
WHY DO YOU WANT TO BE FRIENDS WITH MAJIMA SO BADLY ANYWAY?
HE'S AN INSENSITIVE JERK! AND TO BE HONEST, YOU GUYS DIDN'T SEEM LIKE YOU WERE EXACTLY HITTING IT OFF, EITHER!
TH... THAT'S...
BUT...
I WAS IN THE SAME CLASS WITH MAJIMA-KUN IN SENIOR YEAR OF JUNIOR HIGH, TOO ...
I'M SHY, SO WHEN WE CHANGED CLASSES I WASN'T ABLE TO MAKE NEW FRIENDS EASILY...
MAJIMA IN THIRD YEAR OF JUNIOR HIGH.
ONLY HIS GLASSES AND UNIFORM ARE DIFFERENT.
THAT'S WHEN I BEGAN WALKING HOME WITH MAJIMA-KUN, WHO HAPPENED TO LIVE IN THE SAME DIRECTION AS ME.

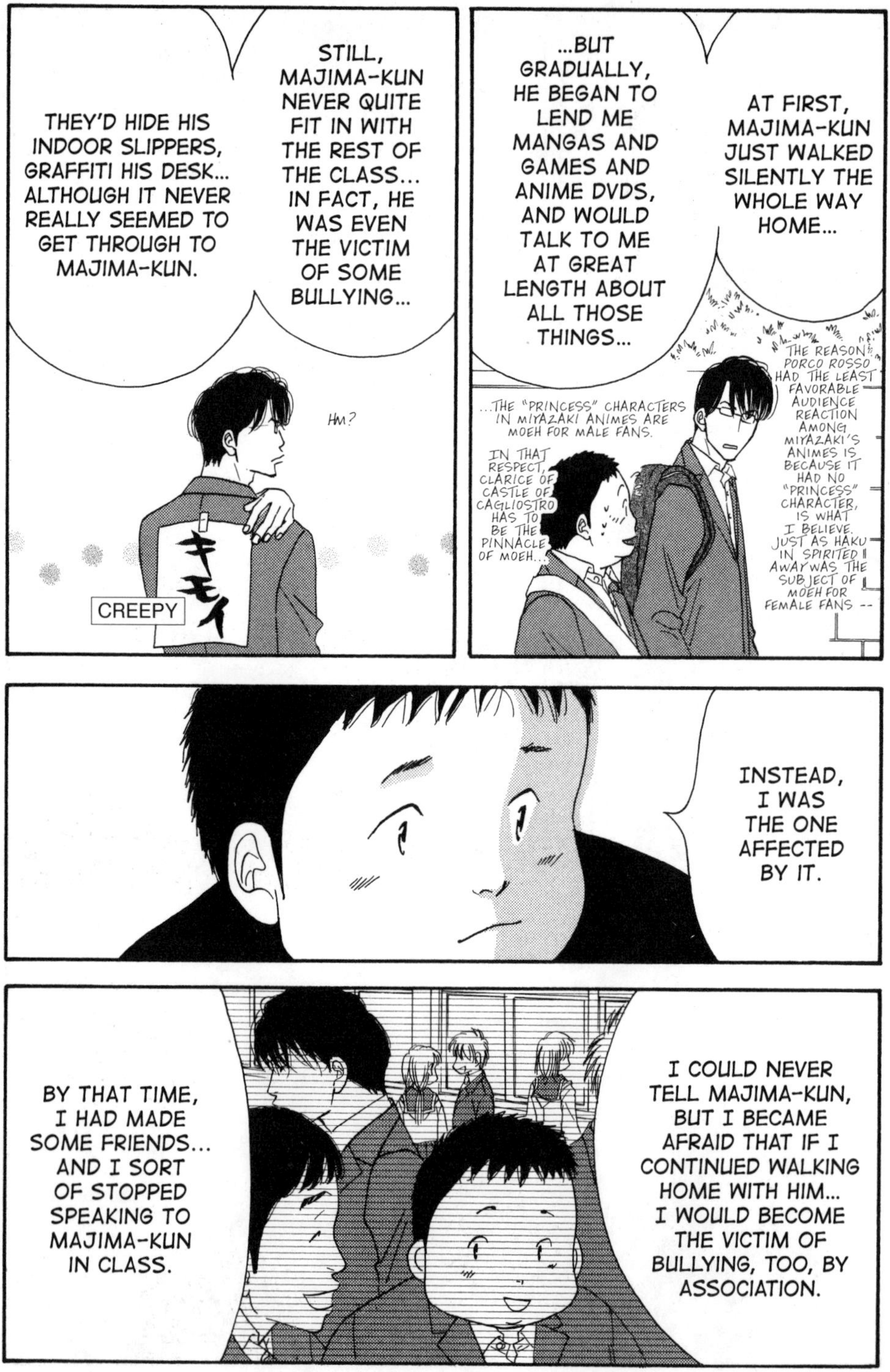
AT FIRST, MAJIMA-KUN JUST WALKED SILENTLY THE WHOLE WAY HOME...
...BUT GRADUALLY, HE BEGAN TO LEND ME MANGAS AND GAMES AND ANIME DVDS, AND WOULD TALK TO ME AT GREAT LENGTH ABOUT ALL THOSE THINGS...
THE REASON PORCO ROSSO HAD THE LEAST FAVORABLE AUDIENCE REACTION AMONG MIYAZAKI'S ANIMES IS BECAUSE IT HAD NO "PRINCESS" CHARACTER, IS WHAT I BELIEVE. JUST AS HAKU IN SPIRITED AWAY WAS THE SUBJECT OF MOEH FOR FEMALE FANS --
...THE "PRINCESS" CHARACTERS IN MIYAZAKI ANIMES ARE MOEH FOR MALE FANS.
IN THAT RESPECT, CLARICE OF CASTLE OF CAGLIOSTRO HAS TO BE THE PINNACLE OF MOEH...
STILL, MAJIMA-KUN NEVER QUITE FIT IN WITH THE REST OF THE CLASS... IN FACT, HE WAS EVEN THE VICTIM OF SOME BULLYING...
THEY'D HIDE HIS INDOOR SLIPPERS, GRAFFITI HIS DESK... ALTHOUGH IT NEVER REALLY SEEMED TO GET THROUGH TO MAJIMA-KUN.
HM?
キモイ
CREEPY
INSTEAD, I WAS THE ONE AFFECTED BY IT.
I COULD NEVER TELL MAJIMA-KUN, BUT I BECAME AFRAID THAT IF I CONTINUED WALKING HOME WITH HIM... I WOULD BECOME THE VICTIM OF BULLYING, TOO, BY ASSOCIATION.
BY THAT TIME, I HAD MADE SOME FRIENDS... AND I SORT OF STOPPED SPEAKING TO MAJIMA-KUN IN CLASS.

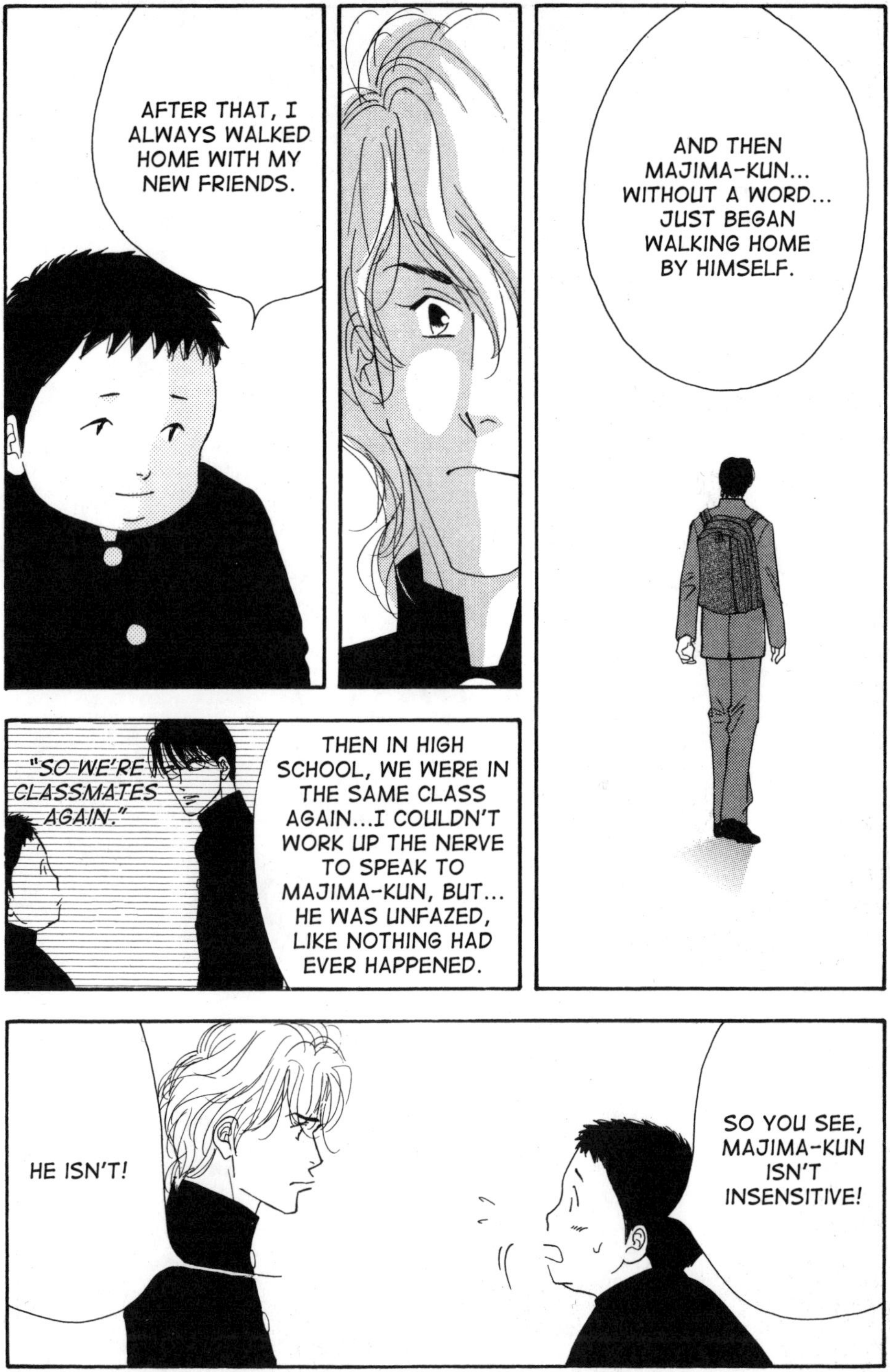
AND THEN MAJIMA-KUN... WITHOUT A WORD... JUST BEGAN WALKING HOME BY HIMSELF.
AFTER THAT, I ALWAYS WALKED HOME WITH MY NEW FRIENDS.
THEN IN HIGH SCHOOL, WE WERE IN THE SAME CLASS AGAIN...I COULDN'T WORK UP THE NERVE TO SPEAK TO MAJIMA-KUN, BUT... HE WAS UNFAZED, LIKE NOTHING HAD EVER HAPPENED.
"SO WE'RE CLASSMATES AGAIN."
SO YOU SEE, MAJIMA-KUN ISN'T INSENSITIVE!
HE ISN'T!

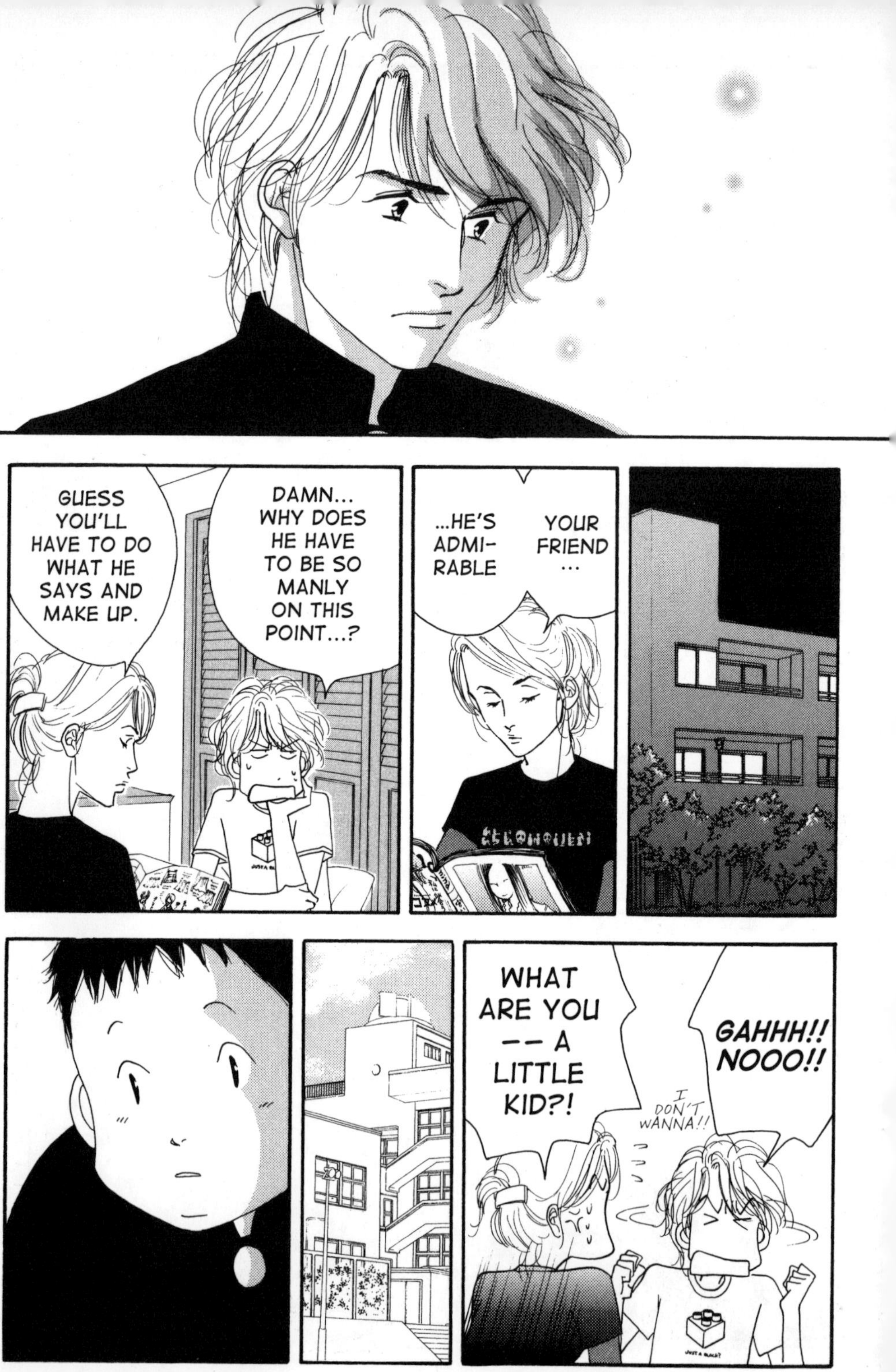
YOUR FRIEND ... ...HE'S ADMIRABLE
DAMN... WHY DOES HE HAVE TO BE SO MANLY ON THIS POINT...?
GUESS YOU'LL HAVE TO DO WHAT HE SAYS AND MAKE UP.
GAHHH!! NOOO!!
I DON'T WANNA!!
WHAT ARE YOU -- A LITTLE KID?!

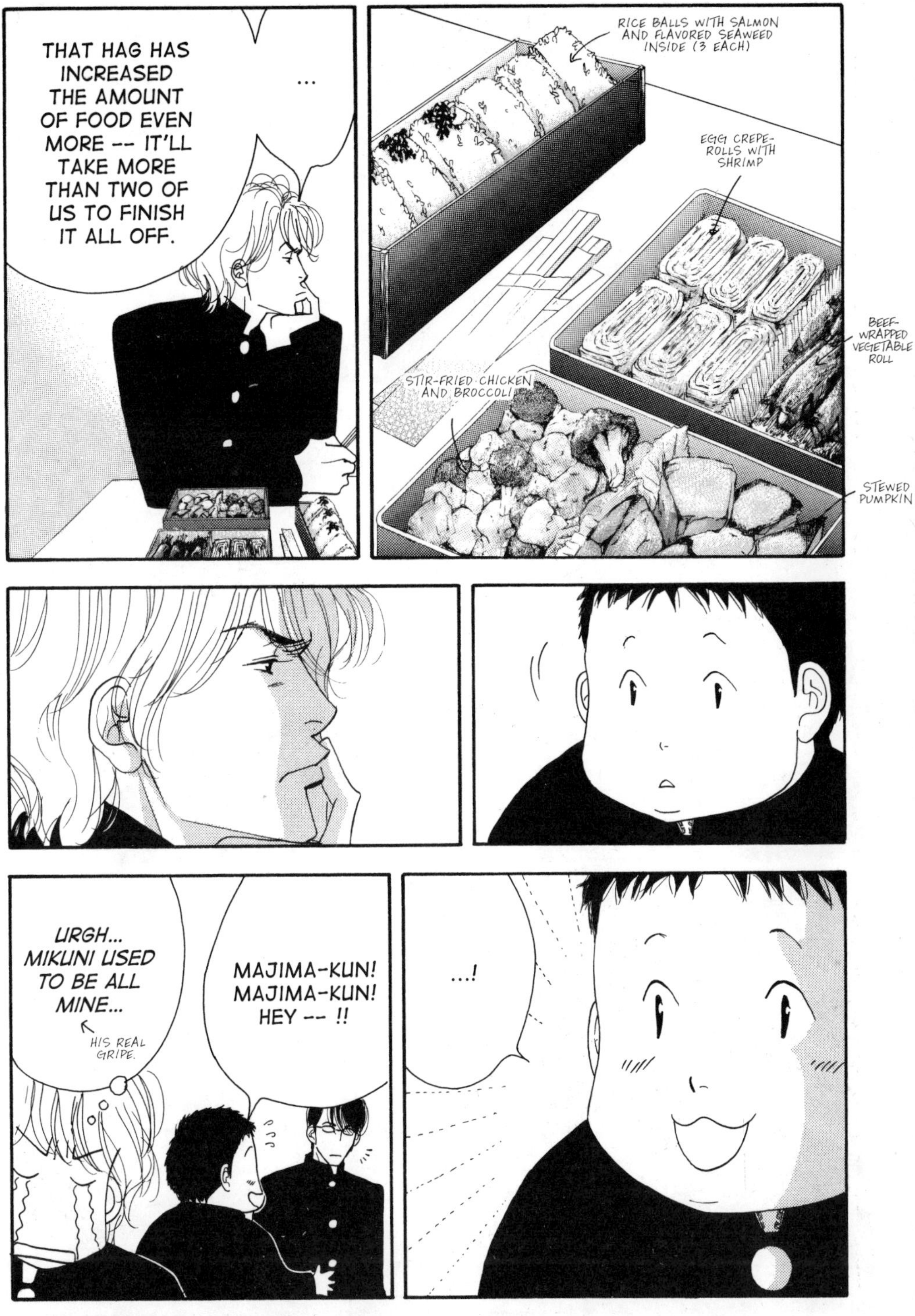
RICE BALLS WITH SALMON AND FLAVORED SEAWEED INSIDE (3 EACH)
EGG CREPE-ROLLS WITH SHRIMP
BEEF-WRAPPED VEGETABLE ROLL
STIR-FRIED CHICKEN AND BROCCOLI
STEWED PUMPKIN
...
THAT HAG HAS INCREASED THE AMOUNT OF FOOD EVEN MORE -- IT'LL TAKE MORE THAN TWO OF US TO FINISH IT ALL OFF.
...!
MAJIMA-KUN! MAJIMA-KUN! HEY -- !!
URGH... MIKUNI USED TO BE ALL MINE...
HIS REAL GRIPE.

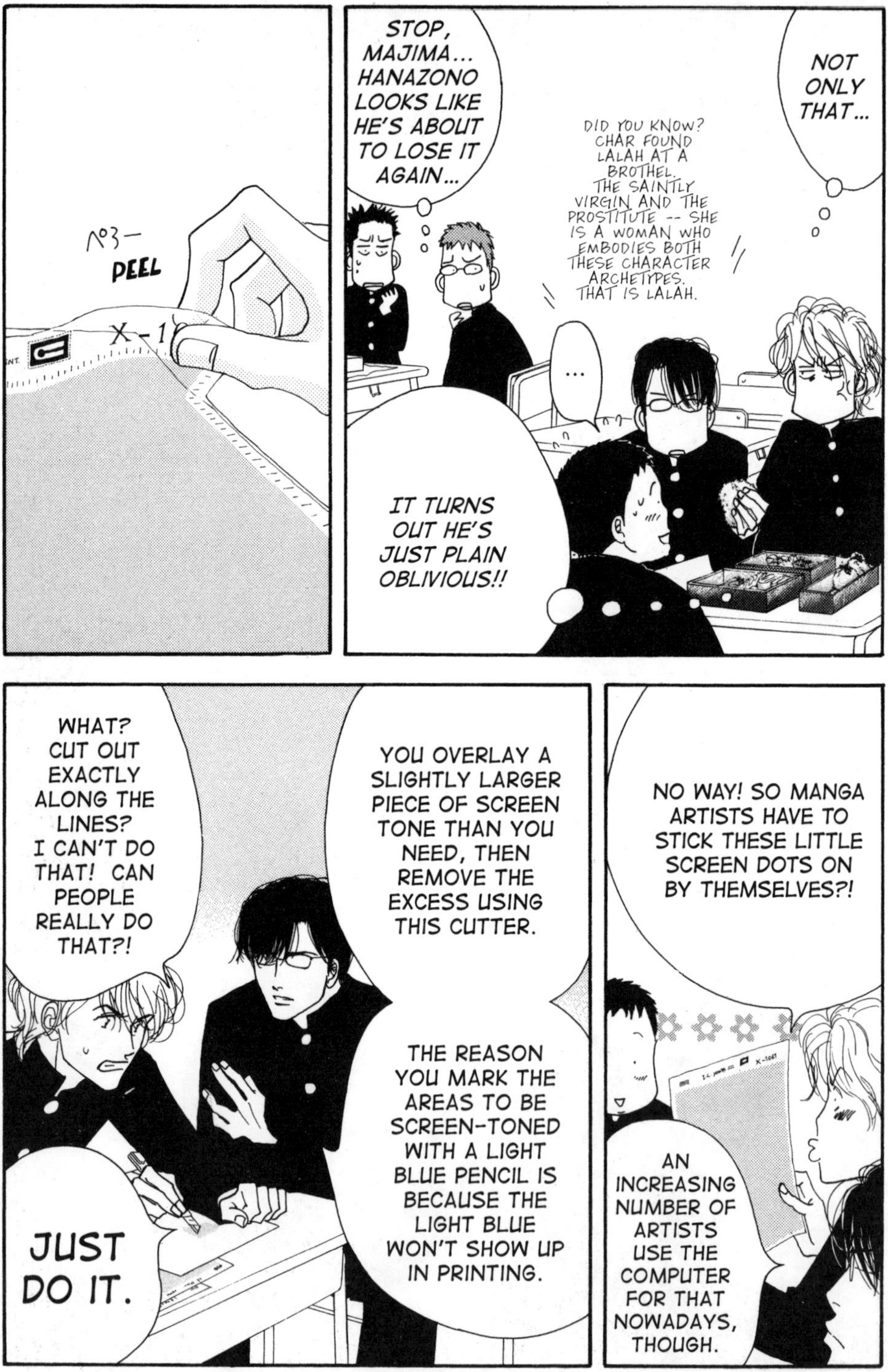
NOT ONLY THAT...
DID YOU KNOW? CHAR FOUND LALAH AT A BROTHEL. THE SAINTLY VIRGIN AND THE PROSTITUTE -- SHE IS A WOMAN WHO EMBODIES BOTH THESE CHARACTER ARCHETYPES. THAT IS LALAH.
STOP, MAJIMA... HANAZONO LOOKS LIKE HE'S ABOUT TO LOSE IT AGAIN...
...
IT TURNS OUT HE'S JUST PLAIN OBLIVIOUS!!
PEEL
NO WAY! SO MANGA ARTISTS HAVE TO STICK THESE LITTLE SCREEN DOTS ON BY THEMSELVES?!
AN INCREASING NUMBER OF ARTISTS USE THE COMPUTER FOR THAT NOWADAYS, THOUGH.
YOU OVERLAY A SLIGHTLY LARGER PIECE OF SCREEN TONE THAN YOU NEED, THEN REMOVE THE EXCESS USING THIS CUTTER.
WHAT? CUT OUT EXACTLY ALONG THE LINES? I CAN'T DO THAT! CAN PEOPLE REALLY DO THAT?!
THE REASON YOU MARK THE AREAS TO BE SCREEN-TONED WITH A LIGHT BLUE PENCIL IS BECAUSE THE LIGHT BLUE WON'T SHOW UP IN PRINTING.
JUST DO IT.

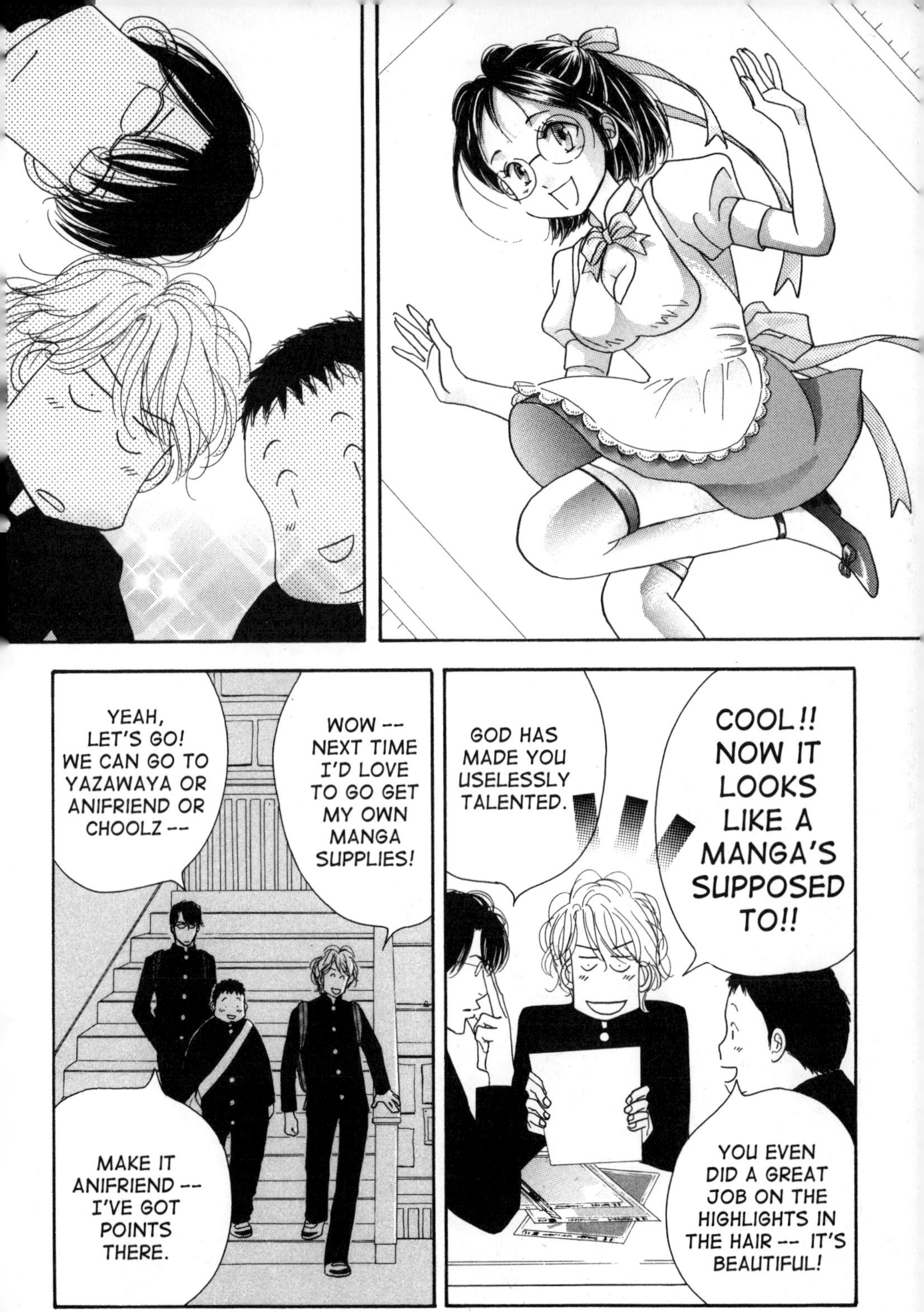
COOL!! NOW IT LOOKS LIKE A MANGA'S SUPPOSED TO!!
GOD HAS MADE YOU USELESSLY TALENTED.
YOU EVEN DID A GREAT JOB ON THE HIGHLIGHTS IN THE HAIR -- IT'S BEAUTIFUL!
WOW -- NEXT TIME I'D LOVE TO GO GET MY OWN MANGA SUPPLIES!
YEAH, LET'S GO! WE CAN GO TO YAZAWAYA OR ANIFRIEND OR CHOOLZ --
MAKE IT ANIFRIEND -- I'VE GOT POINTS THERE.

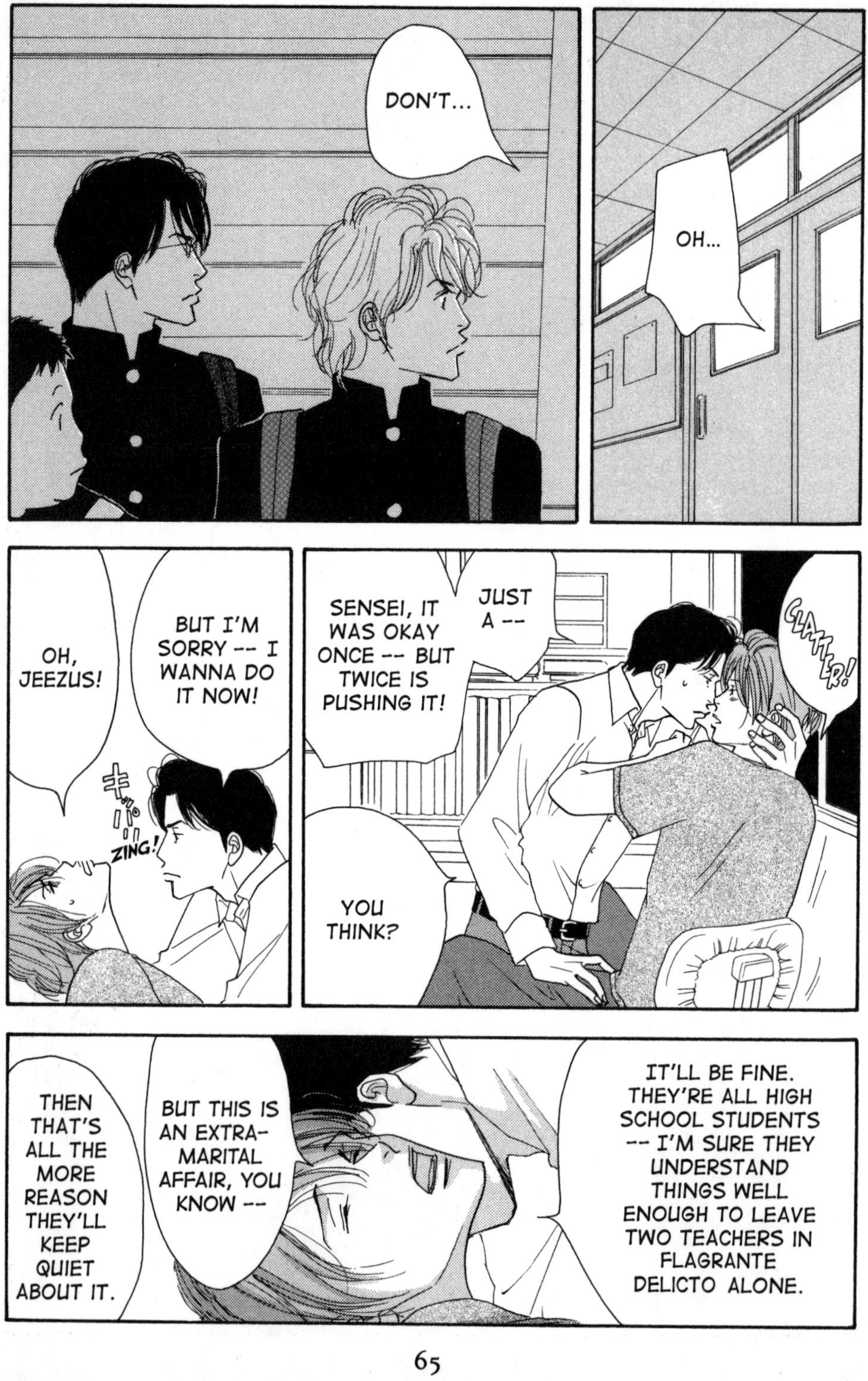
OH...
DON'T...
CLATTER!
JUST A --
SENSEI, IT WAS OKAY ONCE -- BUT TWICE IS PUSHING IT!
YOU THINK?
BUT I'M SORRY -- I WANNA DO IT NOW!
OH, JEEZUS!
ZING!
IT'LL BE FINE. THEY'RE ALL HIGH SCHOOL STUDENTS -- I'M SURE THEY UNDERSTAND THINGS WELL ENOUGH TO LEAVE TWO TEACHERS IN FLAGRANTE DELICTO ALONE.
BUT THIS IS AN EXTRA-MARITAL AFFAIR, YOU KNOW --
THEN THAT'S ALL THE MORE REASON THEY'LL KEEP QUIET ABOUT IT.

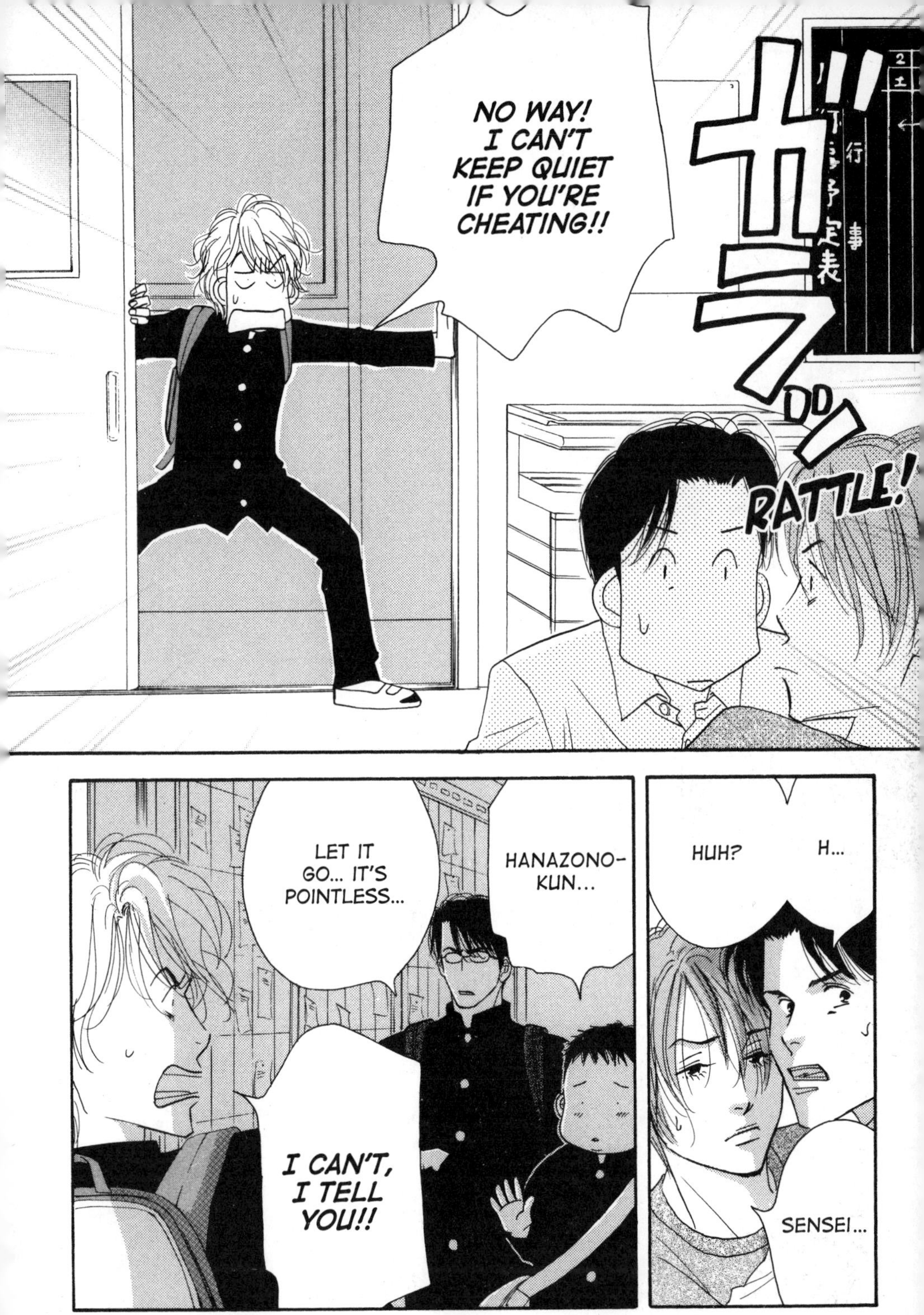

RATTLE!
NO WAY! I CAN'T KEEP QUIET IF YOU'RE CHEATING!!
H...
HUH?
SENSEI...
HANAZONO-KUN...
LET IT GO... IT'S POINTLESS...
I CAN'T, I TELL YOU!!

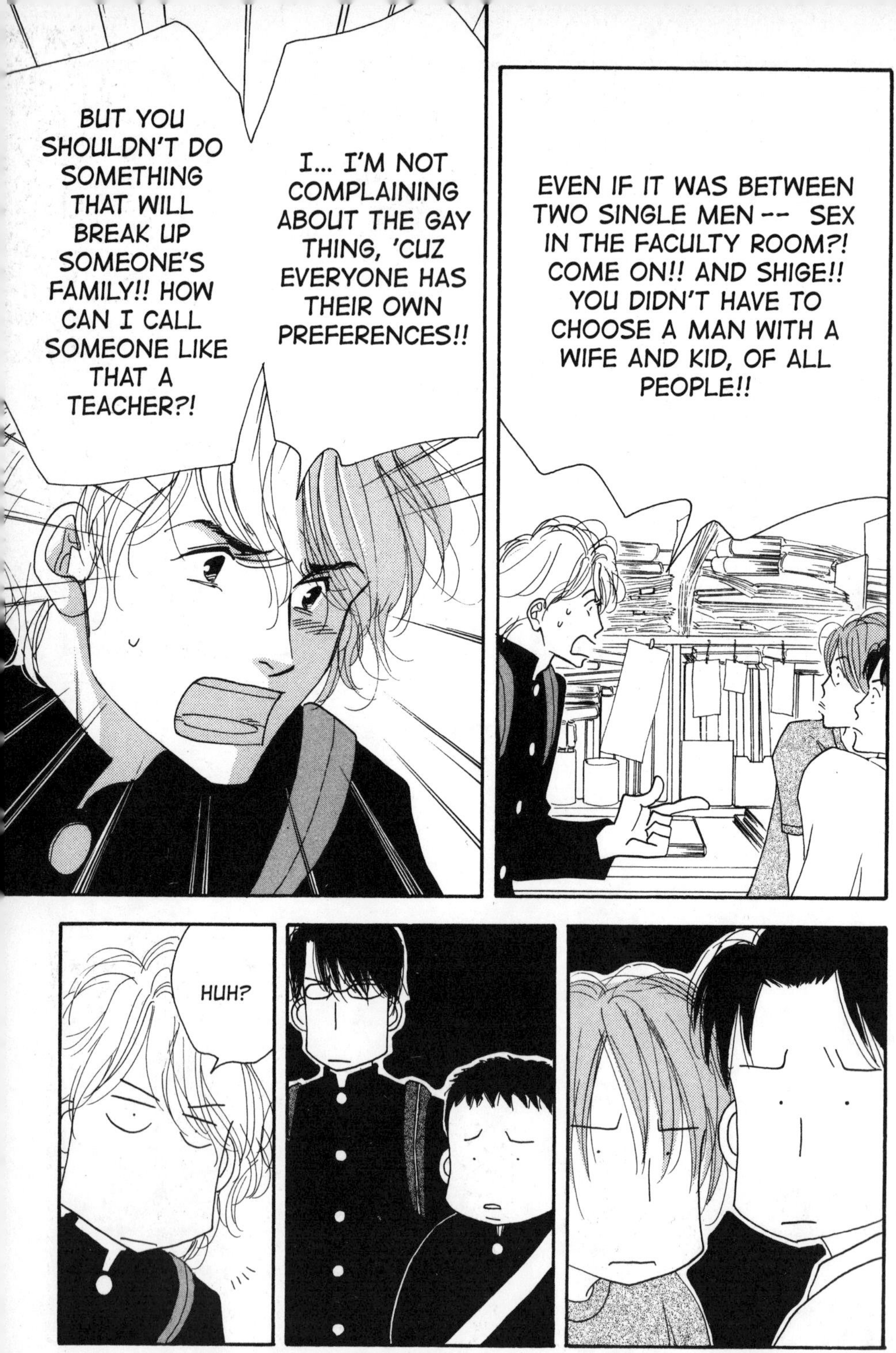
EVEN IF IT WAS BETWEEN TWO SINGLE MEN -- SEX IN THE FACULTY ROOM?! COME ON!! AND SHIGE!! YOU DIDN'T HAVE TO CHOOSE A MAN WITH A WIFE AND KID, OF ALL PEOPLE!!
I... I'M NOT COMPLAINING ABOUT THE GAY THING, 'CUZ EVERYONE HAS THEIR OWN PREFERENCES!!
BUT YOU SHOULDN'T DO SOMETHING THAT WILL BREAK UP SOMEONE'S FAMILY!! HOW CAN I CALL SOMEONE LIKE THAT A TEACHER?!
HUH?

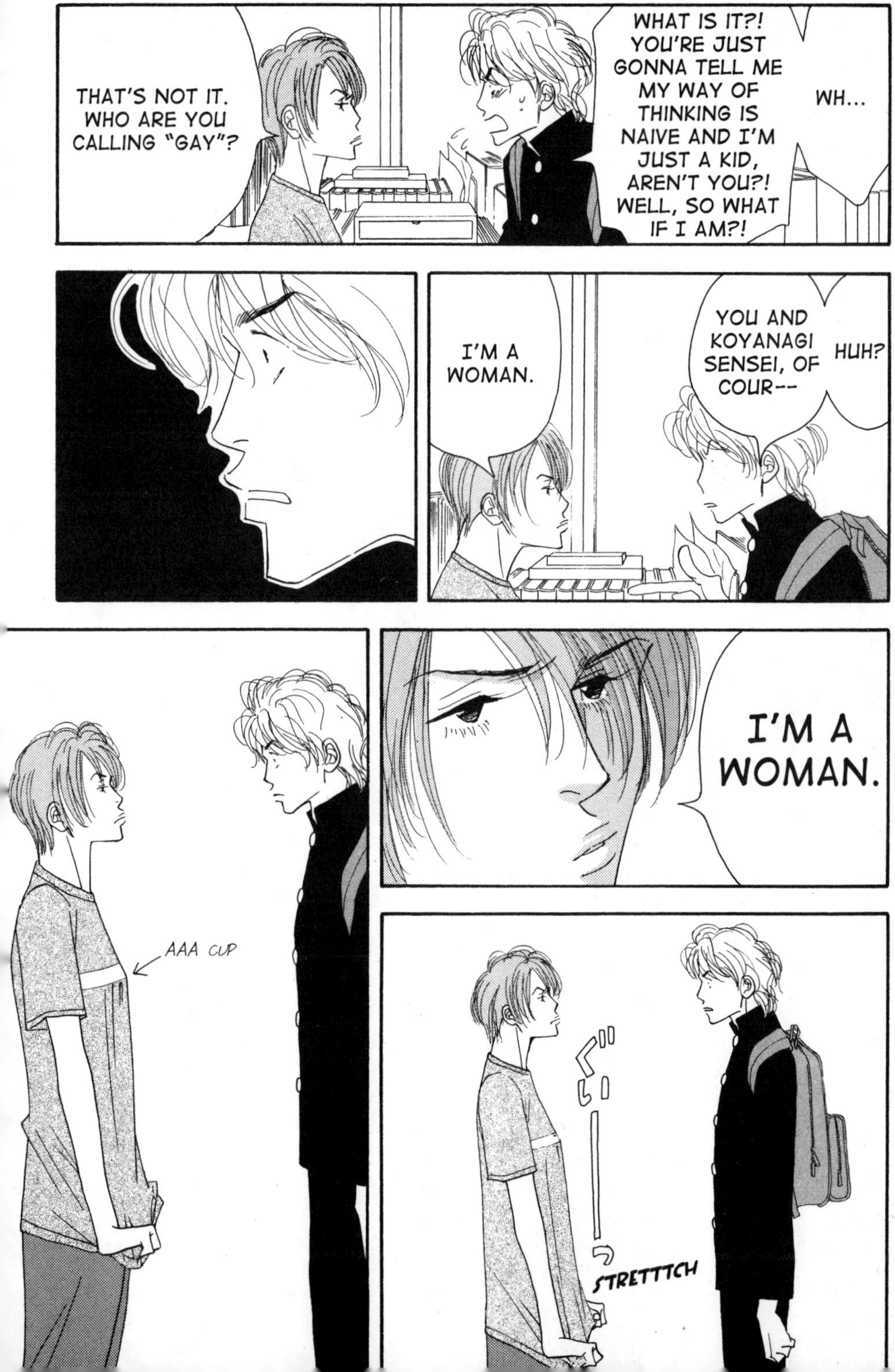
WH...
WHAT IS IT?! YOU'RE JUST GONNA TELL ME MY WAY OF THINKING IS NAIVE AND I'M JUST A KID, AREN'T YOU?! WELL, SO WHAT IF I AM?!
THAT'S NOT IT. WHO ARE YOU CALLING "GAY"?
HUH?
YOU AND KOYANAGI SENSEI, OF COUR--
I'M A WOMAN.
I'M A WOMAN.
STRETTTCH
AAA CUP

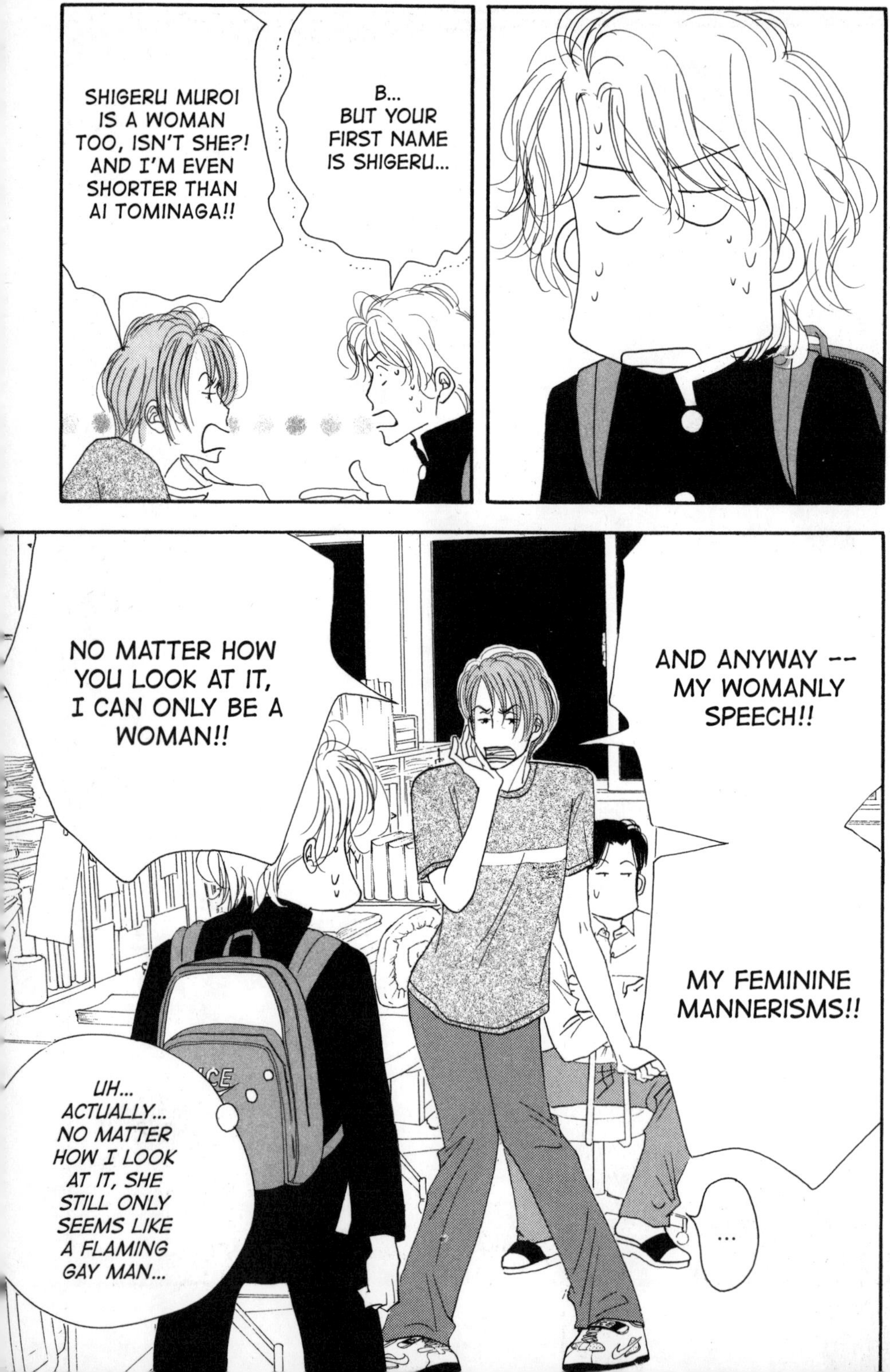
B... BUT YOUR FIRST NAME IS SHIGERU...
SHIGERU MUROI IS A WOMAN TOO, ISN'T SHE?! AND I'M EVEN SHORTER THAN AI TOMINAGA!!
NO MATTER HOW YOU LOOK AT IT, I CAN ONLY BE A WOMAN!!
AND ANYWAY -- MY WOMANLY SPEECH!!
MY FEMININE MANNERISMS!!
...
UH... ACTUALLY... NO MATTER HOW I LOOK AT IT, SHE STILL ONLY SEEMS LIKE A FLAMING GAY MAN...

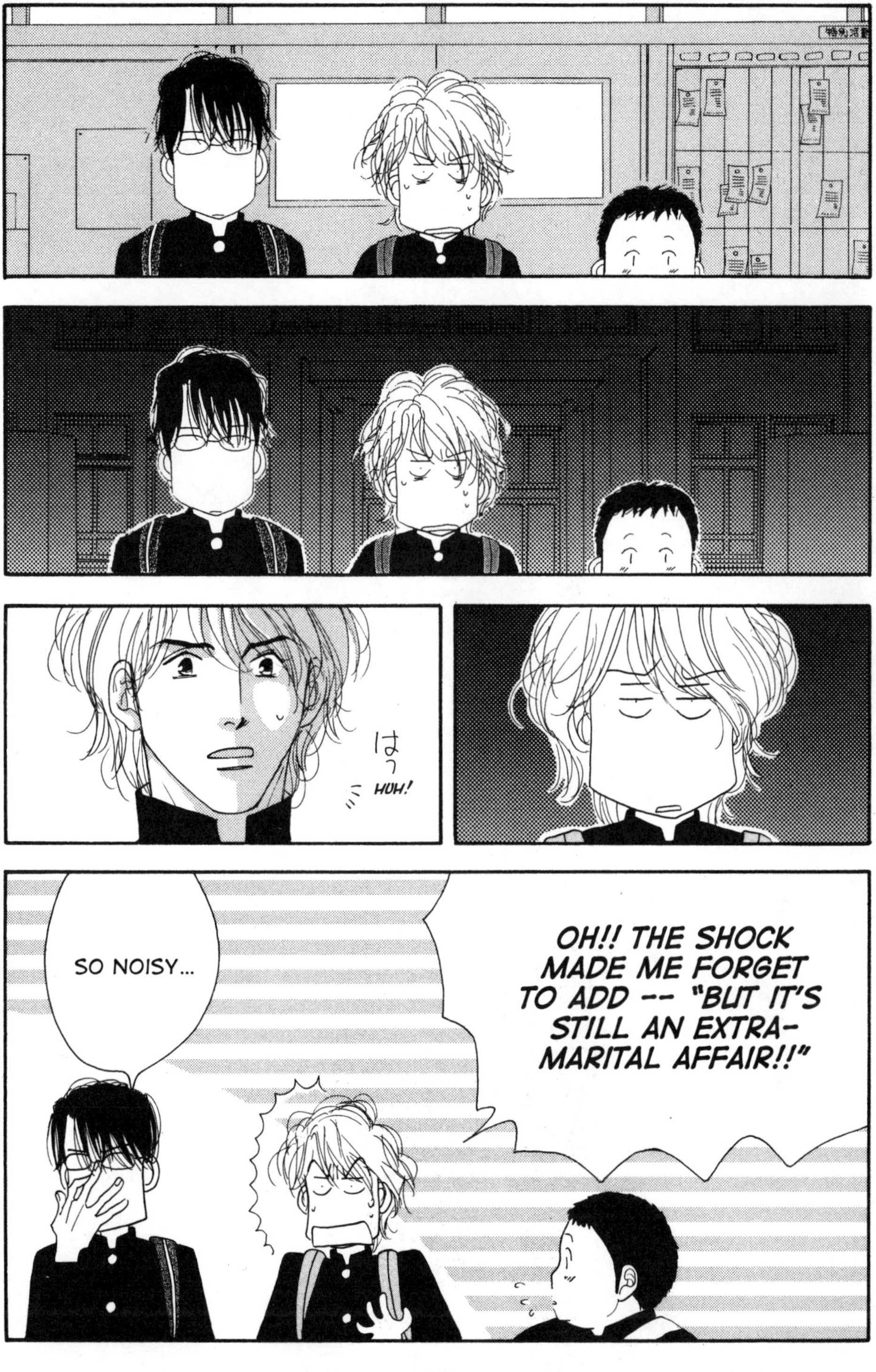
はっ
HUH!
OH!! THE SHOCK MADE ME FORGET TO ADD -- "BUT IT'S STILL AN EXTRA-MARITAL AFFAIR!!"
SO NOISY...

#3

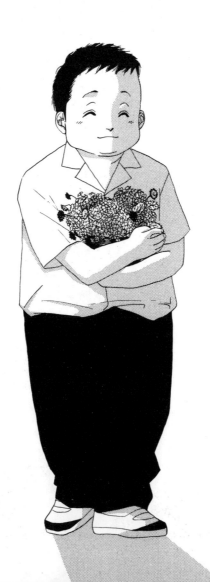

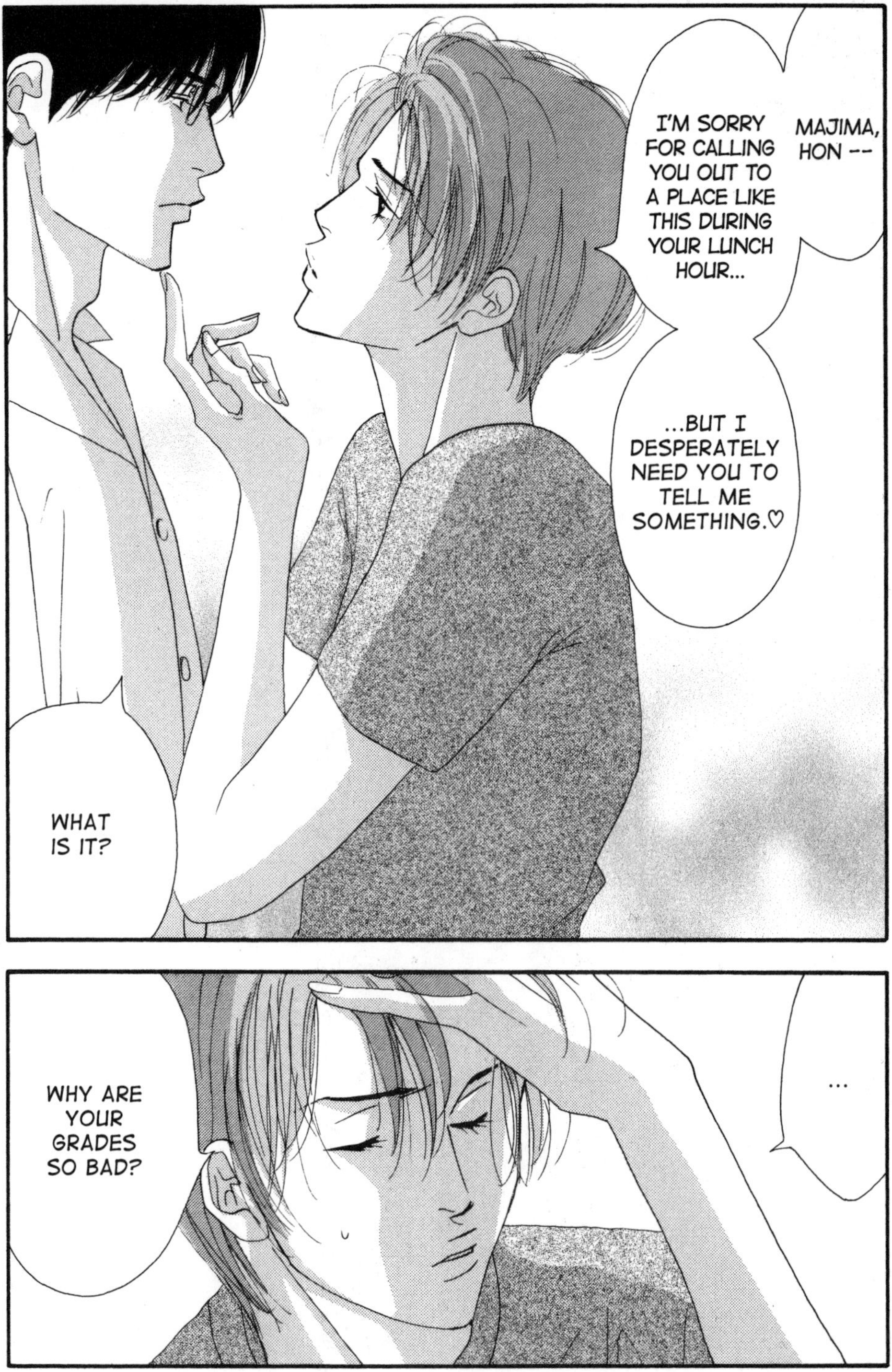
MAJIMA, HON --
I'M SORRY FOR CALLING YOU OUT TO A PLACE LIKE THIS DURING YOUR LUNCH HOUR...
...BUT I DESPERATELY NEED YOU TO TELL ME SOMETHING.♡
WHAT IS IT?
...
WHY ARE YOUR GRADES SO BAD?

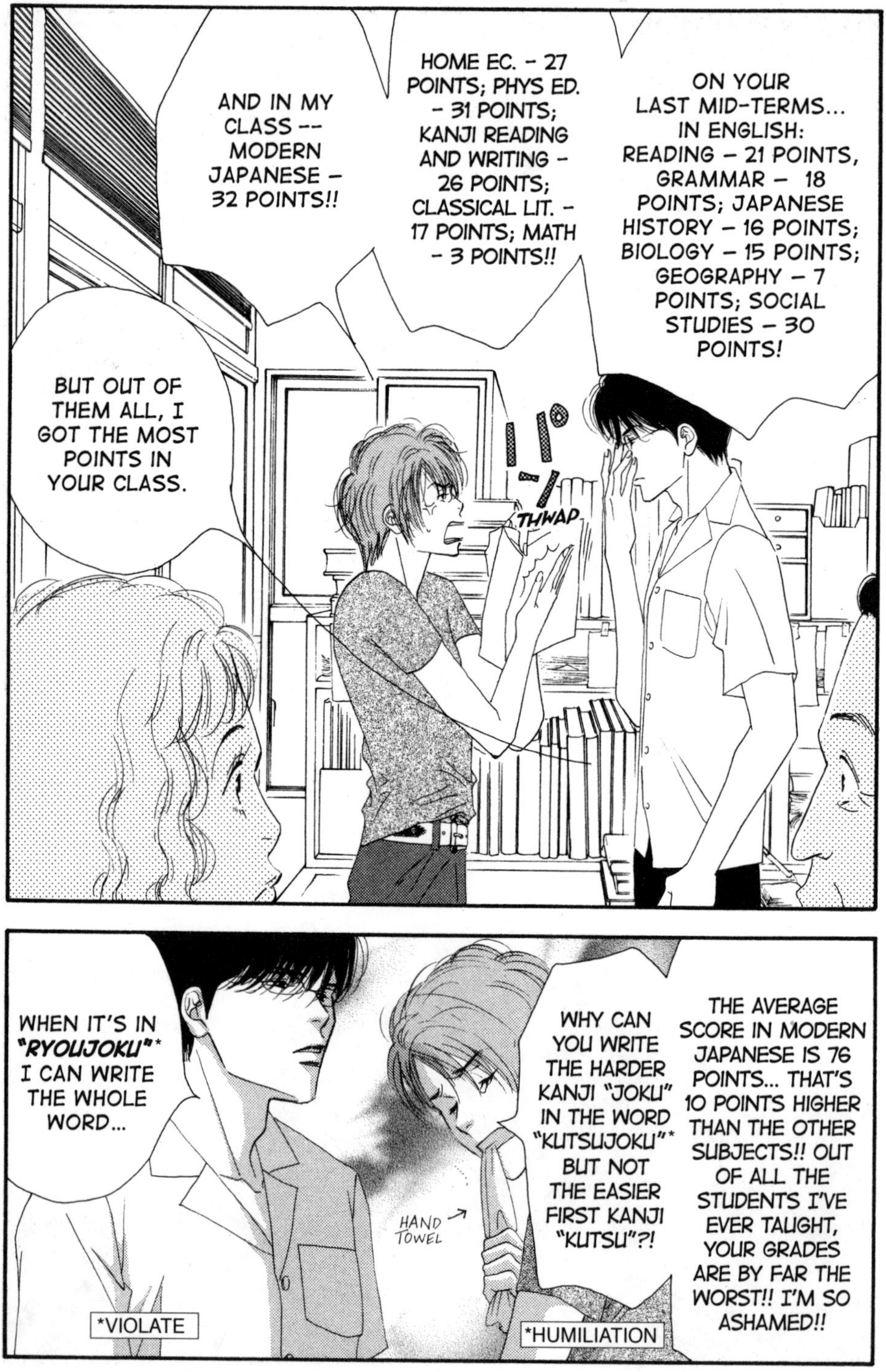
ON YOUR LAST MID-TERMS... IN ENGLISH: READING – 21 POINTS, GRAMMAR – 18 POINTS; JAPANESE HISTORY – 16 POINTS; BIOLOGY – 15 POINTS; GEOGRAPHY – 7 POINTS; SOCIAL STUDIES – 30 POINTS!
HOME EC. - 27 POINTS; PHYS ED. - 31 POINTS; KANJI READING AND WRITING - 26 POINTS; CLASSICAL LIT. - 17 POINTS; MATH - 3 POINTS!!
AND IN MY CLASS -- MODERN JAPANESE – 32 POINTS!!
BUT OUT OF THEM ALL, I GOT THE MOST POINTS IN YOUR CLASS.
THWAP
THE AVERAGE SCORE IN MODERN JAPANESE IS 76 POINTS... THAT'S 10 POINTS HIGHER THAN THE OTHER SUBJECTS!! OUT OF ALL THE STUDENTS I'VE EVER TAUGHT, YOUR GRADES ARE BY FAR THE WORST!! I'M SO ASHAMED!!
WHY CAN YOU WRITE THE HARDER KANJI "JOKU" IN THE WORD "KUTSUJOKU"* BUT NOT THE EASIER FIRST KANJI "KUTSU"?!
*HUMILIATION
HAND TOWEL
WHEN IT'S IN "RYOUJOKU"* I CAN WRITE THE WHOLE WORD...
*VIOLATE

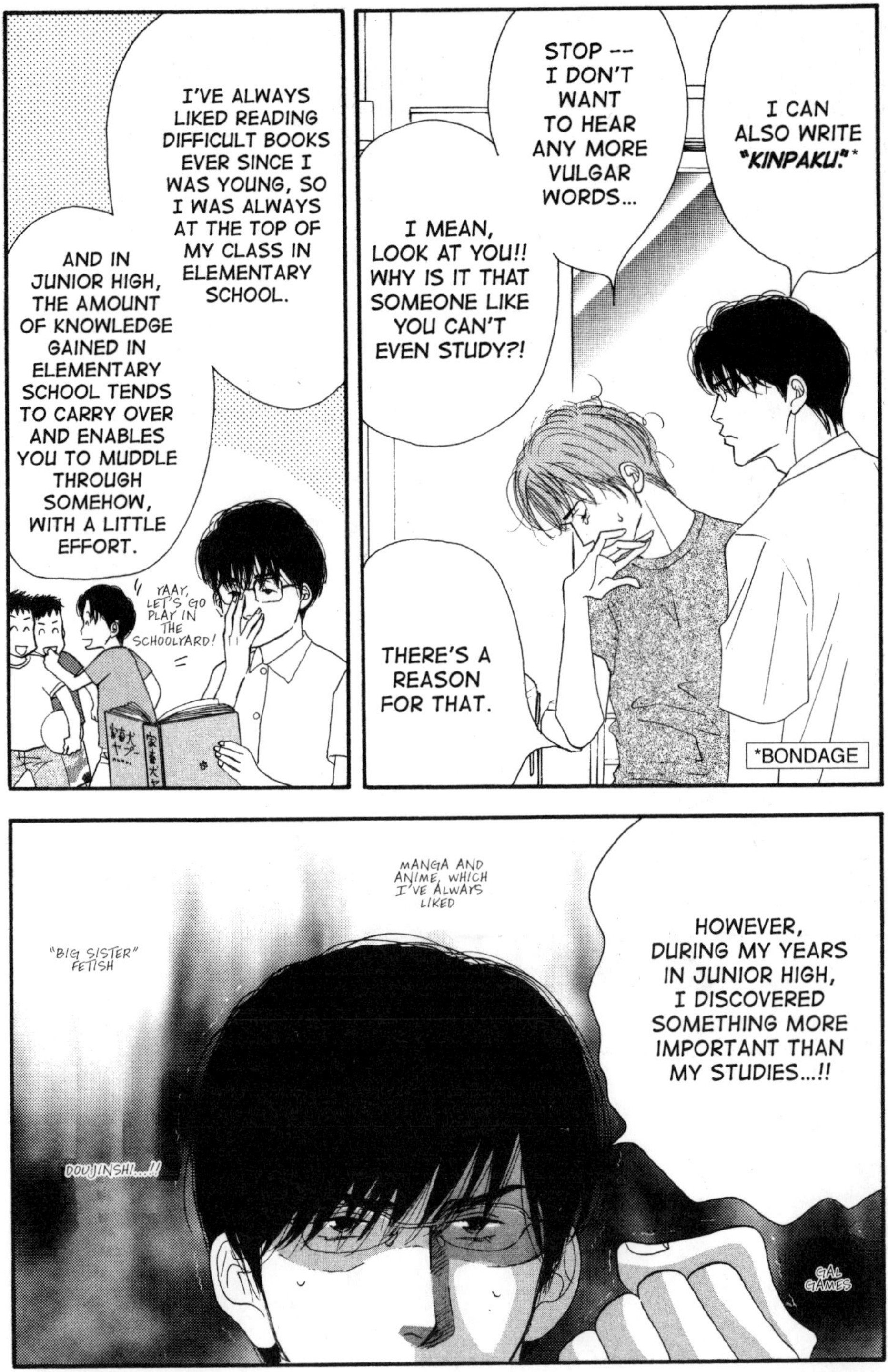
I CAN ALSO WRITE "KINPAKU."*
STOP -- I DON'T WANT TO HEAR ANY MORE VULGAR WORDS...
I MEAN, LOOK AT YOU!! WHY IS IT THAT SOMEONE LIKE YOU CAN'T EVEN STUDY?!
THERE'S A REASON FOR THAT.
*BONDAGE
I'VE ALWAYS LIKED READING DIFFICULT BOOKS EVER SINCE I WAS YOUNG, SO I WAS ALWAYS AT THE TOP OF MY CLASS IN ELEMENTARY SCHOOL.
AND IN JUNIOR HIGH, THE AMOUNT OF KNOWLEDGE GAINED IN ELEMENTARY SCHOOL TENDS TO CARRY OVER AND ENABLES YOU TO MUDDLE THROUGH SOMEHOW, WITH A LITTLE EFFORT.
YAAY, LET'S GO PLAY IN THE SCHOOLYARD!
HOWEVER, DURING MY YEARS IN JUNIOR HIGH, I DISCOVERED SOMETHING MORE IMPORTANT THAN MY STUDIES...!!
MANGA AND ANIME, WHICH I'VE ALWAYS LIKED
"BIG SISTER" FETISH
GAL GAMES
DOUJINSHI...!!

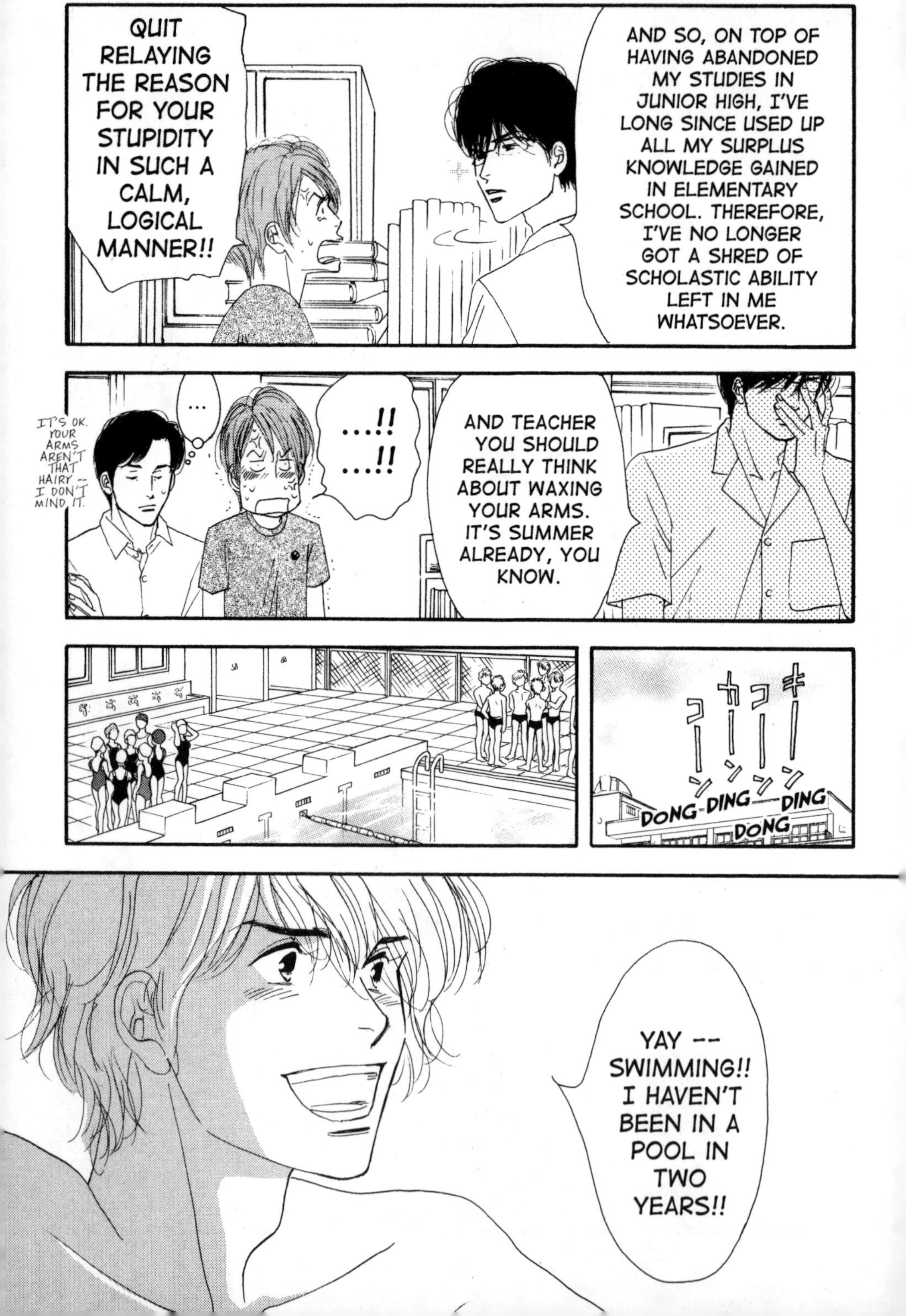
AND SO, ON TOP OF HAVING ABANDONED MY STUDIES IN JUNIOR HIGH, I'VE LONG SINCE USED UP ALL MY SURPLUS KNOWLEDGE GAINED IN ELEMENTARY SCHOOL. THEREFORE, I'VE NO LONGER GOT A SHRED OF SCHOLASTIC ABILITY LEFT IN ME WHATSOEVER.
QUIT RELAYING THE REASON FOR YOUR STUPIDITY IN SUCH A CALM, LOGICAL MANNER!!
AND TEACHER YOU SHOULD REALLY THINK ABOUT WAXING YOUR ARMS. IT'S SUMMER ALREADY, YOU KNOW.
...!! ...!!
...
IT'S OK. YOUR ARMS AREN'T THAT HAIRY -- I DON'T MIND IT.
キーンコーンカーンコーン
DONG-DING—DING
DONG
YAY -- SWIMMING!! I HAVEN'T BEEN IN A POOL IN TWO YEARS!!

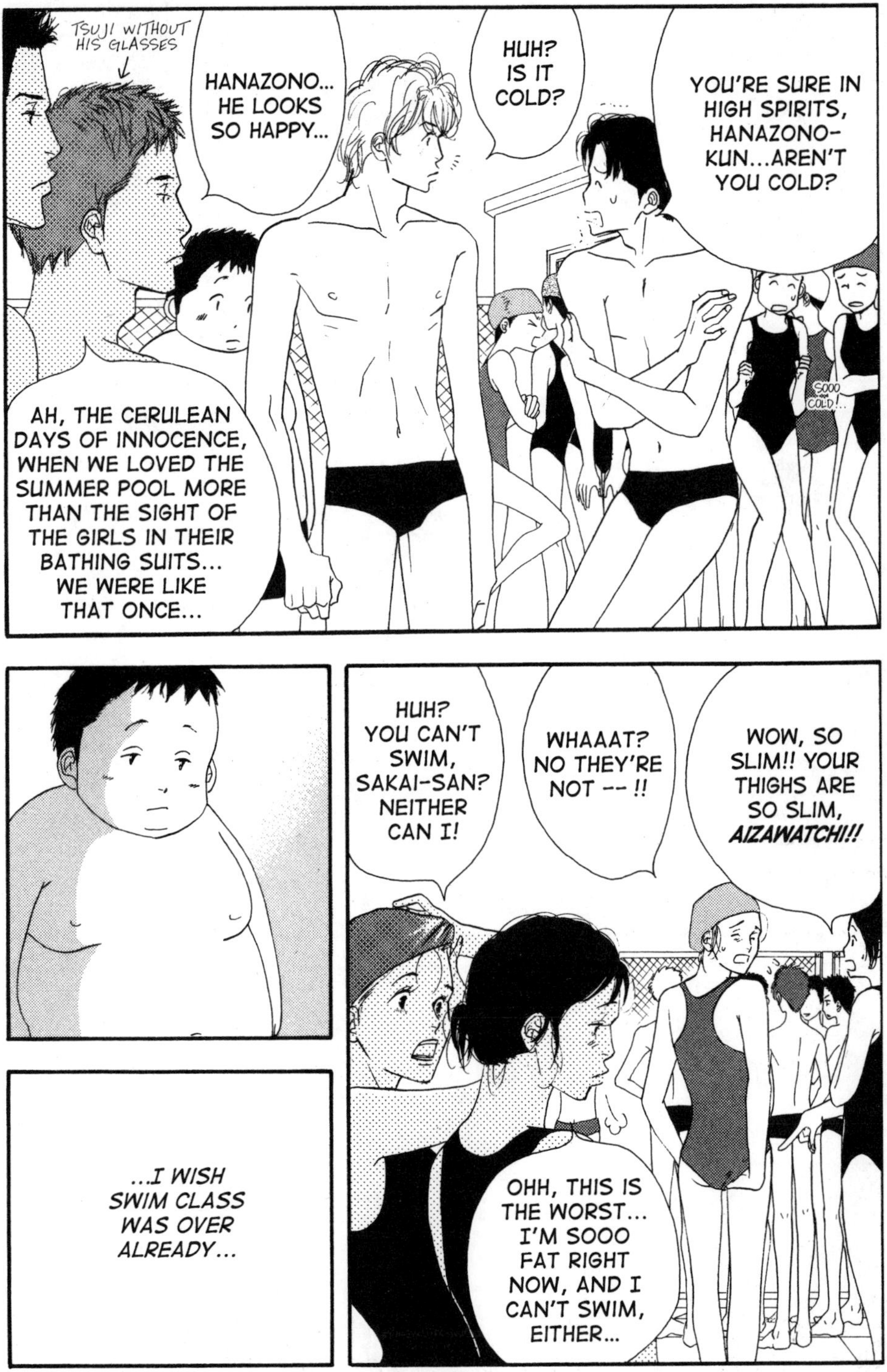
YOU'RE SURE IN HIGH SPIRITS, HANAZONO-KUN...AREN'T YOU COLD?
HUH? IS IT COLD?
SOOO COLD!..
HANAZONO... HE LOOKS SO HAPPY...
TSUJI WITHOUT HIS GLASSES
AH, THE CERULEAN DAYS OF INNOCENCE, WHEN WE LOVED THE SUMMER POOL MORE THAN THE SIGHT OF THE GIRLS IN THEIR BATHING SUITS... WE WERE LIKE THAT ONCE...
WOW, SO SLIM!! YOUR THIGHS ARE SO SLIM, AIZAWATCHI!!
WHAAAT? NO THEY'RE NOT -- !!
HUH? YOU CAN'T SWIM, SAKAI-SAN? NEITHER CAN I!
OHH, THIS IS THE WORST... I'M SOOO FAT RIGHT NOW, AND I CAN'T SWIM, EITHER...
...I WISH SWIM CLASS WAS OVER ALREADY...

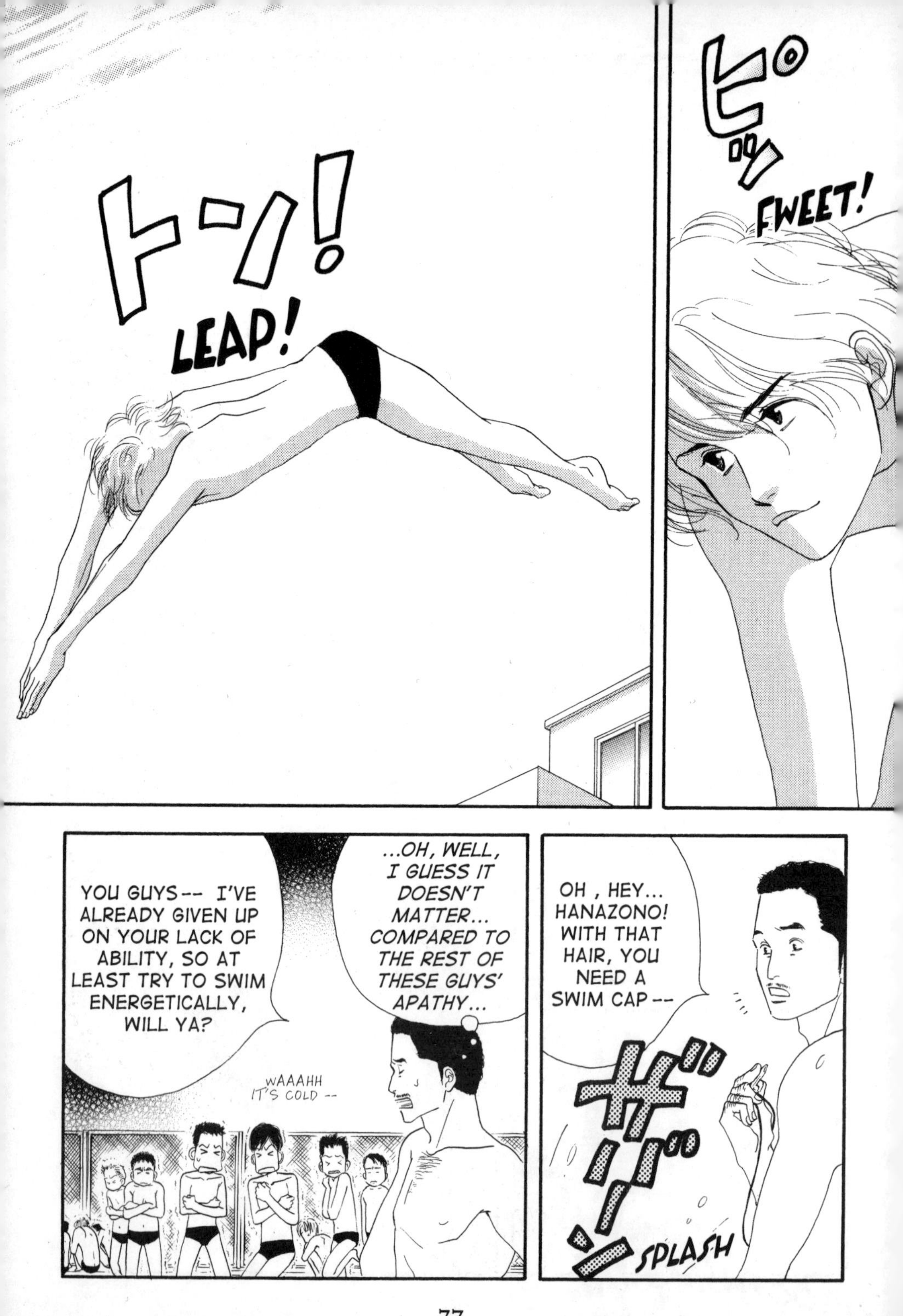

ピッ
FWEET!
トーン!
LEAP!
OH , HEY... HANAZONO! WITH THAT HAIR, YOU NEED A SWIM CAP --
ザブーン
SPLASH
...OH, WELL, I GUESS IT DOESN'T MATTER... COMPARED TO THE REST OF THESE GUYS' APATHY...
YOU GUYS -- I'VE ALREADY GIVEN UP ON YOUR LACK OF ABILITY, SO AT LEAST TRY TO SWIM ENERGETICALLY, WILL YA?
WAAAHH IT'S COLD --

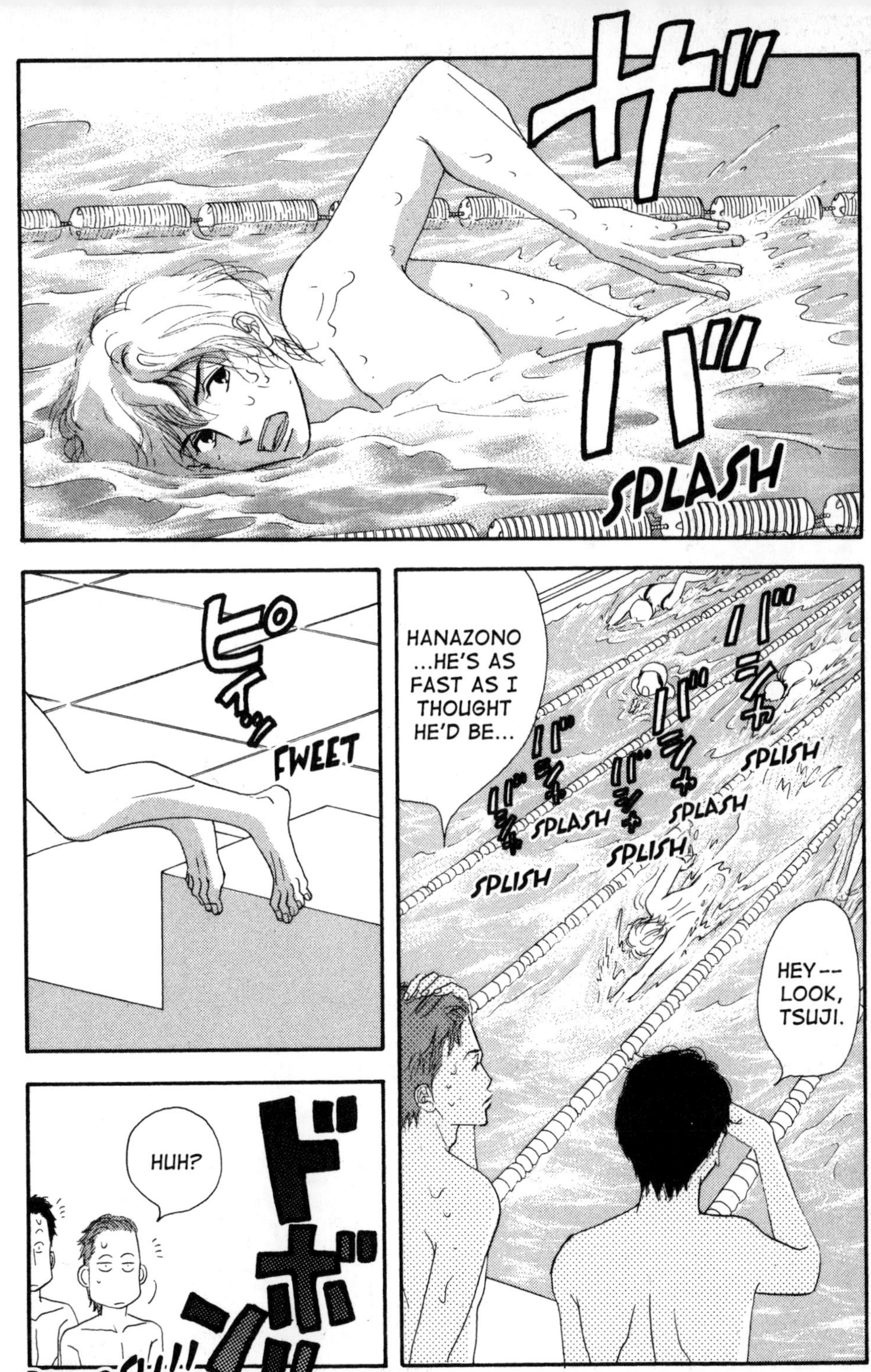
SPLASH
HANAZONO ...HE'S AS FAST AS I THOUGHT HE'D BE...
SPLISH
SPLASH
SPLASH
SPLISH
SPLASH
SPLISH
HEY-- LOOK, TSUJI.
FWEET
HUH?
SPLOOSH!!!

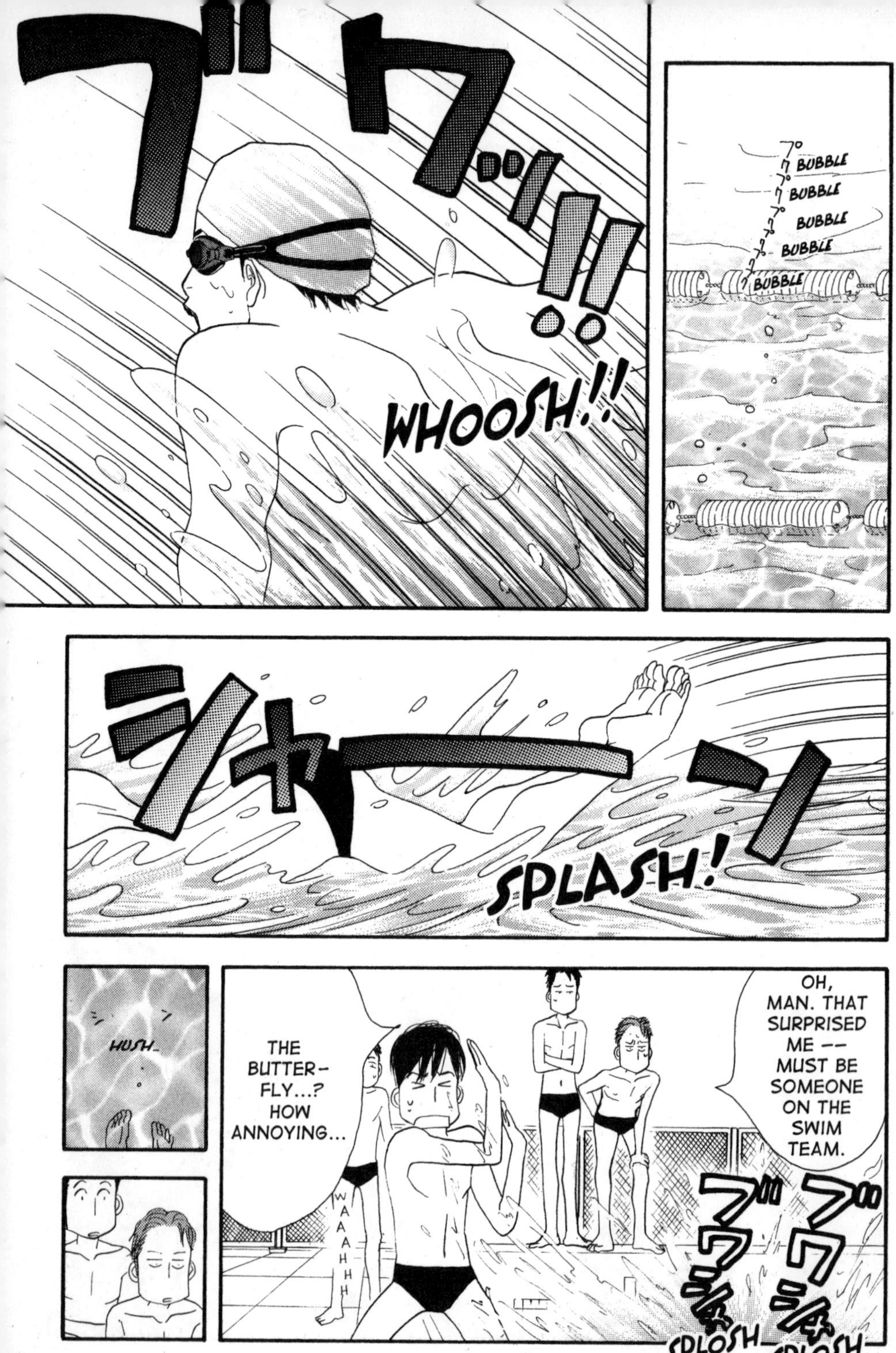
BUBBLE
BUBBLE
BUBBLE
BUBBLE
BUBBLE
ブワッ!!
WHOOSH!!
シャーーッ
SPLASH!
OH, MAN. THAT SURPRISED ME -- MUST BE SOMEONE ON THE SWIM TEAM.
THE BUTTER-FLY...? HOW ANNOYING...
WAAAHHH
ブワシャ
SPLOSH
ブワシャ
SPLOSH
HUSH

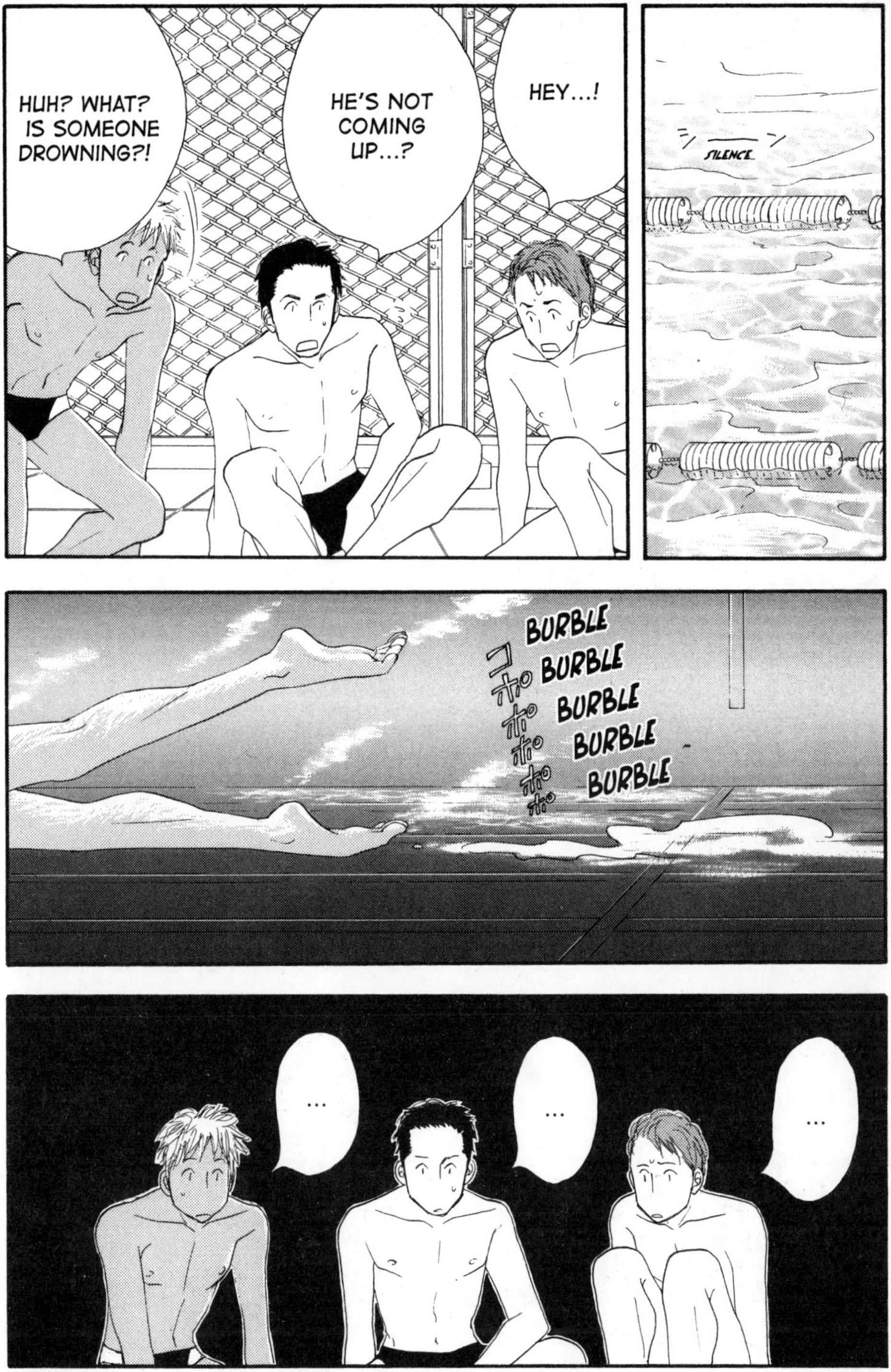
SILENCE
HEY...!
HE'S NOT COMING UP...?
HUH? WHAT? IS SOMEONE DROWNING?!
BURBLE BURBLE BURBLE BURBLE BURBLE
...
...
...

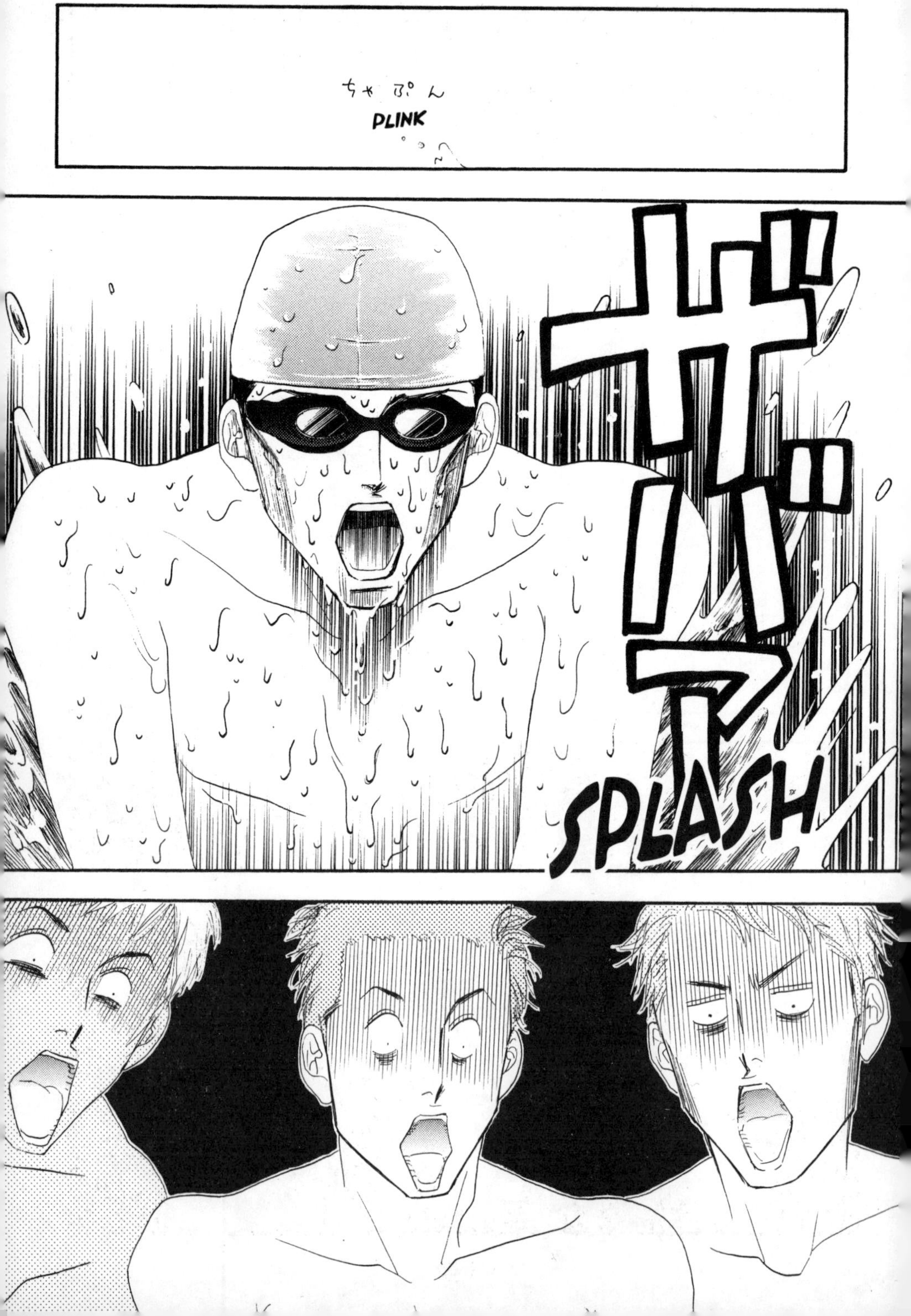
ちゃぷん
PLINK
ザバア
SPLASH

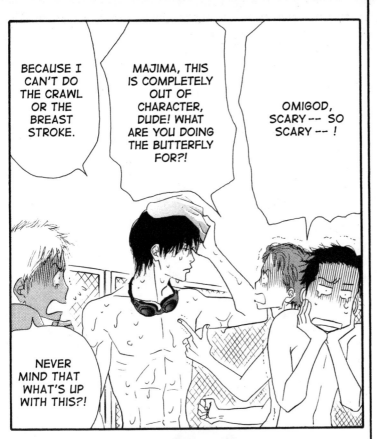

キャーアーアー
EEEEEK--

OMIGOD, SCARY -- SO SCARY -- !
MAJIMA, THIS IS COMPLETELY OUT OF CHARACTER, DUDE! WHAT ARE YOU DOING THE BUTTERFLY FOR?!
BECAUSE I CAN'T DO THE CRAWL OR THE BREAST STROKE.
NEVER MIND THAT WHAT'S UP WITH THIS?!
THOSE ABS!!
THEY'RE WAY TOO RIPPED!!
NOT ONLY THAT -- YOU'RE *THAT* YOKED...

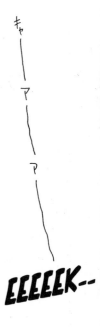

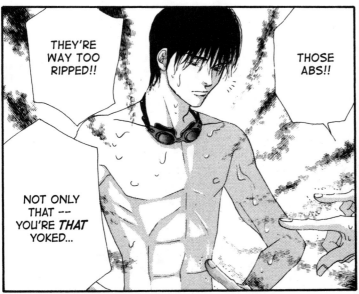

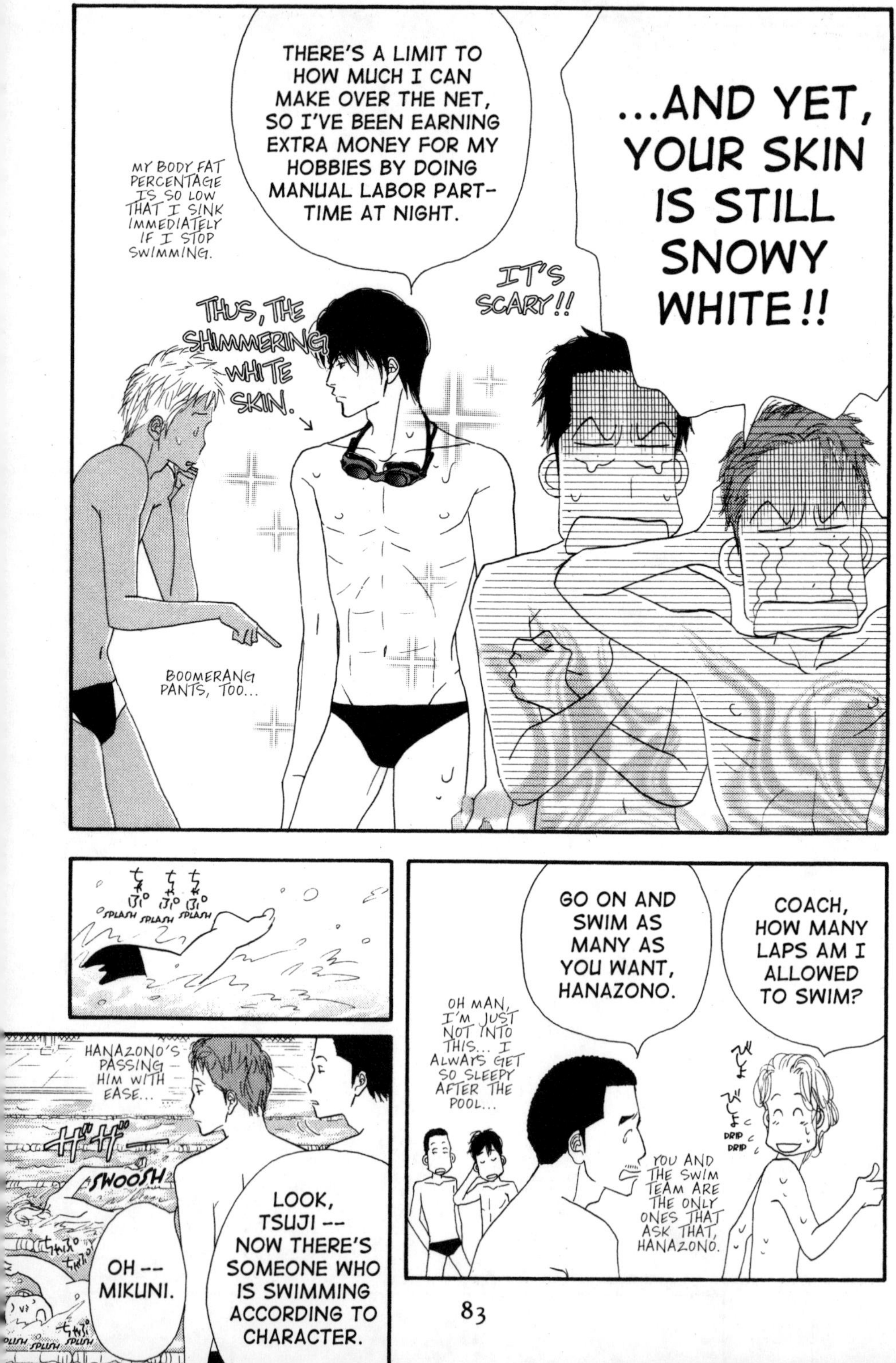
...AND YET, YOUR SKIN IS STILL SNOWY WHITE!!
IT'S SCARY!!
THERE'S A LIMIT TO HOW MUCH I CAN MAKE OVER THE NET, SO I'VE BEEN EARNING EXTRA MONEY FOR MY HOBBIES BY DOING MANUAL LABOR PART-TIME AT NIGHT.
THUS, THE SHIMMERING WHITE SKIN.
MY BODY FAT PERCENTAGE IS SO LOW THAT I SINK IMMEDIATELY IF I STOP SWIMMING.
BOOMERANG PANTS, TOO...
COACH, HOW MANY LAPS AM I ALLOWED TO SWIM?
GO ON AND SWIM AS MANY AS YOU WANT, HANAZONO.
OH MAN, I'M JUST NOT INTO THIS... I ALWAYS GET SO SLEEPY AFTER THE POOL...
DRIP DRIP
YOU AND THE SWIM TEAM ARE THE ONLY ONES THAT ASK THAT, HANAZONO.
SPLASH SPLASH SPLASH
HANAZONO'S PASSING HIM WITH EASE...
SWOOSH
LOOK, TSUJI -- NOW THERE'S SOMEONE WHO IS SWIMMING ACCORDING TO CHARACTER.
OH -- MIKUNI.
SPLISH SPLISH SPLISH

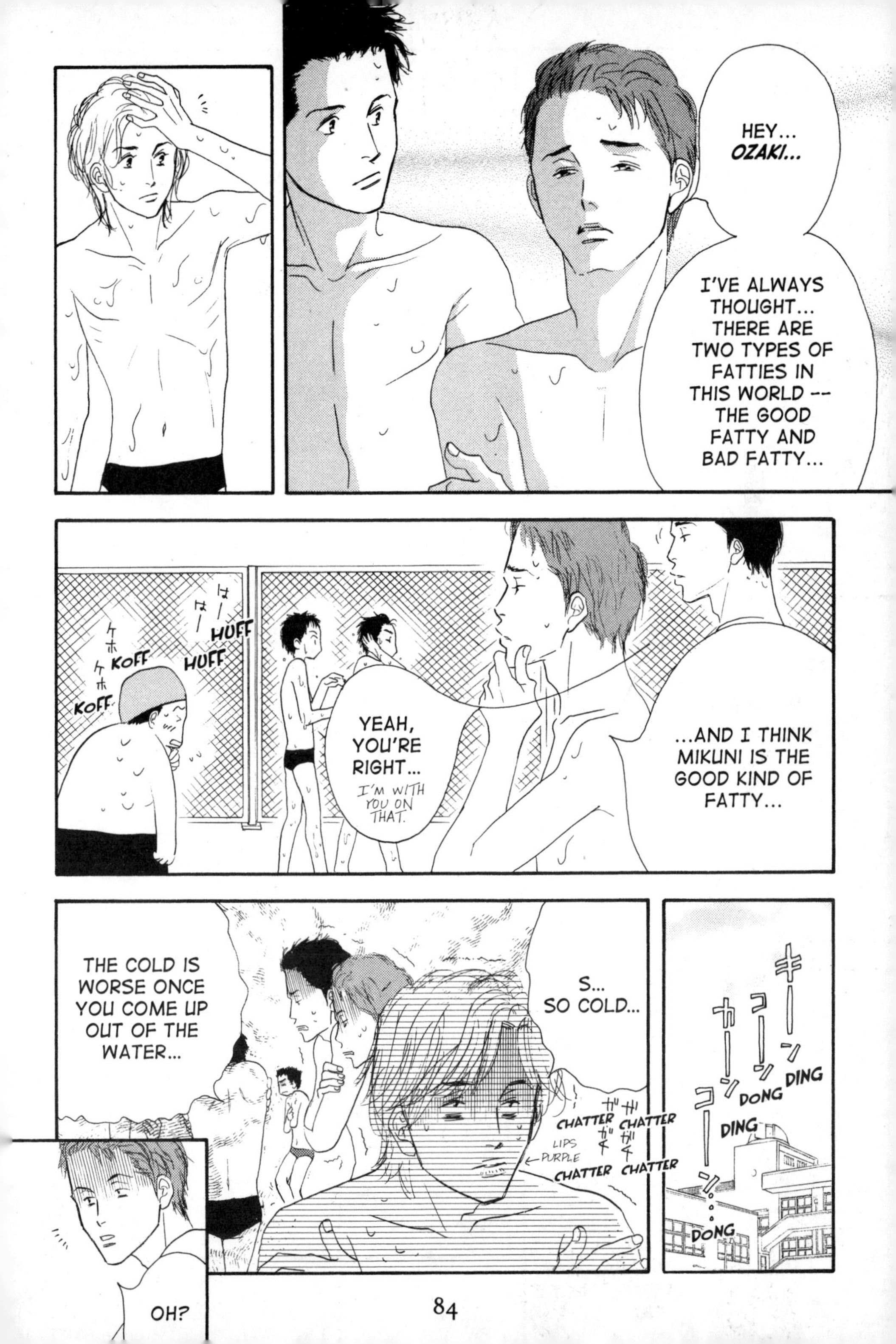

HEY... OZAKI...
I'VE ALWAYS THOUGHT... THERE ARE TWO TYPES OF FATTIES IN THIS WORLD -- THE GOOD FATTY AND BAD FATTY...
...AND I THINK MIKUNI IS THE GOOD KIND OF FATTY...
YEAH, YOU'RE RIGHT...
I'M WITH YOU ON THAT.
はー はー
HUFF HUFF
ケホ ケホ
KOFF KOFF
キーンコーンカーンコーン
DING DONG DING DONG
S... SO COLD...
ガチ ガチ ガチ ガチ
CHATTER CHATTER CHATTER CHATTER
LIPS PURPLE
THE COLD IS WORSE ONCE YOU COME UP OUT OF THE WATER...
OH?

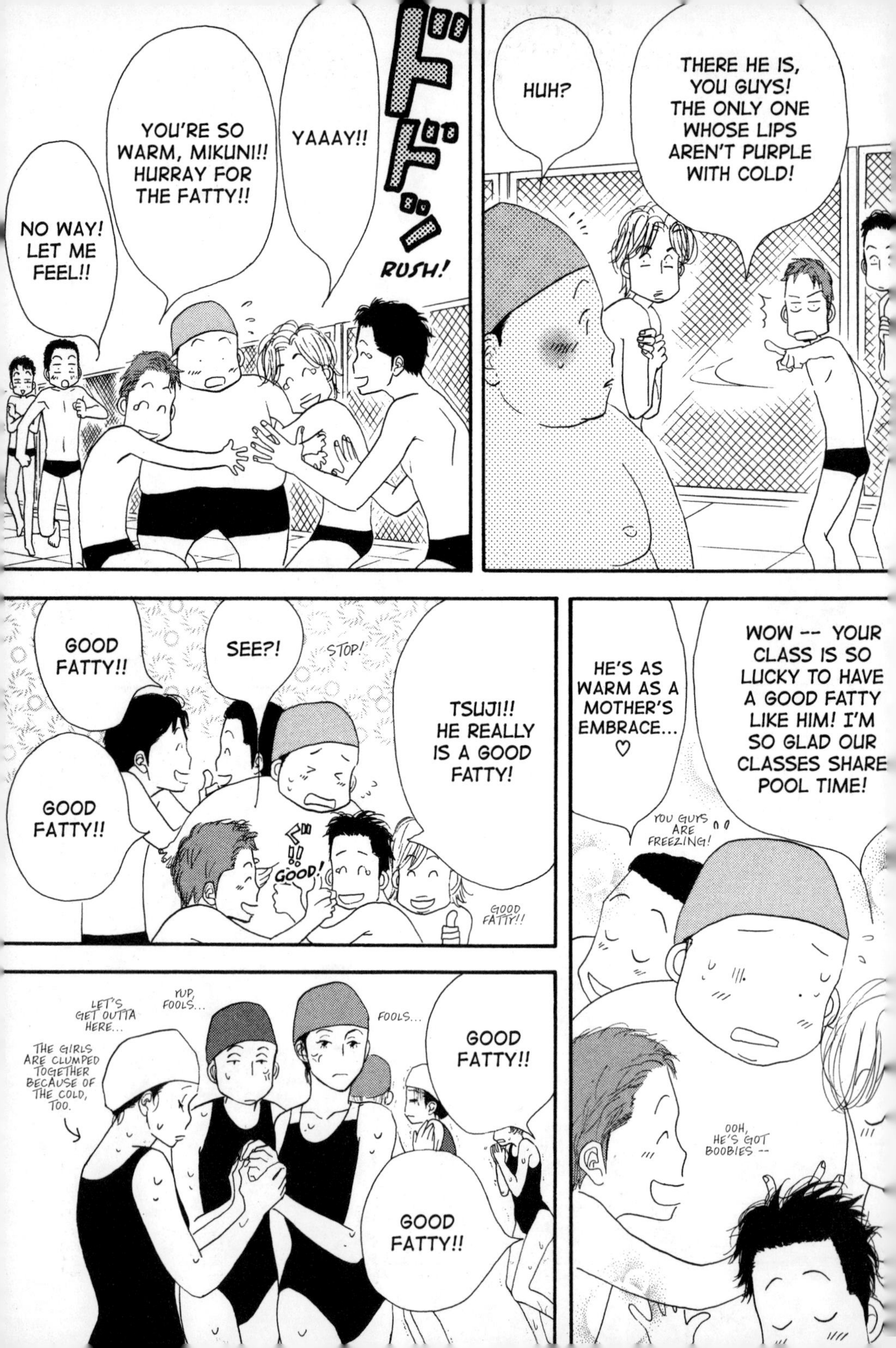
THERE HE IS, YOU GUYS! THE ONLY ONE WHOSE LIPS AREN'T PURPLE WITH COLD!
HUH?
RUSH!
YAAAY!!
YOU'RE SO WARM, MIKUNI!! HURRAY FOR THE FATTY!!
NO WAY! LET ME FEEL!!
WOW -- YOUR CLASS IS SO LUCKY TO HAVE A GOOD FATTY LIKE HIM! I'M SO GLAD OUR CLASSES SHARE POOL TIME!
HE'S AS WARM AS A MOTHER'S EMBRACE... ♡
YOU GUYS ARE FREEZING!
OOH, HE'S GOT BOOBIES --
TSUJI!! HE REALLY IS A GOOD FATTY!
STOP!
SEE?!
GOOD FATTY!!
GOOD FATTY!!
GOOD!
GOOD FATTY!!
GOOD FATTY!!
FOOLS...
YUP, FOOLS...
LET'S GET OUTTA HERE...
THE GIRLS ARE CLUMPED TOGETHER BECAUSE OF THE COLD, TOO.
GOOD FATTY!!

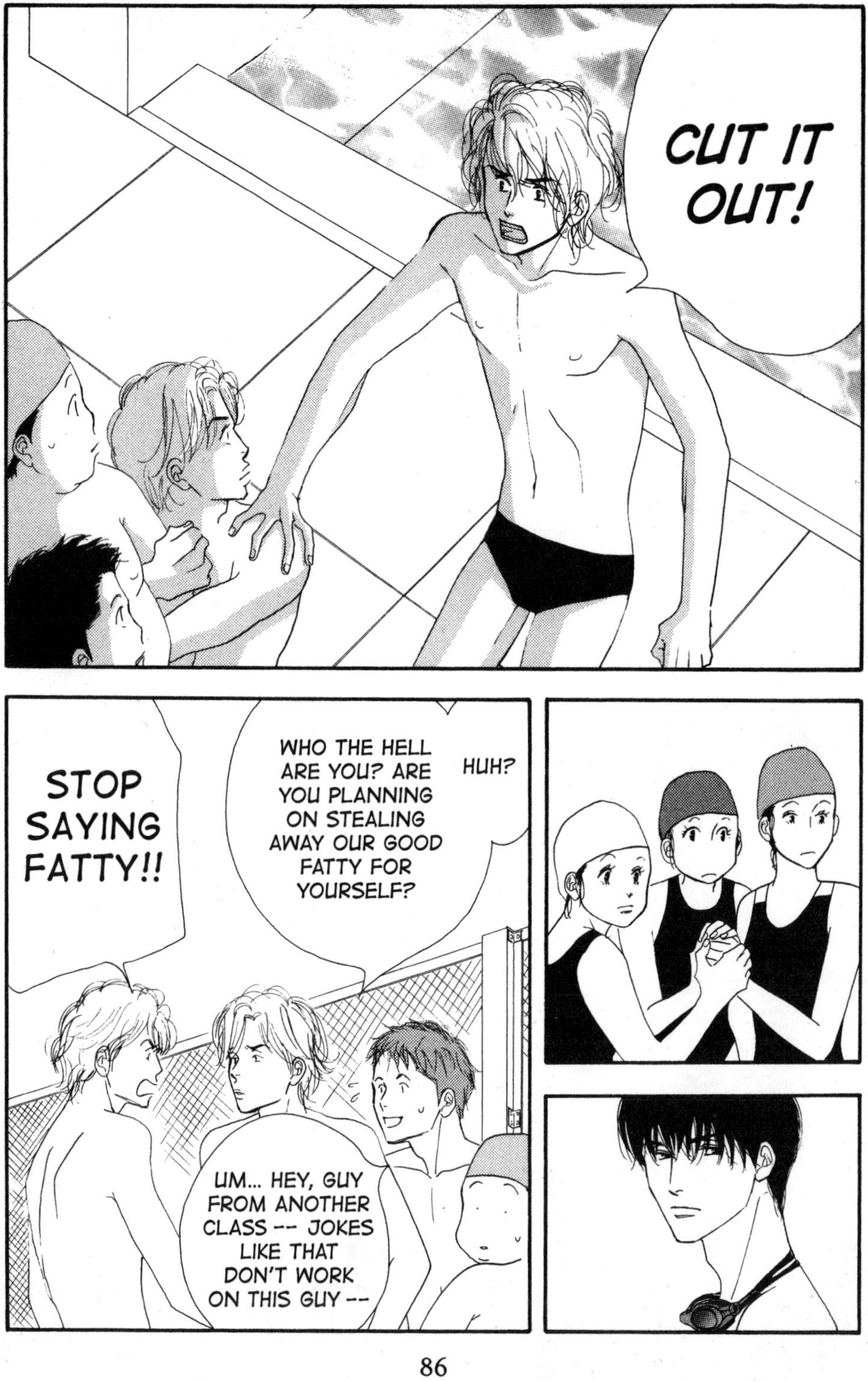
CUT IT OUT!
HUH?
WHO THE HELL ARE YOU? ARE YOU PLANNING ON STEALING AWAY OUR GOOD FATTY FOR YOURSELF?
STOP SAYING FATTY!!
UM... HEY, GUY FROM ANOTHER CLASS -- JOKES LIKE THAT DON'T WORK ON THIS GUY --

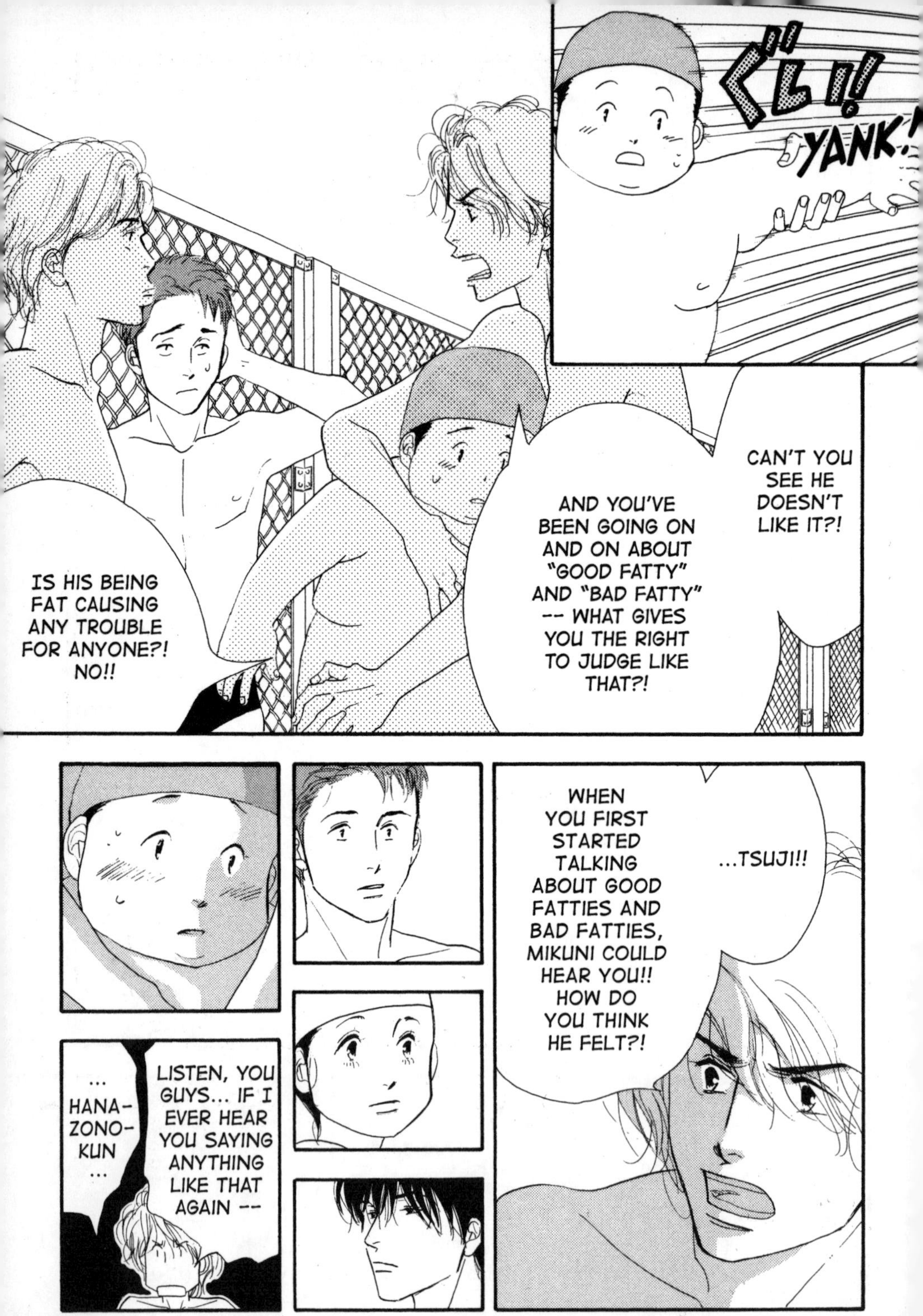
ぐい!!
YANK!
CAN'T YOU SEE HE DOESN'T LIKE IT?!
AND YOU'VE BEEN GOING ON AND ON ABOUT "GOOD FATTY" AND "BAD FATTY" -- WHAT GIVES YOU THE RIGHT TO JUDGE LIKE THAT?!
IS HIS BEING FAT CAUSING ANY TROUBLE FOR ANYONE?! NO!!
...TSUJI!!
WHEN YOU FIRST STARTED TALKING ABOUT GOOD FATTIES AND BAD FATTIES, MIKUNI COULD HEAR YOU!! HOW DO YOU THINK HE FELT?!
LISTEN, YOU GUYS... IF I EVER HEAR YOU SAYING ANYTHING LIKE THAT AGAIN --
... HANA-ZONO-KUN ...

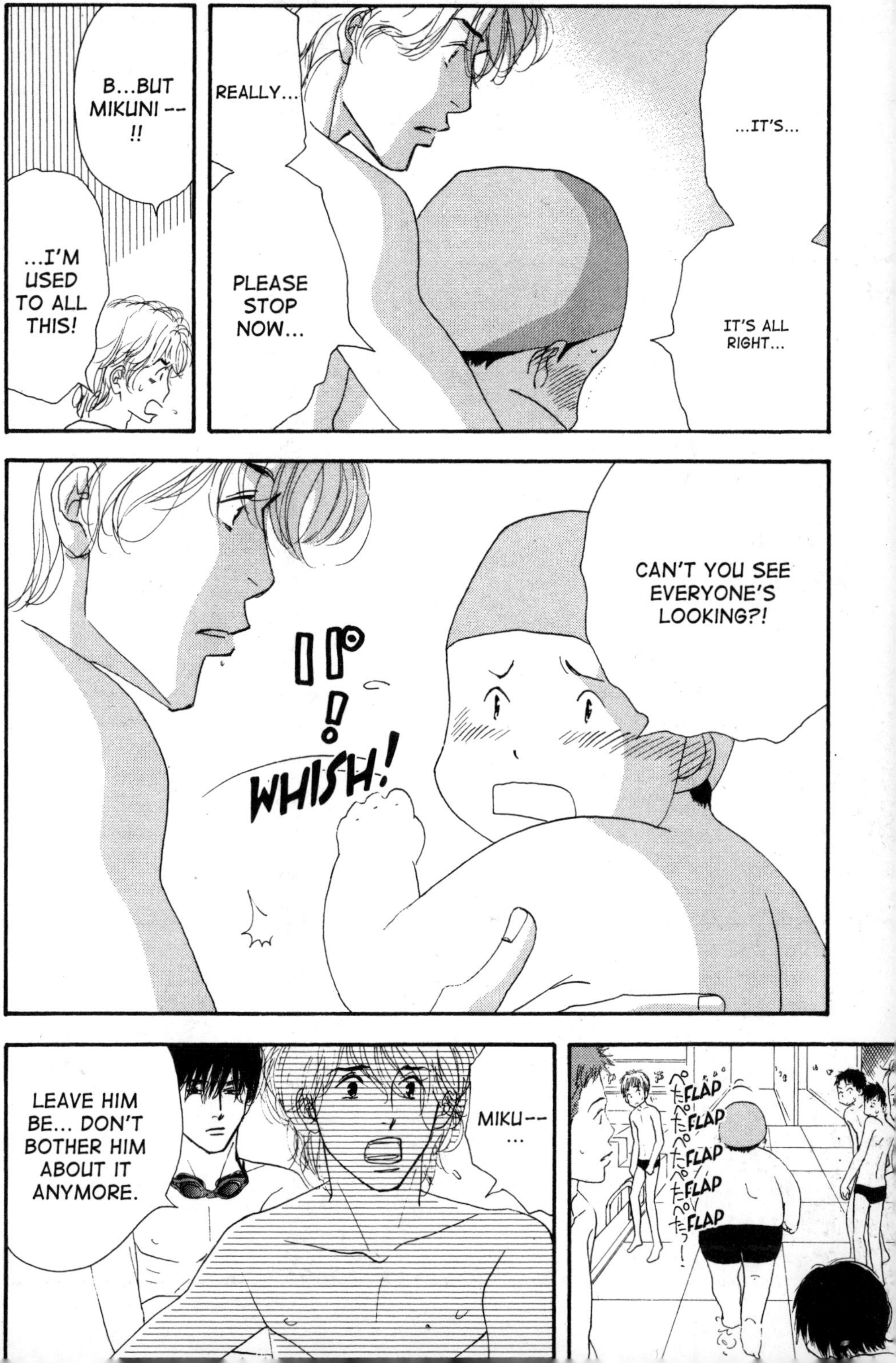
...IT'S...
IT'S ALL RIGHT...
REALLY...
PLEASE STOP NOW...
B...BUT MIKUNI -- !!
...I'M USED TO ALL THIS!
CAN'T YOU SEE EVERYONE'S LOOKING?!
!!
WHISH!
FLAP
FLAP
FLAP
FLAP
FLAP
MIKU-- ...
LEAVE HIM BE... DON'T BOTHER HIM ABOUT IT ANYMORE.

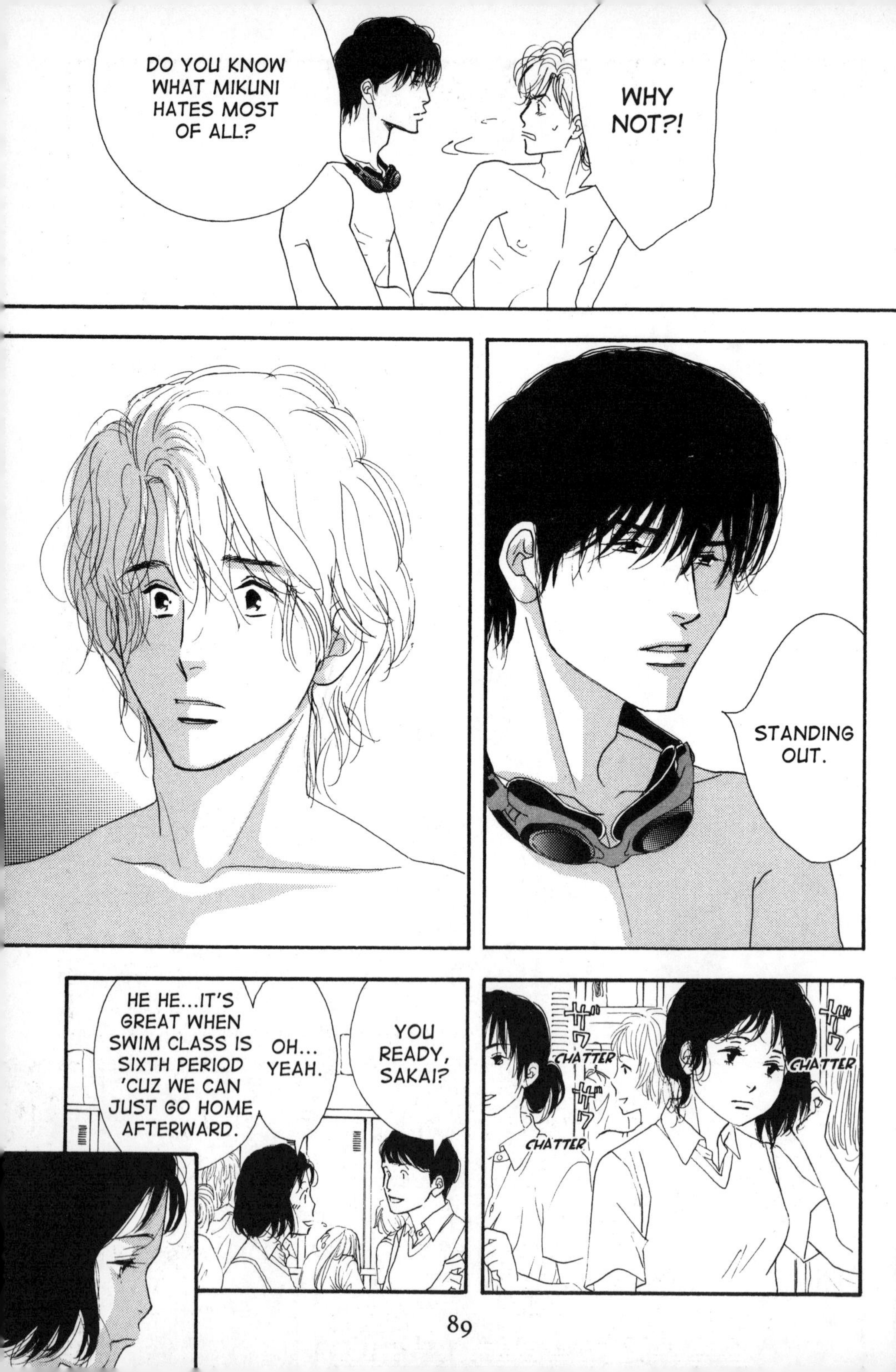
WHY NOT?!
DO YOU KNOW WHAT MIKUNI HATES MOST OF ALL?
STANDING OUT.
CHATTER
CHATTER
CHATTER
YOU READY, SAKAI?
OH... YEAH.
HE HE...IT'S GREAT WHEN SWIM CLASS IS SIXTH PERIOD 'CUZ WE CAN JUST GO HOME AFTERWARD.

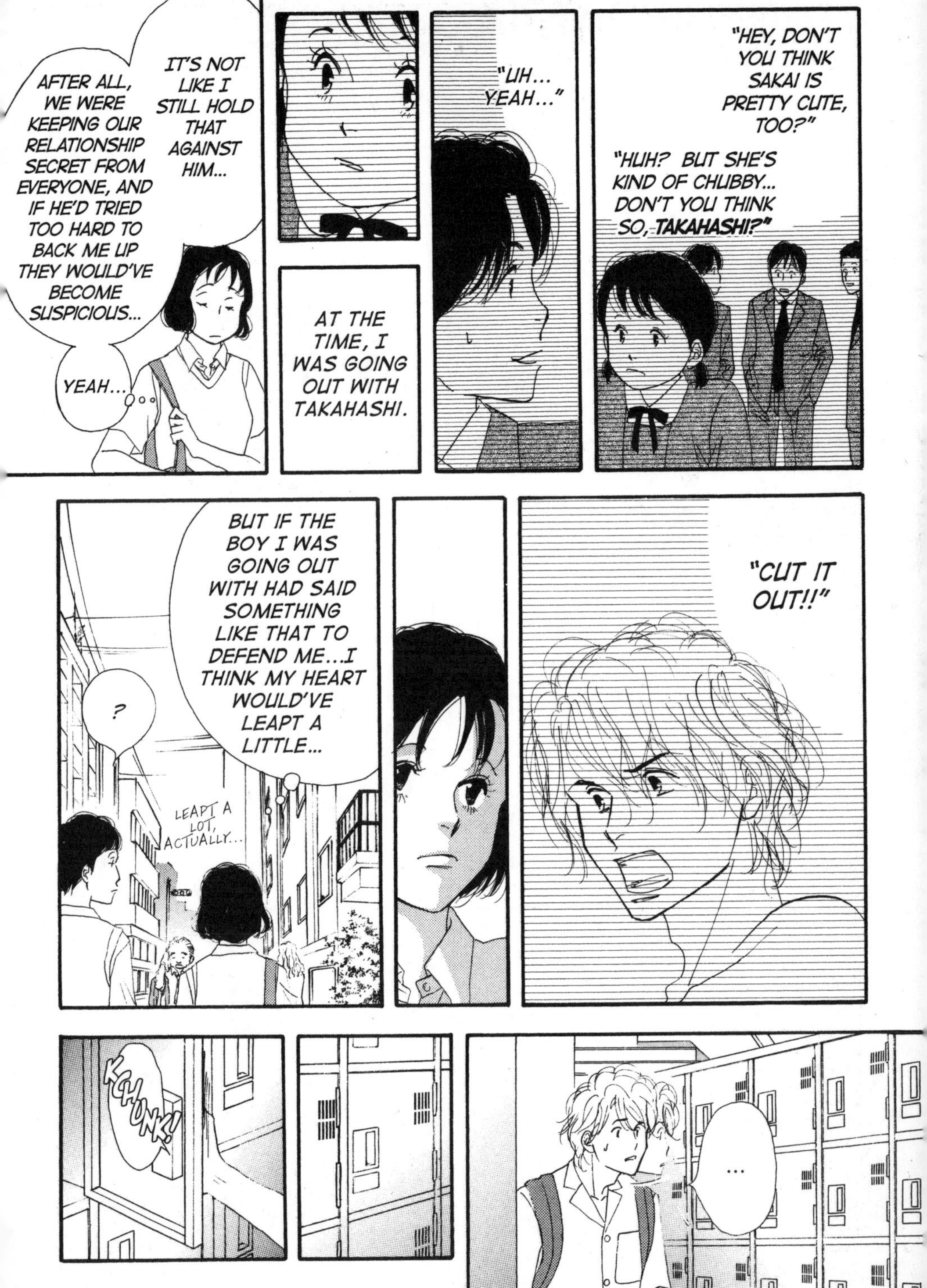
"HEY, DON'T YOU THINK SAKAI IS PRETTY CUTE, TOO?"
"HUH? BUT SHE'S KIND OF CHUBBY... DON'T YOU THINK SO, TAKAHASHI?"
"UH... YEAH..."
AT THE TIME, I WAS GOING OUT WITH TAKAHASHI.
IT'S NOT LIKE I STILL HOLD THAT AGAINST HIM...
AFTER ALL, WE WERE KEEPING OUR RELATIONSHIP SECRET FROM EVERYONE, AND IF HE'D TRIED TOO HARD TO BACK ME UP THEY WOULD'VE BECOME SUSPICIOUS...
YEAH...
"CUT IT OUT!!"
BUT IF THE BOY I WAS GOING OUT WITH HAD SAID SOMETHING LIKE THAT TO DEFEND ME...I THINK MY HEART WOULD'VE LEAPT A LITTLE...
?
LEAPT A LOT, ACTUALLY...
...
KCHUNK!

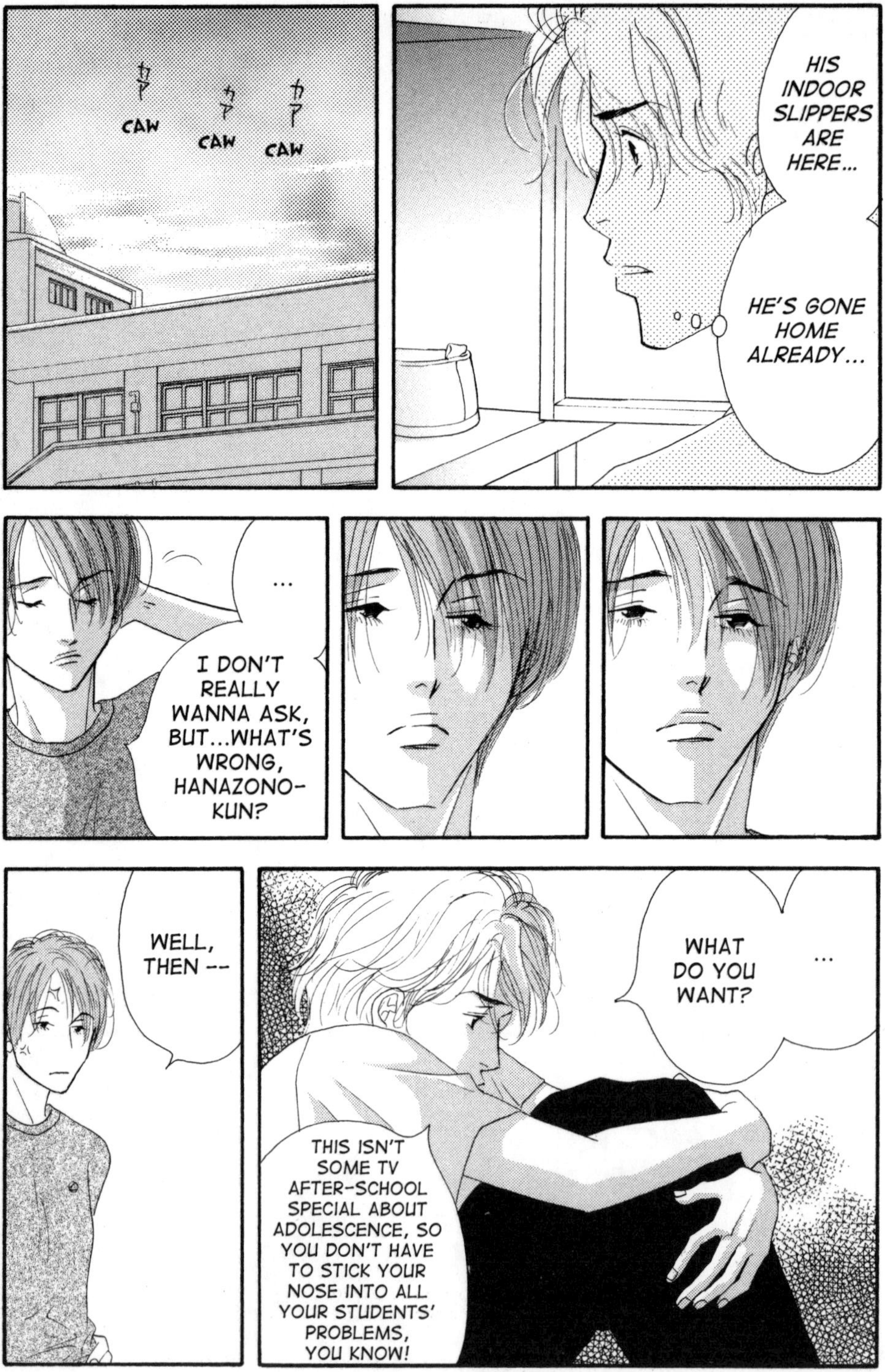
HIS INDOOR SLIPPERS ARE HERE...
HE'S GONE HOME ALREADY...
カア CAW
カア CAW
カア CAW
...
I DON'T REALLY WANNA ASK, BUT...WHAT'S WRONG, HANAZONO-KUN?
...
WHAT DO YOU WANT?
THIS ISN'T SOME TV AFTER-SCHOOL SPECIAL ABOUT ADOLESCENCE, SO YOU DON'T HAVE TO STICK YOUR NOSE INTO ALL YOUR STUDENTS' PROBLEMS, YOU KNOW!
WELL, THEN --

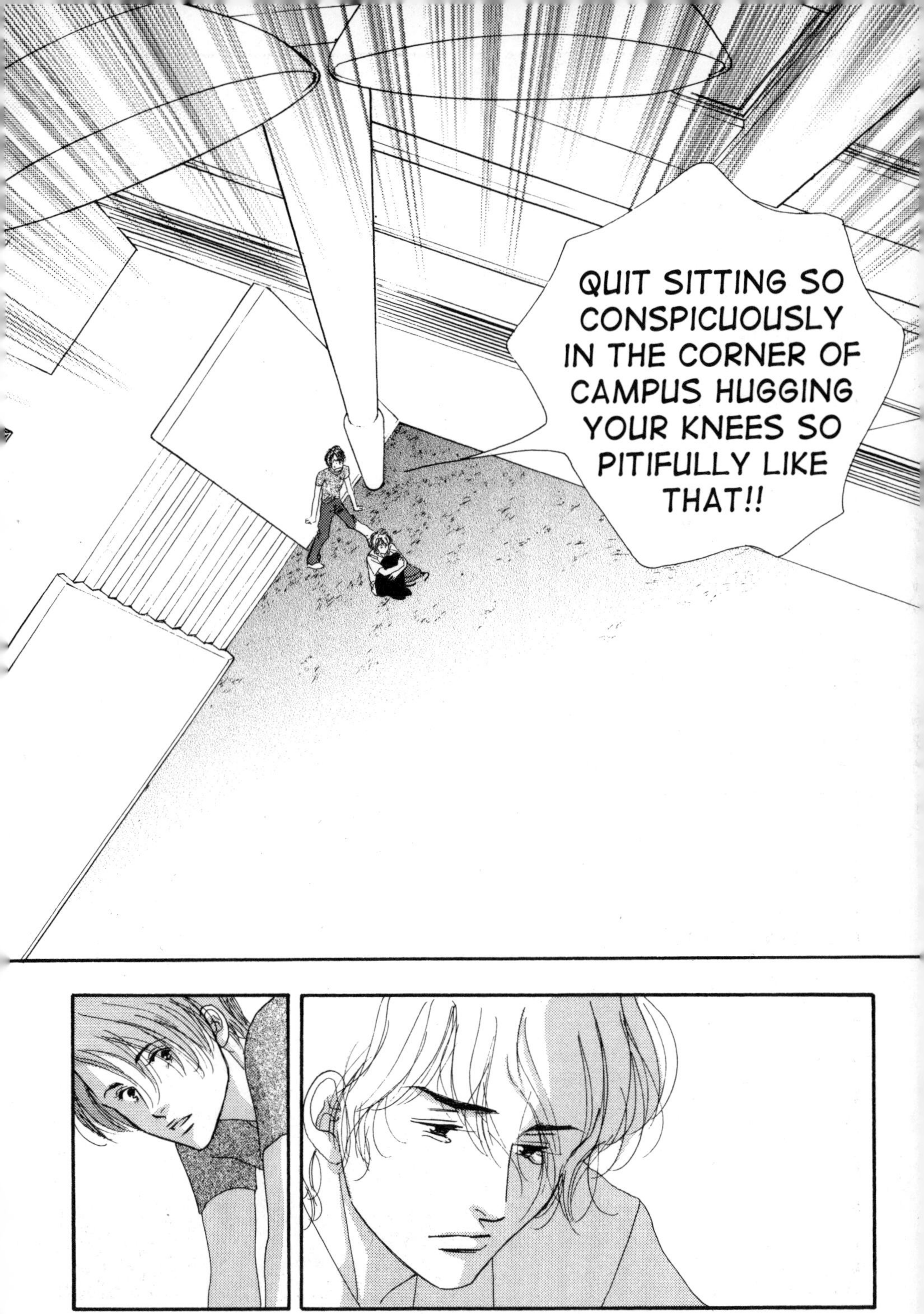
QUIT SITTING SO CONSPICUOUSLY IN THE CORNER OF CAMPUS HUGGING YOUR KNEES SO PITIFULLY LIKE THAT!!

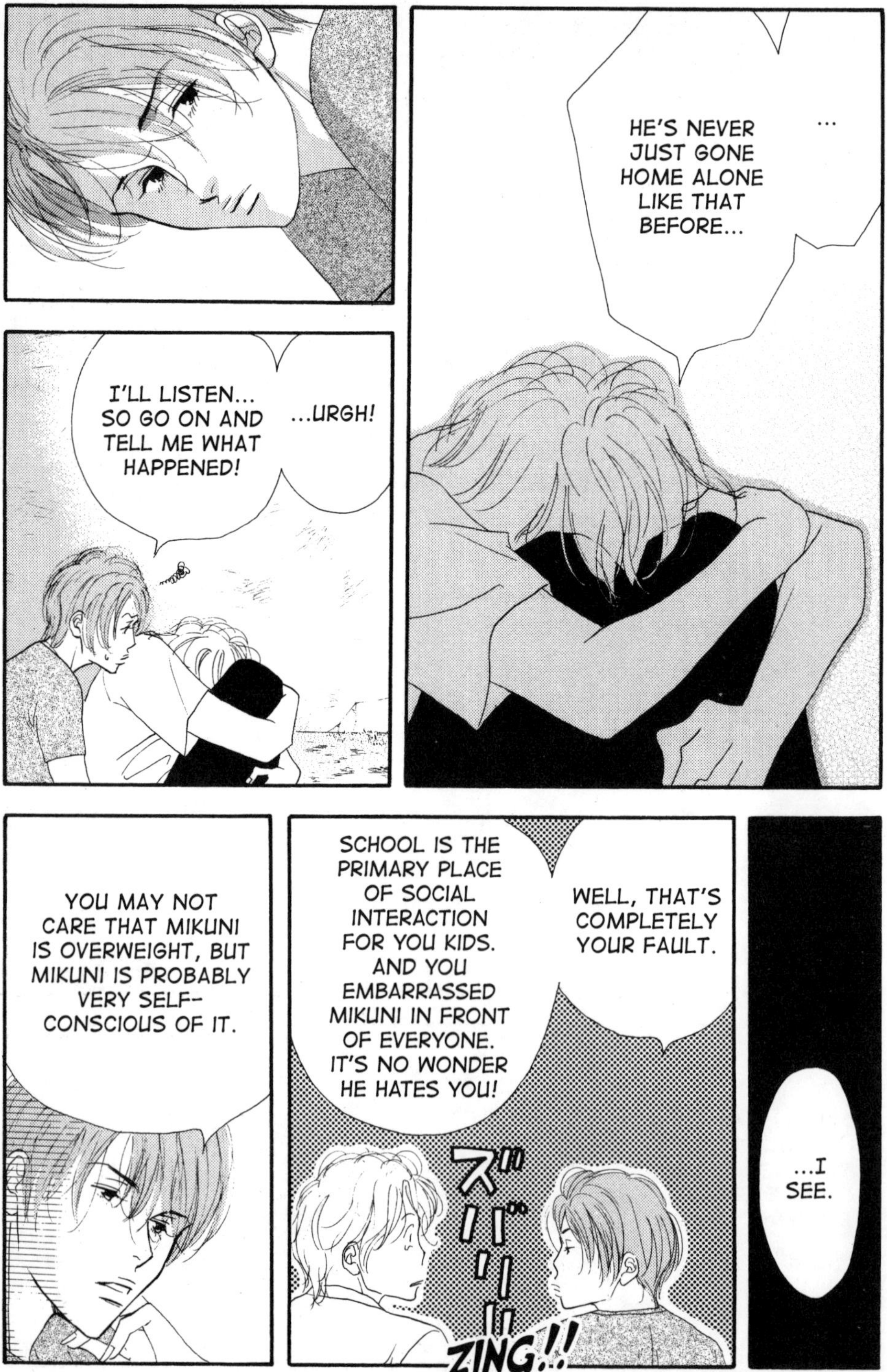
...
HE'S NEVER JUST GONE HOME ALONE LIKE THAT BEFORE...
I'LL LISTEN... SO GO ON AND TELL ME WHAT HAPPENED!
...URGH!
...I SEE.
WELL, THAT'S COMPLETELY YOUR FAULT.
SCHOOL IS THE PRIMARY PLACE OF SOCIAL INTERACTION FOR YOU KIDS. AND YOU EMBARRASSED MIKUNI IN FRONT OF EVERYONE. IT'S NO WONDER HE HATES YOU!
ズバーッ
ZING!!
YOU MAY NOT CARE THAT MIKUNI IS OVERWEIGHT, BUT MIKUNI IS PROBABLY VERY SELF-CONSCIOUS OF IT.

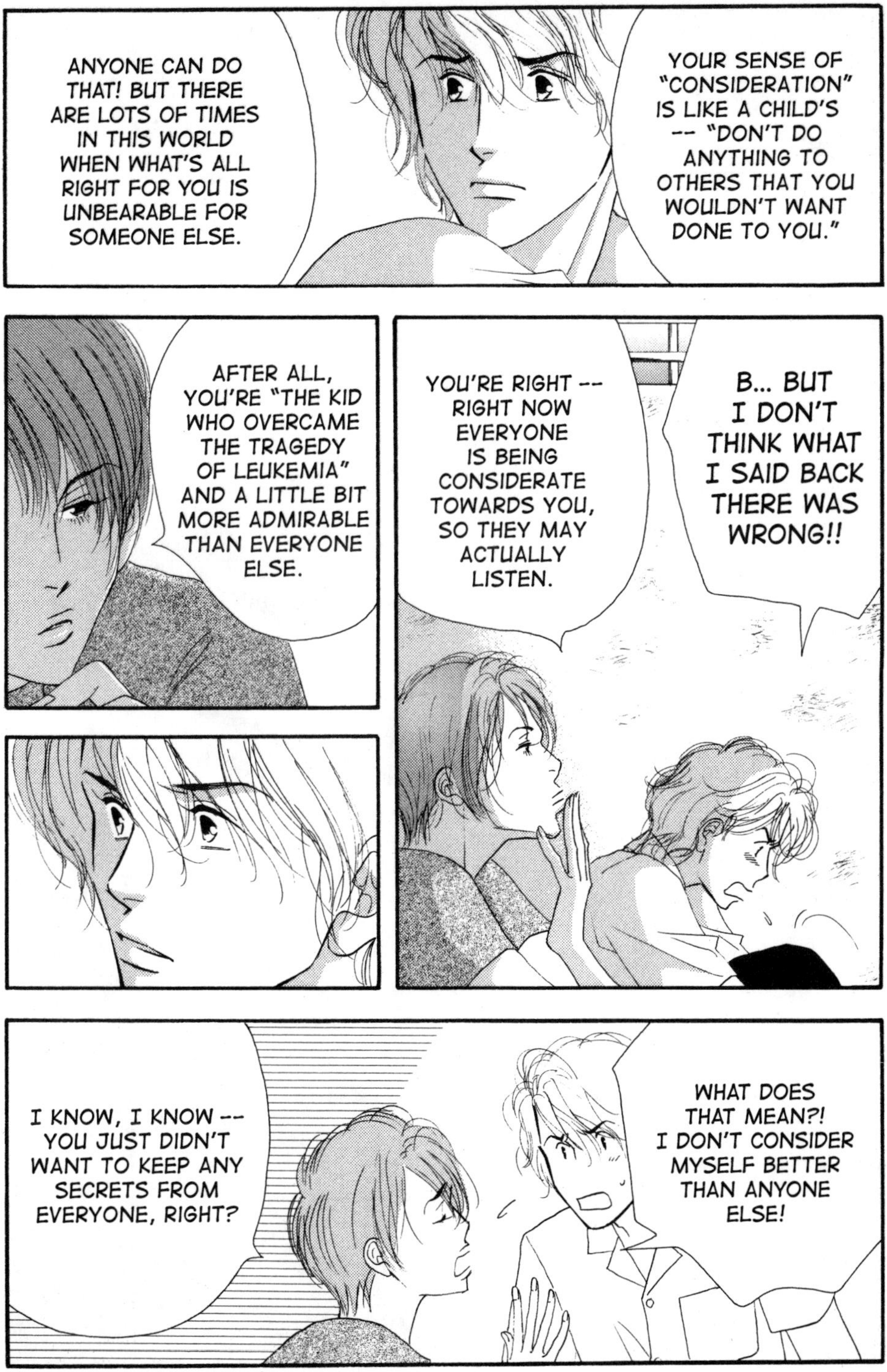
YOUR SENSE OF "CONSIDERATION" IS LIKE A CHILD'S -- "DON'T DO ANYTHING TO OTHERS THAT YOU WOULDN'T WANT DONE TO YOU."
ANYONE CAN DO THAT! BUT THERE ARE LOTS OF TIMES IN THIS WORLD WHEN WHAT'S ALL RIGHT FOR YOU IS UNBEARABLE FOR SOMEONE ELSE.
B... BUT I DON'T THINK WHAT I SAID BACK THERE WAS WRONG!!
YOU'RE RIGHT -- RIGHT NOW EVERYONE IS BEING CONSIDERATE TOWARDS YOU, SO THEY MAY ACTUALLY LISTEN.
AFTER ALL, YOU'RE "THE KID WHO OVERCAME THE TRAGEDY OF LEUKEMIA" AND A LITTLE BIT MORE ADMIRABLE THAN EVERYONE ELSE.
WHAT DOES THAT MEAN?! I DON'T CONSIDER MYSELF BETTER THAN ANYONE ELSE!
I KNOW, I KNOW -- YOU JUST DIDN'T WANT TO KEEP ANY SECRETS FROM EVERYONE, RIGHT?

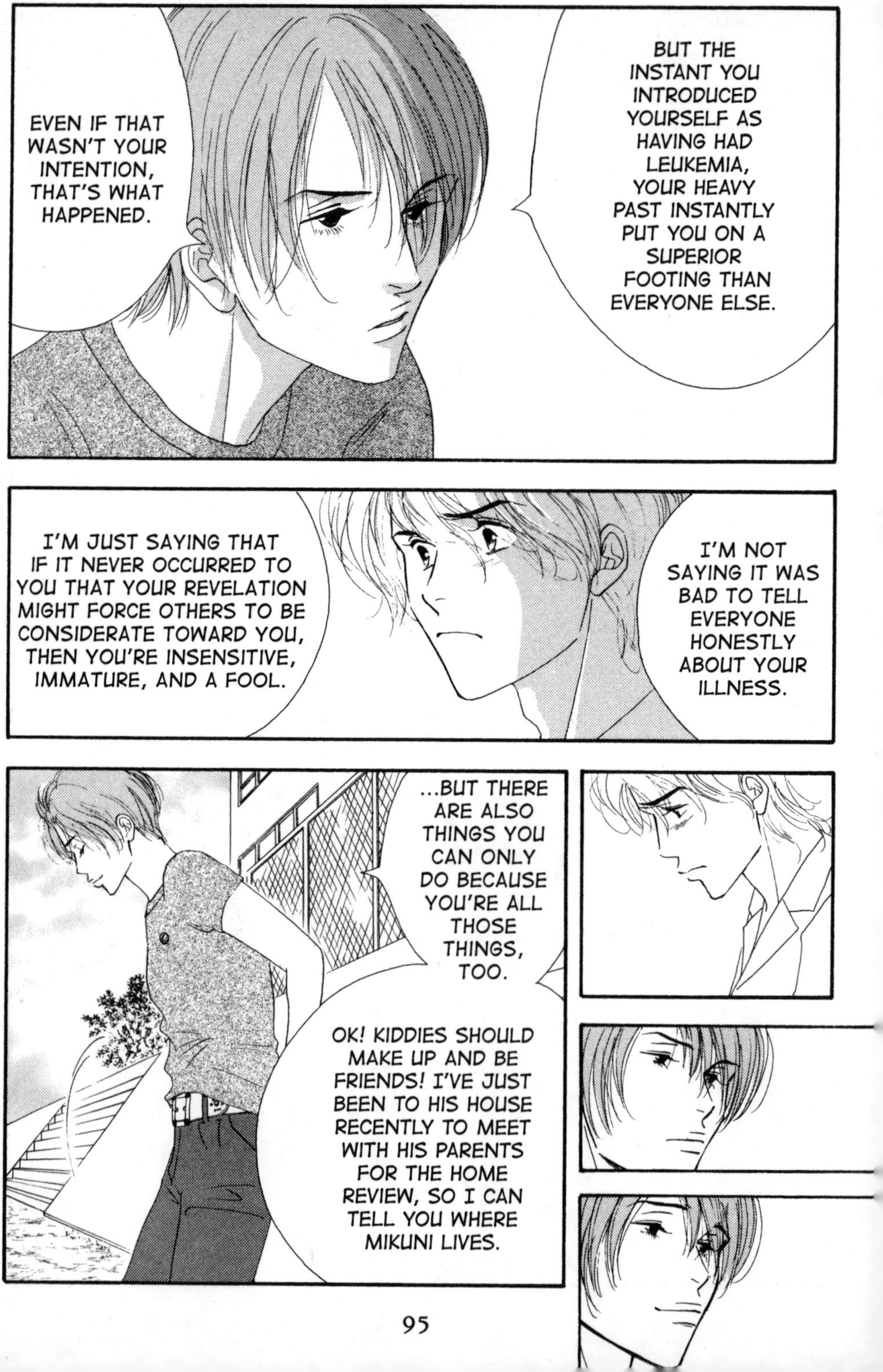
BUT THE INSTANT YOU INTRODUCED YOURSELF AS HAVING HAD LEUKEMIA, YOUR HEAVY PAST INSTANTLY PUT YOU ON A SUPERIOR FOOTING THAN EVERYONE ELSE.
EVEN IF THAT WASN'T YOUR INTENTION, THAT'S WHAT HAPPENED.
I'M NOT SAYING IT WAS BAD TO TELL EVERYONE HONESTLY ABOUT YOUR ILLNESS.
I'M JUST SAYING THAT IF IT NEVER OCCURRED TO YOU THAT YOUR REVELATION MIGHT FORCE OTHERS TO BE CONSIDERATE TOWARD YOU, THEN YOU'RE INSENSITIVE, IMMATURE, AND A FOOL.
...BUT THERE ARE ALSO THINGS YOU CAN ONLY DO BECAUSE YOU'RE ALL THOSE THINGS, TOO.
OK! KIDDIES SHOULD MAKE UP AND BE FRIENDS! I'VE JUST BEEN TO HIS HOUSE RECENTLY TO MEET WITH HIS PARENTS FOR THE HOME REVIEW, SO I CAN TELL YOU WHERE MIKUNI LIVES.

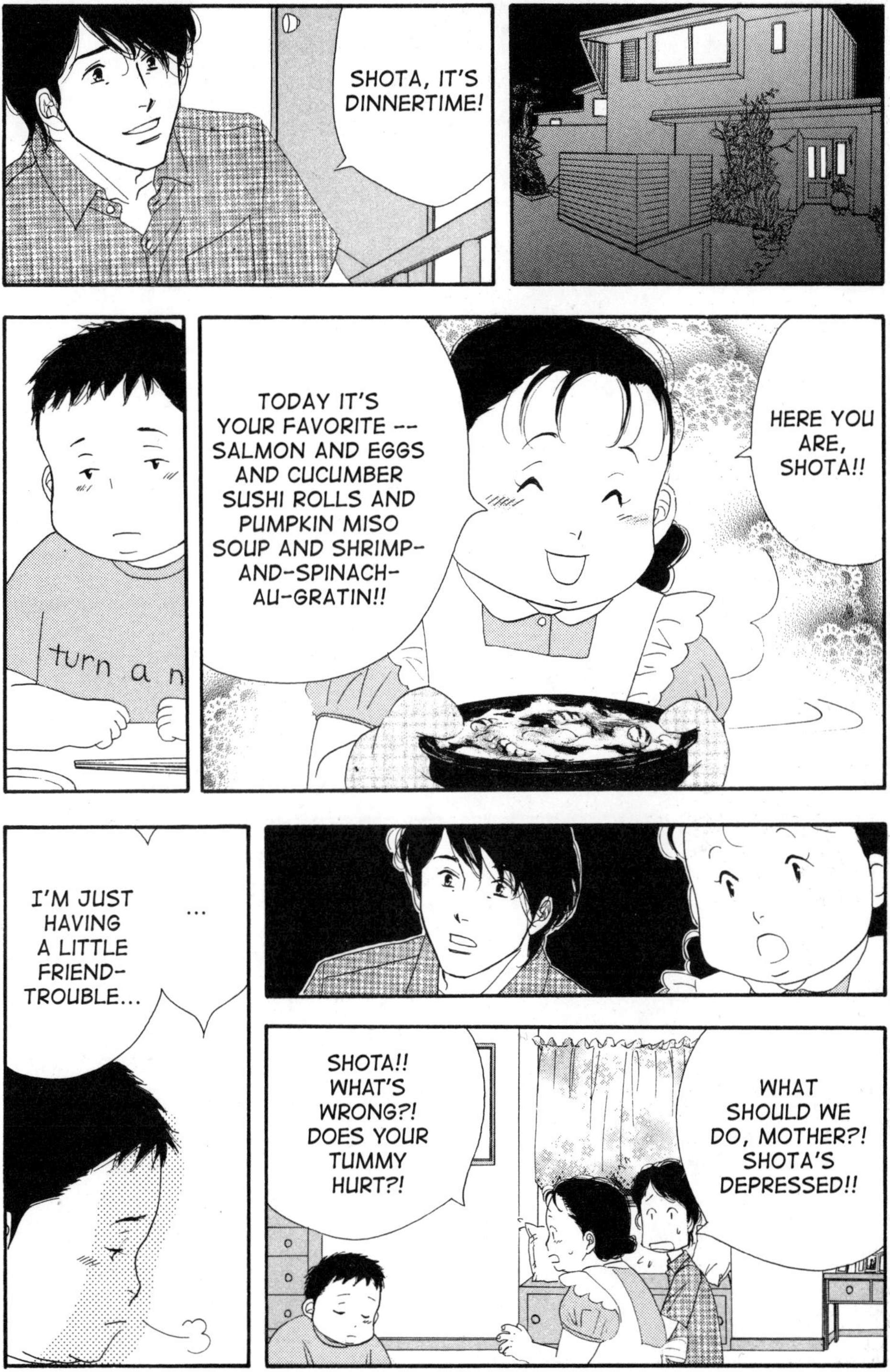
SHOTA, IT'S DINNERTIME!
HERE YOU ARE, SHOTA!!
TODAY IT'S YOUR FAVORITE -- SALMON AND EGGS AND CUCUMBER SUSHI ROLLS AND PUMPKIN MISO SOUP AND SHRIMP-AND-SPINACH-AU-GRATIN!!
turn a n
WHAT SHOULD WE DO, MOTHER?! SHOTA'S DEPRESSED!!
SHOTA!! WHAT'S WRONG?! DOES YOUR TUMMY HURT?!
...
I'M JUST HAVING A LITTLE FRIEND-TROUBLE...

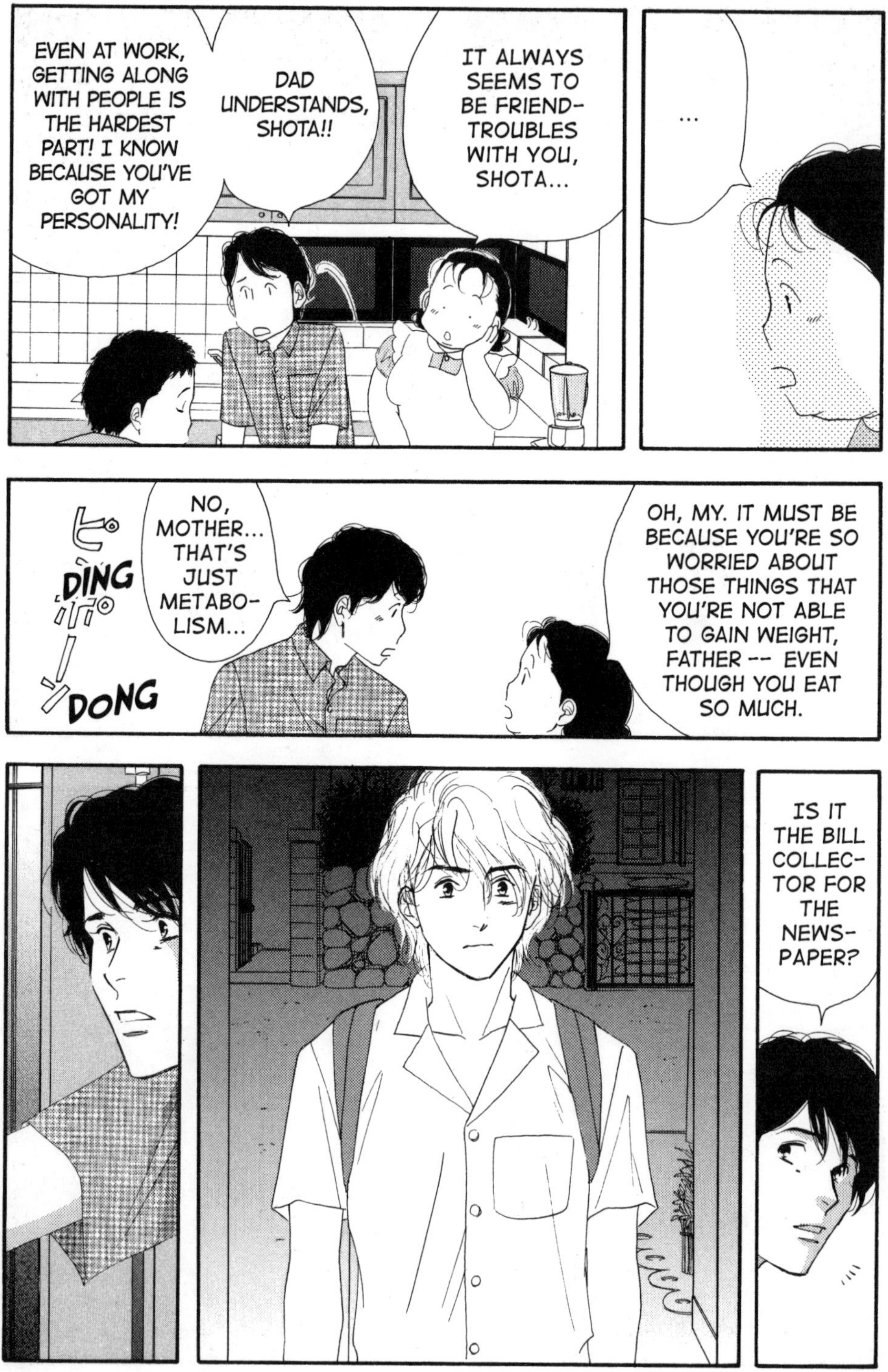
...
IT ALWAYS SEEMS TO BE FRIEND-TROUBLES WITH YOU, SHOTA...
DAD UNDERSTANDS, SHOTA!!
EVEN AT WORK, GETTING ALONG WITH PEOPLE IS THE HARDEST PART! I KNOW BECAUSE YOU'VE GOT MY PERSONALITY!
OH, MY. IT MUST BE BECAUSE YOU'RE SO WORRIED ABOUT THOSE THINGS THAT YOU'RE NOT ABLE TO GAIN WEIGHT, FATHER -- EVEN THOUGH YOU EAT SO MUCH.
NO, MOTHER... THAT'S JUST METABO-LISM...
ピンポーン
DING DONG
IS IT THE BILL COLLEC-TOR FOR THE NEWS-PAPER?

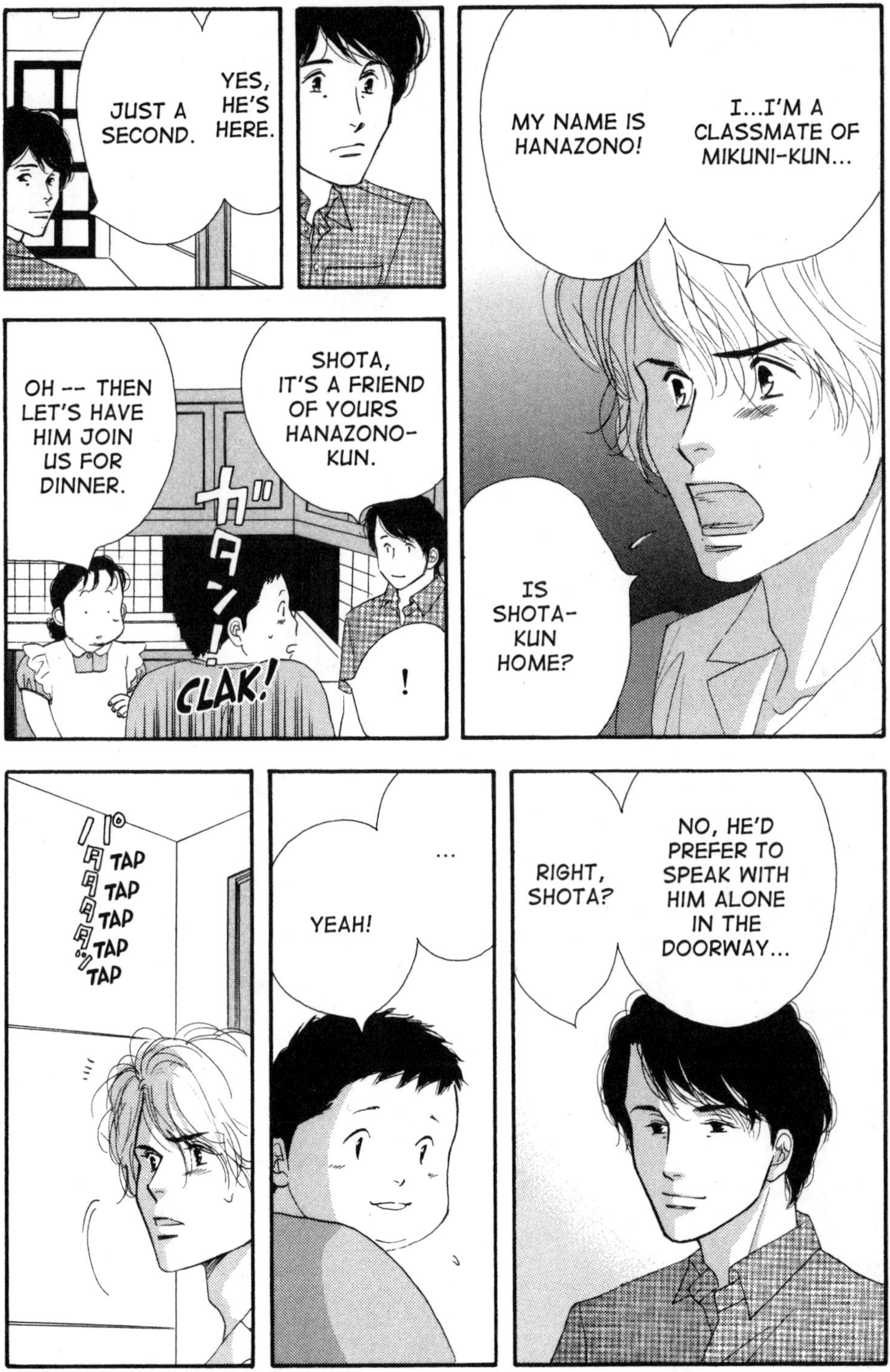
I...I'M A CLASSMATE OF MIKUNI-KUN...
MY NAME IS HANAZONO!
IS SHOTA-KUN HOME?
YES, HE'S HERE.
JUST A SECOND.
SHOTA, IT'S A FRIEND OF YOURS HANAZONO-KUN.
OH -- THEN LET'S HAVE HIM JOIN US FOR DINNER.
!
CLAK!
NO, HE'D PREFER TO SPEAK WITH HIM ALONE IN THE DOORWAY...
RIGHT, SHOTA?
...
YEAH!
TAP TAP TAP TAP TAP

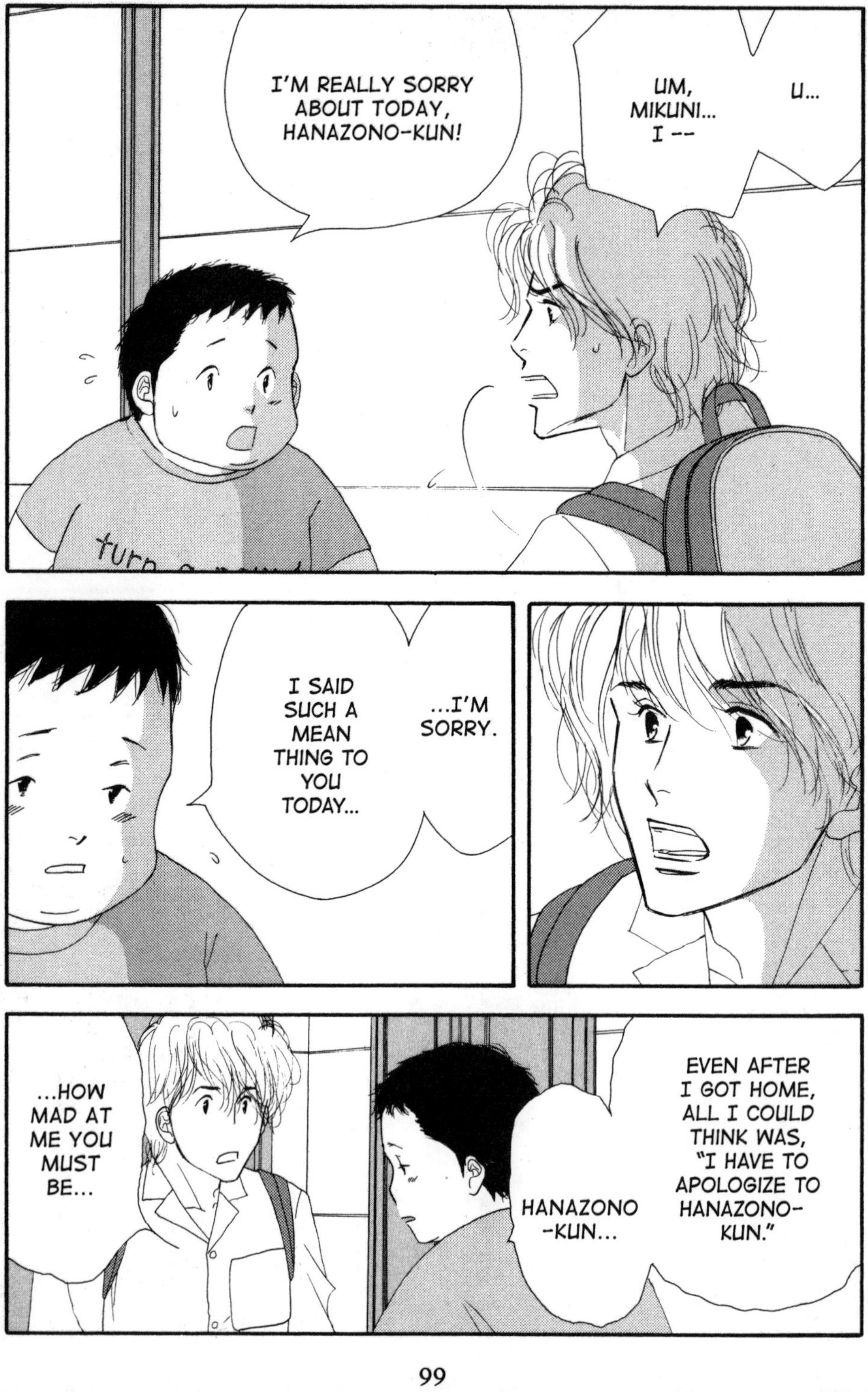
U...
UM, MIKUNI... I --
I'M REALLY SORRY ABOUT TODAY, HANAZONO-KUN!
...I'M SORRY.
I SAID SUCH A MEAN THING TO YOU TODAY...
EVEN AFTER I GOT HOME, ALL I COULD THINK WAS, "I HAVE TO APOLOGIZE TO HANAZONO-KUN."
HANAZONO-KUN...
...HOW MAD AT ME YOU MUST BE...

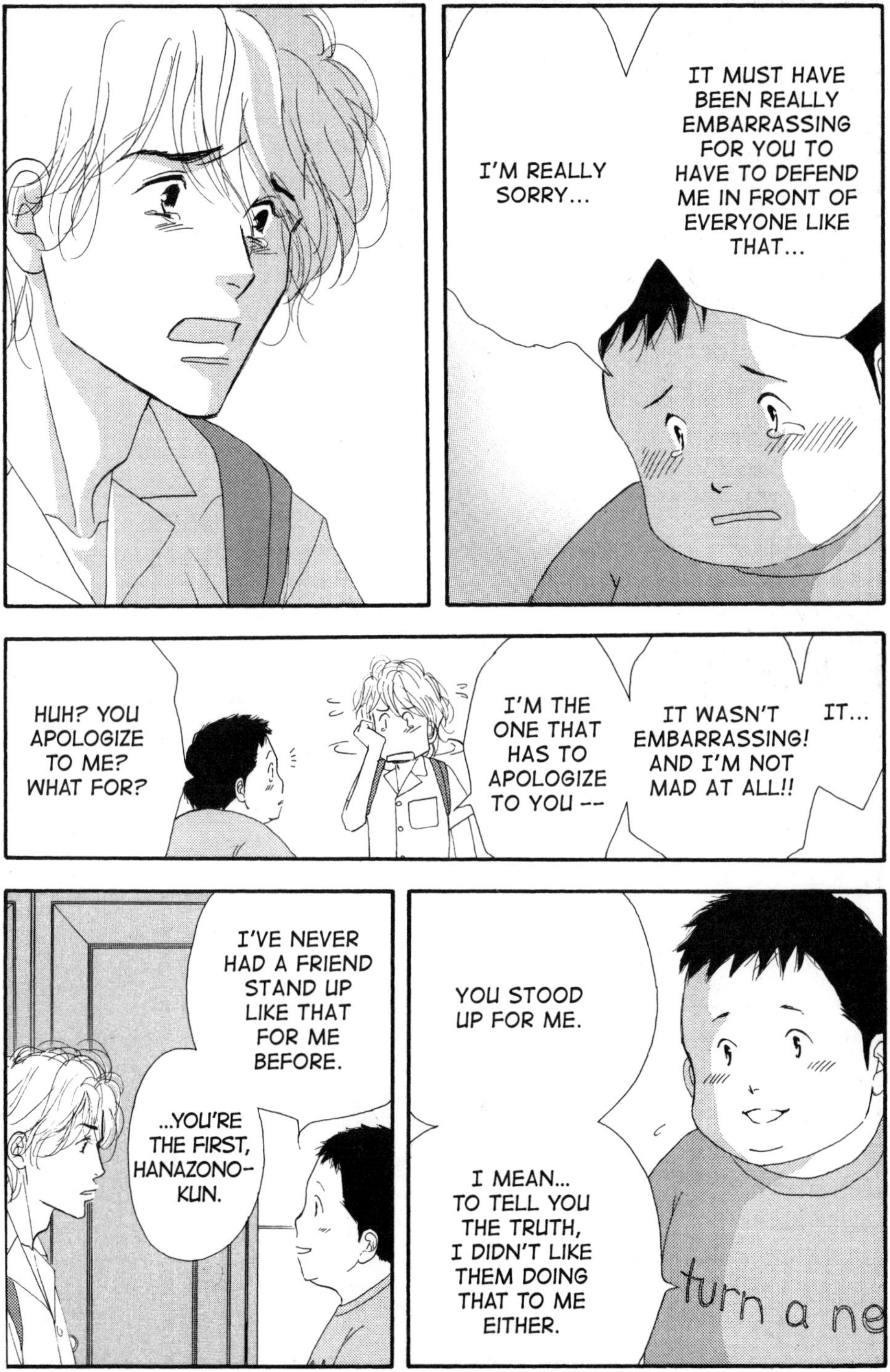
IT MUST HAVE BEEN REALLY EMBARRASSING FOR YOU TO HAVE TO DEFEND ME IN FRONT OF EVERYONE LIKE THAT...
I'M REALLY SORRY...
IT...
IT WASN'T EMBARRASSING! AND I'M NOT MAD AT ALL!!
I'M THE ONE THAT HAS TO APOLOGIZE TO YOU --
HUH? YOU APOLOGIZE TO ME? WHAT FOR?
YOU STOOD UP FOR ME.
I MEAN... TO TELL YOU THE TRUTH, I DIDN'T LIKE THEM DOING THAT TO ME EITHER.
I'VE NEVER HAD A FRIEND STAND UP LIKE THAT FOR ME BEFORE.
...YOU'RE THE FIRST, HANAZONO-KUN.

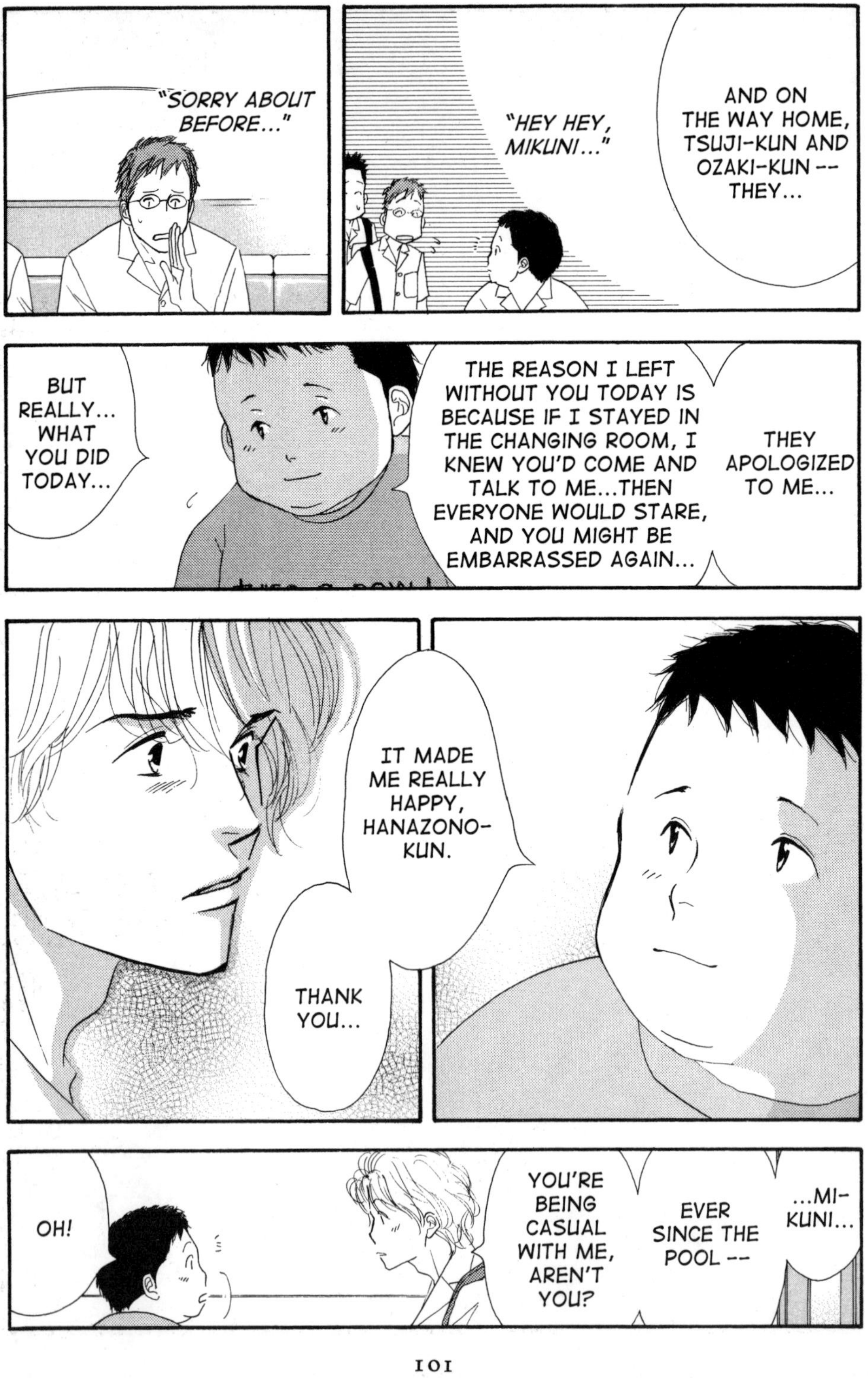
AND ON THE WAY HOME, TSUJI-KUN AND OZAKI-KUN -- THEY...
"HEY HEY, MIKUNI..."
"SORRY ABOUT BEFORE..."
THEY APOLOGIZED TO ME...
THE REASON I LEFT WITHOUT YOU TODAY IS BECAUSE IF I STAYED IN THE CHANGING ROOM, I KNEW YOU'D COME AND TALK TO ME...THEN EVERYONE WOULD STARE, AND YOU MIGHT BE EMBARRASSED AGAIN...
BUT REALLY... WHAT YOU DID TODAY...
IT MADE ME REALLY HAPPY, HANAZONO-KUN.
THANK YOU...
...MI-KUNI...
EVER SINCE THE POOL --
YOU'RE BEING CASUAL WITH ME, AREN'T YOU?
OH!

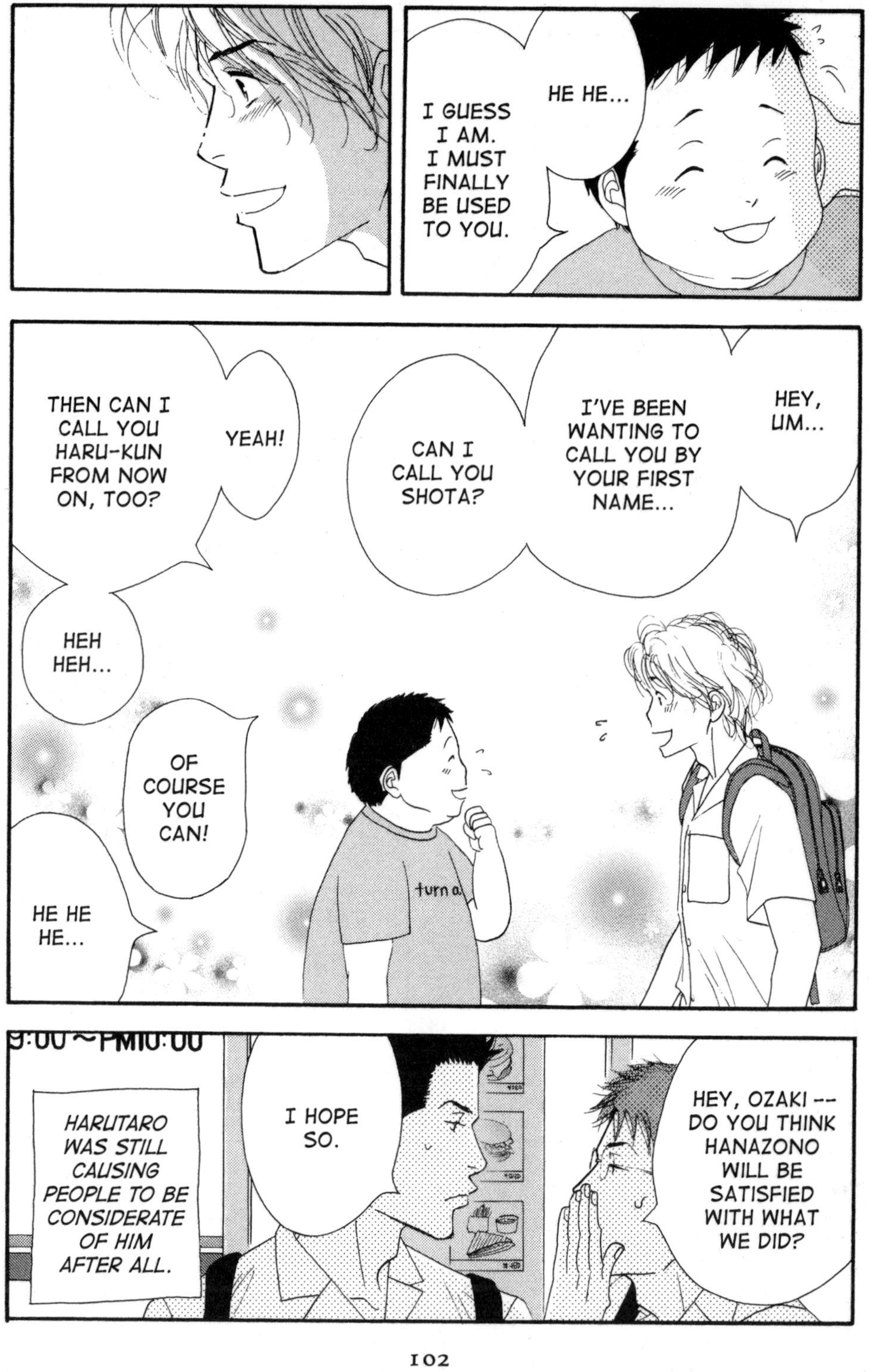
HE HE...
I GUESS I AM. I MUST FINALLY BE USED TO YOU.
HEY, UM...
I'VE BEEN WANTING TO CALL YOU BY YOUR FIRST NAME...
CAN I CALL YOU SHOTA?
YEAH!
THEN CAN I CALL YOU HARU-KUN FROM NOW ON, TOO?
HEH HEH...
OF COURSE YOU CAN!
turn a.
HE HE HE...
HEY, OZAKI -- DO YOU THINK HANAZONO WILL BE SATISFIED WITH WHAT WE DID?
I HOPE SO.
HARUTARO WAS STILL CAUSING PEOPLE TO BE CONSIDERATE OF HIM AFTER ALL.

#4

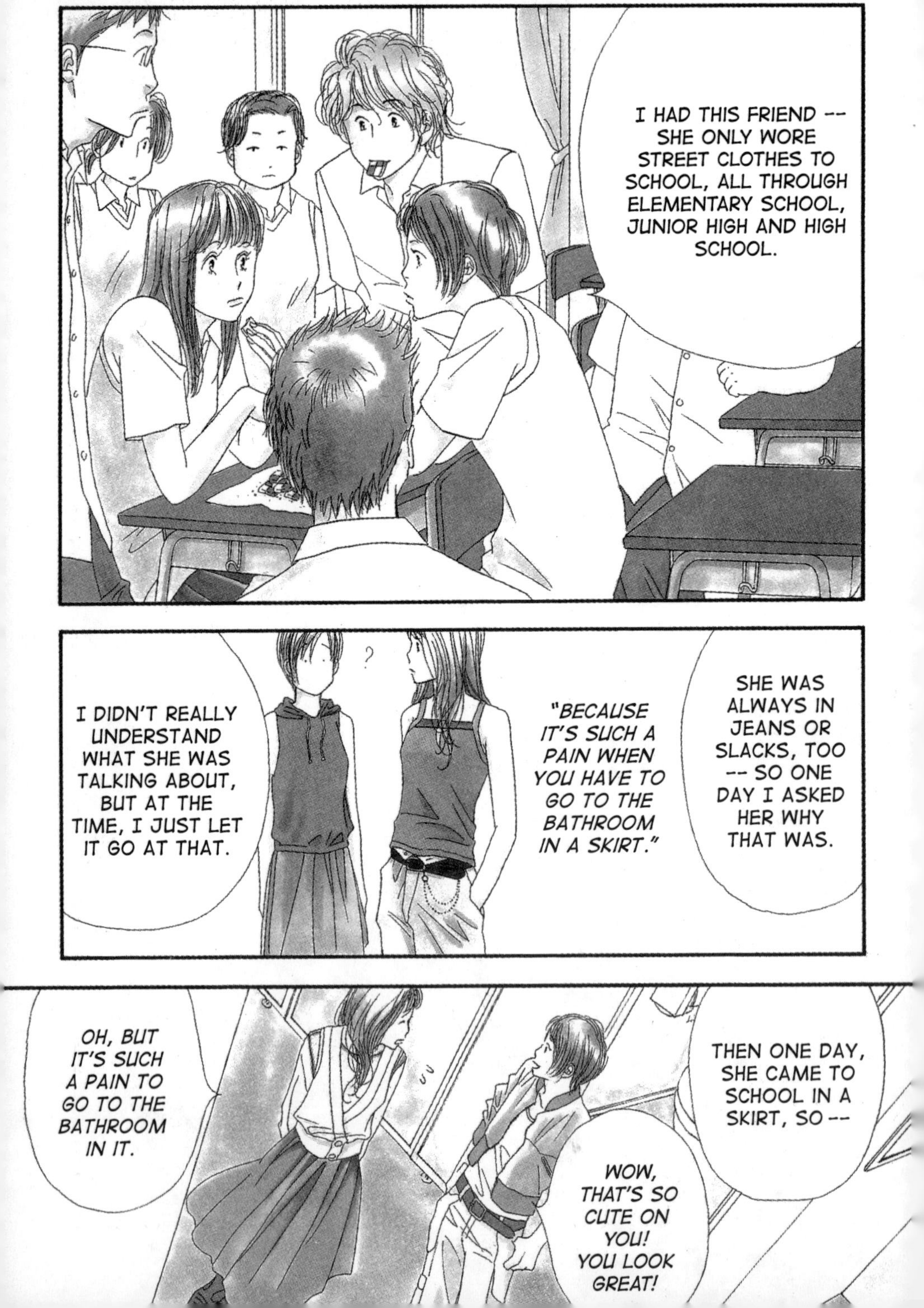
I HAD THIS FRIEND -- SHE ONLY WORE STREET CLOTHES TO SCHOOL, ALL THROUGH ELEMENTARY SCHOOL, JUNIOR HIGH AND HIGH SCHOOL.
SHE WAS ALWAYS IN JEANS OR SLACKS, TOO -- SO ONE DAY I ASKED HER WHY THAT WAS.
"BECAUSE IT'S SUCH A PAIN WHEN YOU HAVE TO GO TO THE BATHROOM IN A SKIRT."
?
I DIDN'T REALLY UNDERSTAND WHAT SHE WAS TALKING ABOUT, BUT AT THE TIME, I JUST LET IT GO AT THAT.
THEN ONE DAY, SHE CAME TO SCHOOL IN A SKIRT, SO --
WOW, THAT'S SO CUTE ON YOU! YOU LOOK GREAT!
OH, BUT IT'S SUCH A PAIN TO GO TO THE BATHROOM IN IT.

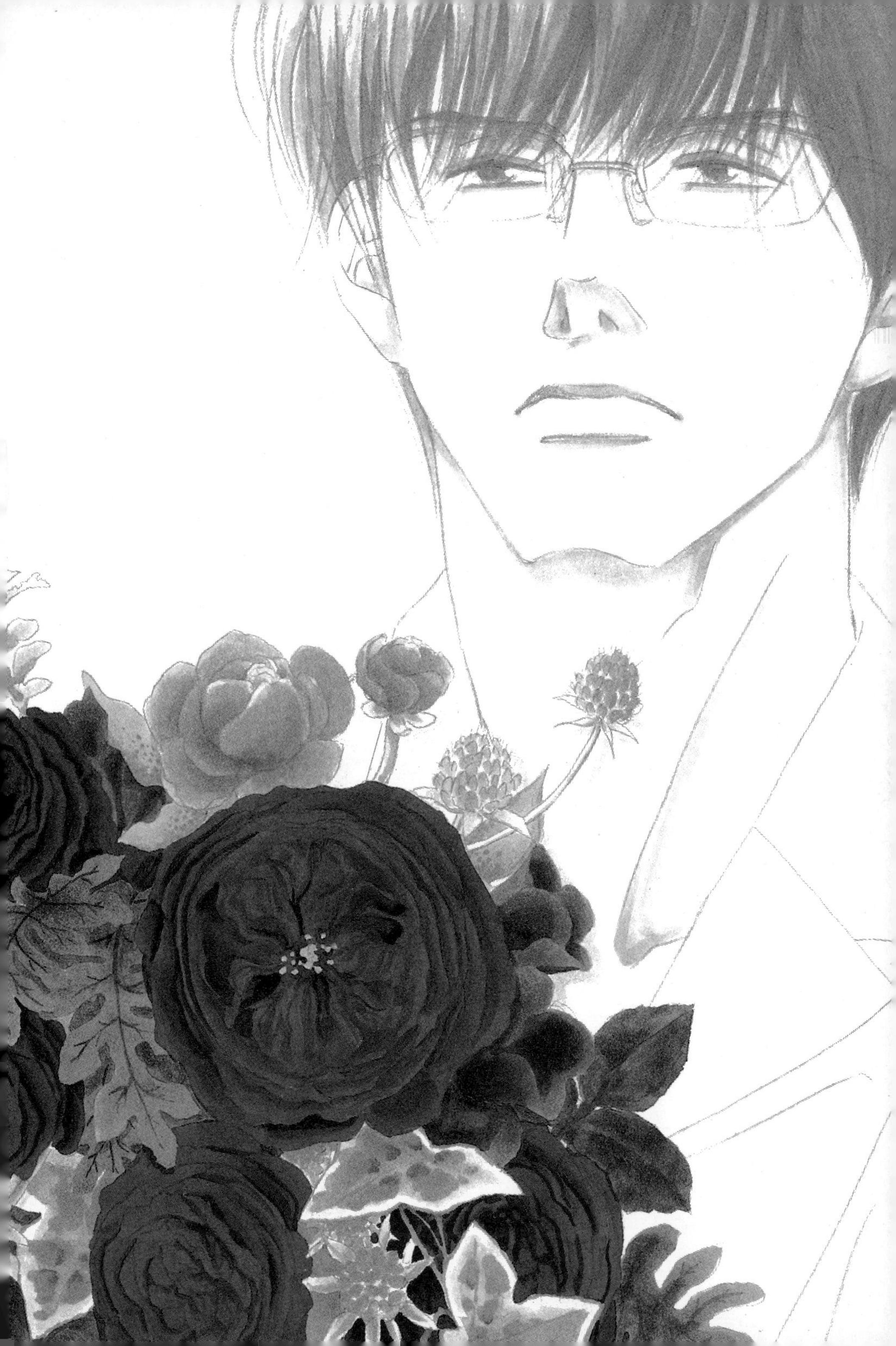

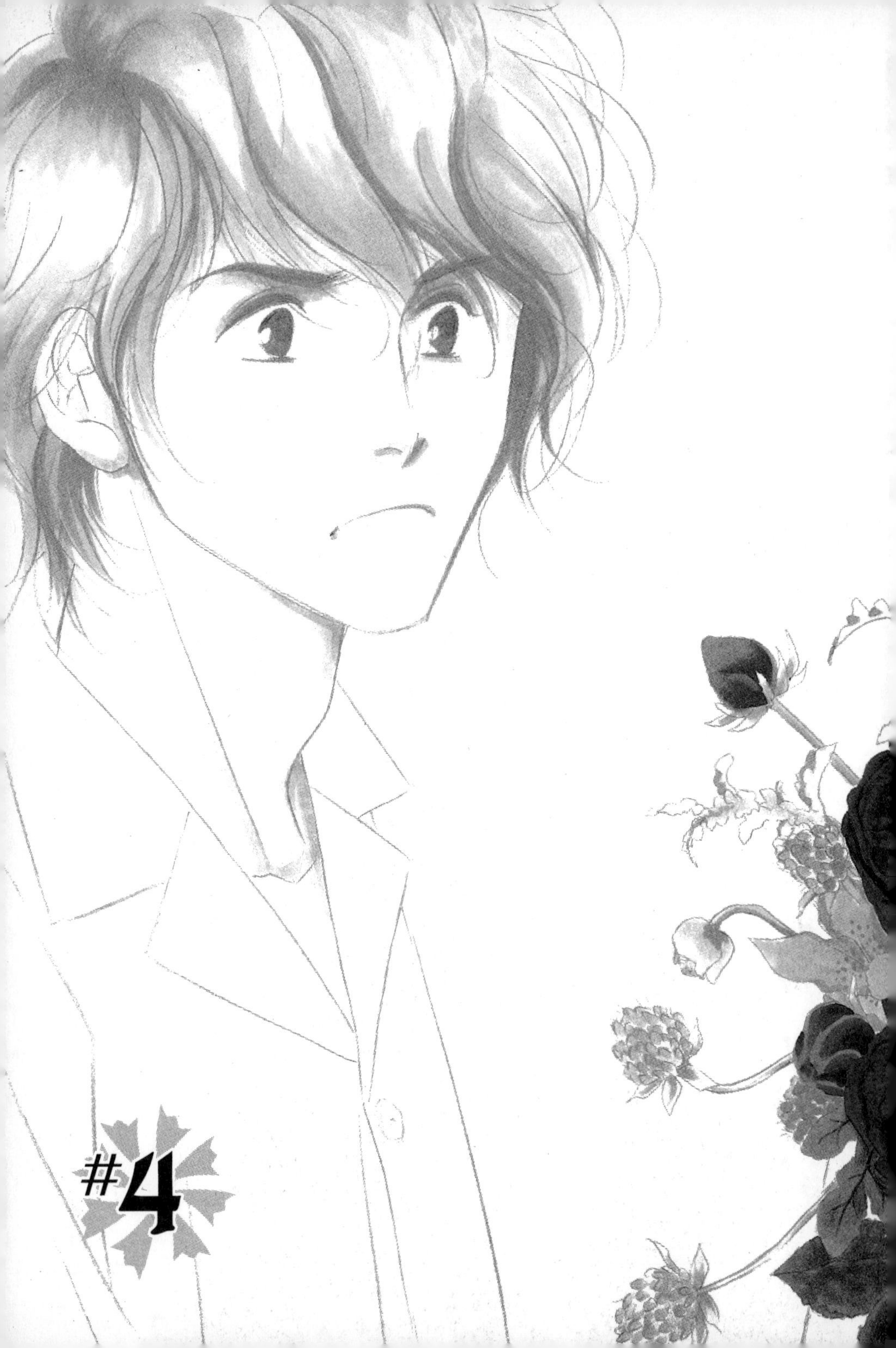
#4

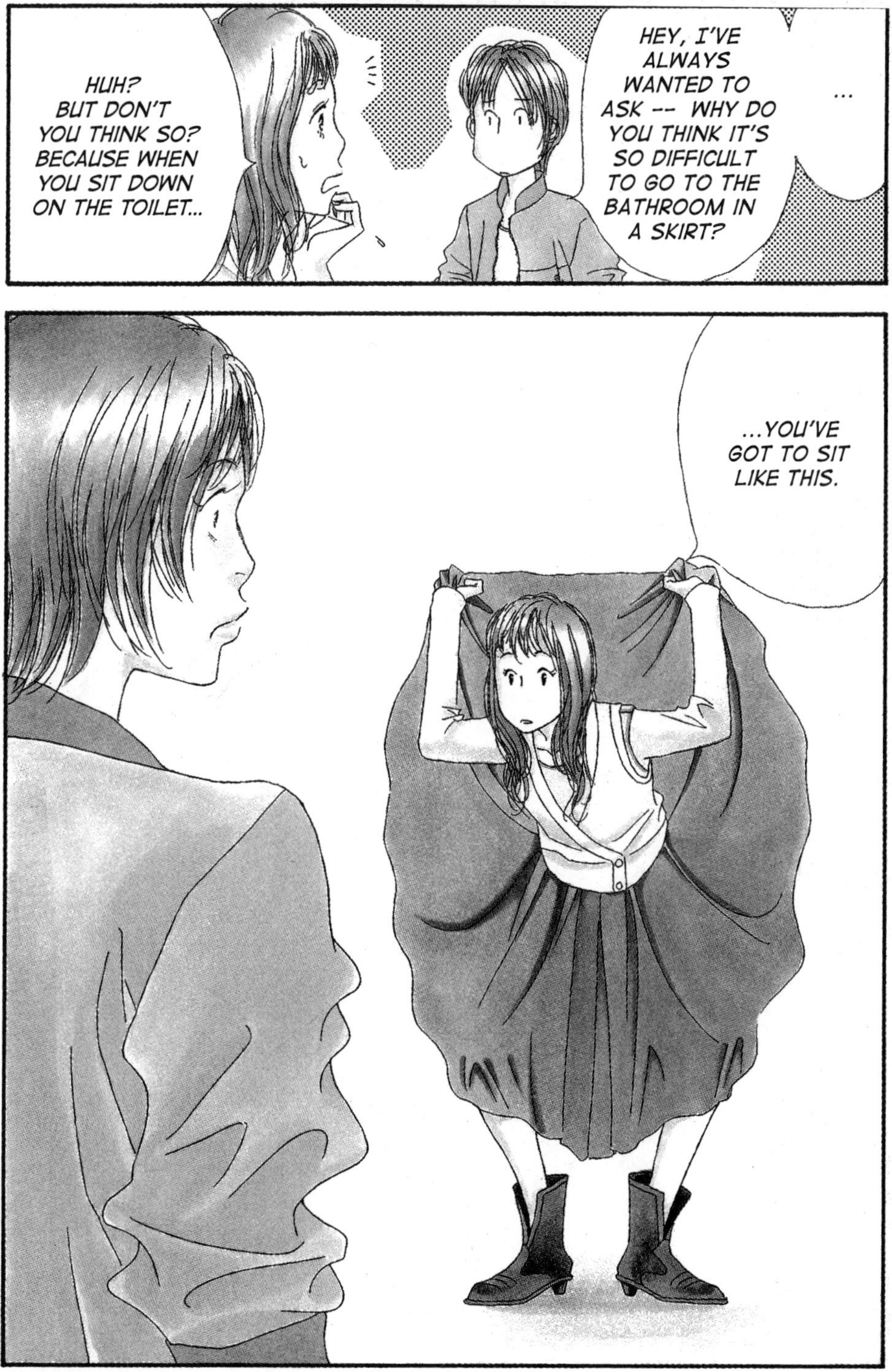
...
HEY, I'VE ALWAYS WANTED TO ASK -- WHY DO YOU THINK IT'S SO DIFFICULT TO GO TO THE BATHROOM IN A SKIRT?
HUH? BUT DON'T YOU THINK SO? BECAUSE WHEN YOU SIT DOWN ON THE TOILET...
...YOU'VE GOT TO SIT LIKE THIS.

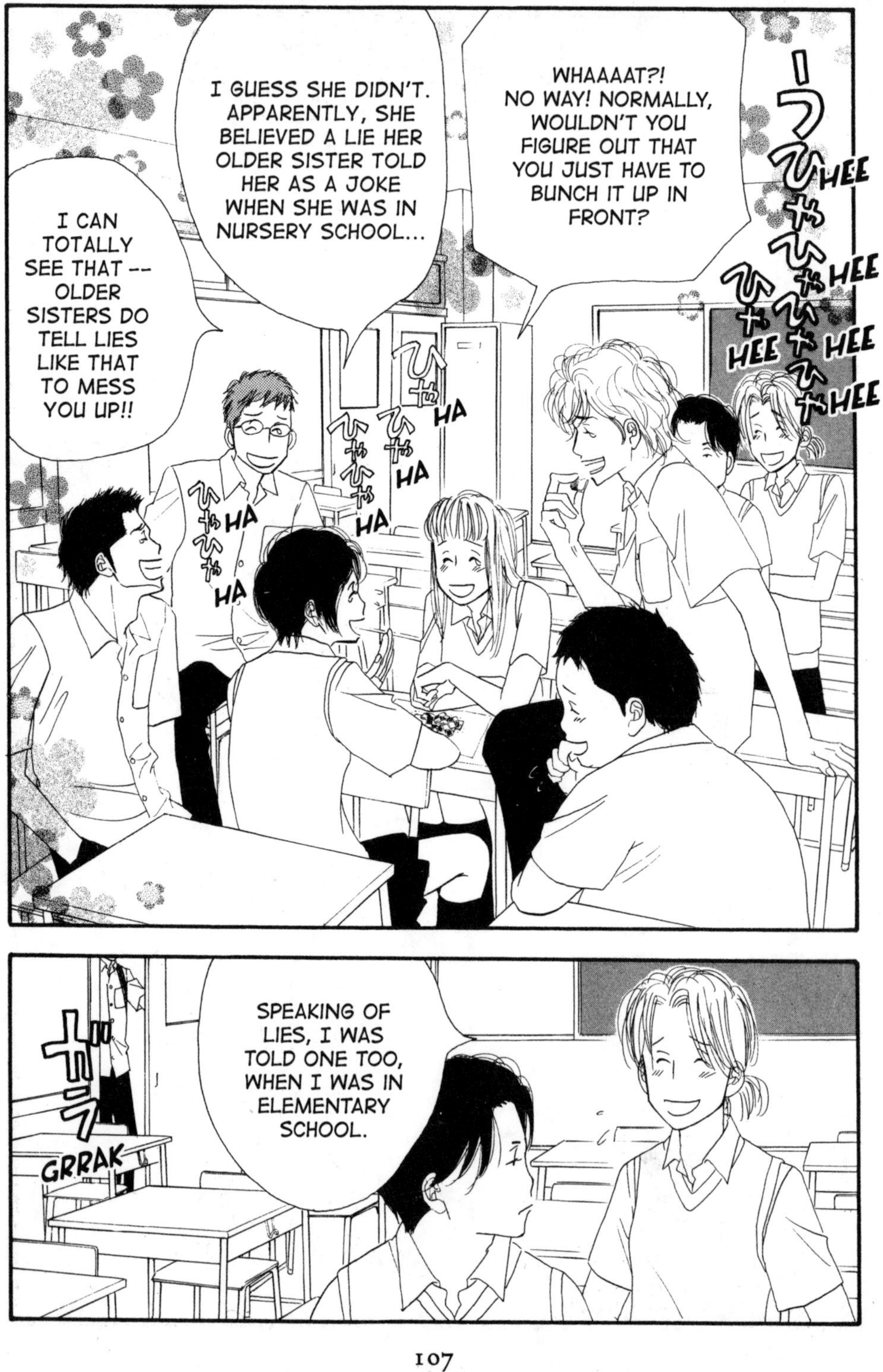
HEE HEE HEE HEE HEE
WHAAAAT?! NO WAY! NORMALLY, WOULDN'T YOU FIGURE OUT THAT YOU JUST HAVE TO BUNCH IT UP IN FRONT?
I GUESS SHE DIDN'T. APPARENTLY, SHE BELIEVED A LIE HER OLDER SISTER TOLD HER AS A JOKE WHEN SHE WAS IN NURSERY SCHOOL...
HA HA HA HA HA
I CAN TOTALLY SEE THAT -- OLDER SISTERS DO TELL LIES LIKE THAT TO MESS YOU UP!!
SPEAKING OF LIES, I WAS TOLD ONE TOO, WHEN I WAS IN ELEMENTARY SCHOOL.
GRRAK

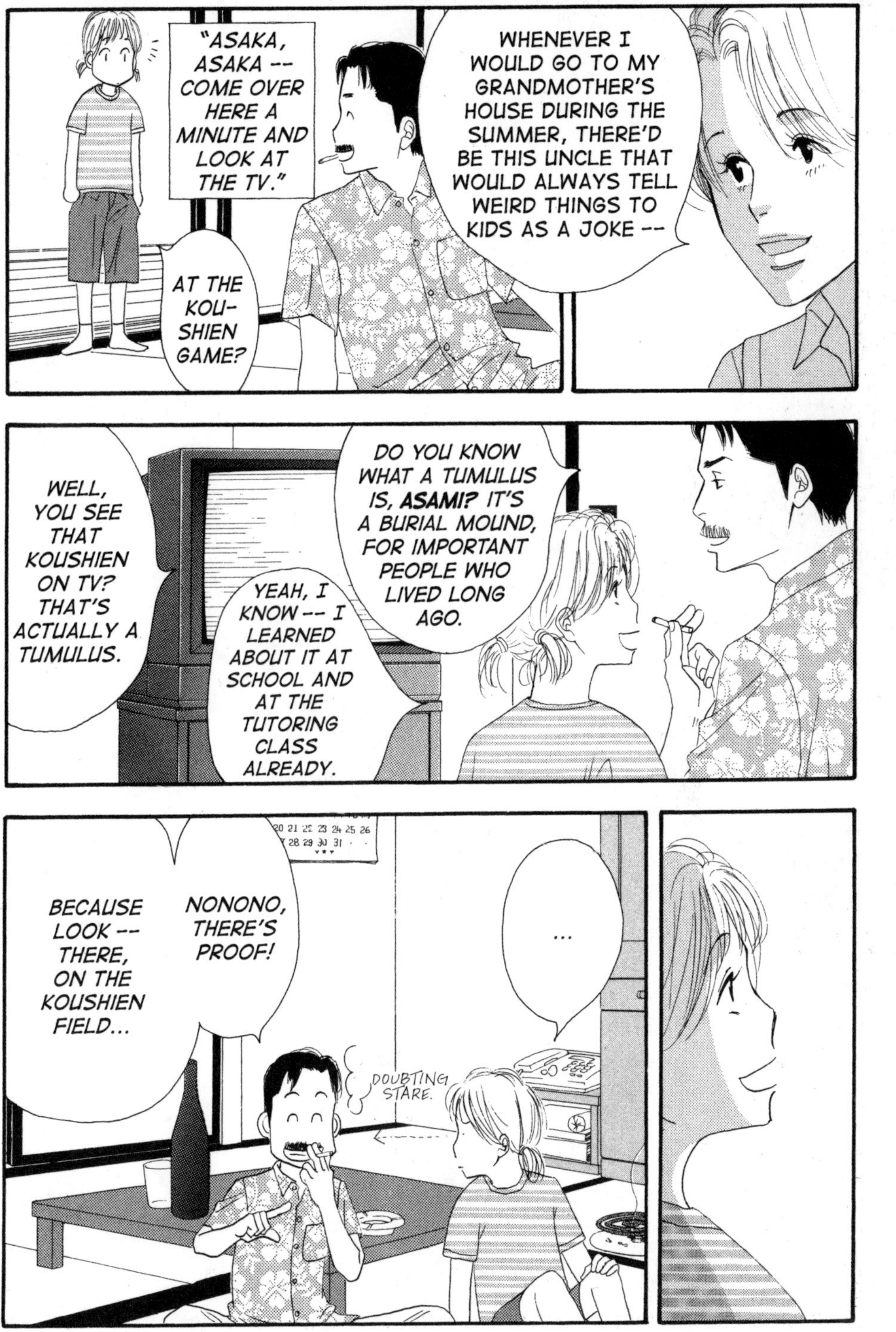
WHENEVER I WOULD GO TO MY GRANDMOTHER'S HOUSE DURING THE SUMMER, THERE'D BE THIS UNCLE THAT WOULD ALWAYS TELL WEIRD THINGS TO KIDS AS A JOKE --
"ASAKA, ASAKA -- COME OVER HERE A MINUTE AND LOOK AT THE TV."
AT THE KOU-SHIEN GAME?
DO YOU KNOW WHAT A TUMULUS IS, ASAMI? IT'S A BURIAL MOUND, FOR IMPORTANT PEOPLE WHO LIVED LONG AGO.
YEAH, I KNOW -- I LEARNED ABOUT IT AT SCHOOL AND AT THE TUTORING CLASS ALREADY.
WELL, YOU SEE THAT KOUSHIEN ON TV? THAT'S ACTUALLY A TUMULUS.
...
NONONO, THERE'S PROOF!
BECAUSE LOOK -- THERE, ON THE KOUSHIEN FIELD...
DOUBTING STARE.

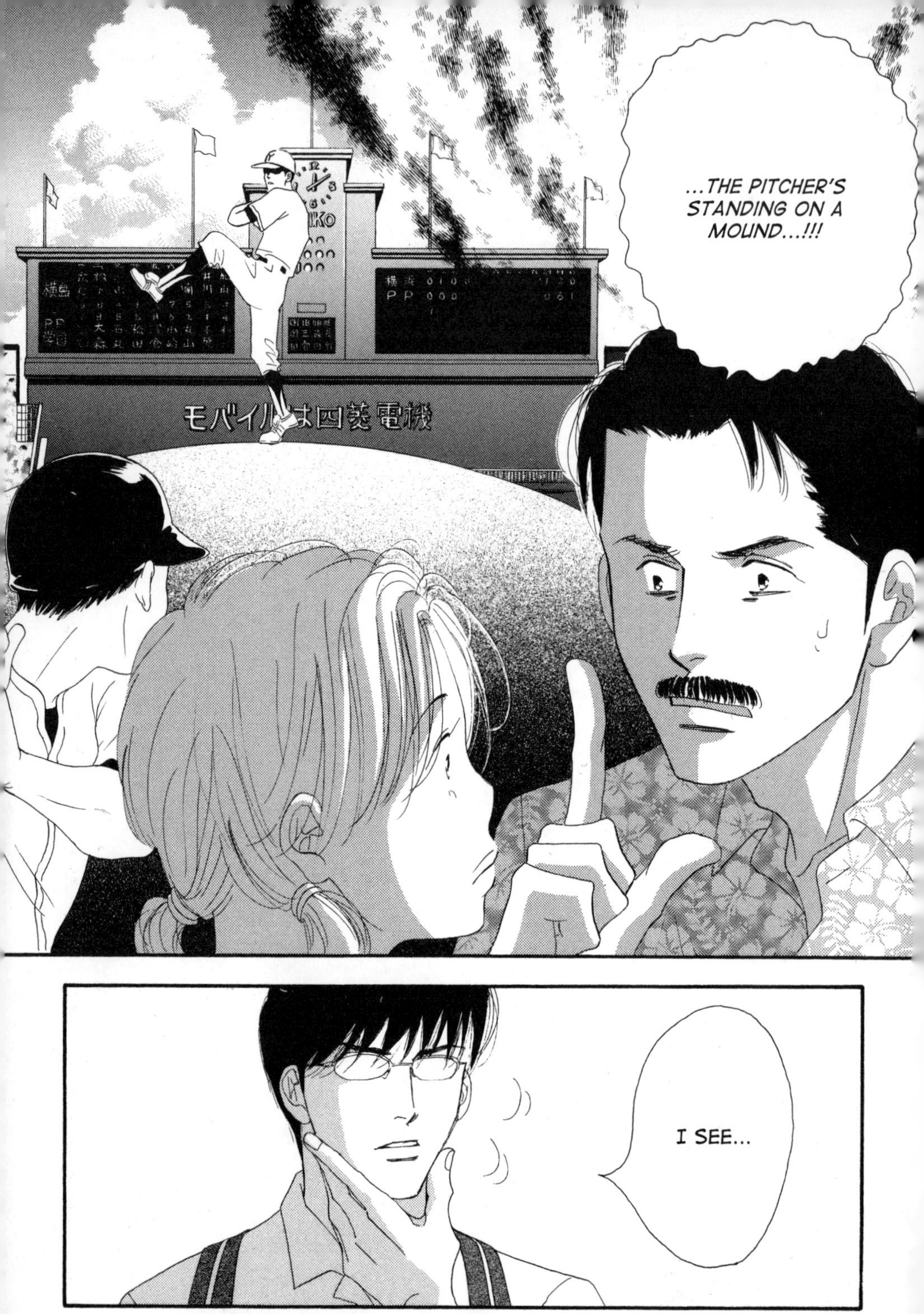
...THE PITCHER'S STANDING ON A MOUND...!!!
I SEE...

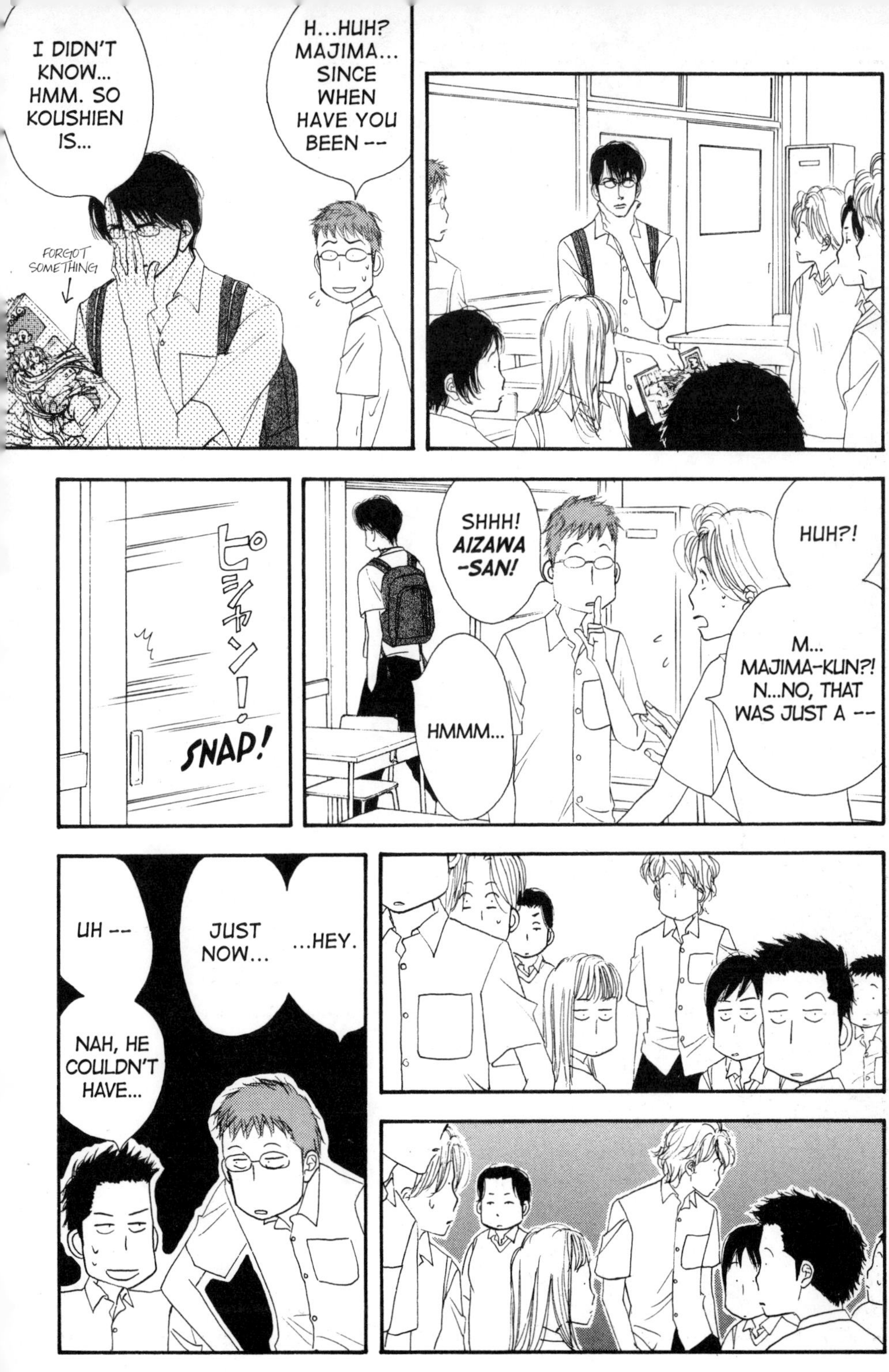

H...HUH? MAJIMA... SINCE WHEN HAVE YOU BEEN --
I DIDN'T KNOW... HMM. SO KOUSHIEN IS...
FORGOT SOMETHING
HUH?!
SHHH! AIZAWA-SAN!
M... MAJIMA-KUN?! N...NO, THAT WAS JUST A --
HMMM...
ピシャン！
SNAP!
...HEY.
JUST NOW...
UH --
NAH, HE COULDN'T HAVE...

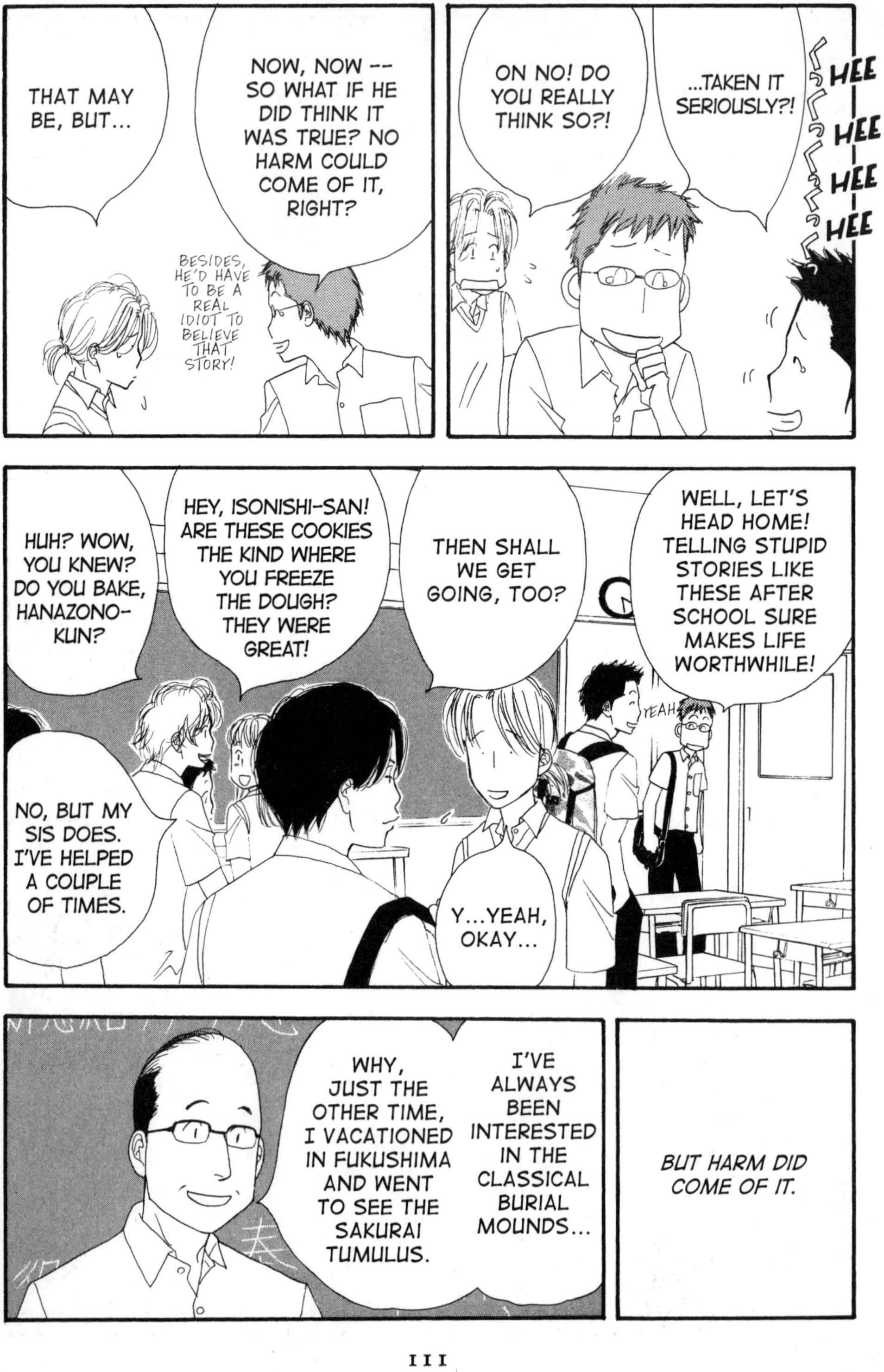
HEE HEE HEE HEE
...TAKEN IT SERIOUSLY?!
ON NO! DO YOU REALLY THINK SO?!
NOW, NOW -- SO WHAT IF HE DID THINK IT WAS TRUE? NO HARM COULD COME OF IT, RIGHT?
BESIDES, HE'D HAVE TO BE A REAL IDIOT TO BELIEVE THAT STORY!
THAT MAY BE, BUT...
WELL, LET'S HEAD HOME! TELLING STUPID STORIES LIKE THESE AFTER SCHOOL SURE MAKES LIFE WORTHWHILE!
YEAH
THEN SHALL WE GET GOING, TOO?
Y...YEAH, OKAY...
HEY, ISONISHI-SAN! ARE THESE COOKIES THE KIND WHERE YOU FREEZE THE DOUGH? THEY WERE GREAT!
HUH? WOW, YOU KNEW? DO YOU BAKE, HANAZONO-KUN?
NO, BUT MY SIS DOES. I'VE HELPED A COUPLE OF TIMES.
BUT HARM DID COME OF IT.
I'VE ALWAYS BEEN INTERESTED IN THE CLASSICAL BURIAL MOUNDS...
WHY, JUST THE OTHER TIME, I VACATIONED IN FUKUSHIMA AND WENT TO SEE THE SAKURAI TUMULUS.

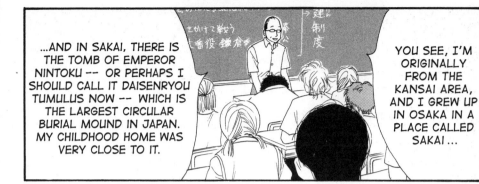

YOU SEE, I'M ORIGINALLY FROM THE KANSAI AREA, AND I GREW UP IN OSAKA IN A PLACE CALLED SAKAI ...
...AND IN SAKAI, THERE IS THE TOMB OF EMPEROR NINTOKU -- OR PERHAPS I SHOULD CALL IT DAISENRYOU TUMULUS NOW -- WHICH IS THE LARGEST CIRCULAR BURIAL MOUND IN JAPAN. MY CHILDHOOD HOME WAS VERY CLOSE TO IT.
A TUMULUS IS ISOLATED, WHICH MEANS THAT IT IS ESSENTIALLY IN A BIG FOREST.
THAT'S WHY EVEN THOUGH OSAKA'S SUMMERS ARE MUCH HARSHER THAN IN TOKYO, WE COULD OPEN THE DOOR TO OUR HOUSE AND A COOL BREEZE WOULD COME BLOWING IN FROM THAT FOREST...
AH, WE NEVER EVEN NEEDED A FAN... AFTER I ENTERED SCHOOL AND LEARNED THAT THE PLACE WAS ACTUALLY A BURIAL MOUND, A CURIOUS FEELING CAME OVER ME, I CAN TELL YOU!
AH, WELL, WE'VE LONG SINCE FINISHED UP WITH THE TUMULUS PERIOD IN CLASS, SO I'VE RAMBLED A BIT, BUT --
HA HA... IT'S JUST AN EXAMPLE OF HOW THE ORIGINS OF SOMEONE'S INTERESTS CAN BE FOUND UNEXPECTEDLY CLOSE BY.
...
...
SO... HOW ABOUT YOU? IS THERE ANYONE HERE WHO HAS ACTUALLY SEEN A TUMULUS FOR THEMSELVES?
OH, MAJIMA-KUN! YOU HAVE?
CLATTER!
YES!!

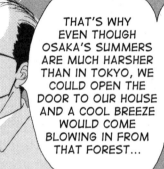

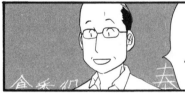

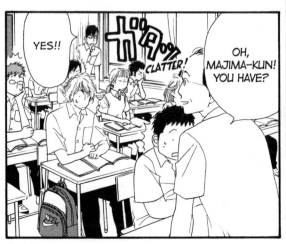

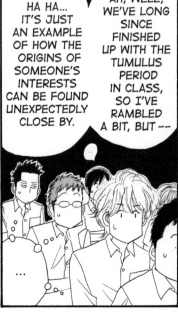

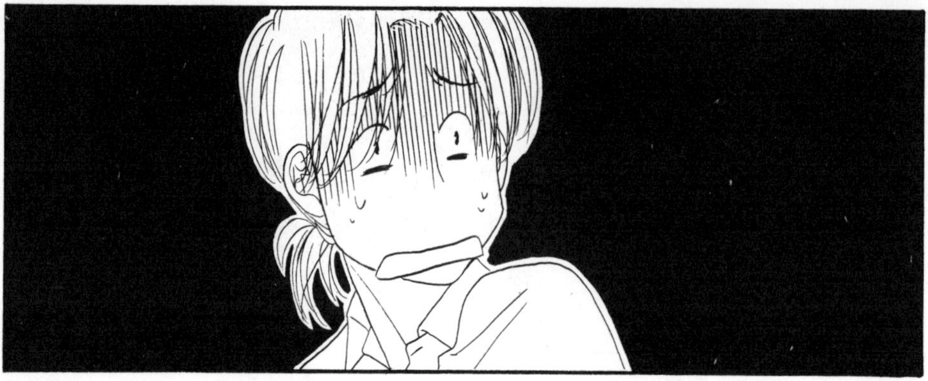

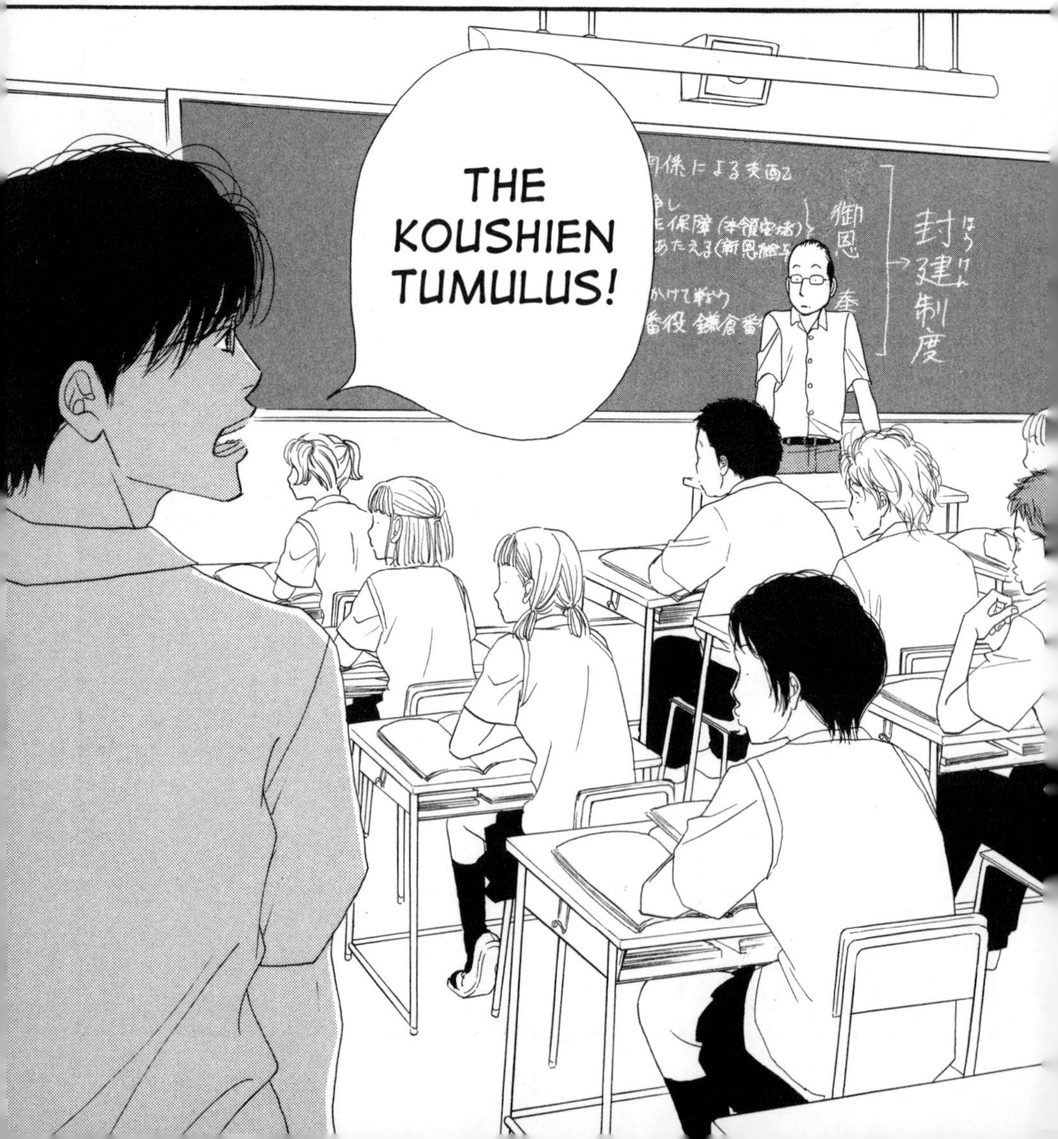
THE KOUSHIEN TUMULUS!
御恩
封建制度

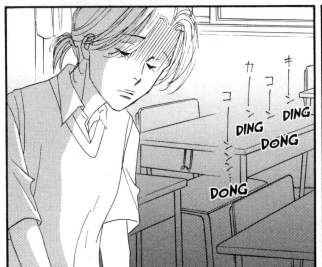

DING DING
DONG
DONG

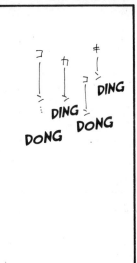

DING DING
DONG DONG

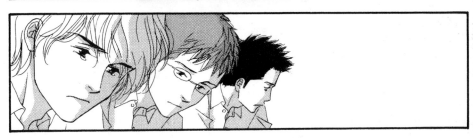

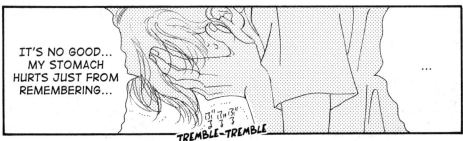

IT'S NO GOOD...
MY STOMACH
HURTS JUST FROM
REMEMBERING...

...

TREMBLE-TREMBLE

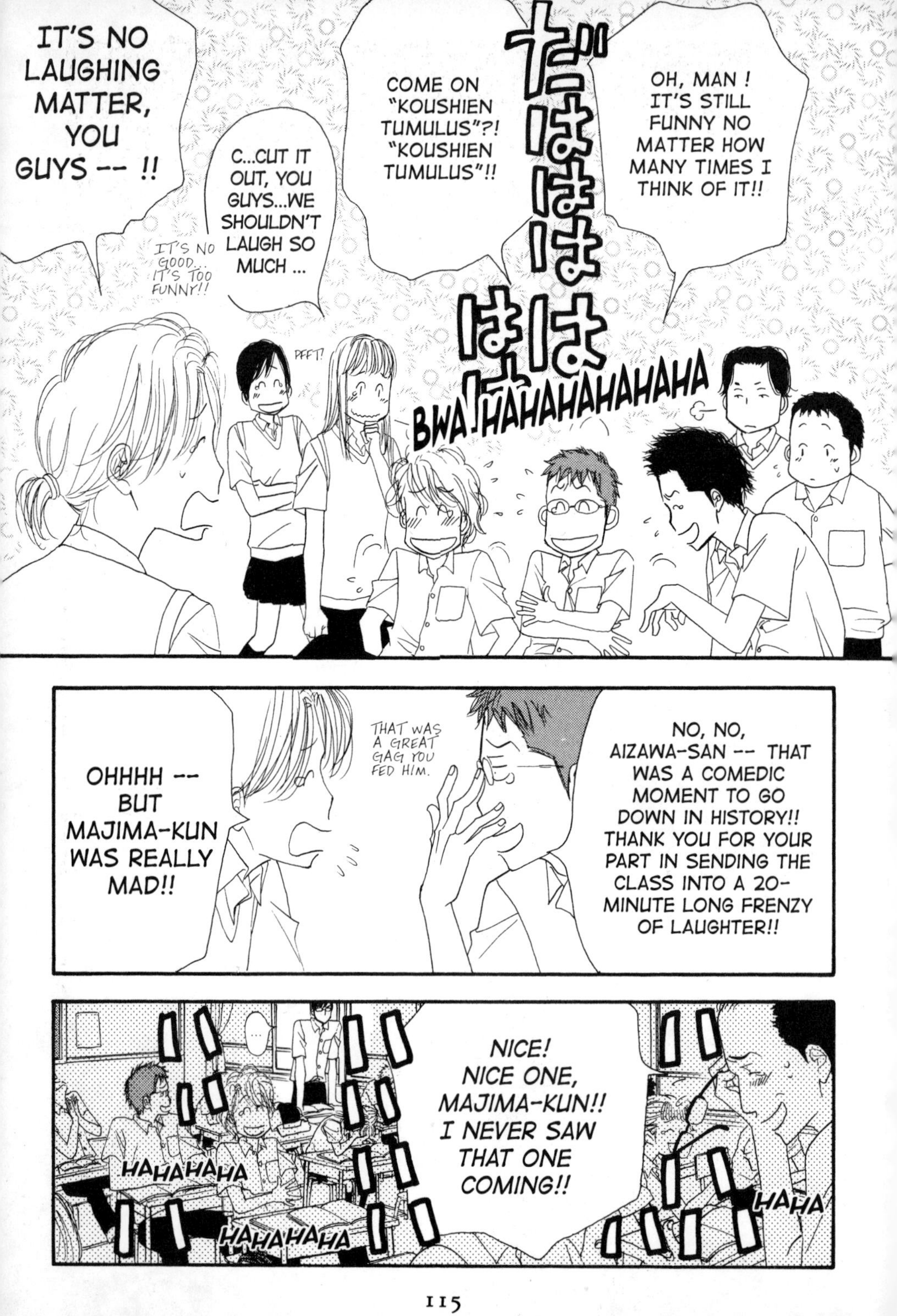
OH, MAN ! IT'S STILL FUNNY NO MATTER HOW MANY TIMES I THINK OF IT!!
だははははは
COME ON "KOUSHIEN TUMULUS"?! "KOUSHIEN TUMULUS"!!
C...CUT IT OUT, YOU GUYS...WE SHOULDN'T LAUGH SO MUCH ...
IT'S NO GOOD... IT'S TOO FUNNY!!
IT'S NO LAUGHING MATTER, YOU GUYS -- !!
BWAHAHAHAHAHAHA
PFFT!
NO, NO, AIZAWA-SAN -- THAT WAS A COMEDIC MOMENT TO GO DOWN IN HISTORY!! THANK YOU FOR YOUR PART IN SENDING THE CLASS INTO A 20-MINUTE LONG FRENZY OF LAUGHTER!!
THAT WAS A GREAT GAG YOU FED HIM.
OHHHH -- BUT MAJIMA-KUN WAS REALLY MAD!!
HAHA
NICE! NICE ONE, MAJIMA-KUN!! I NEVER SAW THAT ONE COMING!!
...
HAHAHAHA
HAHAHAHA

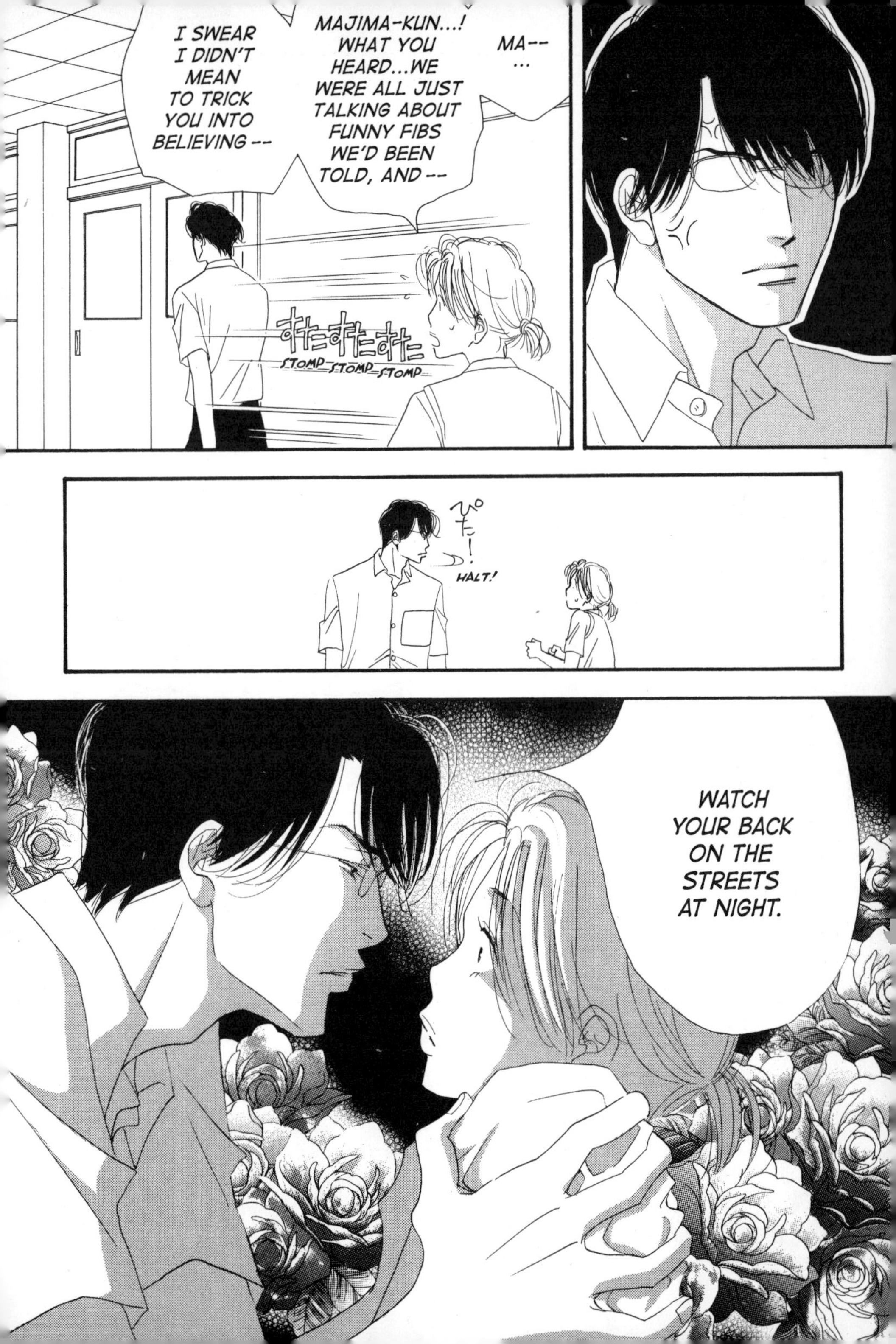
MA-- ...
MAJIMA-KUN...! WHAT YOU HEARD...WE WERE ALL JUST TALKING ABOUT FUNNY FIBS WE'D BEEN TOLD, AND --
I SWEAR I DIDN'T MEAN TO TRICK YOU INTO BELIEVING --
すたすたすた
STOMP STOMP STOMP
ぴた!
HALT!
WATCH YOUR BACK ON THE STREETS AT NIGHT.

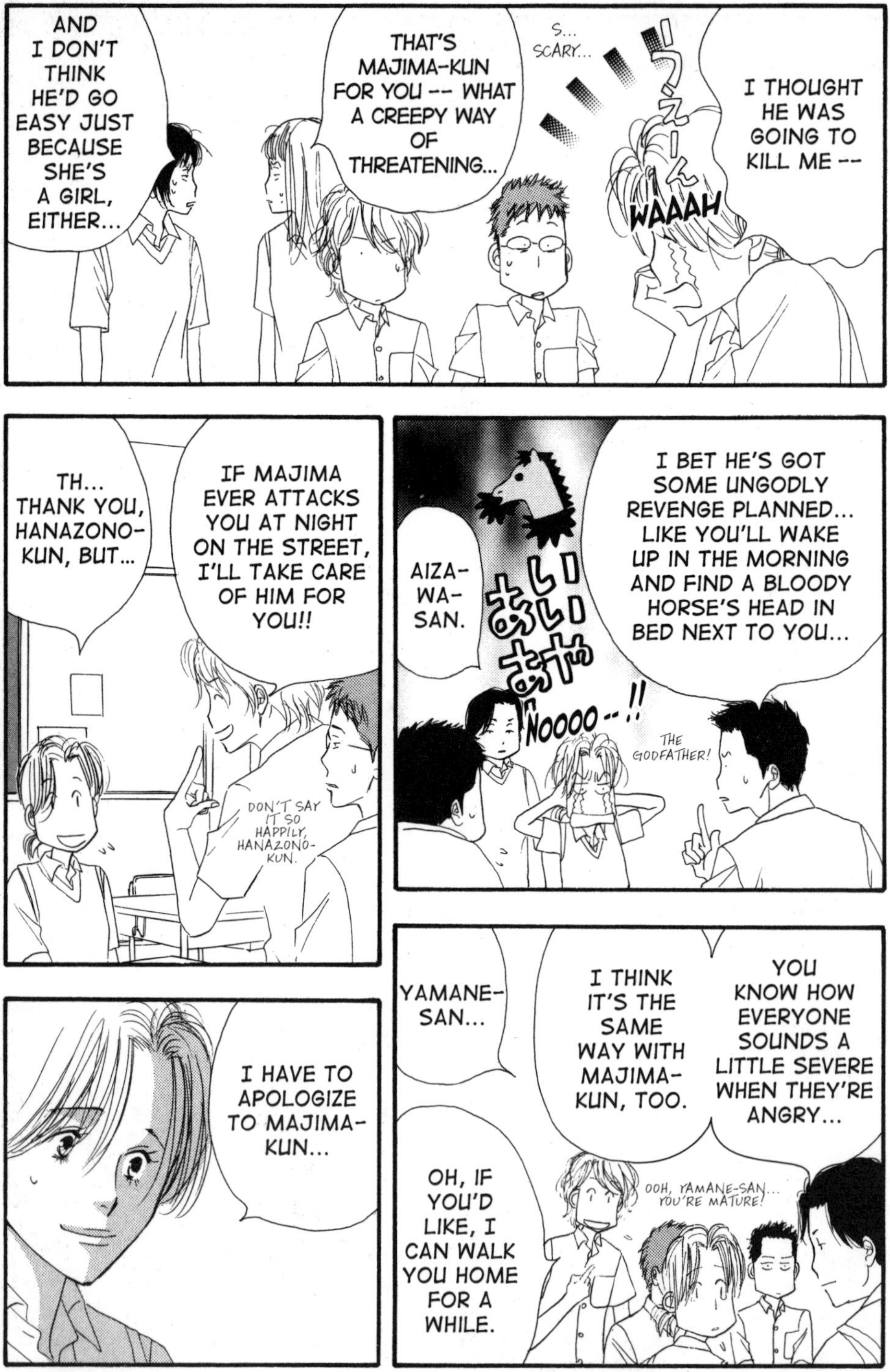
I THOUGHT HE WAS GOING TO KILL ME --
WAAAH
S... SCARY...
THAT'S MAJIMA-KUN FOR YOU -- WHAT A CREEPY WAY OF THREATENING...
AND I DON'T THINK HE'D GO EASY JUST BECAUSE SHE'S A GIRL, EITHER...
I BET HE'S GOT SOME UNGODLY REVENGE PLANNED... LIKE YOU'LL WAKE UP IN THE MORNING AND FIND A BLOODY HORSE'S HEAD IN BED NEXT TO YOU...
AIZA-WA-SAN.
NOOOO--!!
THE GODFATHER!
IF MAJIMA EVER ATTACKS YOU AT NIGHT ON THE STREET, I'LL TAKE CARE OF HIM FOR YOU!!
TH... THANK YOU, HANAZONO-KUN, BUT...
DON'T SAY IT SO HAPPILY, HANAZONO-KUN.
YOU KNOW HOW EVERYONE SOUNDS A LITTLE SEVERE WHEN THEY'RE ANGRY...
I THINK IT'S THE SAME WAY WITH MAJIMA-KUN, TOO.
YAMANE-SAN...
OOH, YAMANE-SAN... YOU'RE MATURE!
OH, IF YOU'D LIKE, I CAN WALK YOU HOME FOR A WHILE.
I HAVE TO APOLOGIZE TO MAJIMA-KUN...

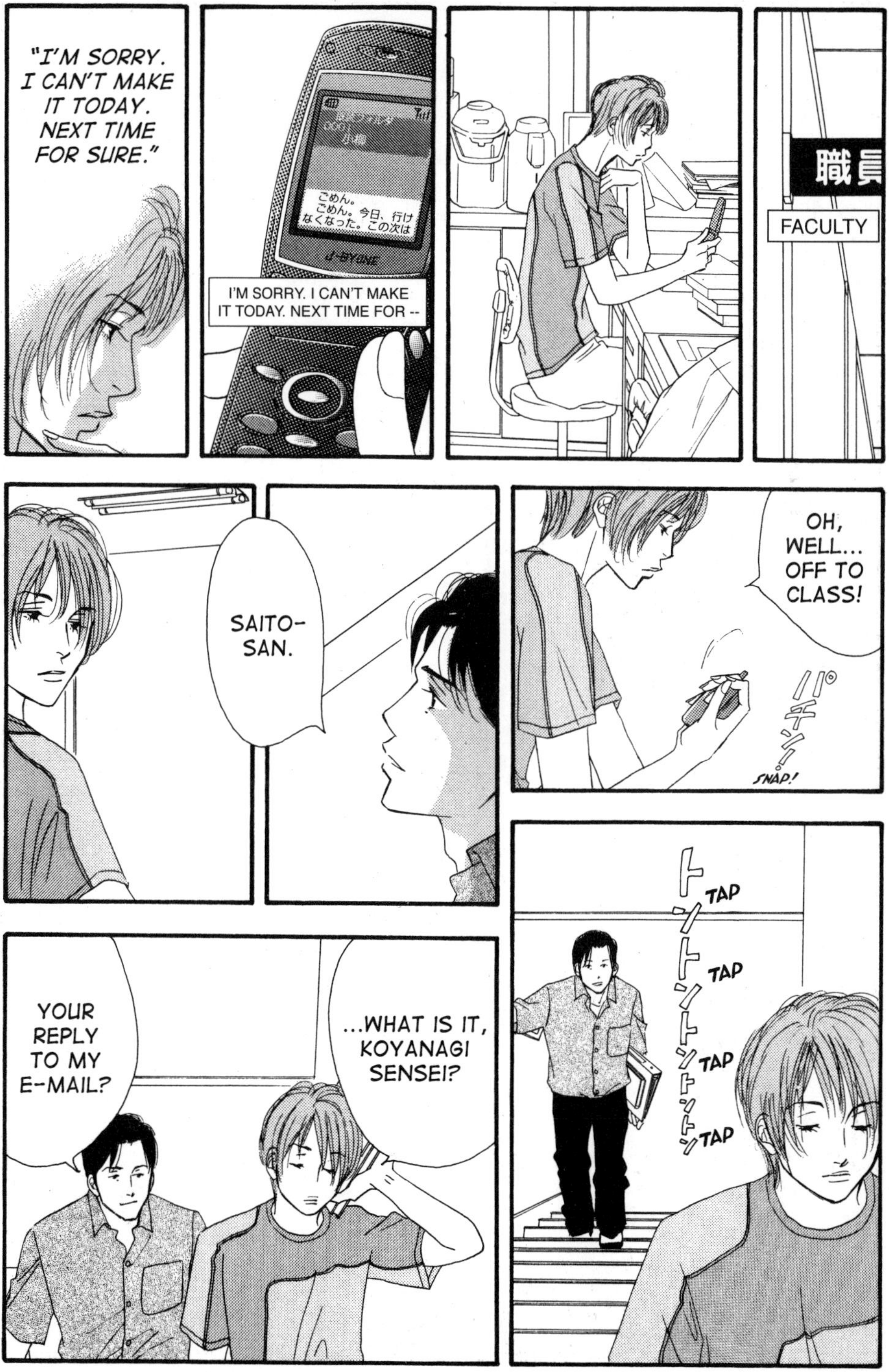
職員
FACULTY
ごめん。
ごめん。今日、行けなくなった。この次は
I'M SORRY. I CAN'T MAKE IT TODAY. NEXT TIME FOR --
"I'M SORRY. I CAN'T MAKE IT TODAY. NEXT TIME FOR SURE."
OH, WELL... OFF TO CLASS!
パチン!
SNAP!
SAITO-SAN.
トントントントン
TAP TAP TAP TAP
...WHAT IS IT, KOYANAGI SENSEI?
YOUR REPLY TO MY E-MAIL?

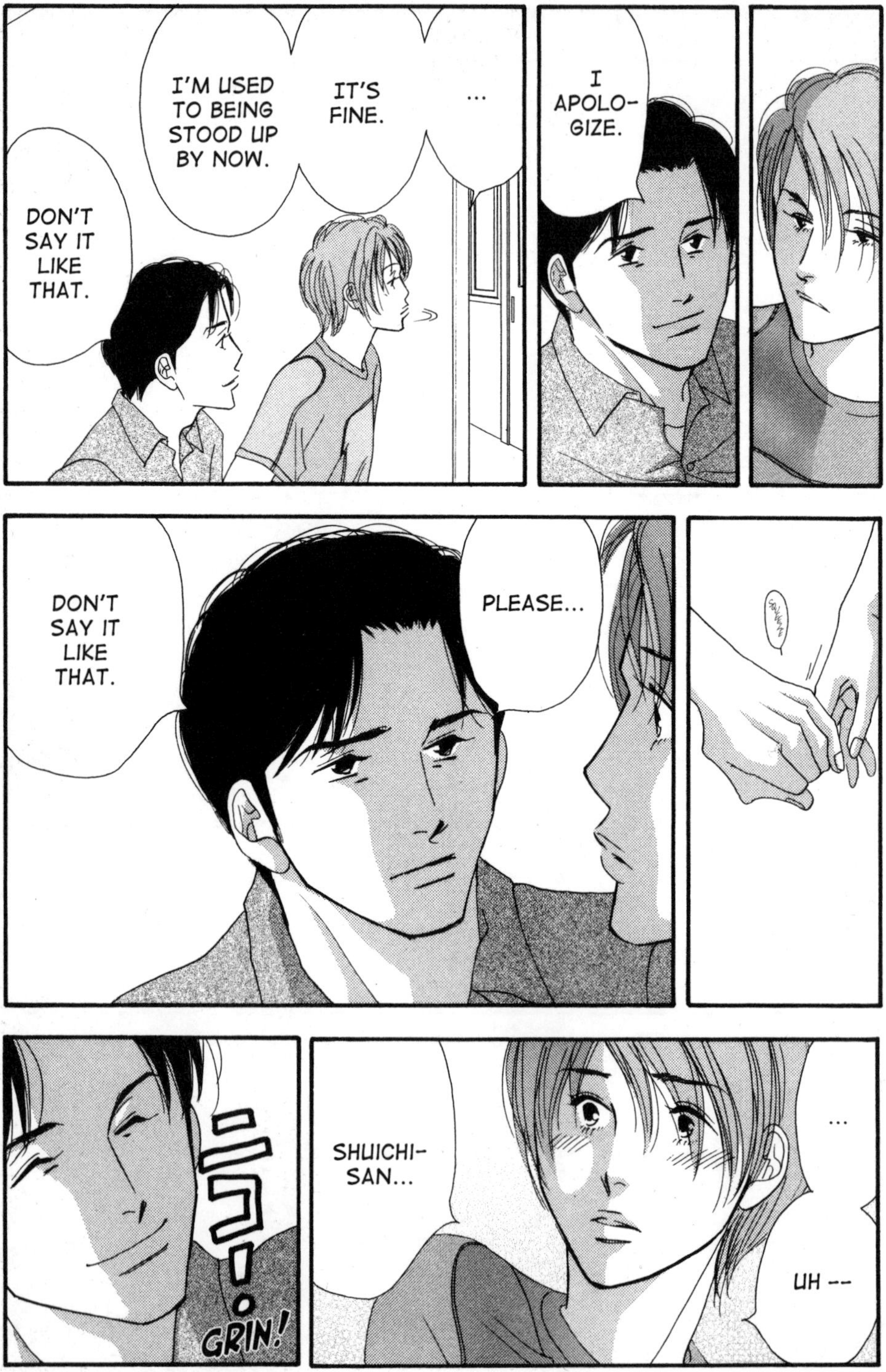
I APOLOGIZE.
...
IT'S FINE.
I'M USED TO BEING STOOD UP BY NOW.
DON'T SAY IT LIKE THAT.
PLEASE...
DON'T SAY IT LIKE THAT.
...
SHUICHI-SAN...
UH --
GRIN!

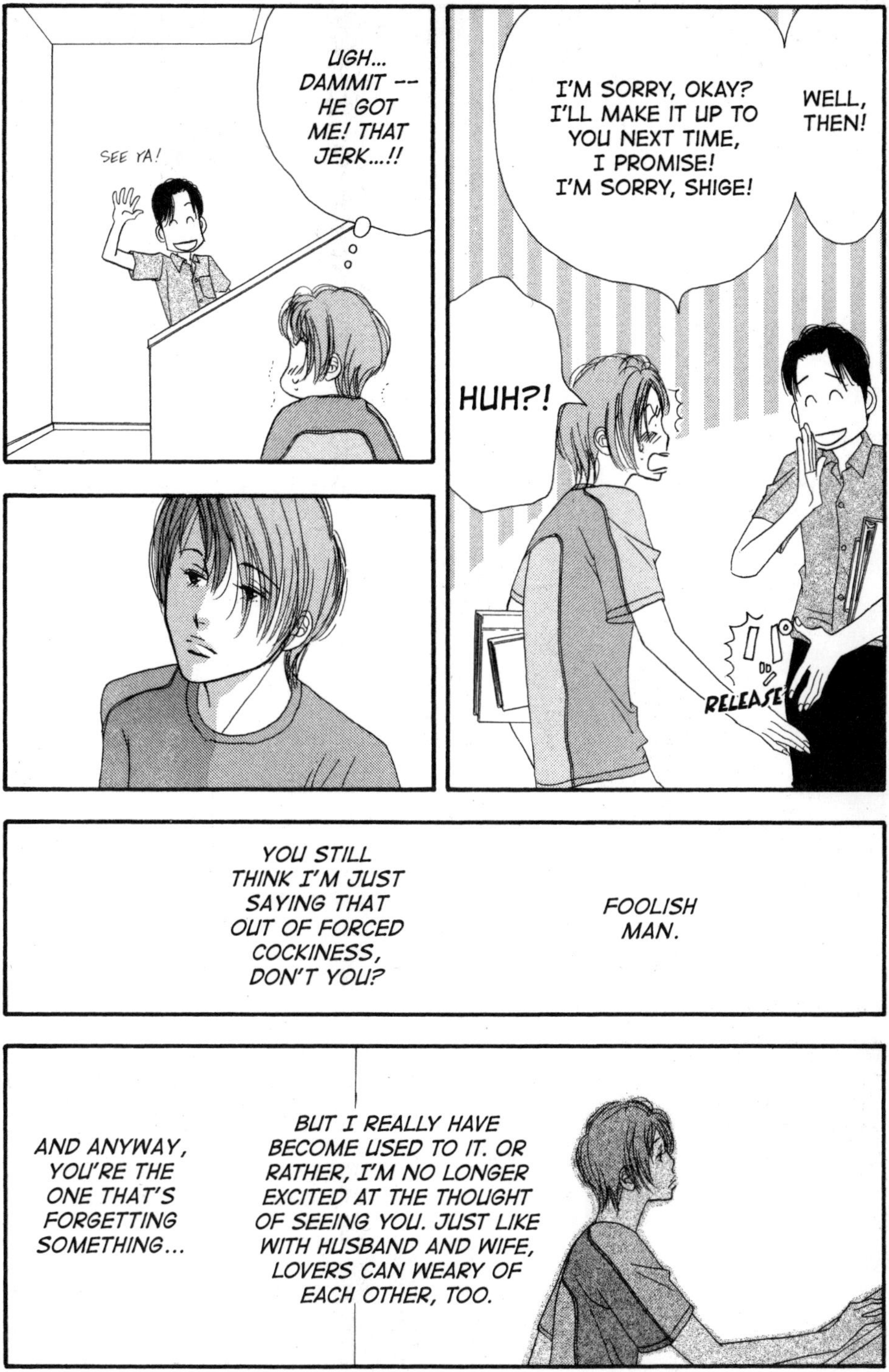
WELL, THEN!
I'M SORRY, OKAY? I'LL MAKE IT UP TO YOU NEXT TIME, I PROMISE! I'M SORRY, SHIGE!
HUH?!
RELEASE
UGH... DAMMIT -- HE GOT ME! THAT JERK...!!
SEE YA!
FOOLISH MAN.
YOU STILL THINK I'M JUST SAYING THAT OUT OF FORCED COCKINESS, DON'T YOU?
BUT I REALLY HAVE BECOME USED TO IT. OR RATHER, I'M NO LONGER EXCITED AT THE THOUGHT OF SEEING YOU. JUST LIKE WITH HUSBAND AND WIFE, LOVERS CAN WEARY OF EACH OTHER, TOO.
AND ANYWAY, YOU'RE THE ONE THAT'S FORGETTING SOMETHING...

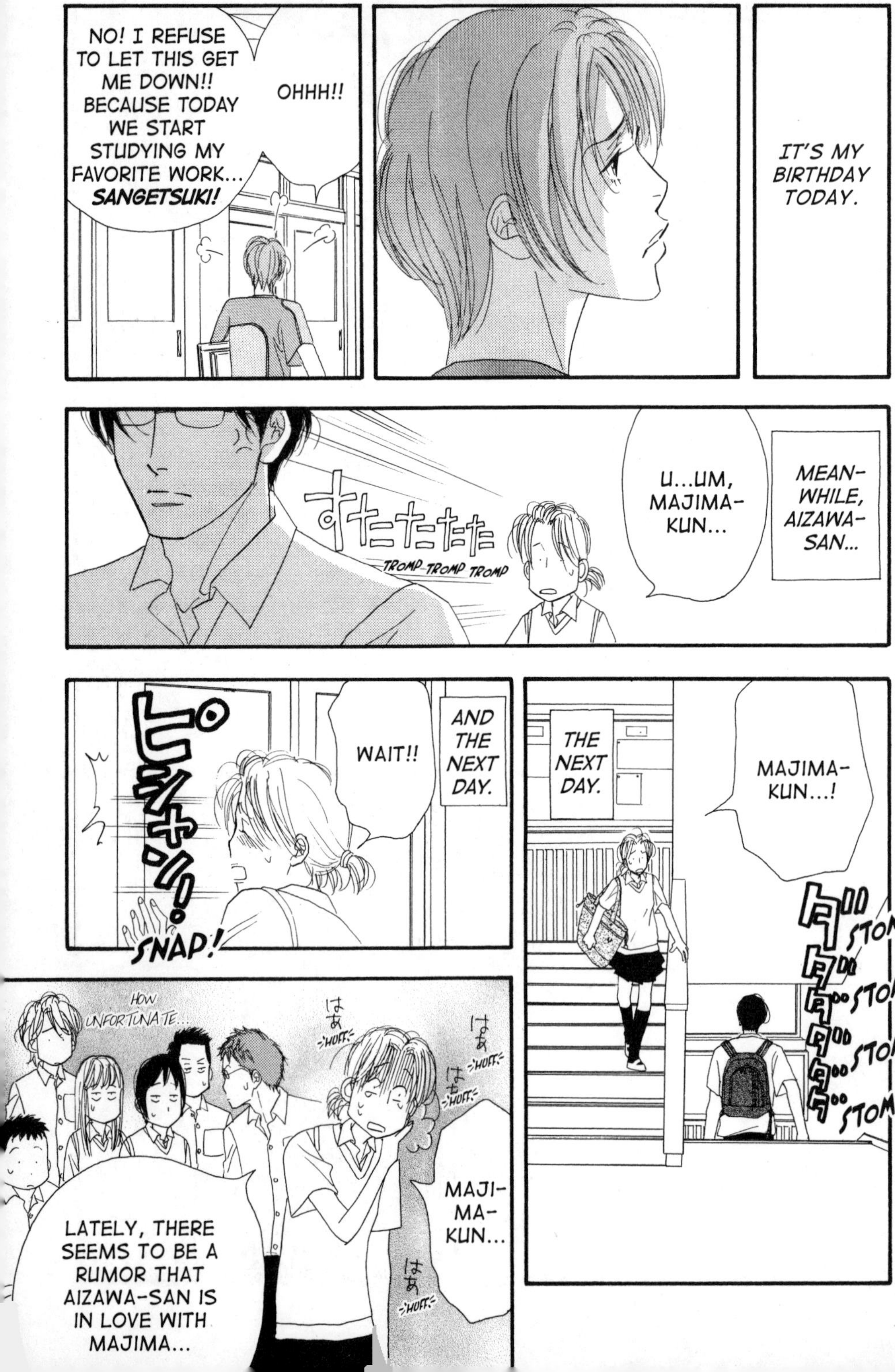
IT'S MY BIRTHDAY TODAY.
NO! I REFUSE TO LET THIS GET ME DOWN!! BECAUSE TODAY WE START STUDYING MY FAVORITE WORK... **SANGETSUKI!**
OHHH!!
MEAN-WHILE, AIZAWA-SAN...
U...UM, MAJIMA-KUN...
すたたたたた
TROMP-TROMP TROMP
MAJIMA-KUN...!
THE NEXT DAY.
STOMP STOMP STOMP STOMP
AND THE NEXT DAY.
WAIT!!
ピシャッ!
SNAP!
はあ HUFF
はあ HUFF
はあ HUFF
MAJI-MA-KUN...
はあ HUFF
HOW UNFORTUNATE...
LATELY, THERE SEEMS TO BE A RUMOR THAT AIZAWA-SAN IS IN LOVE WITH MAJIMA...

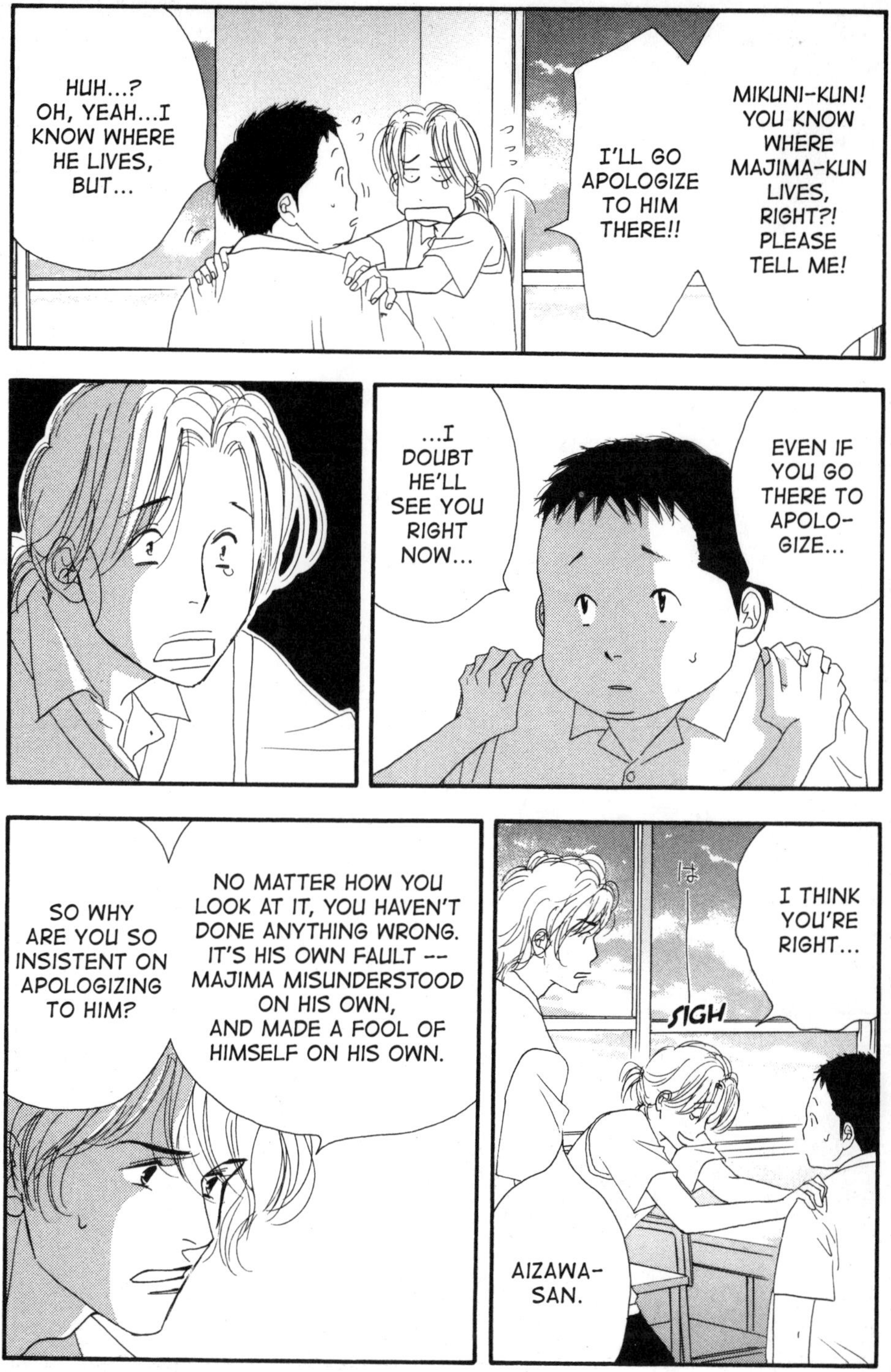
MIKUNI-KUN! YOU KNOW WHERE MAJIMA-KUN LIVES, RIGHT?! PLEASE TELL ME!
I'LL GO APOLOGIZE TO HIM THERE!!
HUH...? OH, YEAH...I KNOW WHERE HE LIVES, BUT...
EVEN IF YOU GO THERE TO APOLO-GIZE...
...I DOUBT HE'LL SEE YOU RIGHT NOW...
I THINK YOU'RE RIGHT...
は—
SIGH
AIZAWA-SAN.
NO MATTER HOW YOU LOOK AT IT, YOU HAVEN'T DONE ANYTHING WRONG. IT'S HIS OWN FAULT -- MAJIMA MISUNDERSTOOD ON HIS OWN, AND MADE A FOOL OF HIMSELF ON HIS OWN.
SO WHY ARE YOU SO INSISTENT ON APOLOGIZING TO HIM?

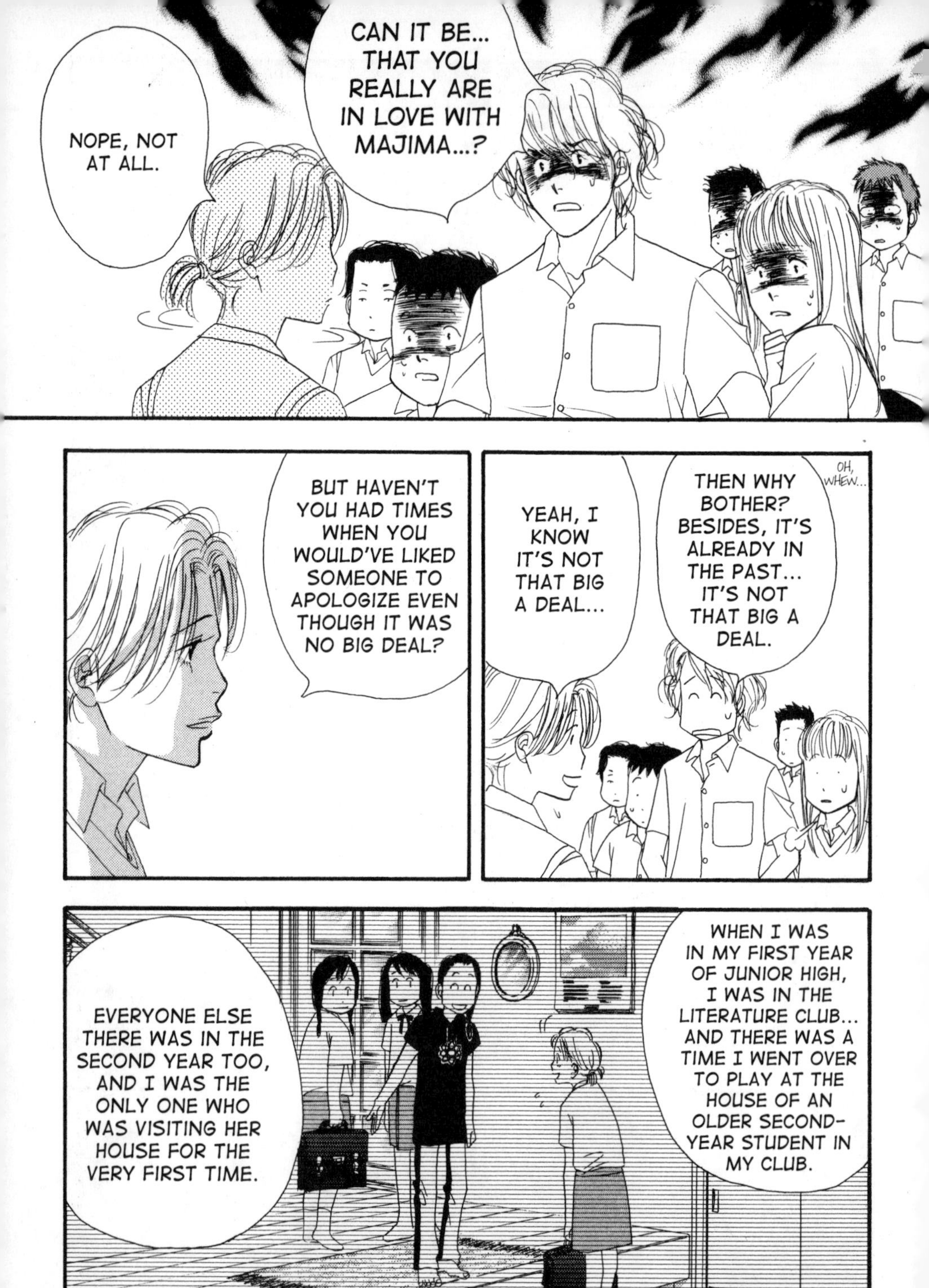
CAN IT BE... THAT YOU REALLY ARE IN LOVE WITH MAJIMA...?
NOPE, NOT AT ALL.
OH, WHEW...
THEN WHY BOTHER? BESIDES, IT'S ALREADY IN THE PAST... IT'S NOT THAT BIG A DEAL.
YEAH, I KNOW IT'S NOT THAT BIG A DEAL...
BUT HAVEN'T YOU HAD TIMES WHEN YOU WOULD'VE LIKED SOMEONE TO APOLOGIZE EVEN THOUGH IT WAS NO BIG DEAL?
WHEN I WAS IN MY FIRST YEAR OF JUNIOR HIGH, I WAS IN THE LITERATURE CLUB... AND THERE WAS A TIME I WENT OVER TO PLAY AT THE HOUSE OF AN OLDER SECOND-YEAR STUDENT IN MY CLUB.
EVERYONE ELSE THERE WAS IN THE SECOND YEAR TOO, AND I WAS THE ONLY ONE WHO WAS VISITING HER HOUSE FOR THE VERY FIRST TIME.

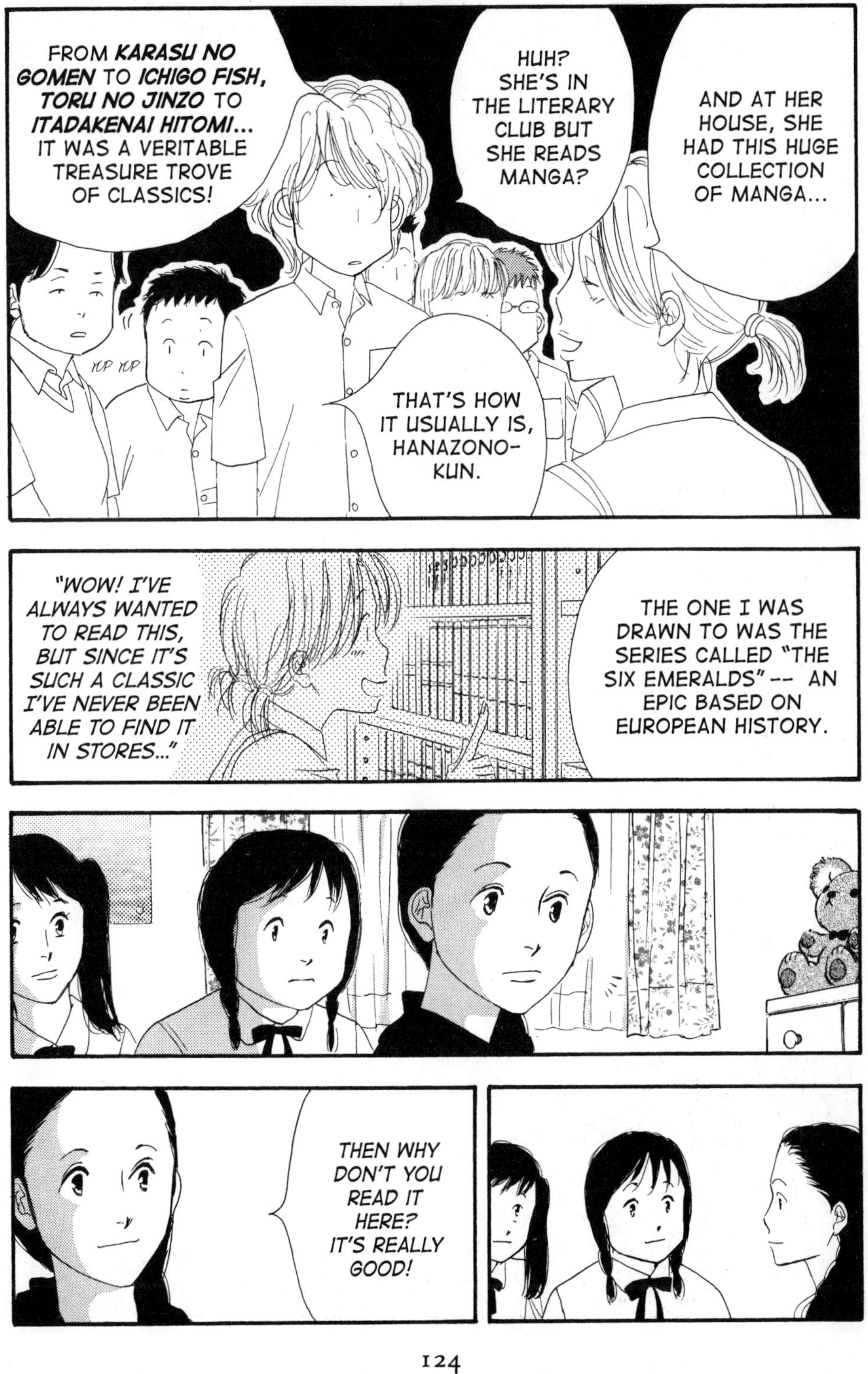
AND AT HER HOUSE, SHE HAD THIS HUGE COLLECTION OF MANGA...
HUH? SHE'S IN THE LITERARY CLUB BUT SHE READS MANGA?
THAT'S HOW IT USUALLY IS, HANAZONO-KUN.
FROM KARASU NO GOMEN TO ICHIGO FISH, TORU NO JINZO TO ITADAKENAI HITOMI... IT WAS A VERITABLE TREASURE TROVE OF CLASSICS!
YUP YUP
THE ONE I WAS DRAWN TO WAS THE SERIES CALLED "THE SIX EMERALDS" -- AN EPIC BASED ON EUROPEAN HISTORY.
"WOW! I'VE ALWAYS WANTED TO READ THIS, BUT SINCE IT'S SUCH A CLASSIC I'VE NEVER BEEN ABLE TO FIND IT IN STORES..."
THEN WHY DON'T YOU READ IT HERE? IT'S REALLY GOOD!

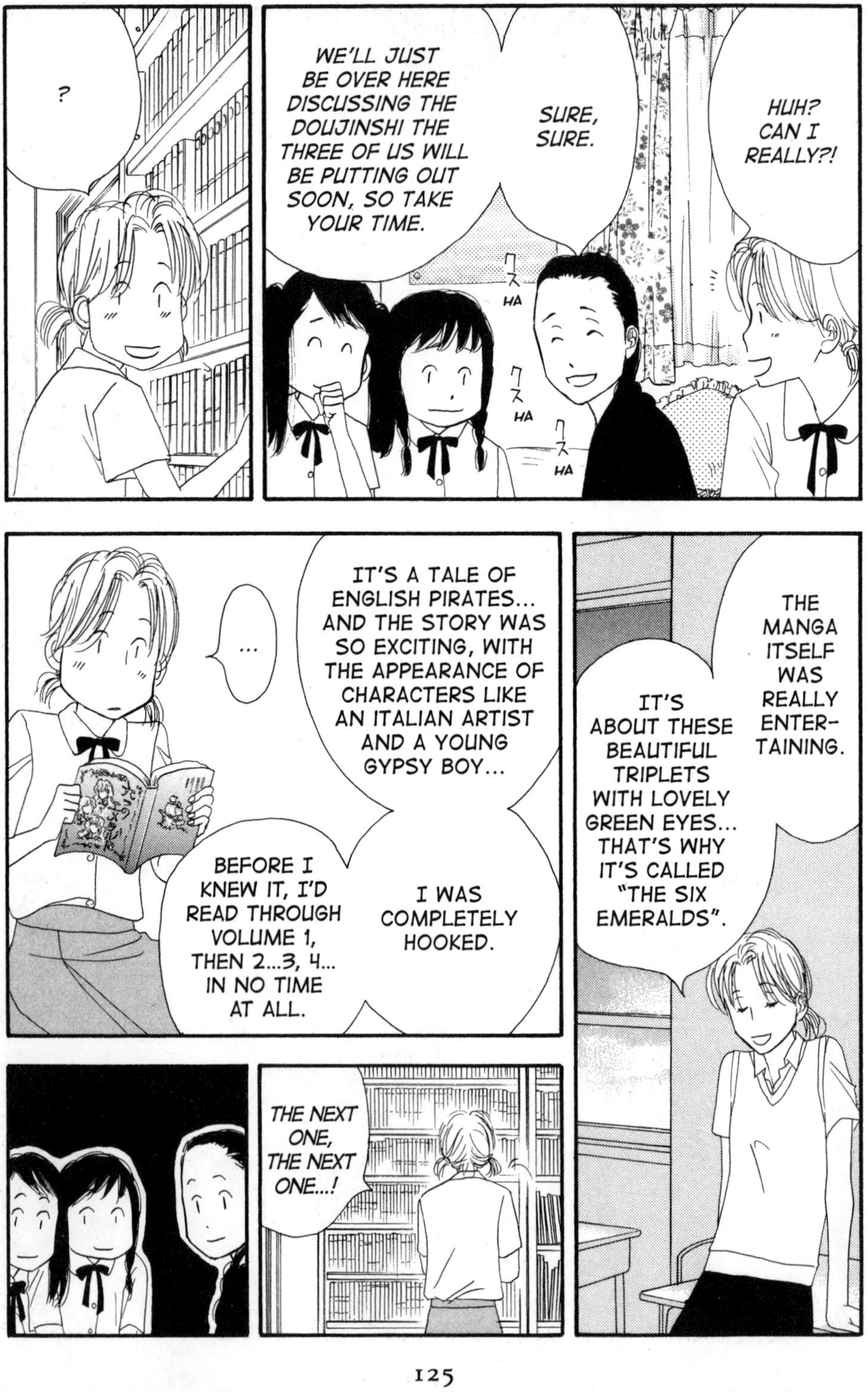
HUH? CAN I REALLY?!
SURE, SURE.
WE'LL JUST BE OVER HERE DISCUSSING THE DOUJINSHI THE THREE OF US WILL BE PUTTING OUT SOON, SO TAKE YOUR TIME.
クス HA
クス HA
クス HA
?
THE MANGA ITSELF WAS REALLY ENTERTAINING.
IT'S ABOUT THESE BEAUTIFUL TRIPLETS WITH LOVELY GREEN EYES... THAT'S WHY IT'S CALLED "THE SIX EMERALDS".
IT'S A TALE OF ENGLISH PIRATES... AND THE STORY WAS SO EXCITING, WITH THE APPEARANCE OF CHARACTERS LIKE AN ITALIAN ARTIST AND A YOUNG GYPSY BOY...
I WAS COMPLETELY HOOKED.
BEFORE I KNEW IT, I'D READ THROUGH VOLUME 1, THEN 2...3, 4... IN NO TIME AT ALL.
...
THE NEXT ONE, THE NEXT ONE...!

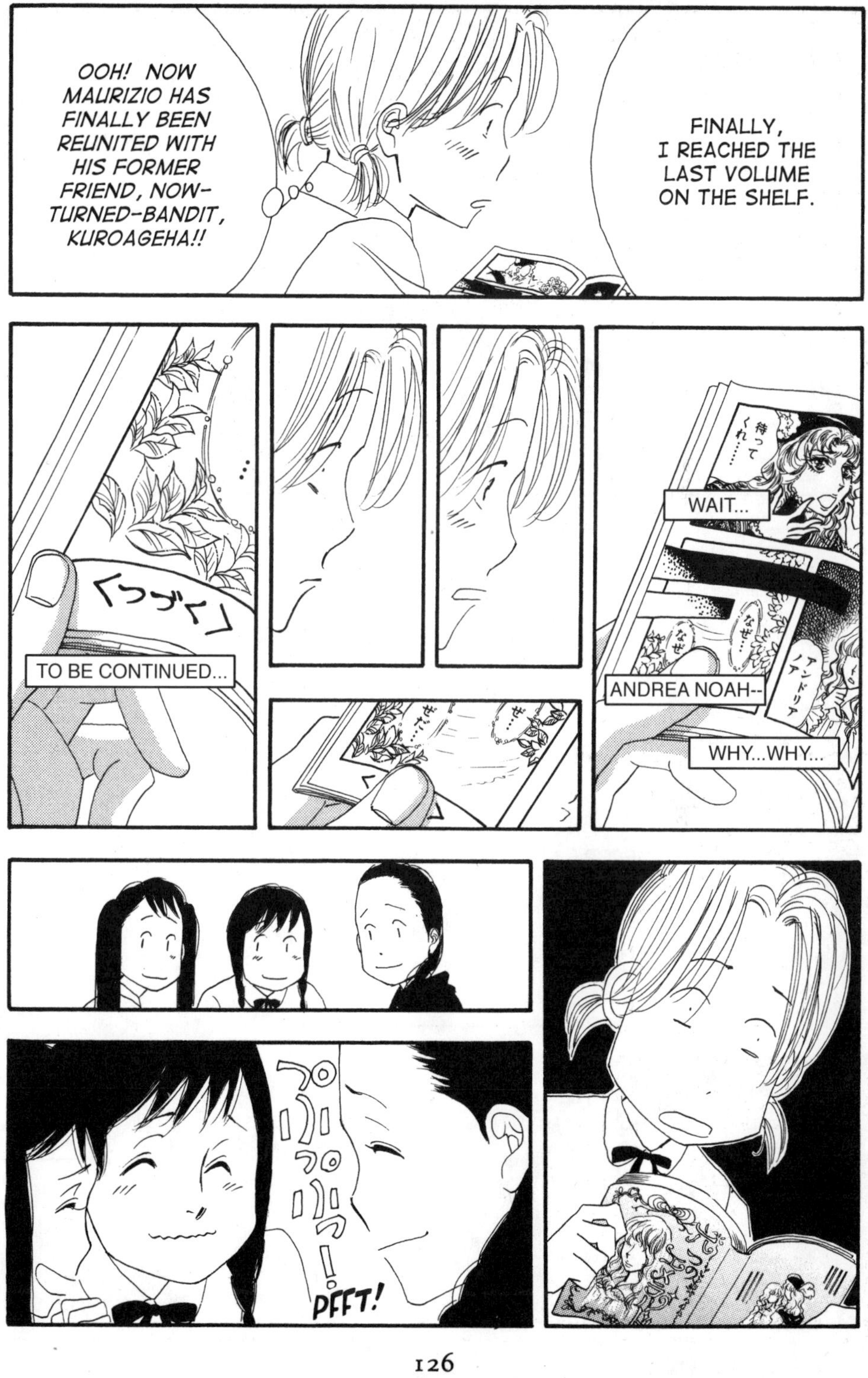
FINALLY, I REACHED THE LAST VOLUME ON THE SHELF.
OOH! NOW MAURIZIO HAS FINALLY BEEN REUNITED WITH HIS FORMER FRIEND, NOW-TURNED-BANDIT, KUROAGEHA!!
待ってくれ……
WAIT...
なぜ……
なぜ
アンドリア ノア
ANDREA NOAH--
WHY...WHY...
...
〈つづく〉
TO BE CONTINUED...
PFFT!

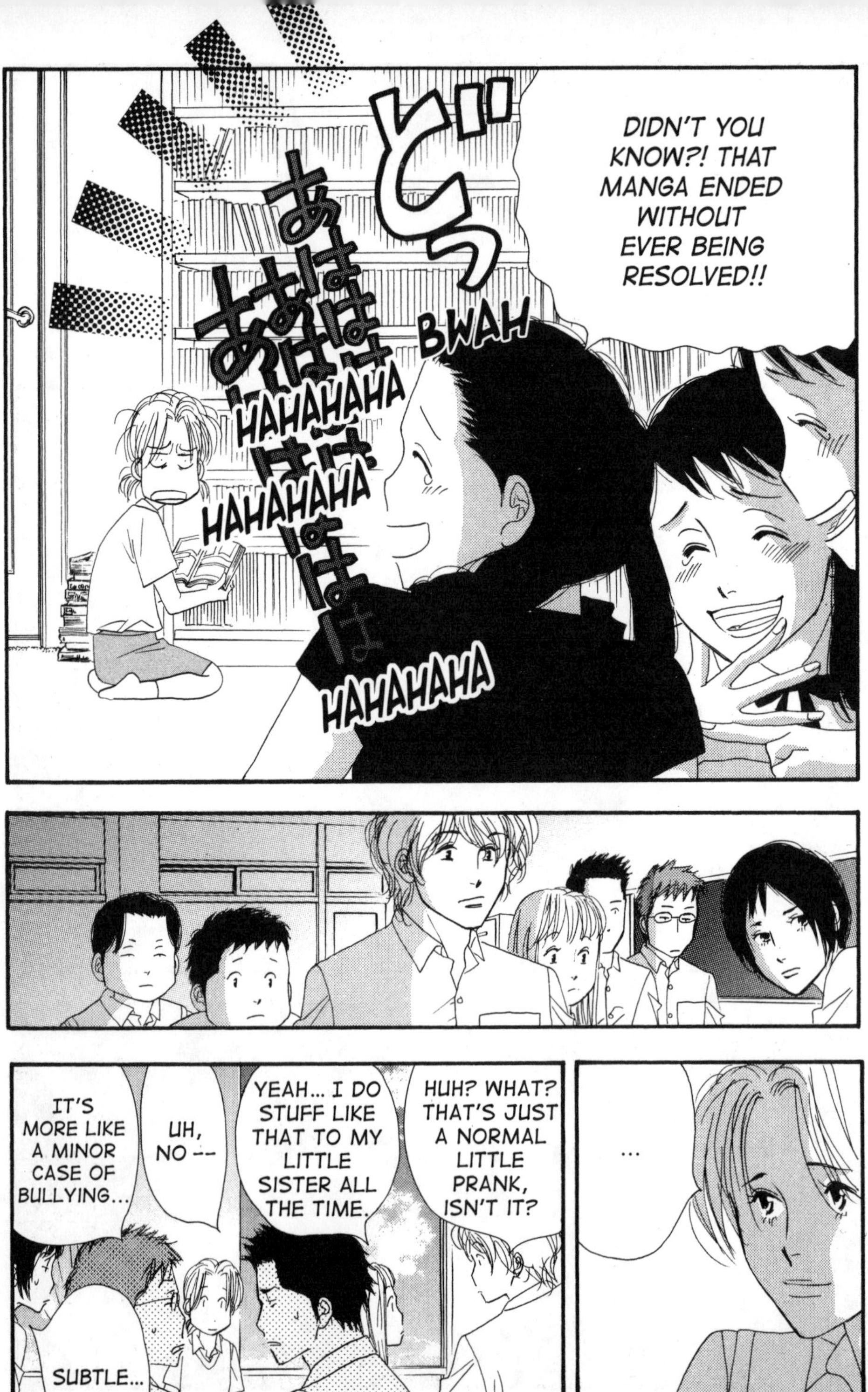
DIDN'T YOU KNOW?! THAT MANGA ENDED WITHOUT EVER BEING RESOLVED!!
BWAH
HAHAHAHA
HAHAHAHA
HAHAHAHA
...
HUH? WHAT? THAT'S JUST A NORMAL LITTLE PRANK, ISN'T IT?
YEAH... I DO STUFF LIKE THAT TO MY LITTLE SISTER ALL THE TIME.
UH, NO --
IT'S MORE LIKE A MINOR CASE OF BULLYING...
SUBTLE...

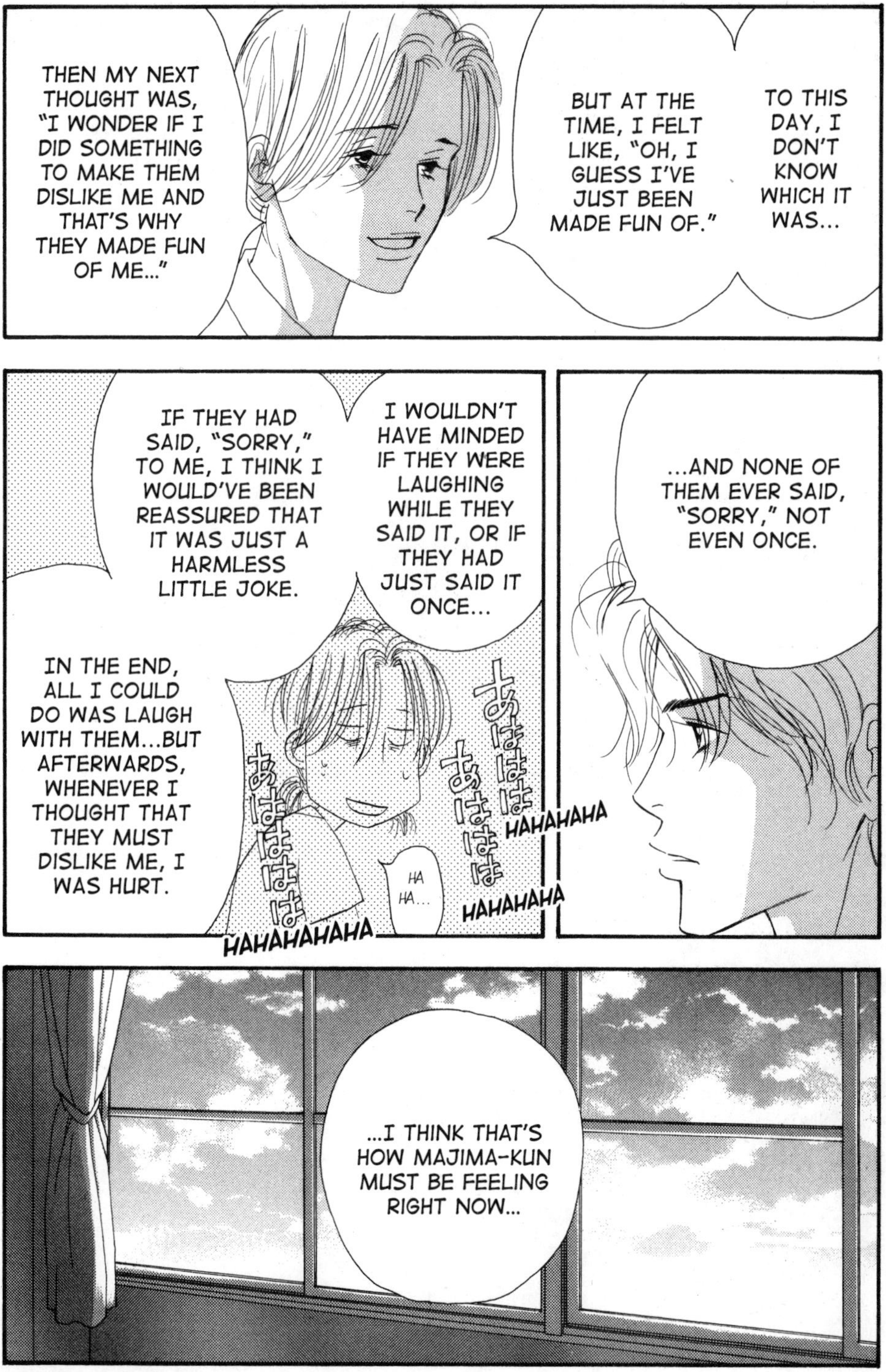

TO THIS DAY, I DON'T KNOW WHICH IT WAS...
BUT AT THE TIME, I FELT LIKE, "OH, I GUESS I'VE JUST BEEN MADE FUN OF."
THEN MY NEXT THOUGHT WAS, "I WONDER IF I DID SOMETHING TO MAKE THEM DISLIKE ME AND THAT'S WHY THEY MADE FUN OF ME..."
...AND NONE OF THEM EVER SAID, "SORRY," NOT EVEN ONCE.
I WOULDN'T HAVE MINDED IF THEY WERE LAUGHING WHILE THEY SAID IT, OR IF THEY HAD JUST SAID IT ONCE...
IF THEY HAD SAID, "SORRY," TO ME, I THINK I WOULD'VE BEEN REASSURED THAT IT WAS JUST A HARMLESS LITTLE JOKE.
あははは
HAHAHAHA
あははは
HAHAHAHA
あははは
HAHAHAHAHA
HA HA...
IN THE END, ALL I COULD DO WAS LAUGH WITH THEM...BUT AFTERWARDS, WHENEVER I THOUGHT THAT THEY MUST DISLIKE ME, I WAS HURT.
...I THINK THAT'S HOW MAJIMA-KUN MUST BE FEELING RIGHT NOW...

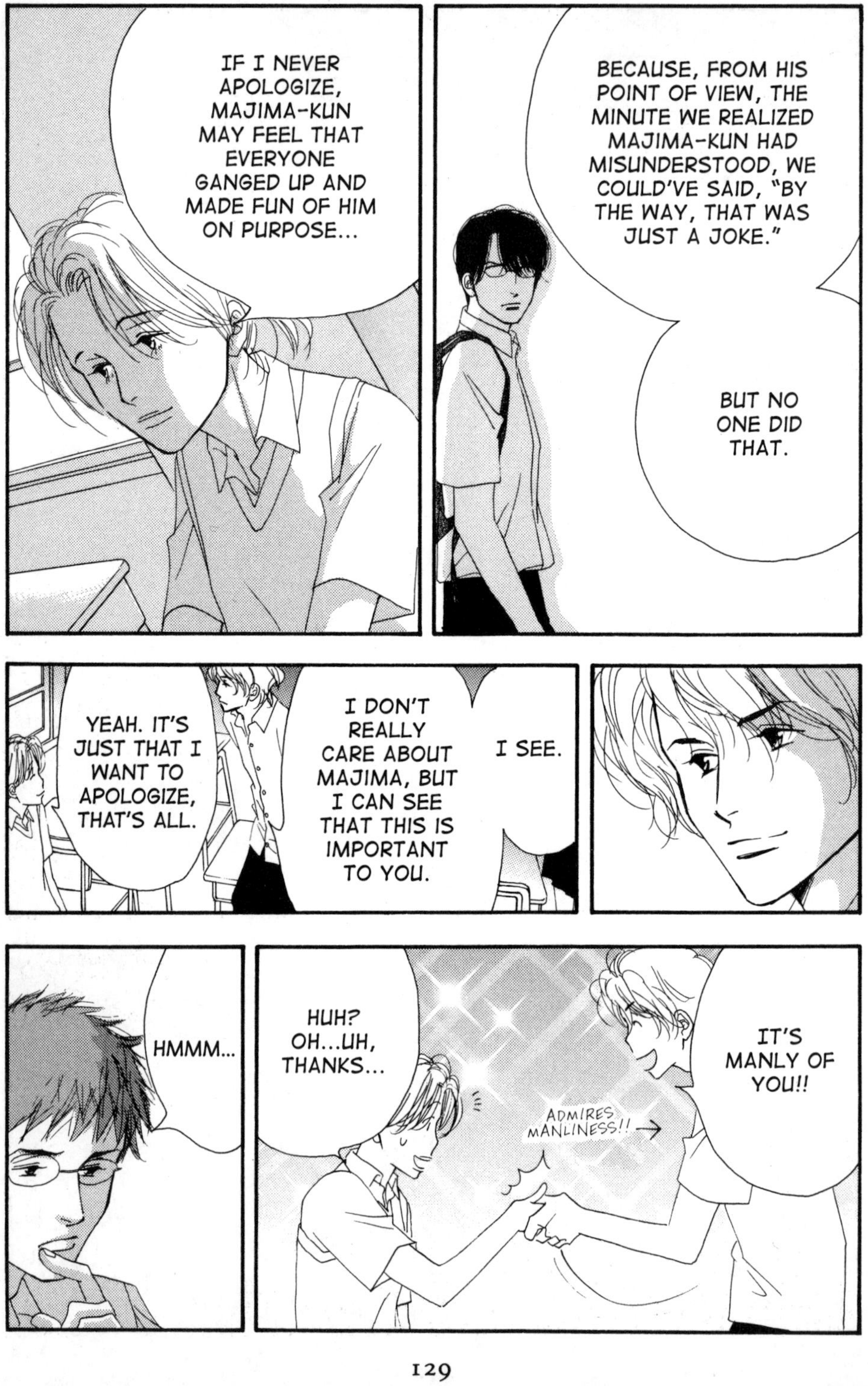

BECAUSE, FROM HIS POINT OF VIEW, THE MINUTE WE REALIZED MAJIMA-KUN HAD MISUNDERSTOOD, WE COULD'VE SAID, "BY THE WAY, THAT WAS JUST A JOKE."
BUT NO ONE DID THAT.
IF I NEVER APOLOGIZE, MAJIMA-KUN MAY FEEL THAT EVERYONE GANGED UP AND MADE FUN OF HIM ON PURPOSE...
I SEE.
I DON'T REALLY CARE ABOUT MAJIMA, BUT I CAN SEE THAT THIS IS IMPORTANT TO YOU.
YEAH. IT'S JUST THAT I WANT TO APOLOGIZE, THAT'S ALL.
IT'S MANLY OF YOU!!
ADMIRES MANLINESS!!
HUH? OH...UH, THANKS...
HMMM...

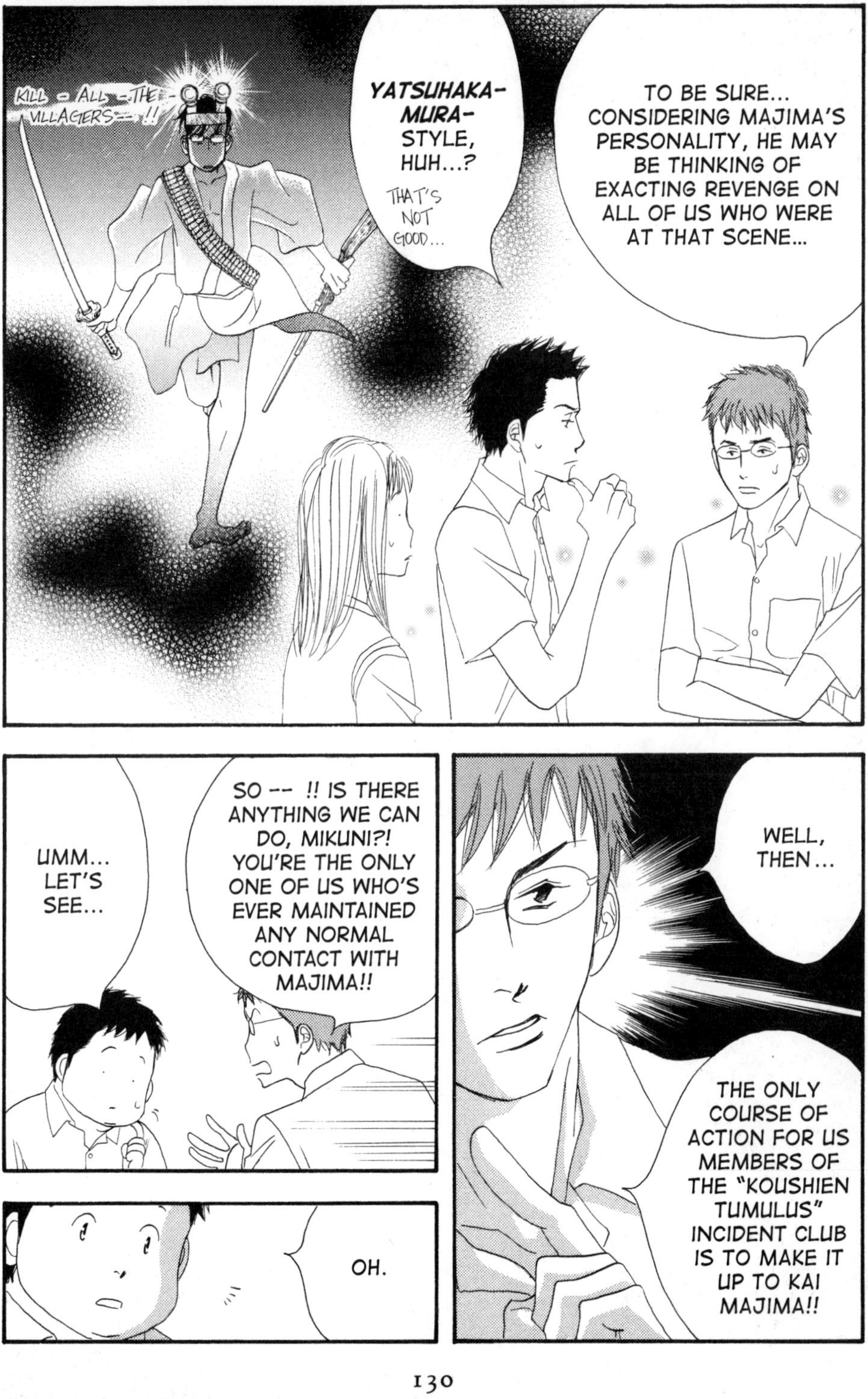
TO BE SURE... CONSIDERING MAJIMA'S PERSONALITY, HE MAY BE THINKING OF EXACTING REVENGE ON ALL OF US WHO WERE AT THAT SCENE...
YATSUHAKA-MURA-STYLE, HUH...?
THAT'S NOT GOOD...
KILL - ALL - THE - VILLAGERS-- !!
WELL, THEN...
THE ONLY COURSE OF ACTION FOR US MEMBERS OF THE "KOUSHIEN TUMULUS" INCIDENT CLUB IS TO MAKE IT UP TO KAI MAJIMA!!
SO -- !! IS THERE ANYTHING WE CAN DO, MIKUNI?! YOU'RE THE ONLY ONE OF US WHO'S EVER MAINTAINED ANY NORMAL CONTACT WITH MAJIMA!!
UMM... LET'S SEE...
OH.

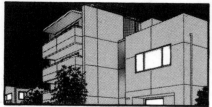

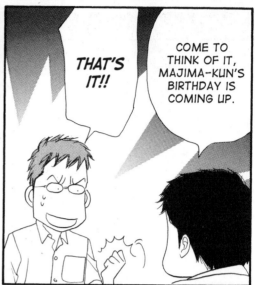

COME TO THINK OF IT, MAJIMA-KUN'S BIRTHDAY IS COMING UP.

THAT'S IT!!

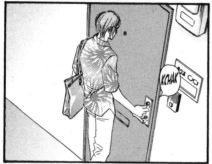

KCHAK

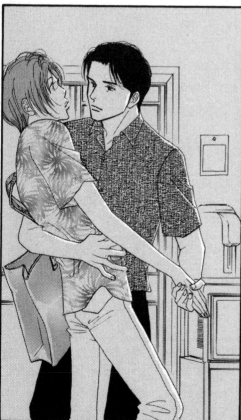

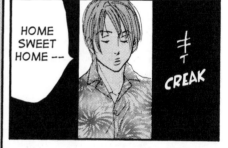

HOME SWEET HOME --

CREAK

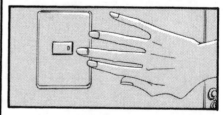

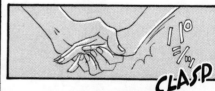

CLASP

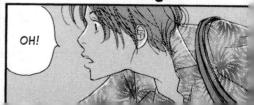

OH!

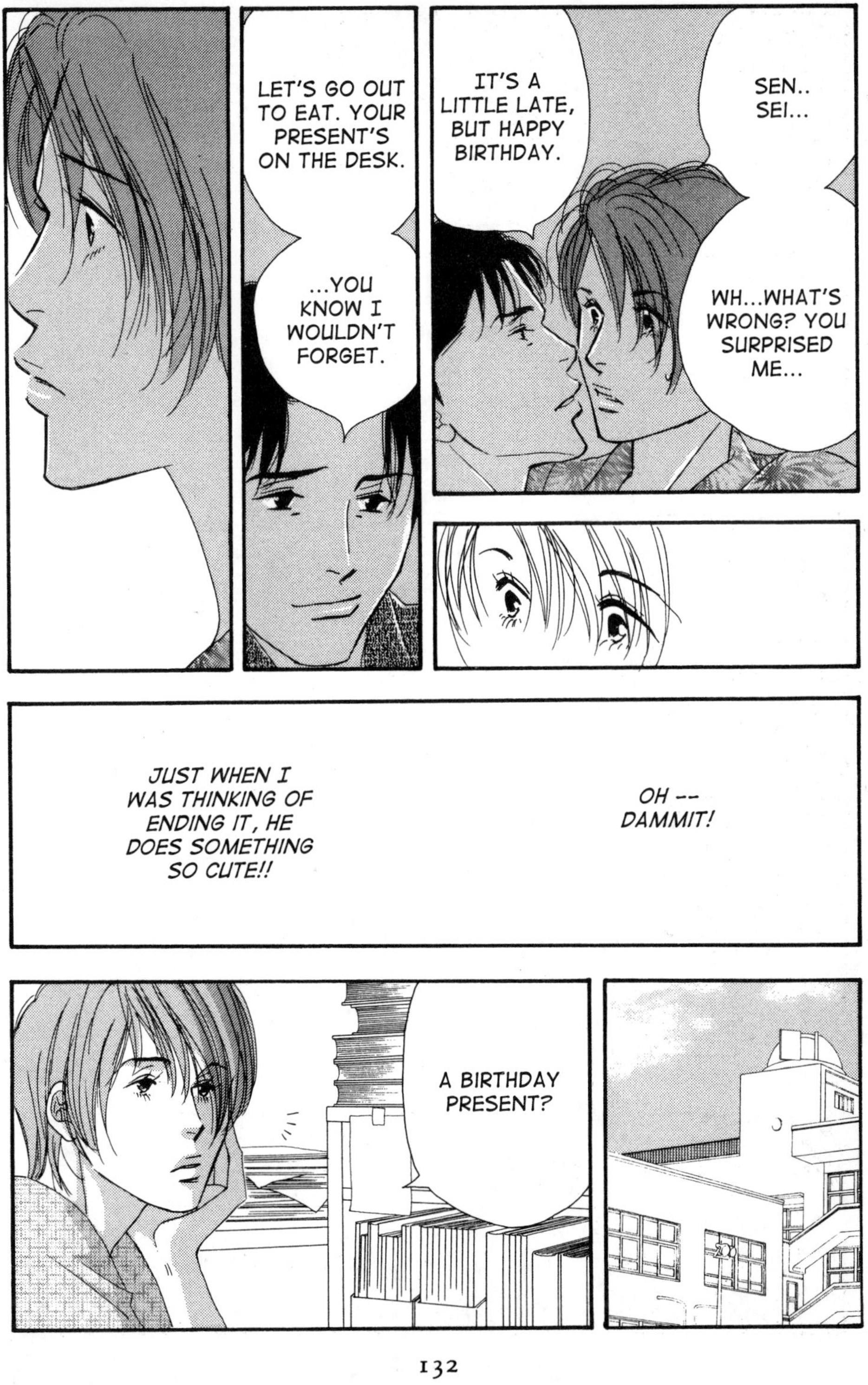
SEN.. SEI...
IT'S A LITTLE LATE, BUT HAPPY BIRTHDAY.
WH...WHAT'S WRONG? YOU SURPRISED ME...
LET'S GO OUT TO EAT. YOUR PRESENT'S ON THE DESK.
...YOU KNOW I WOULDN'T FORGET.
OH -- DAMMIT!
JUST WHEN I WAS THINKING OF ENDING IT, HE DOES SOMETHING SO CUTE!!
A BIRTHDAY PRESENT?

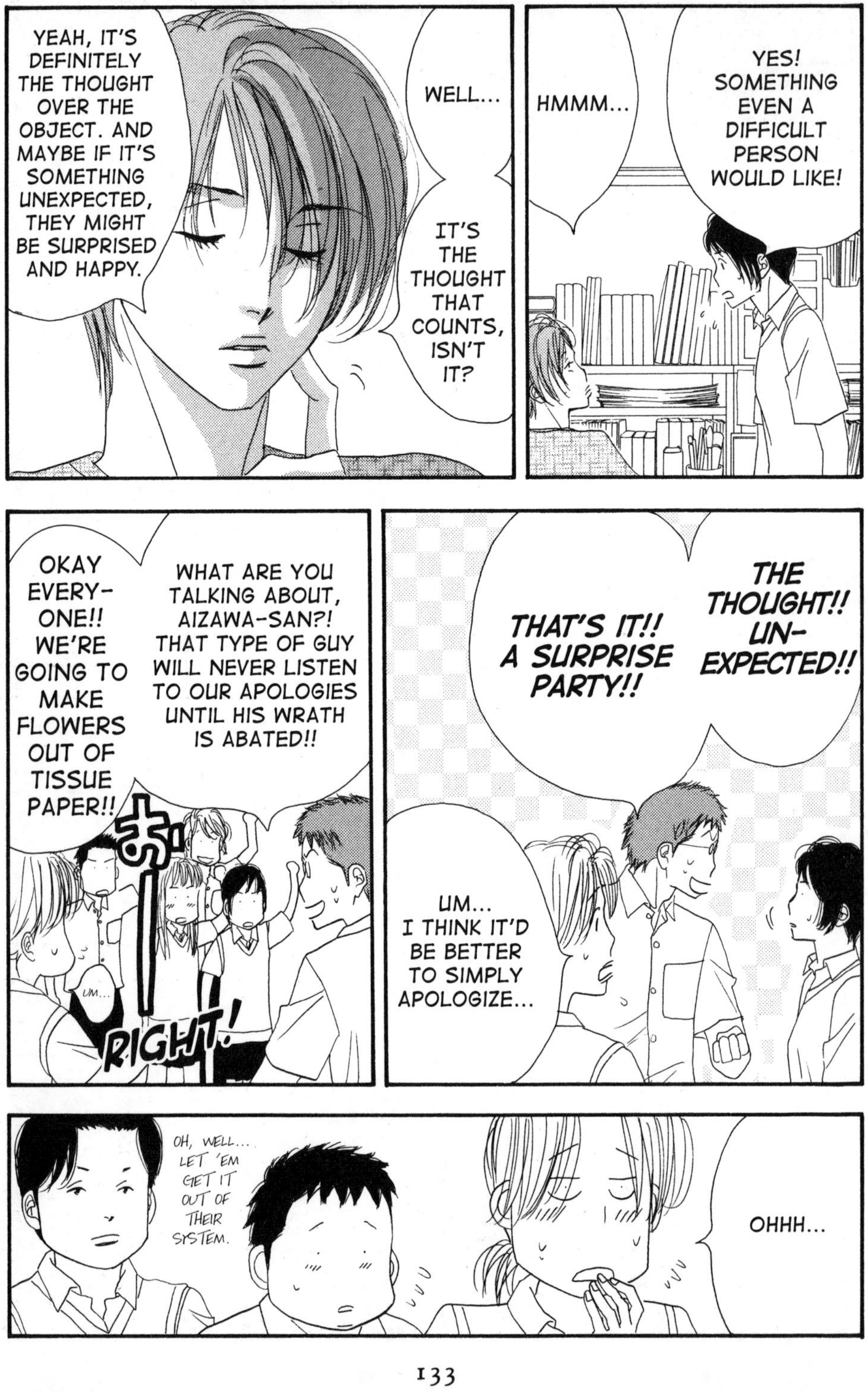
YES! SOMETHING EVEN A DIFFICULT PERSON WOULD LIKE!
HMMM...
WELL...
IT'S THE THOUGHT THAT COUNTS, ISN'T IT?
YEAH, IT'S DEFINITELY THE THOUGHT OVER THE OBJECT. AND MAYBE IF IT'S SOMETHING UNEXPECTED, THEY MIGHT BE SURPRISED AND HAPPY.
THE THOUGHT!! UN-EXPECTED!!
THAT'S IT!! A SURPRISE PARTY!!
UM... I THINK IT'D BE BETTER TO SIMPLY APOLOGIZE...
WHAT ARE YOU TALKING ABOUT, AIZAWA-SAN?! THAT TYPE OF GUY WILL NEVER LISTEN TO OUR APOLOGIES UNTIL HIS WRATH IS ABATED!!
OKAY EVERY-ONE!! WE'RE GOING TO MAKE FLOWERS OUT OF TISSUE PAPER!!
お
RIGHT!
UM...
OHHH...
OH, WELL... LET 'EM GET IT OUT OF THEIR SYSTEM.

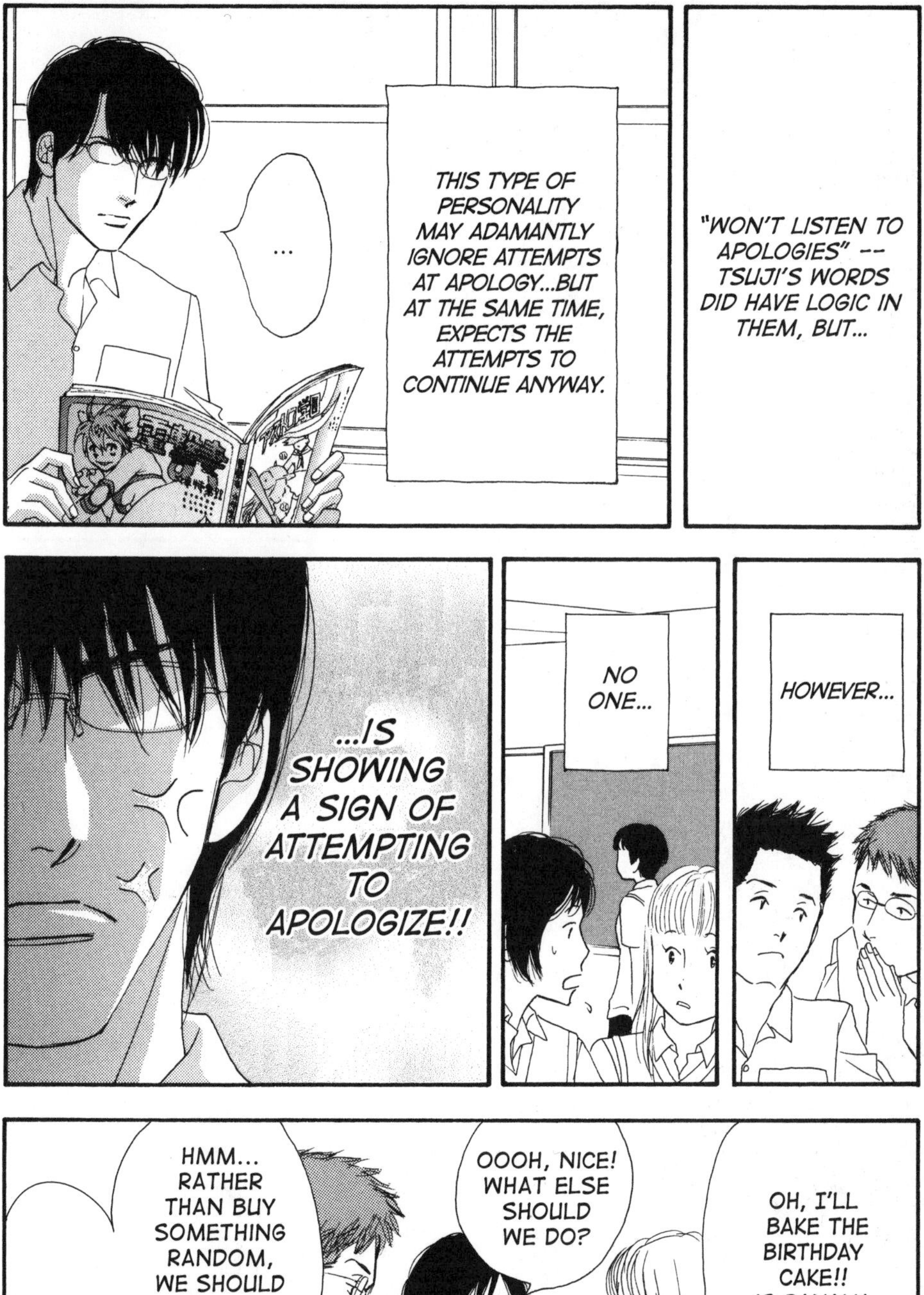
"WON'T LISTEN TO APOLOGIES" -- TSUJI'S WORDS DID HAVE LOGIC IN THEM, BUT...
THIS TYPE OF PERSONALITY MAY ADAMANTLY IGNORE ATTEMPTS AT APOLOGY...BUT AT THE SAME TIME, EXPECTS THE ATTEMPTS TO CONTINUE ANYWAY.
...
HOWEVER...
NO ONE...
...IS SHOWING A SIGN OF ATTEMPTING TO APOLOGIZE!!
OH, I'LL BAKE THE BIRTHDAY CAKE!! IS BANANA CHIFFON OKAY?
OOOH, NICE! WHAT ELSE SHOULD WE DO?
HMM... RATHER THAN BUY SOMETHING RANDOM, WE SHOULD REALLY EXPRESS OUR THOUGHTS...
THOUGHTS ...

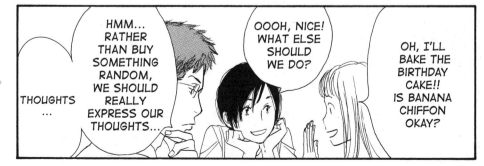

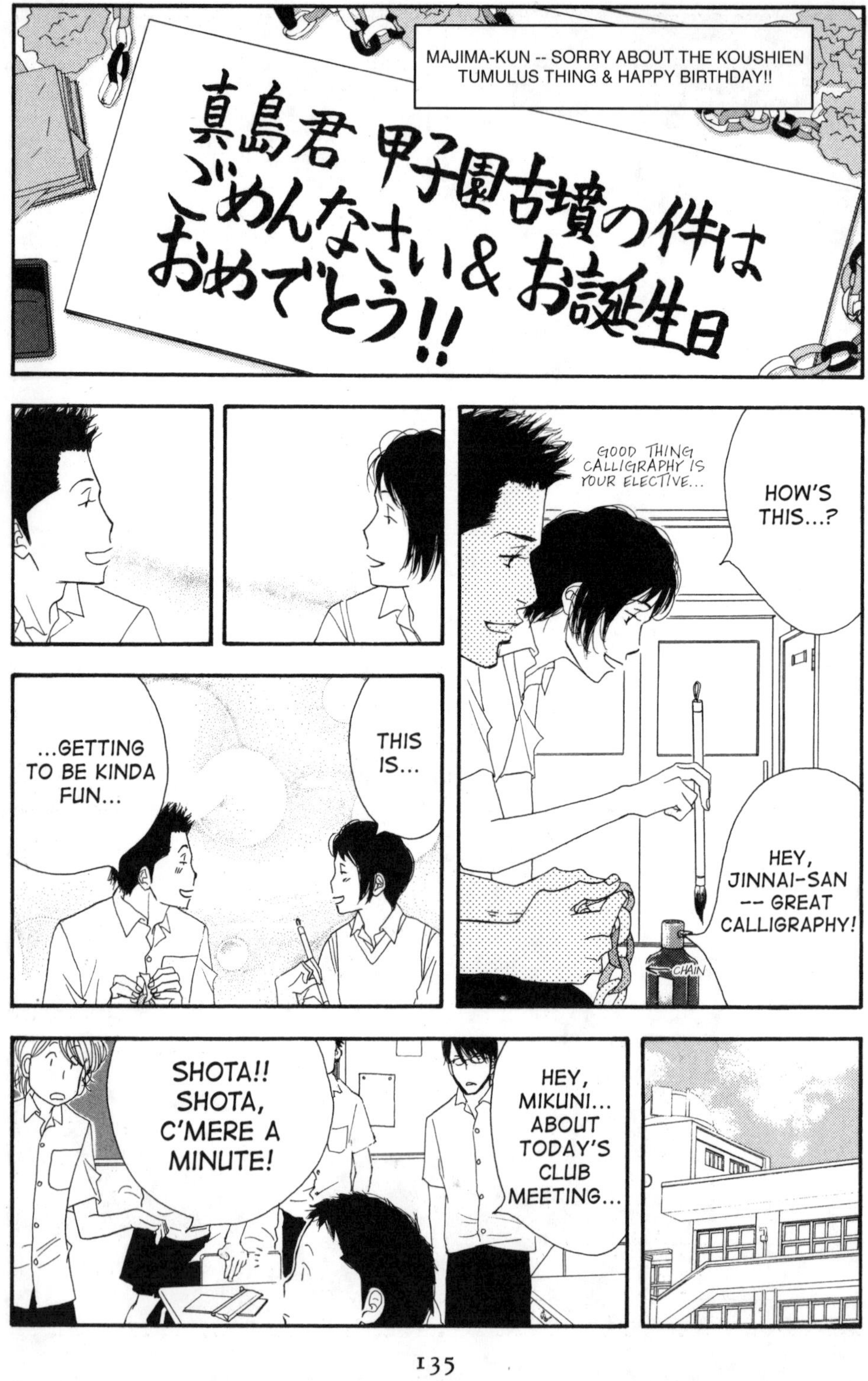
MAJIMA-KUN -- SORRY ABOUT THE KOUSHIEN TUMULUS THING & HAPPY BIRTHDAY!!
真島君 甲子園古墳の件は
ごめんなさい&お誕生日
おめでとう!!
GOOD THING CALLIGRAPHY IS YOUR ELECTIVE...
HOW'S THIS...?
HEY, JINNAI-SAN -- GREAT CALLIGRAPHY!
CHAIN
THIS IS...
...GETTING TO BE KINDA FUN...
HEY, MIKUNI... ABOUT TODAY'S CLUB MEETING...
SHOTA!! SHOTA, C'MERE A MINUTE!

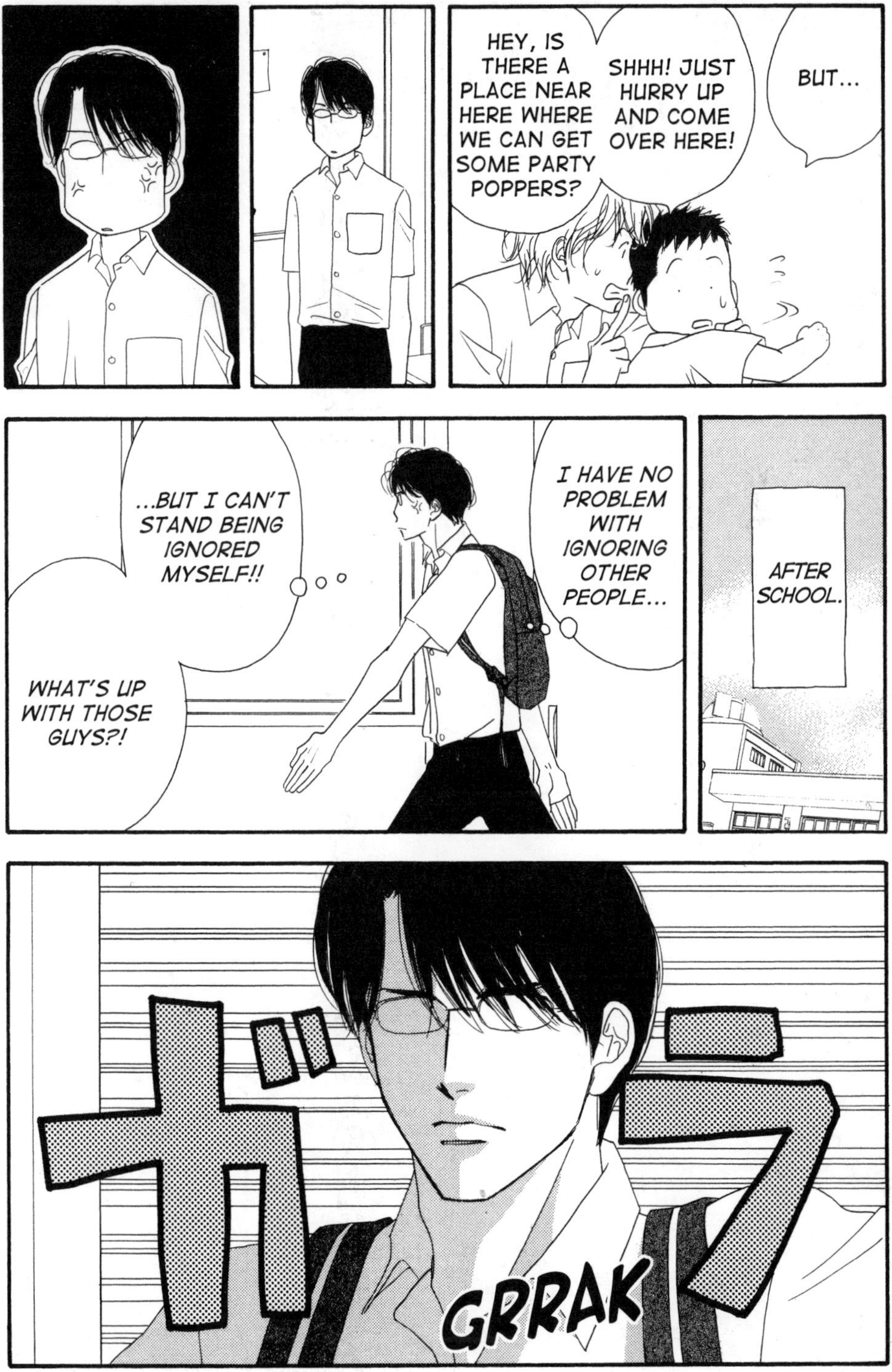
HEY, IS THERE A PLACE NEAR HERE WHERE WE CAN GET SOME PARTY POPPERS?
SHHH! JUST HURRY UP AND COME OVER HERE!
BUT...
AFTER SCHOOL.
I HAVE NO PROBLEM WITH IGNORING OTHER PEOPLE...
...BUT I CAN'T STAND BEING IGNORED MYSELF!!
WHAT'S UP WITH THOSE GUYS?!
ガラ
GRRAK

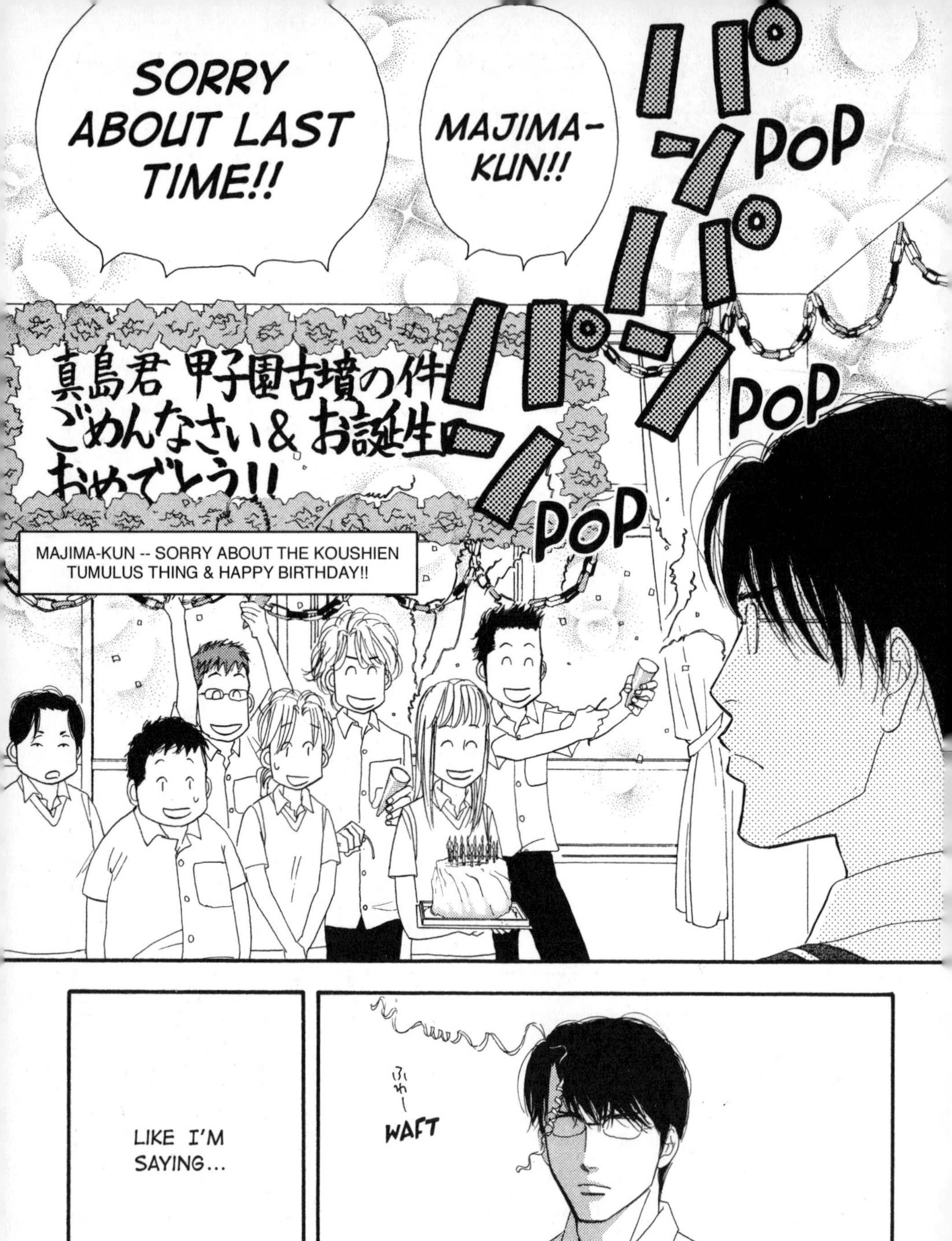
POP
MAJIMA-KUN!!
SORRY ABOUT LAST TIME!!
真島君 甲子園古墳の件
ごめんなさい&お誕生日
おめでとう!!
MAJIMA-KUN -- SORRY ABOUT THE KOUSHIEN TUMULUS THING & HAPPY BIRTHDAY!!
POP
POP
ふわ～
WAFT
LIKE I'M SAYING...

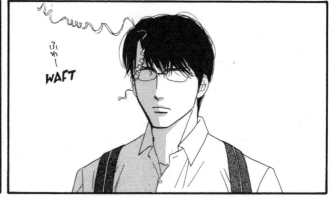

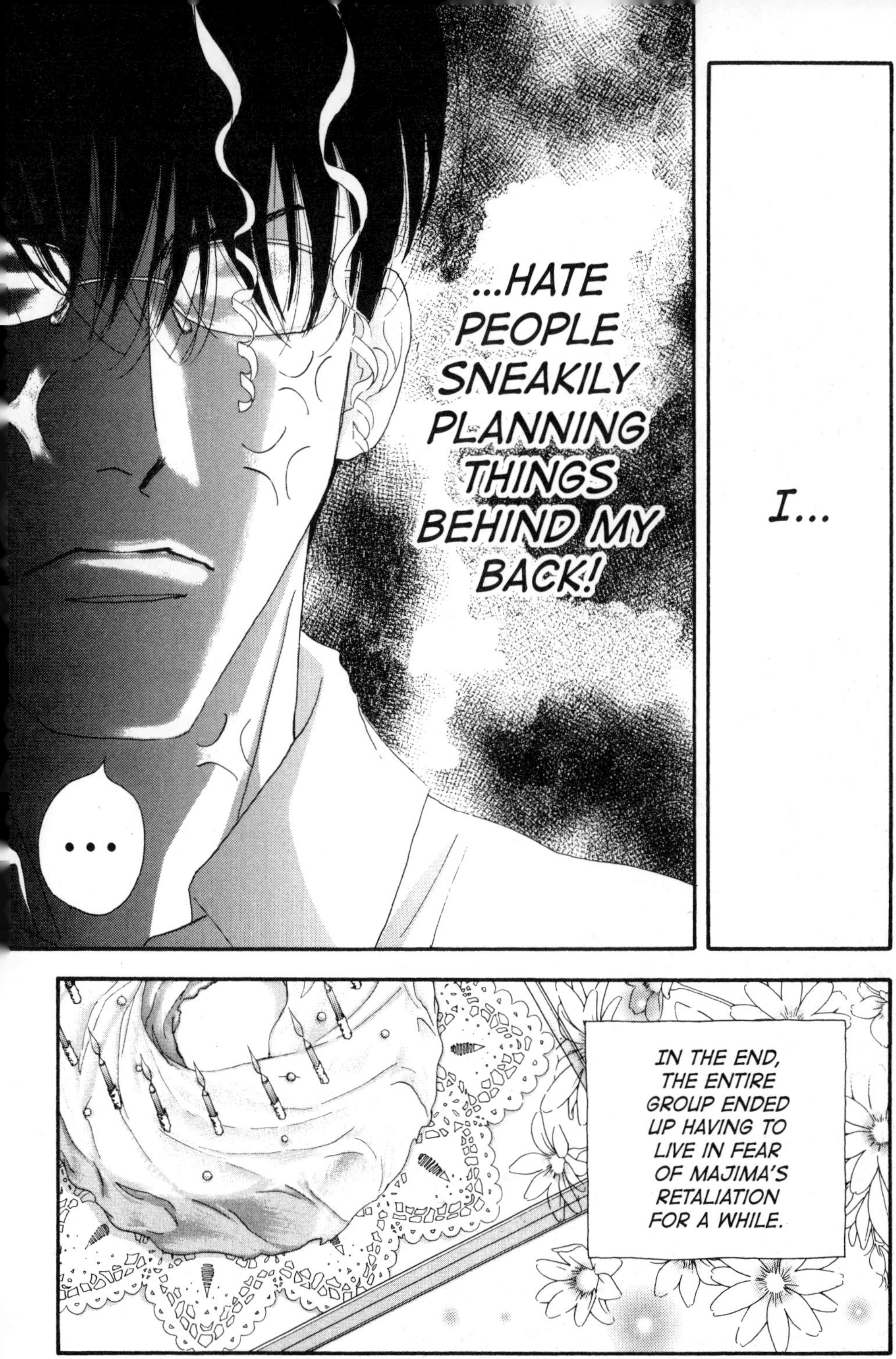
I...
...HATE PEOPLE SNEAKILY PLANNING THINGS BEHIND MY BACK!
...
IN THE END, THE ENTIRE GROUP ENDED UP HAVING TO LIVE IN FEAR OF MAJIMA'S RETALIATION FOR A WHILE.

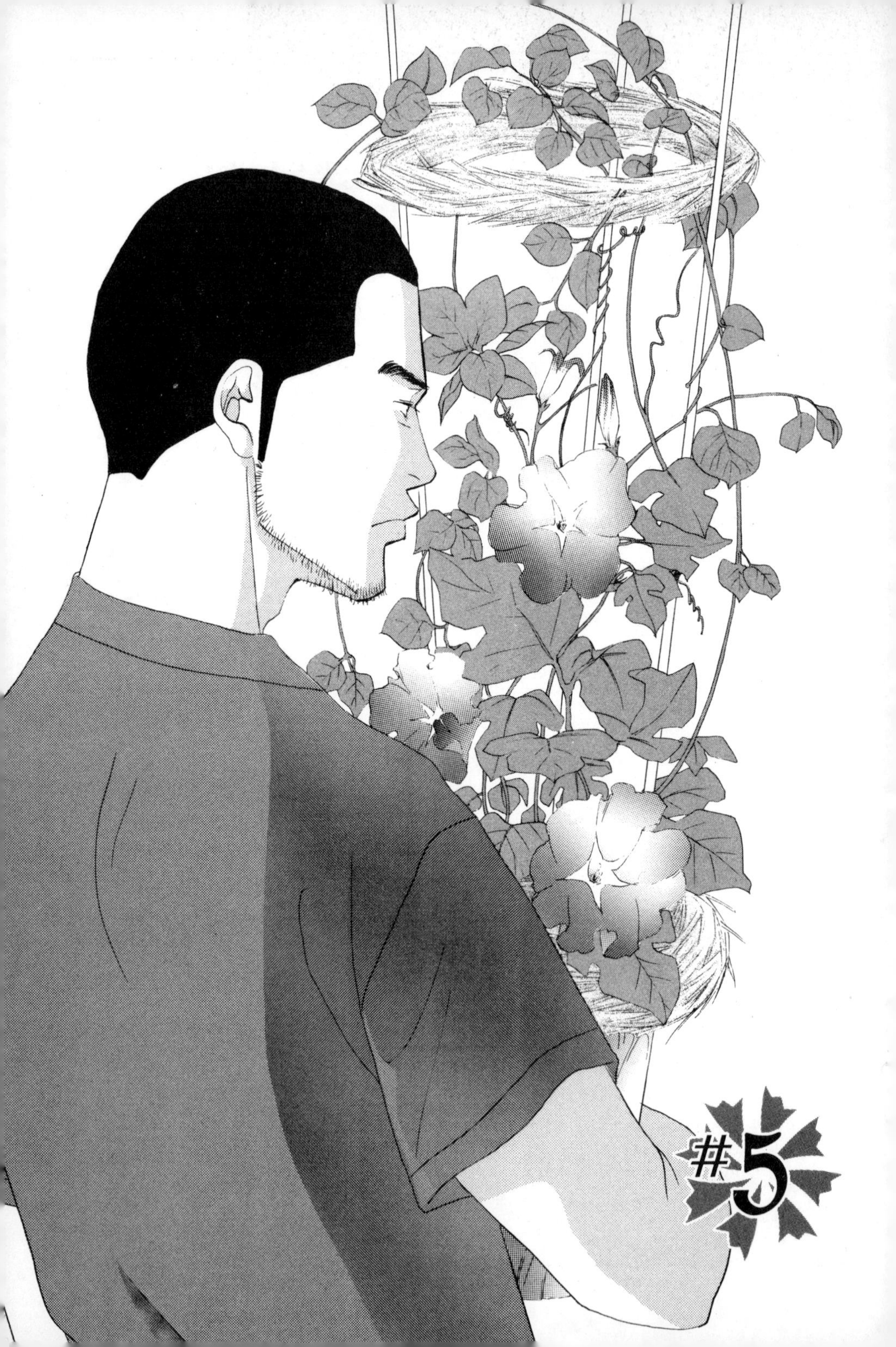
#5

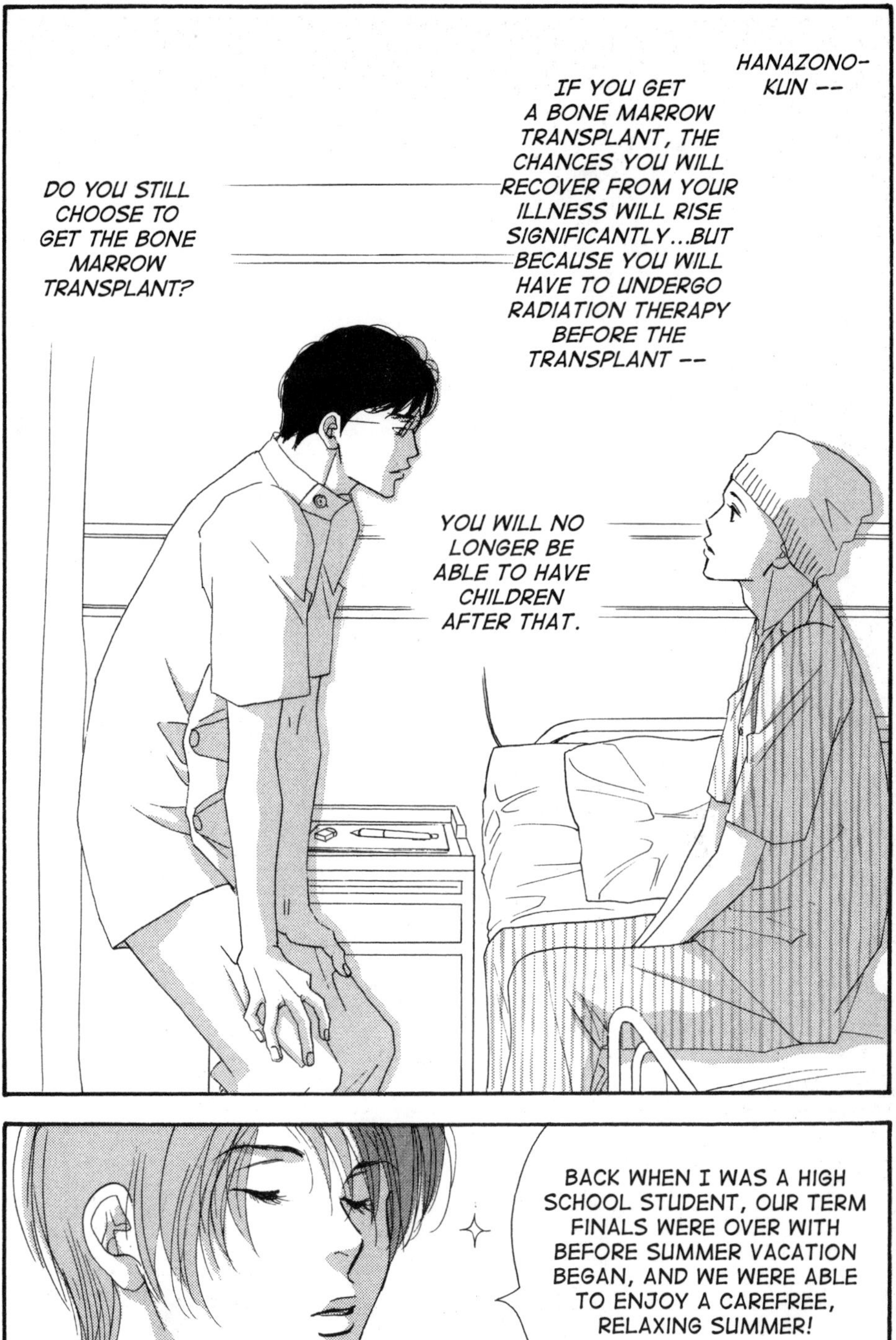
HANAZONO-KUN --
IF YOU GET A BONE MARROW TRANSPLANT, THE CHANCES YOU WILL RECOVER FROM YOUR ILLNESS WILL RISE SIGNIFICANTLY...BUT BECAUSE YOU WILL HAVE TO UNDERGO RADIATION THERAPY BEFORE THE TRANSPLANT --
YOU WILL NO LONGER BE ABLE TO HAVE CHILDREN AFTER THAT.
DO YOU STILL CHOOSE TO GET THE BONE MARROW TRANSPLANT?
BACK WHEN I WAS A HIGH SCHOOL STUDENT, OUR TERM FINALS WERE OVER WITH BEFORE SUMMER VACATION BEGAN, AND WE WERE ABLE TO ENJOY A CAREFREE, RELAXING SUMMER!

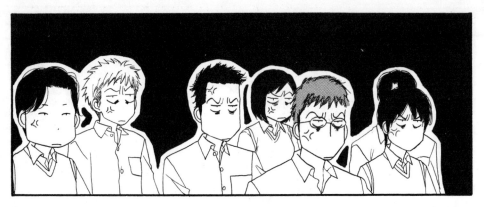

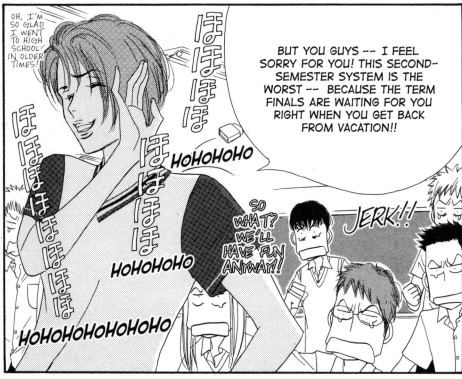

BUT YOU GUYS -- I FEEL SORRY FOR YOU! THIS SECOND-SEMESTER SYSTEM IS THE WORST -- BECAUSE THE TERM FINALS ARE WAITING FOR YOU RIGHT WHEN YOU GET BACK FROM VACATION!!
ほほほほ
HOHOHOHO
JERK!!
SO WHAT? WE'LL HAVE FUN ANYWAY!!
ほほほほ
HOHOHOHO
ほほほほほほほ
HOHOHOHOHOHOHO
OH, I'M SO GLAD I WENT TO HIGH SCHOOL IN OLDER TIMES!

STILL... SUMMER VACATION IS SUMMER VACATION. VARIOUS EVENTS AWAIT.
IN AUGUST, I'M GOING TO MY GRANDMA'S IN SENDAI.

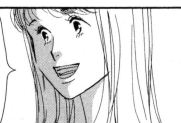

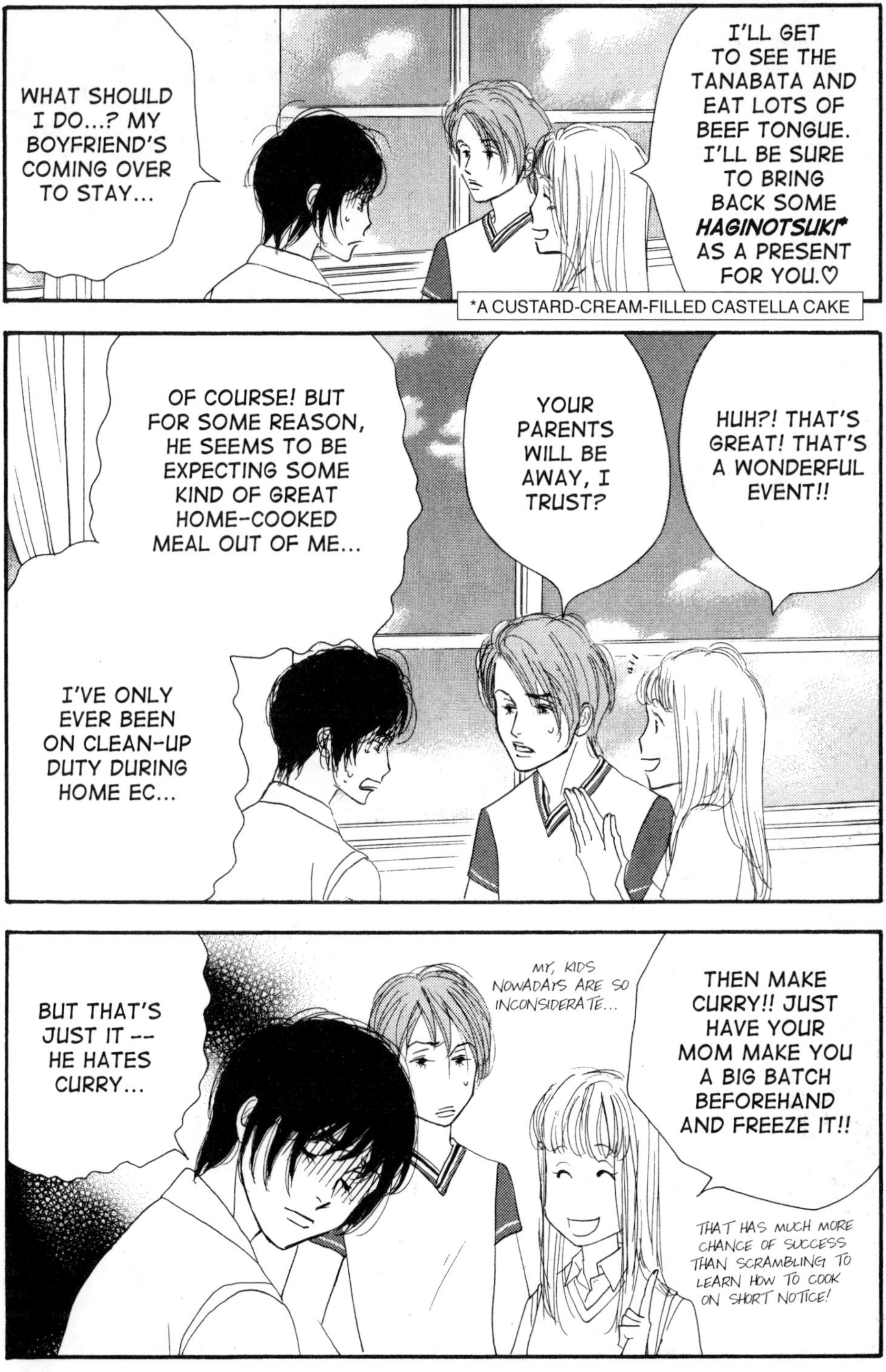
I'LL GET TO SEE THE TANABATA AND EAT LOTS OF BEEF TONGUE. I'LL BE SURE TO BRING BACK SOME ***HAGINOTSUKI**** AS A PRESENT FOR YOU.♡
WHAT SHOULD I DO...? MY BOYFRIEND'S COMING OVER TO STAY...
*A CUSTARD-CREAM-FILLED CASTELLA CAKE
HUH?! THAT'S GREAT! THAT'S A WONDERFUL EVENT!!
YOUR PARENTS WILL BE AWAY, I TRUST?
OF COURSE! BUT FOR SOME REASON, HE SEEMS TO BE EXPECTING SOME KIND OF GREAT HOME-COOKED MEAL OUT OF ME...
I'VE ONLY EVER BEEN ON CLEAN-UP DUTY DURING HOME EC...
THEN MAKE CURRY!! JUST HAVE YOUR MOM MAKE YOU A BIG BATCH BEFOREHAND AND FREEZE IT!!
THAT HAS MUCH MORE CHANCE OF SUCCESS THAN SCRAMBLING TO LEARN HOW TO COOK ON SHORT NOTICE!
MY, KIDS NOWADAYS ARE SO INCONSIDERATE...
BUT THAT'S JUST IT -- HE HATES CURRY...

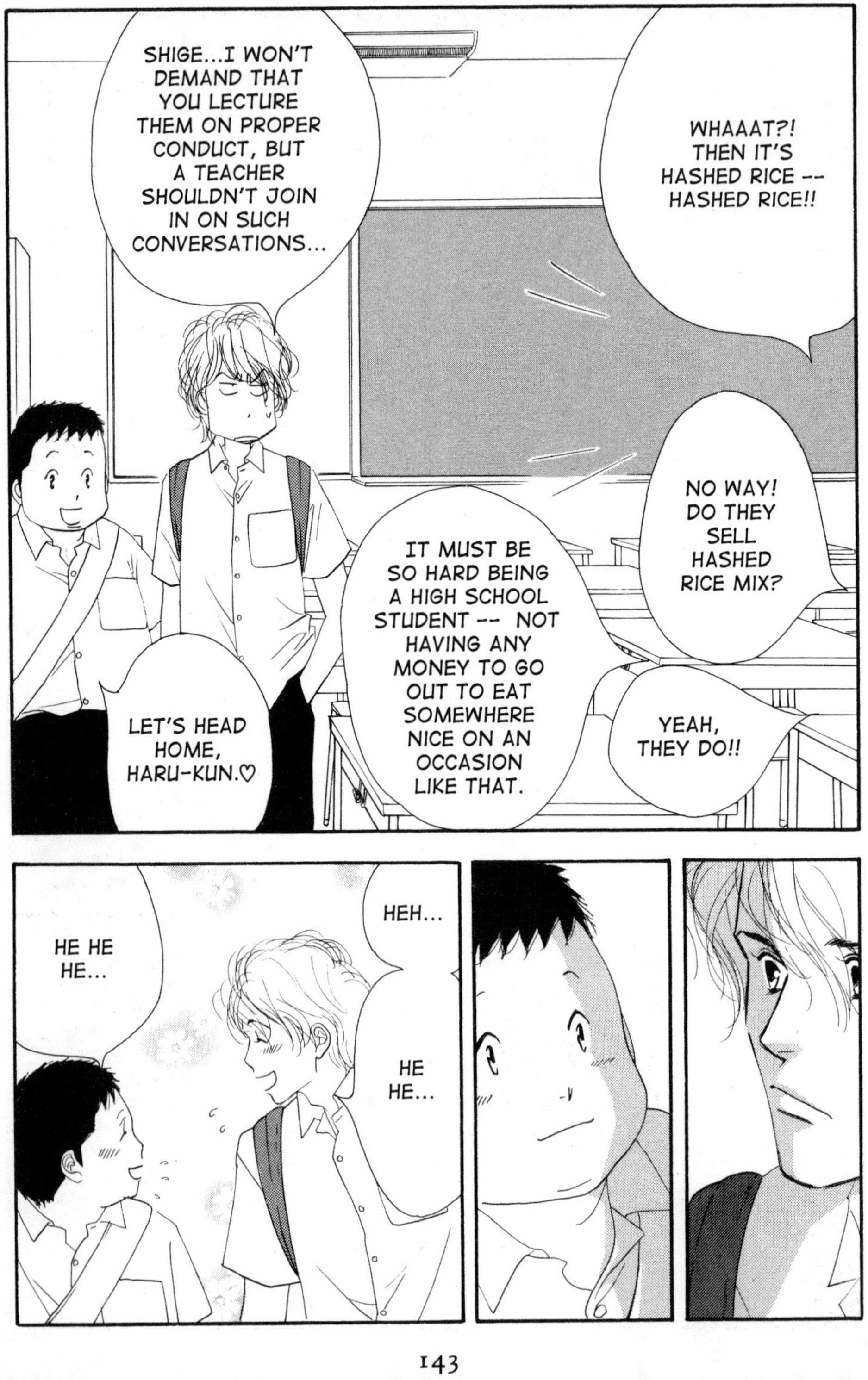
WHAAAT?! THEN IT'S HASHED RICE -- HASHED RICE!!
SHIGE...I WON'T DEMAND THAT YOU LECTURE THEM ON PROPER CONDUCT, BUT A TEACHER SHOULDN'T JOIN IN ON SUCH CONVERSATIONS...
NO WAY! DO THEY SELL HASHED RICE MIX?
IT MUST BE SO HARD BEING A HIGH SCHOOL STUDENT -- NOT HAVING ANY MONEY TO GO OUT TO EAT SOMEWHERE NICE ON AN OCCASION LIKE THAT.
YEAH, THEY DO!!
LET'S HEAD HOME, HARU-KUN.♡
HEH...
HE HE HE...
HE HE...

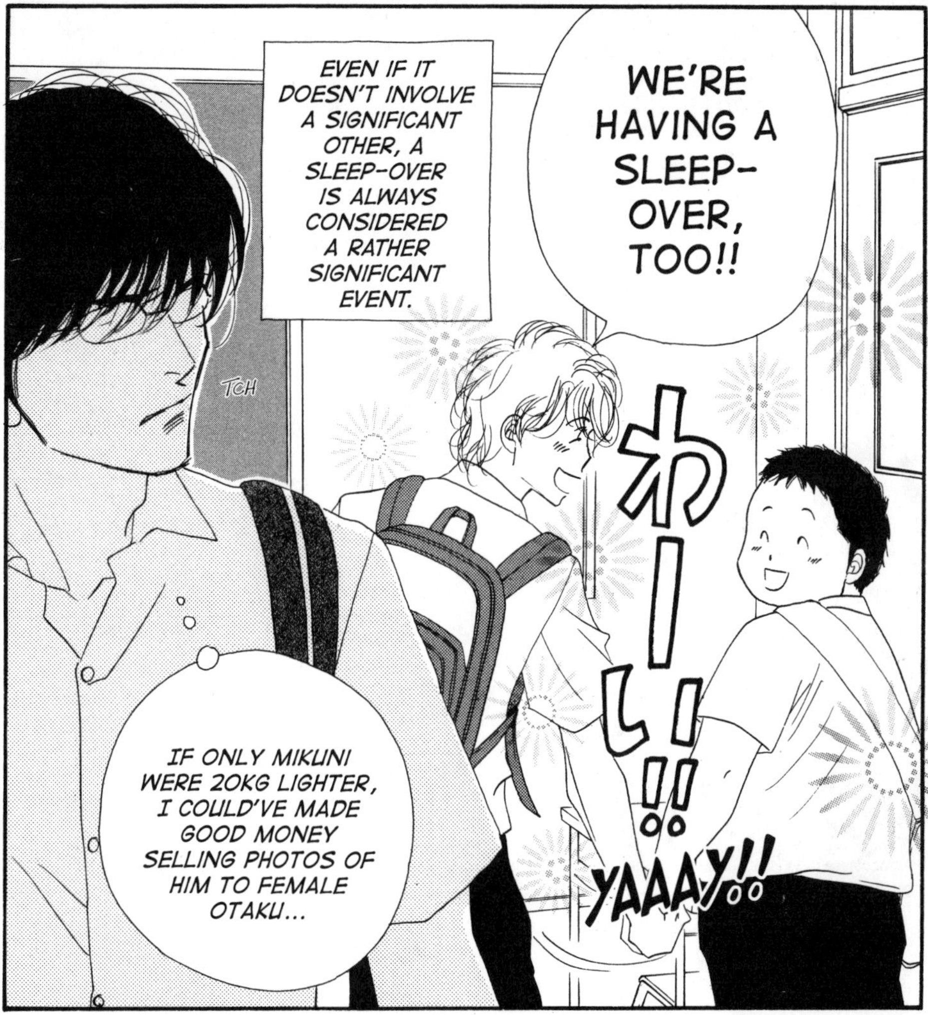
WE'RE HAVING A SLEEP-OVER, TOO!!
EVEN IF IT DOESN'T INVOLVE A SIGNIFICANT OTHER, A SLEEP-OVER IS ALWAYS CONSIDERED A RATHER SIGNIFICANT EVENT.
わーい!!
YAAAY!!
TCH
IF ONLY MIKUNI WERE 20KG LIGHTER, I COULD'VE MADE GOOD MONEY SELLING PHOTOS OF HIM TO FEMALE OTAKU...

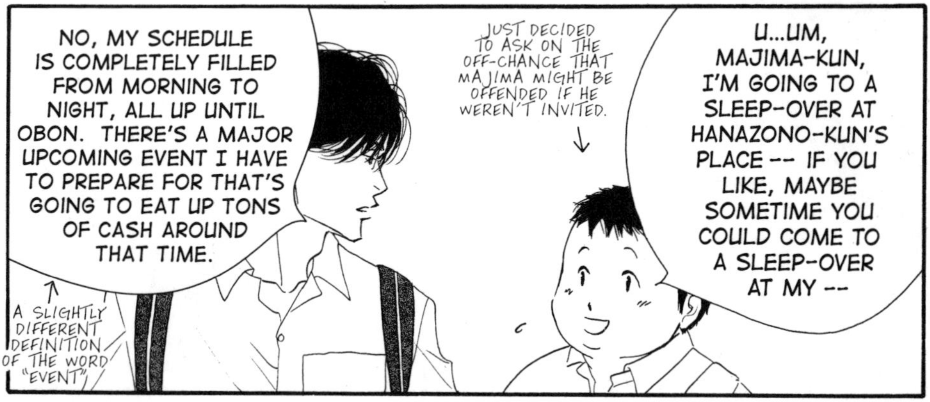
U...UM, MAJIMA-KUN, I'M GOING TO A SLEEP-OVER AT HANAZONO-KUN'S PLACE -- IF YOU LIKE, MAYBE SOMETIME YOU COULD COME TO A SLEEP-OVER AT MY --
JUST DECIDED TO ASK ON THE OFF-CHANCE THAT MAJIMA MIGHT BE OFFENDED IF HE WEREN'T INVITED.
NO, MY SCHEDULE IS COMPLETELY FILLED FROM MORNING TO NIGHT, ALL UP UNTIL OBON. THERE'S A MAJOR UPCOMING EVENT I HAVE TO PREPARE FOR THAT'S GOING TO EAT UP TONS OF CASH AROUND THAT TIME.
A SLIGHTLY DIFFERENT DEFINITION OF THE WORD "EVENT"

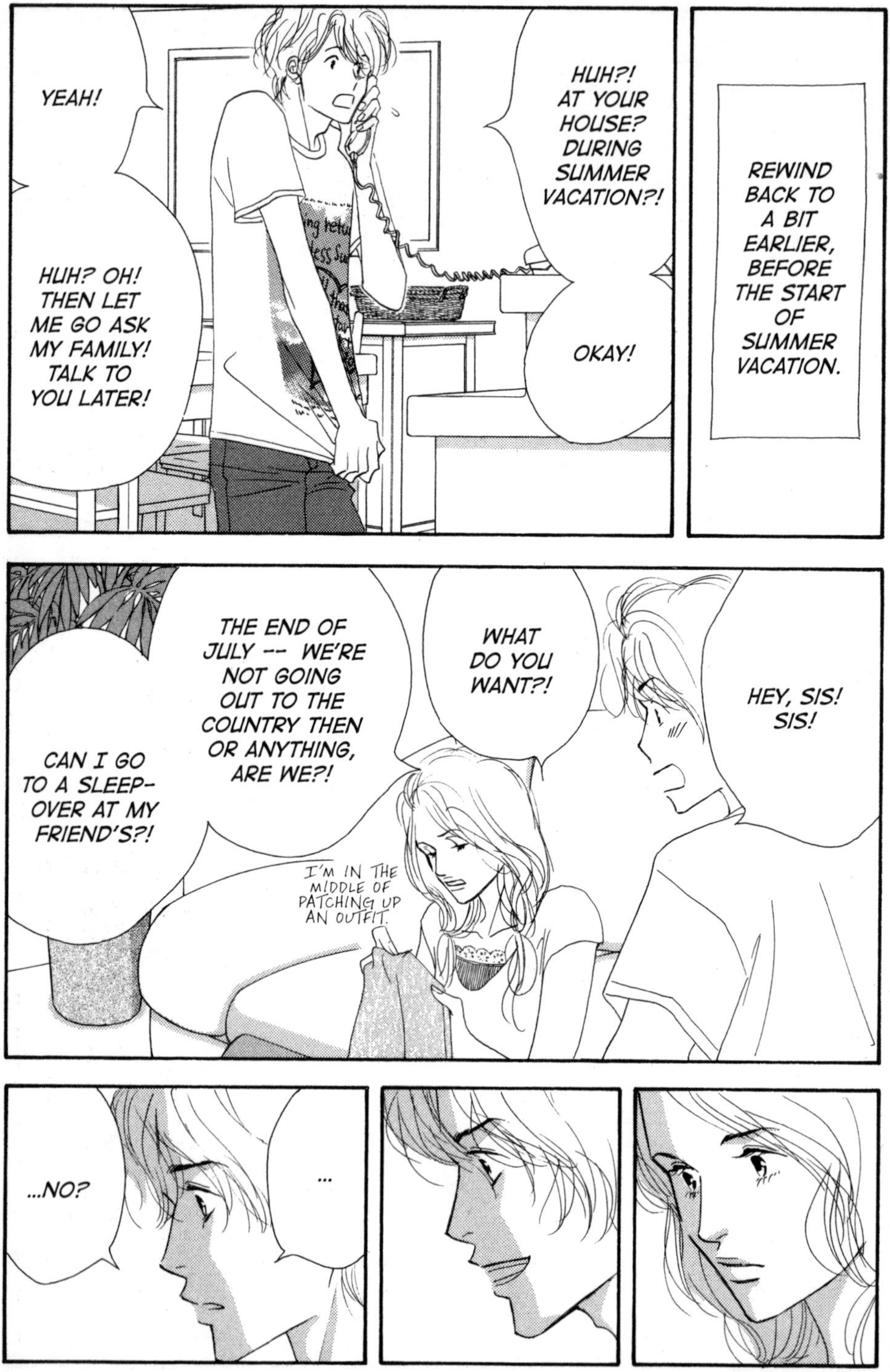
REWIND BACK TO A BIT EARLIER, BEFORE THE START OF SUMMER VACATION.
HUH?! AT YOUR HOUSE? DURING SUMMER VACATION?!
OKAY!
YEAH!
HUH? OH! THEN LET ME GO ASK MY FAMILY! TALK TO YOU LATER!
HEY, SIS! SIS!
WHAT DO YOU WANT?!
I'M IN THE MIDDLE OF PATCHING UP AN OUTFIT.
THE END OF JULY -- WE'RE NOT GOING OUT TO THE COUNTRY THEN OR ANYTHING, ARE WE?!
CAN I GO TO A SLEEP-OVER AT MY FRIEND'S?!
...
...NO?

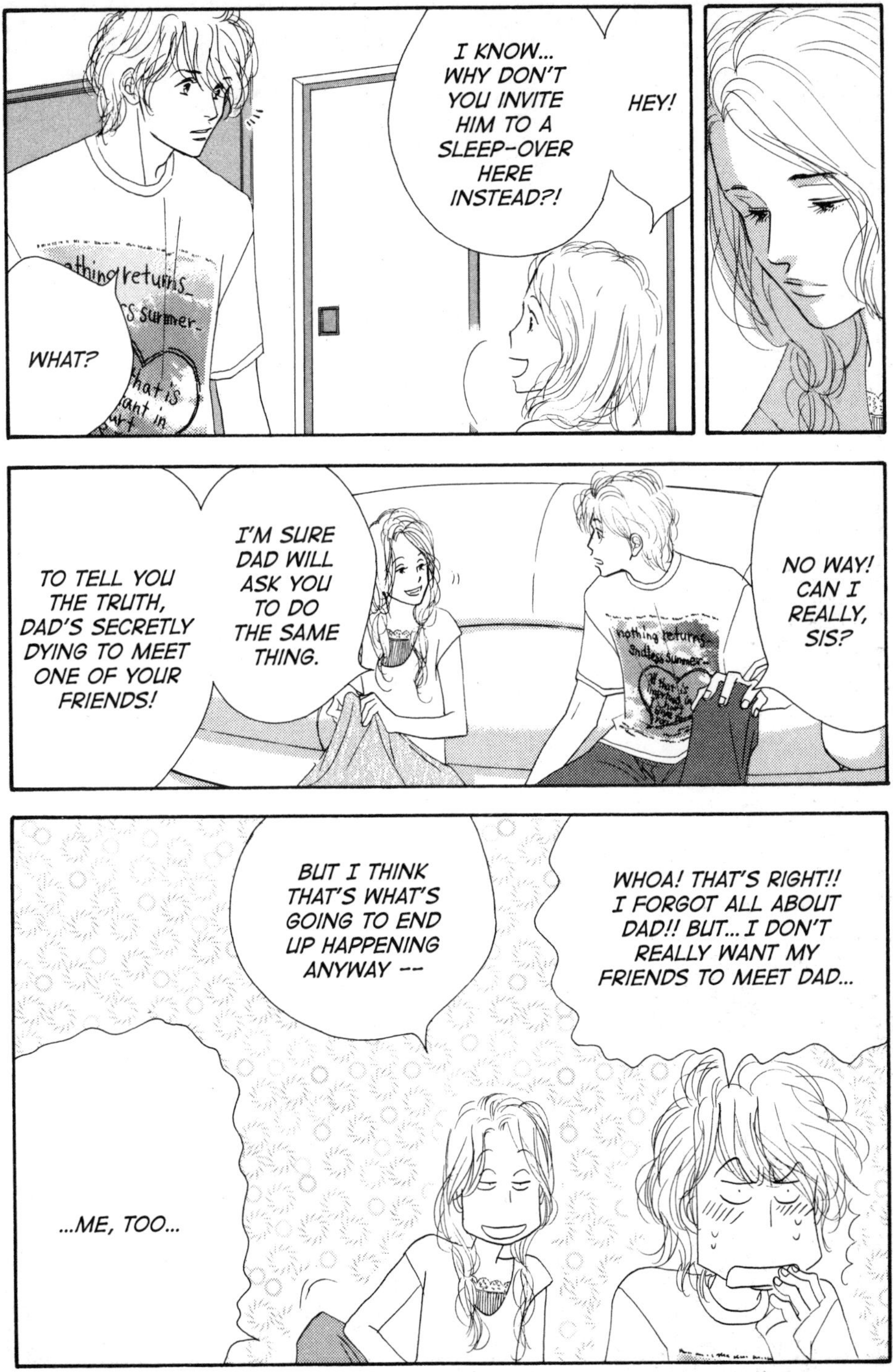
HEY!
I KNOW... WHY DON'T YOU INVITE HIM TO A SLEEP-OVER HERE INSTEAD?!
WHAT?
NO WAY! CAN I REALLY, SIS?
I'M SURE DAD WILL ASK YOU TO DO THE SAME THING.
TO TELL YOU THE TRUTH, DAD'S SECRETLY DYING TO MEET ONE OF YOUR FRIENDS!
WHOA! THAT'S RIGHT!! I FORGOT ALL ABOUT DAD!! BUT... I DON'T REALLY WANT MY FRIENDS TO MEET DAD...
BUT I THINK THAT'S WHAT'S GOING TO END UP HAPPENING ANYWAY --
...ME, TOO...

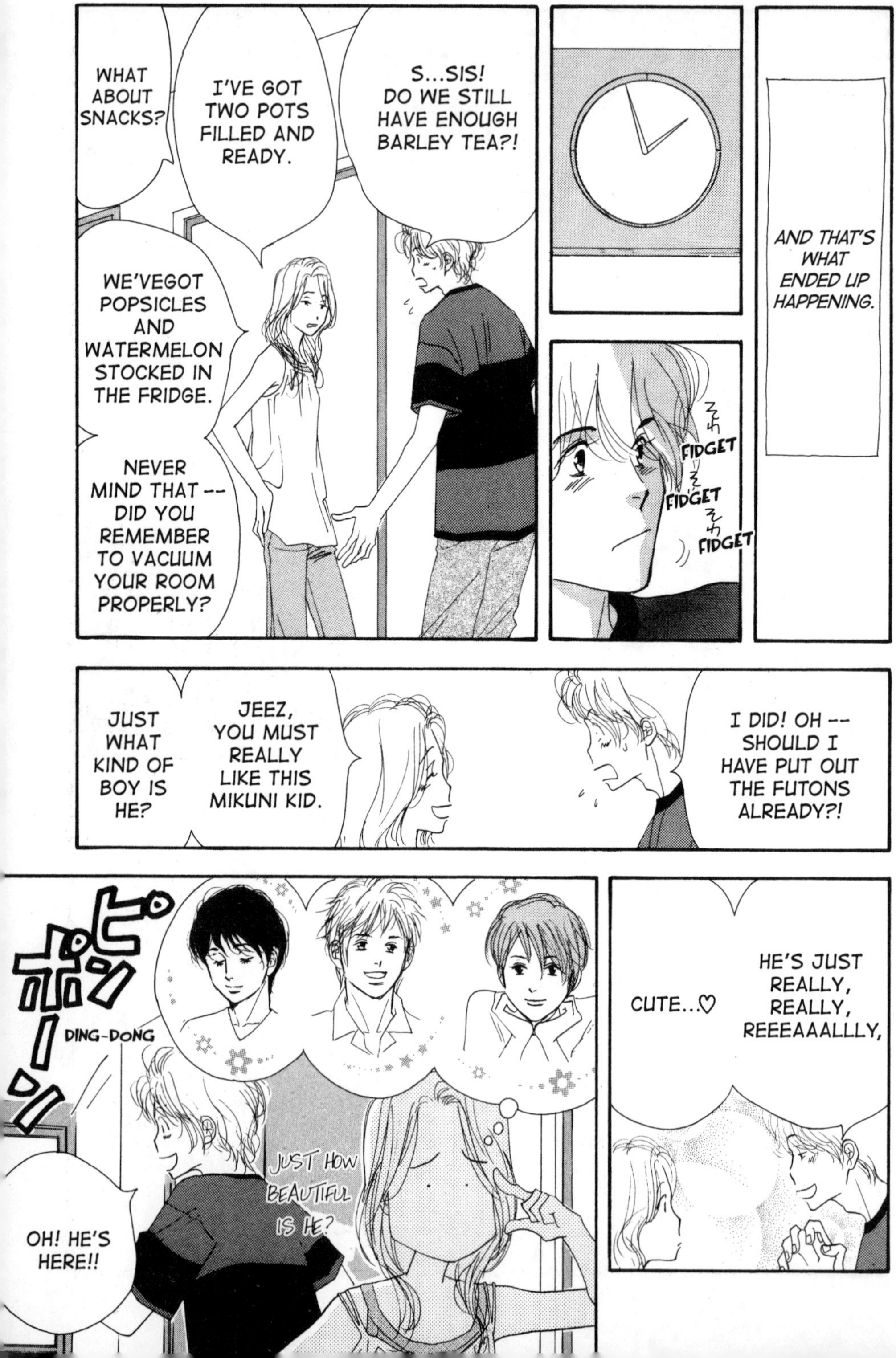
AND THAT'S WHAT ENDED UP HAPPENING.
FIDGET
FIDGET
FIDGET
S...SIS! DO WE STILL HAVE ENOUGH BARLEY TEA?!
I'VE GOT TWO POTS FILLED AND READY.
WHAT ABOUT SNACKS?
WE'VEGOT POPSICLES AND WATERMELON STOCKED IN THE FRIDGE.
NEVER MIND THAT -- DID YOU REMEMBER TO VACUUM YOUR ROOM PROPERLY?
I DID! OH -- SHOULD I HAVE PUT OUT THE FUTONS ALREADY?!
JEEZ, YOU MUST REALLY LIKE THIS MIKUNI KID.
JUST WHAT KIND OF BOY IS HE?
HE'S JUST REALLY, REALLY, REEEAAALLLY,
CUTE...♡
JUST HOW BEAUTIFUL IS HE?
ピンポーン
DING-DONG
OH! HE'S HERE!!

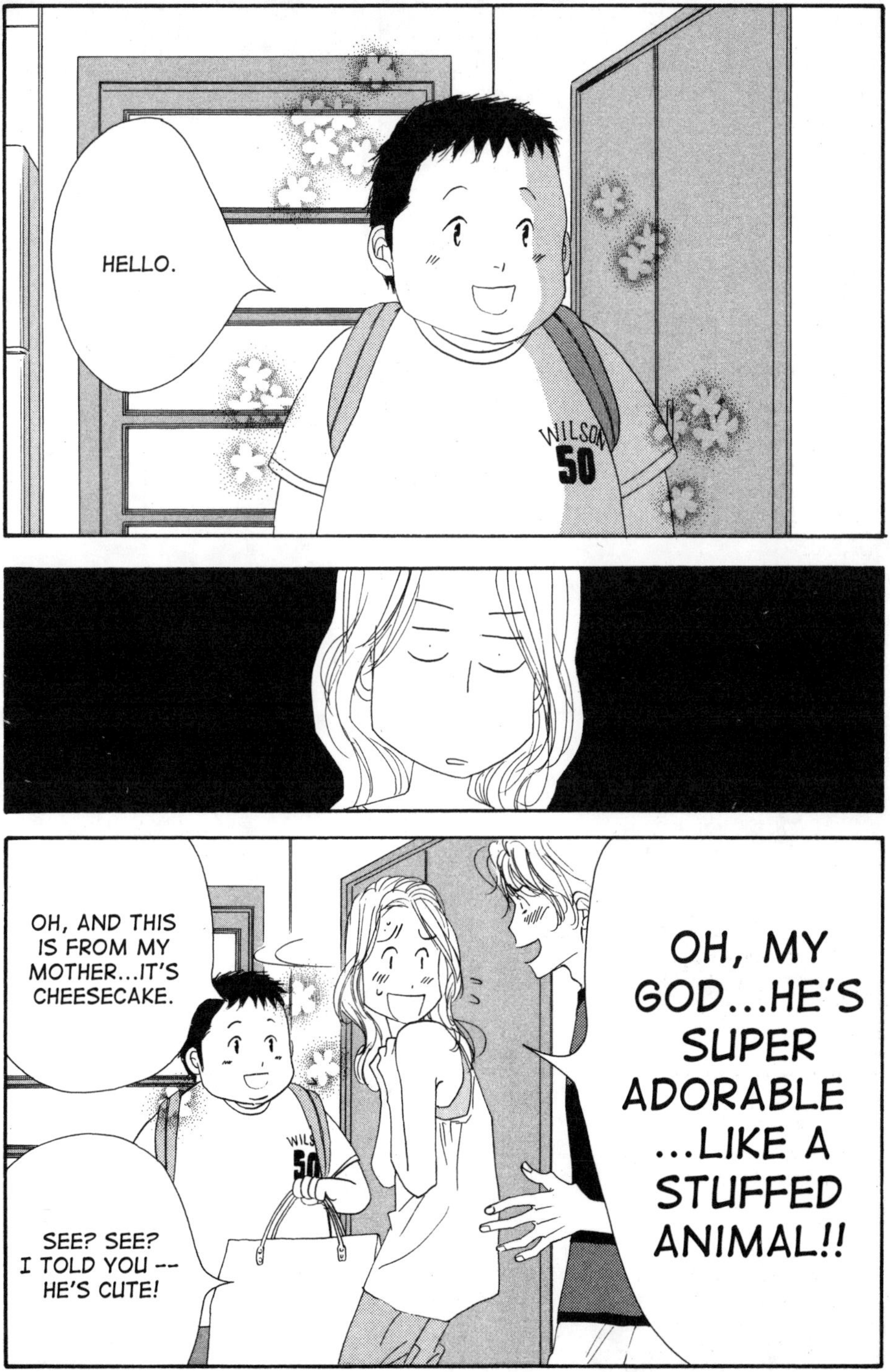
HELLO.
OH, MY GOD...HE'S SUPER ADORABLE ...LIKE A STUFFED ANIMAL!!
OH, AND THIS IS FROM MY MOTHER...IT'S CHEESECAKE.
SEE? SEE? I TOLD YOU -- HE'S CUTE!

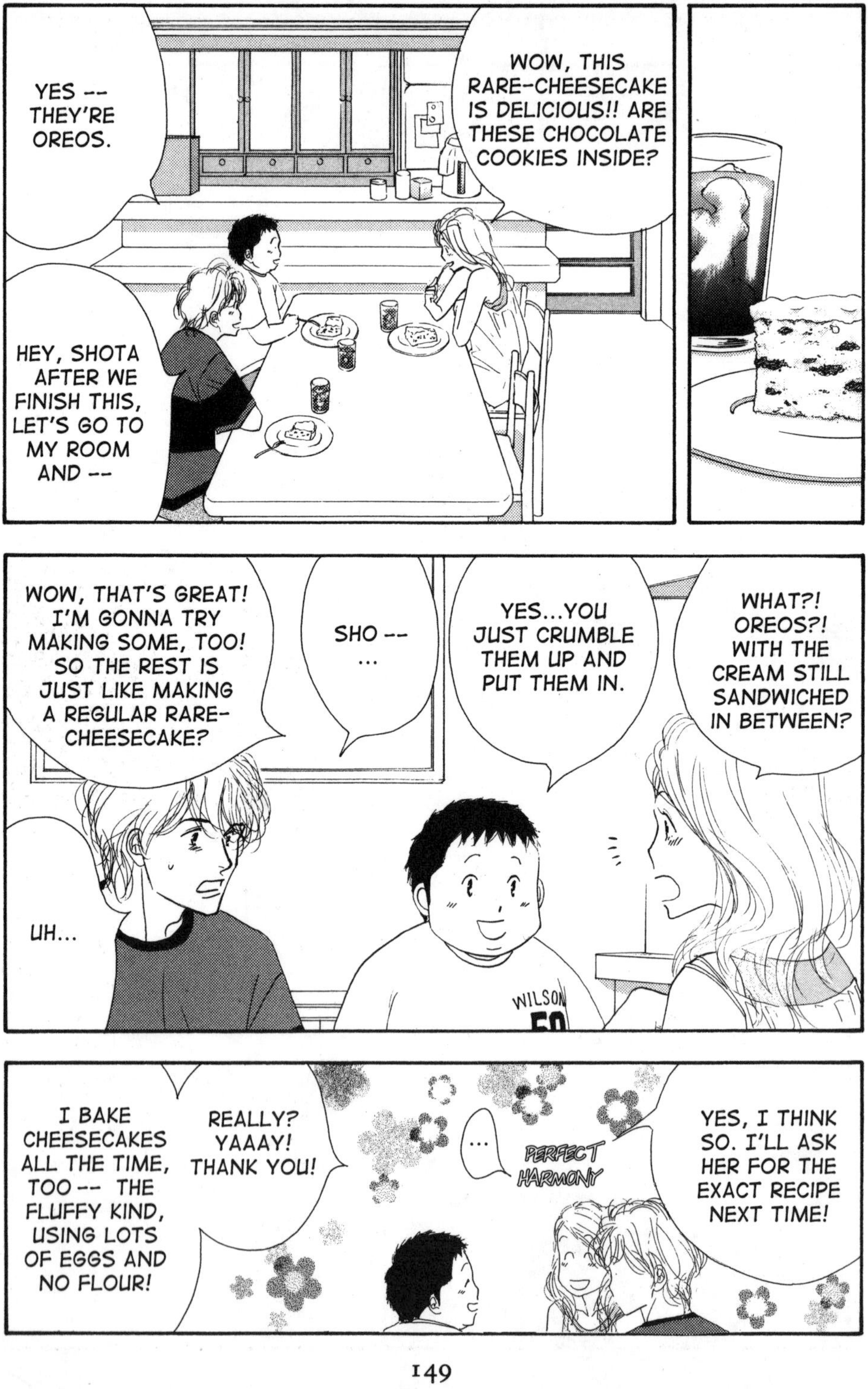
WOW, THIS RARE-CHEESECAKE IS DELICIOUS!! ARE THESE CHOCOLATE COOKIES INSIDE?
YES -- THEY'RE OREOS.
HEY, SHOTA AFTER WE FINISH THIS, LET'S GO TO MY ROOM AND --
WHAT?! OREOS?! WITH THE CREAM STILL SANDWICHED IN BETWEEN?
YES...YOU JUST CRUMBLE THEM UP AND PUT THEM IN.
SHO -- ...
WOW, THAT'S GREAT! I'M GONNA TRY MAKING SOME, TOO! SO THE REST IS JUST LIKE MAKING A REGULAR RARE-CHEESECAKE?
UH...
WILSON
YES, I THINK SO. I'LL ASK HER FOR THE EXACT RECIPE NEXT TIME!
...
PERFECT HARMONY
REALLY? YAAAY! THANK YOU!
I BAKE CHEESECAKES ALL THE TIME, TOO -- THE FLUFFY KIND, USING LOTS OF EGGS AND NO FLOUR!

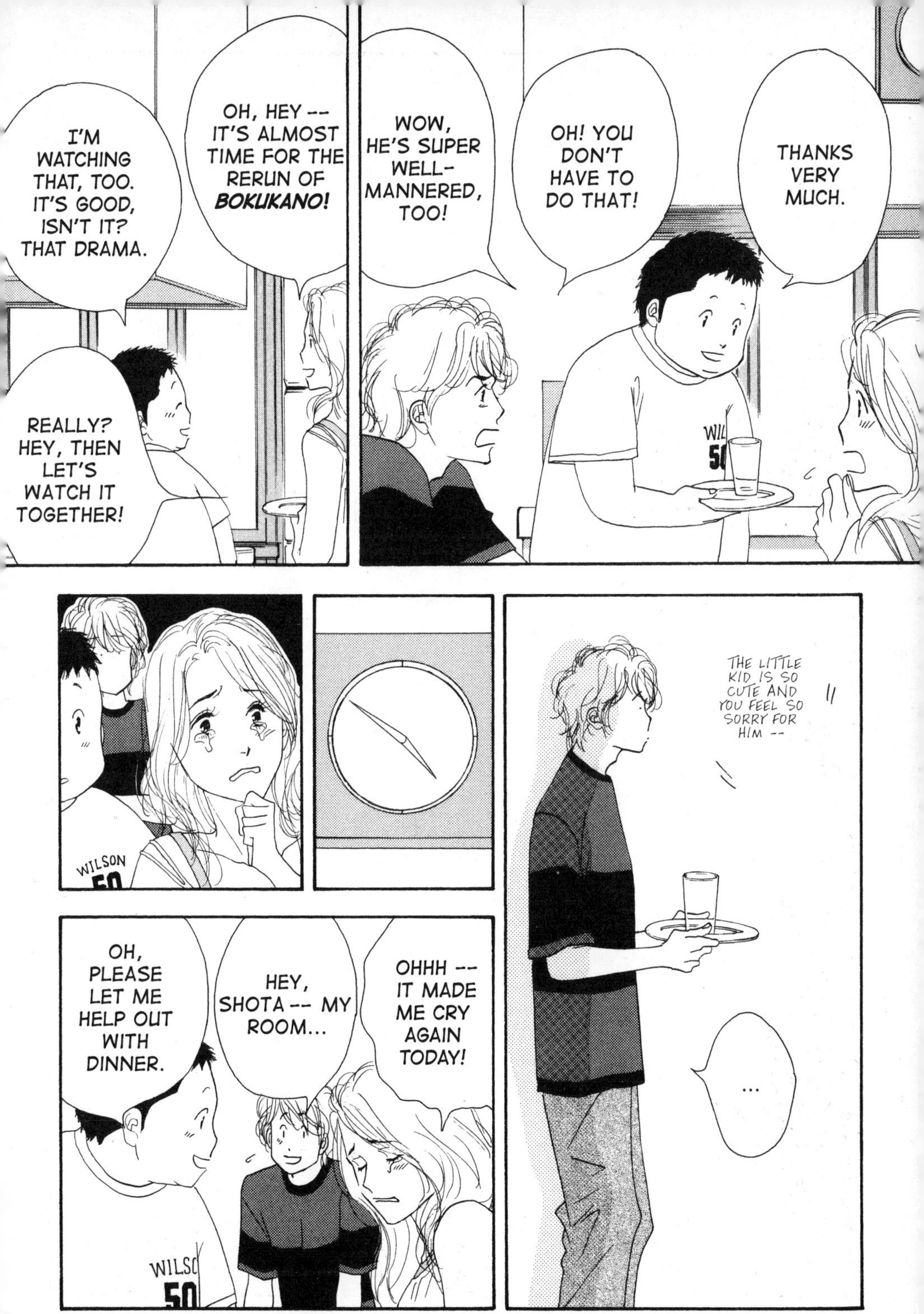
THANKS VERY MUCH.
OH! YOU DON'T HAVE TO DO THAT!
WOW, HE'S SUPER WELL-MANNERED, TOO!
OH, HEY -- IT'S ALMOST TIME FOR THE RERUN OF *BOKUKANO!*
I'M WATCHING THAT, TOO. IT'S GOOD, ISN'T IT? THAT DRAMA.
REALLY? HEY, THEN LET'S WATCH IT TOGETHER!
THE LITTLE KID IS SO CUTE AND YOU FEEL SO SORRY FOR HIM --
...
WILSON 50
OHHH -- IT MADE ME CRY AGAIN TODAY!
HEY, SHOTA -- MY ROOM...
OH, PLEASE LET ME HELP OUT WITH DINNER.

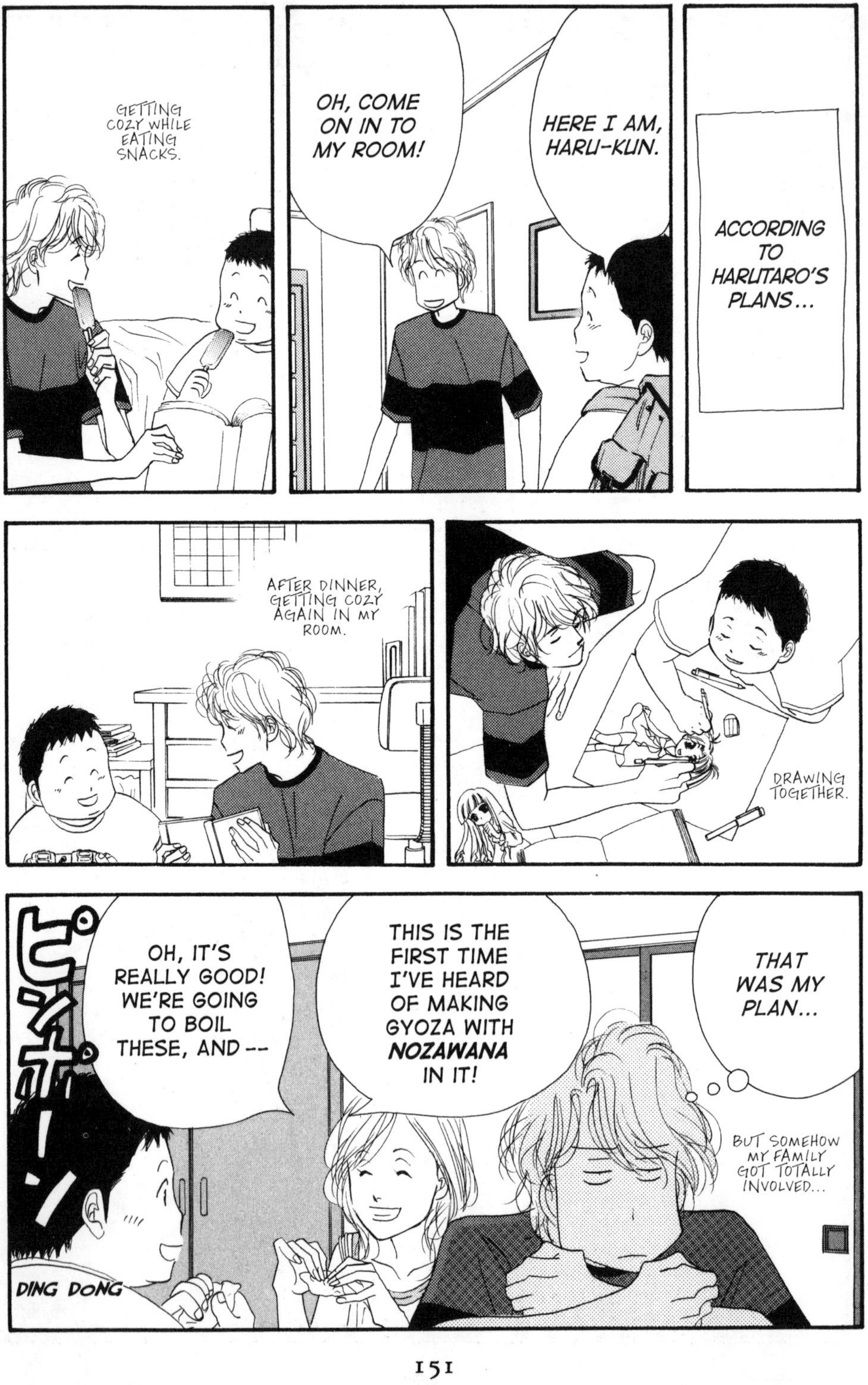
ACCORDING TO HARUTARO'S PLANS...
HERE I AM, HARU-KUN.
OH, COME ON IN TO MY ROOM!
GETTING COZY WHILE EATING SNACKS.
DRAWING TOGETHER.
AFTER DINNER, GETTING COZY AGAIN IN MY ROOM.
THAT WAS MY PLAN...
BUT SOMEHOW MY FAMILY GOT TOTALLY INVOLVED...
THIS IS THE FIRST TIME I'VE HEARD OF MAKING GYOZA WITH **NOZAWANA** IN IT!
OH, IT'S REALLY GOOD! WE'RE GOING TO BOIL THESE, AND --
ピンポーン
DING DONG

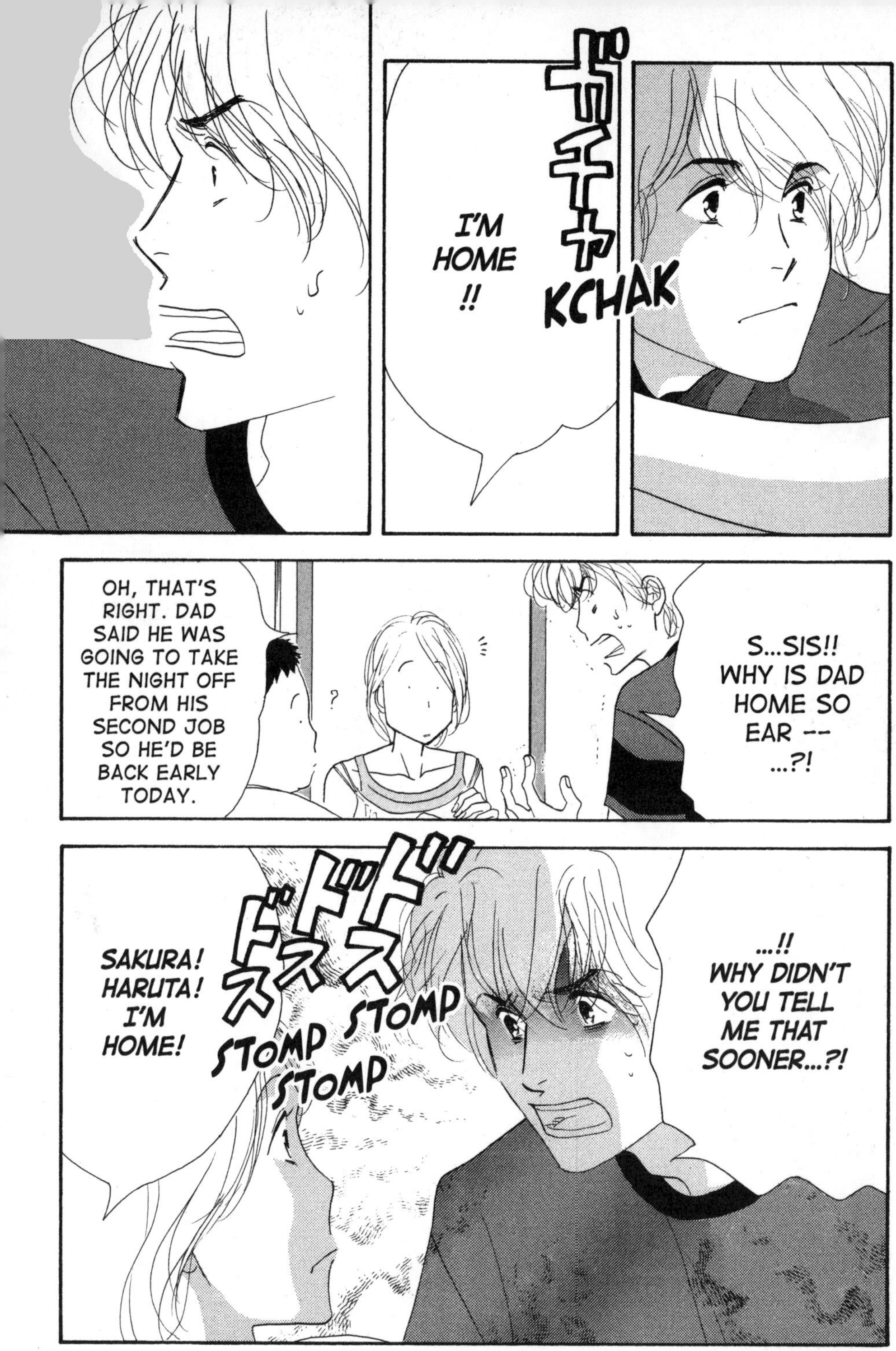
KCHAK
I'M HOME!!
S...SIS!! WHY IS DAD HOME SO EAR -- ...?!
OH, THAT'S RIGHT. DAD SAID HE WAS GOING TO TAKE THE NIGHT OFF FROM HIS SECOND JOB SO HE'D BE BACK EARLY TODAY.
...!! WHY DIDN'T YOU TELL ME THAT SOONER...?!
STOMP STOMP STOMP
SAKURA! HARUTA! I'M HOME!

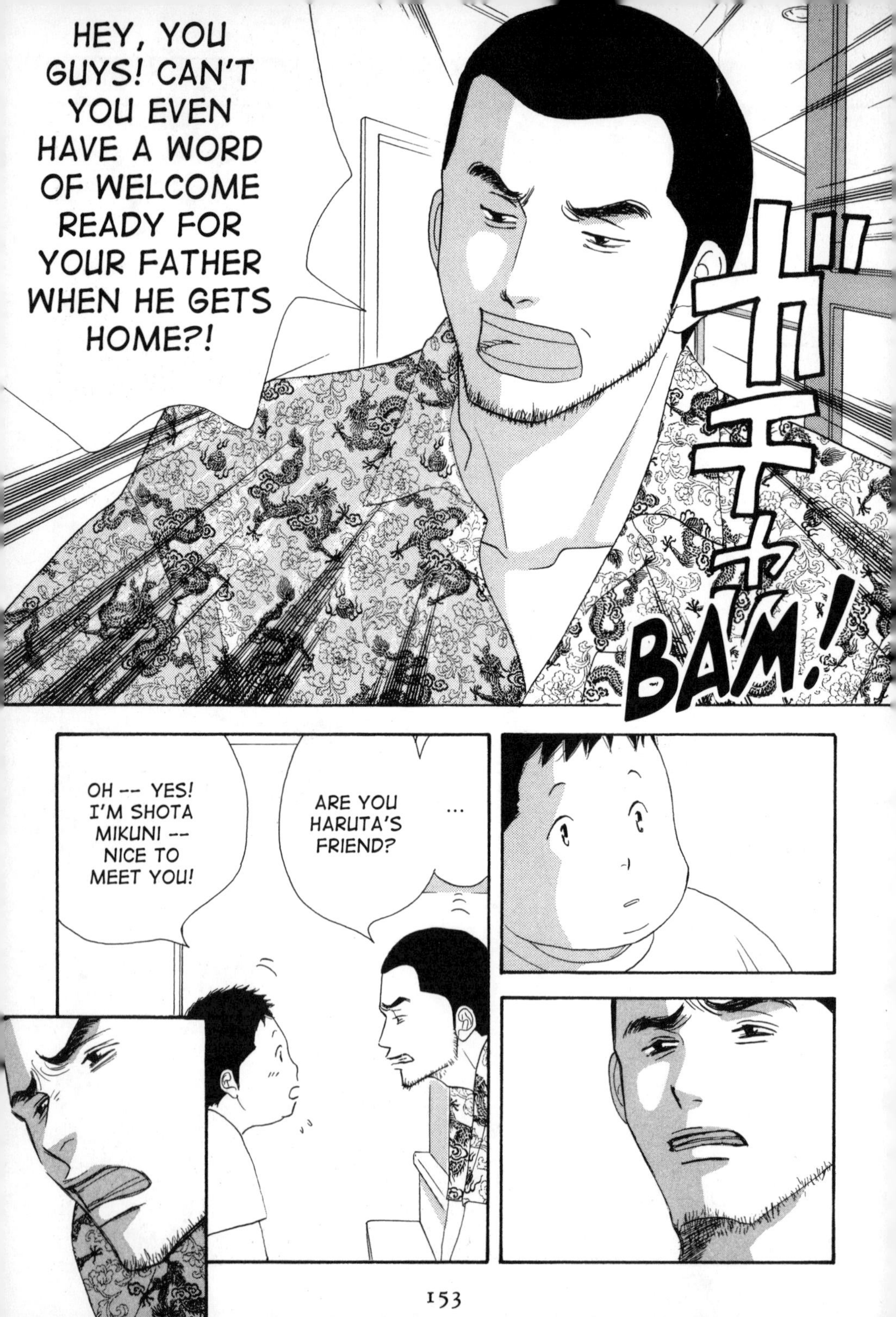
HEY, YOU GUYS! CAN'T YOU EVEN HAVE A WORD OF WELCOME READY FOR YOUR FATHER WHEN HE GETS HOME?!
ガチャ
BAM!
...
ARE YOU HARUTA'S FRIEND?
OH -- YES! I'M SHOTA MIKUNI -- NICE TO MEET YOU!

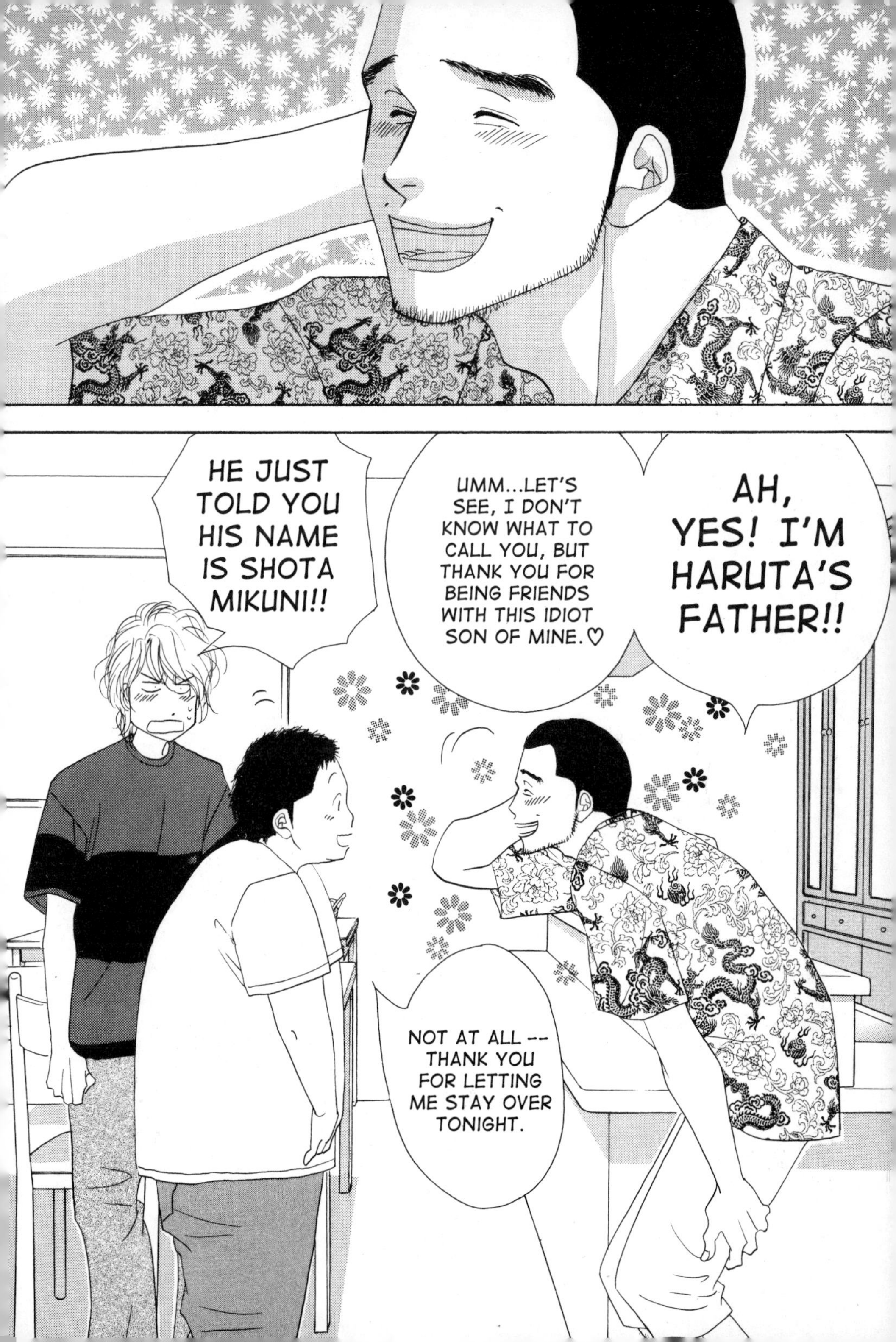
AH, YES! I'M HARUTA'S FATHER!!
UMM...LET'S SEE, I DON'T KNOW WHAT TO CALL YOU, BUT THANK YOU FOR BEING FRIENDS WITH THIS IDIOT SON OF MINE. ♡
HE JUST TOLD YOU HIS NAME IS SHOTA MIKUNI!!
NOT AT ALL -- THANK YOU FOR LETTING ME STAY OVER TONIGHT.

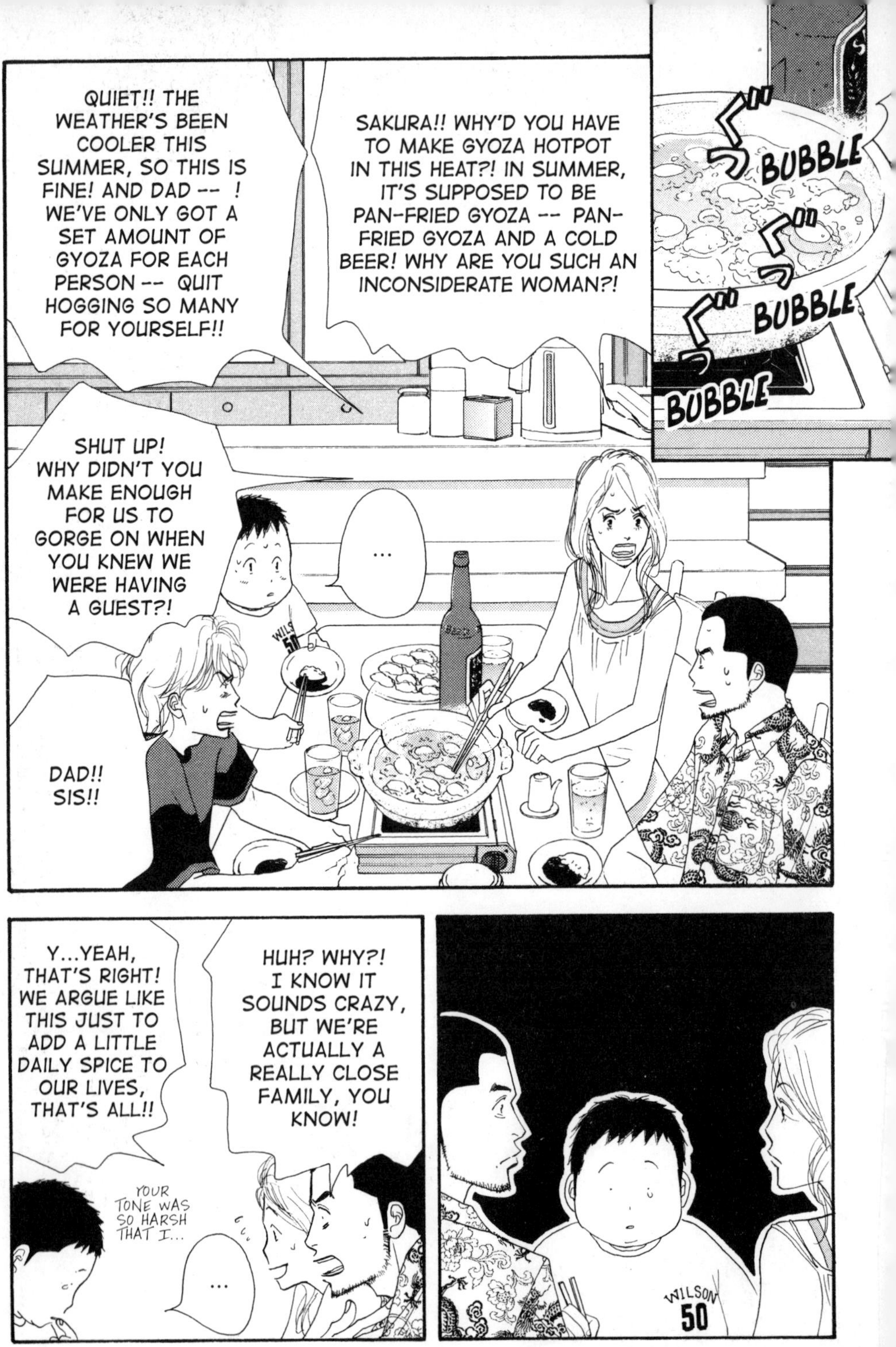
BUBBLE
BUBBLE
BUBBLE
SAKURA!! WHY'D YOU HAVE TO MAKE GYOZA HOTPOT IN THIS HEAT?! IN SUMMER, IT'S SUPPOSED TO BE PAN-FRIED GYOZA -- PAN-FRIED GYOZA AND A COLD BEER! WHY ARE YOU SUCH AN INCONSIDERATE WOMAN?!
QUIET!! THE WEATHER'S BEEN COOLER THIS SUMMER, SO THIS IS FINE! AND DAD -- ! WE'VE ONLY GOT A SET AMOUNT OF GYOZA FOR EACH PERSON -- QUIT HOGGING SO MANY FOR YOURSELF!!
SHUT UP! WHY DIDN'T YOU MAKE ENOUGH FOR US TO GORGE ON WHEN YOU KNEW WE WERE HAVING A GUEST?!
...
DAD!! SIS!!
WILSON 50
HUH? WHY?! I KNOW IT SOUNDS CRAZY, BUT WE'RE ACTUALLY A REALLY CLOSE FAMILY, YOU KNOW!
Y...YEAH, THAT'S RIGHT! WE ARGUE LIKE THIS JUST TO ADD A LITTLE DAILY SPICE TO OUR LIVES, THAT'S ALL!!
YOUR TONE WAS SO HARSH THAT I...
...

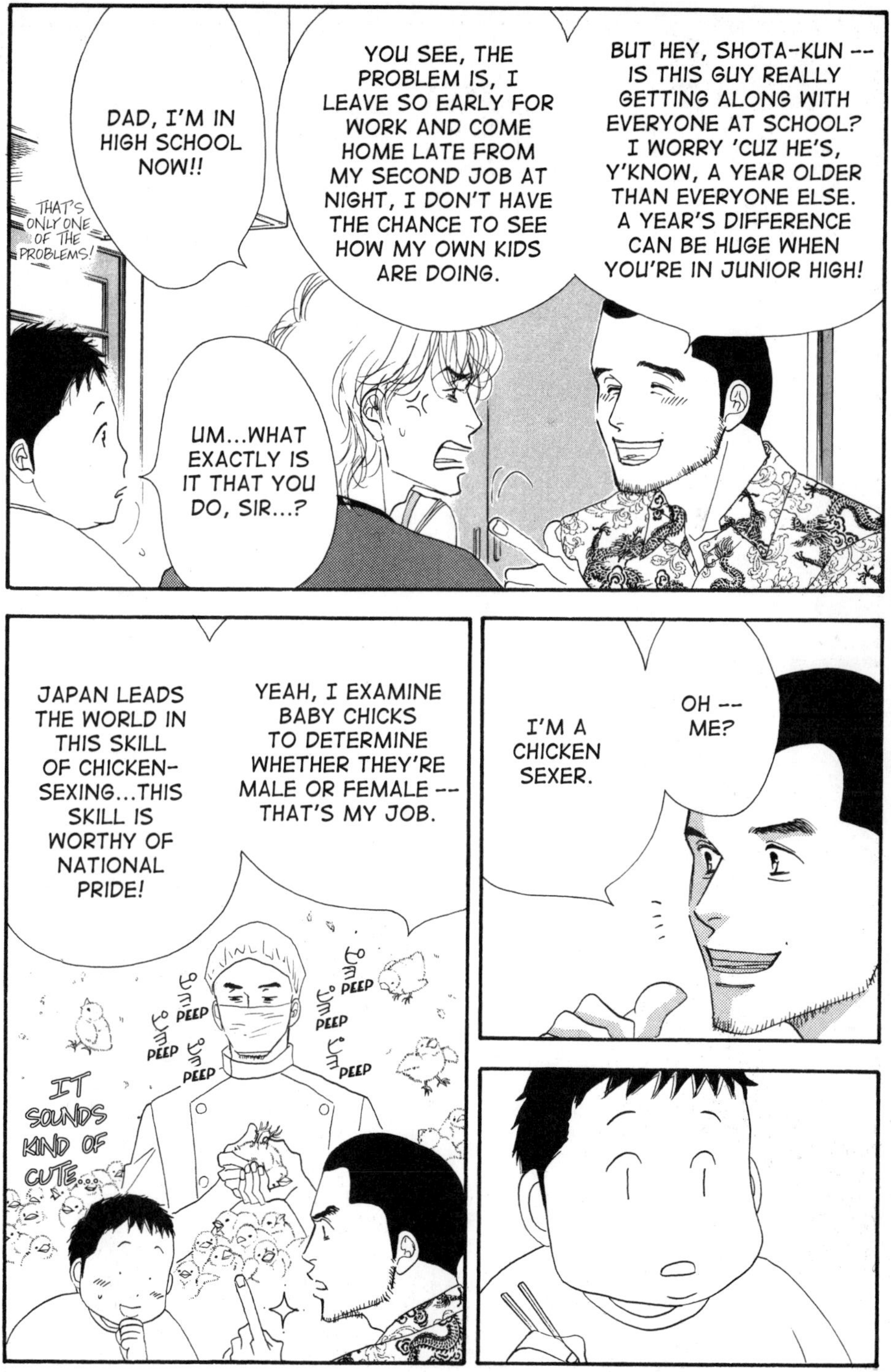
BUT HEY, SHOTA-KUN -- IS THIS GUY REALLY GETTING ALONG WITH EVERYONE AT SCHOOL? I WORRY 'CUZ HE'S, Y'KNOW, A YEAR OLDER THAN EVERYONE ELSE. A YEAR'S DIFFERENCE CAN BE HUGE WHEN YOU'RE IN JUNIOR HIGH!
YOU SEE, THE PROBLEM IS, I LEAVE SO EARLY FOR WORK AND COME HOME LATE FROM MY SECOND JOB AT NIGHT, I DON'T HAVE THE CHANCE TO SEE HOW MY OWN KIDS ARE DOING.
DAD, I'M IN HIGH SCHOOL NOW!!
THAT'S ONLY ONE OF THE PROBLEMS!
UM...WHAT EXACTLY IS IT THAT YOU DO, SIR...?
OH -- ME?
I'M A CHICKEN SEXER.
YEAH, I EXAMINE BABY CHICKS TO DETERMINE WHETHER THEY'RE MALE OR FEMALE -- THAT'S MY JOB.
JAPAN LEADS THE WORLD IN THIS SKILL OF CHICKEN-SEXING...THIS SKILL IS WORTHY OF NATIONAL PRIDE!
ピヨ PEEP
ピヨ PEEP
ピヨ PEEP
ピヨ PEEP
ピヨ PEEP
ピヨ PEEP
IT SOUNDS KIND OF CUTE...

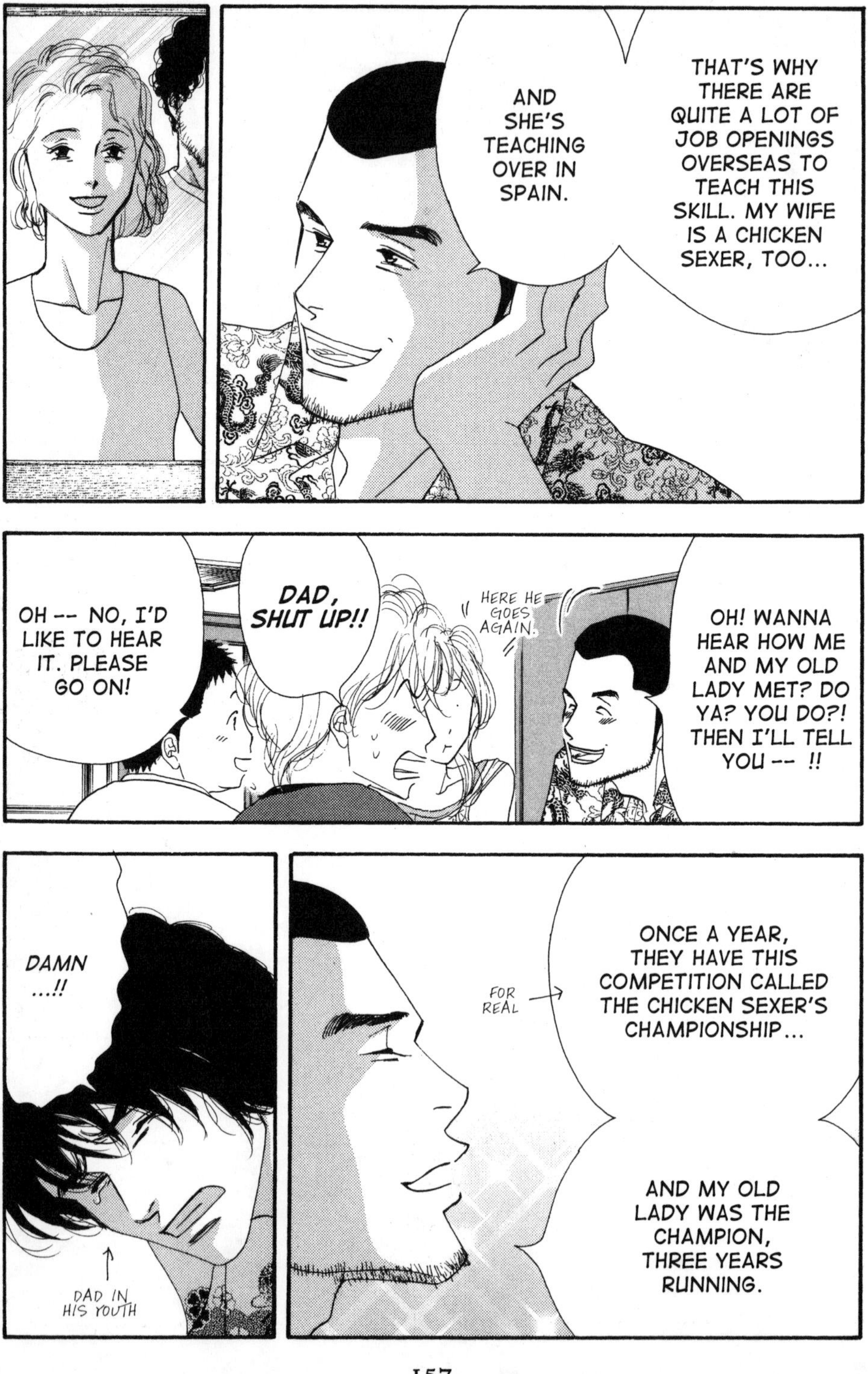
THAT'S WHY THERE ARE QUITE A LOT OF JOB OPENINGS OVERSEAS TO TEACH THIS SKILL. MY WIFE IS A CHICKEN SEXER, TOO...
AND SHE'S TEACHING OVER IN SPAIN.
OH! WANNA HEAR HOW ME AND MY OLD LADY MET? DO YA? YOU DO?! THEN I'LL TELL YOU -- !!
HERE HE GOES AGAIN.
DAD, SHUT UP!!
OH -- NO, I'D LIKE TO HEAR IT. PLEASE GO ON!
ONCE A YEAR, THEY HAVE THIS COMPETITION CALLED THE CHICKEN SEXER'S CHAMPIONSHIP...
FOR REAL
AND MY OLD LADY WAS THE CHAMPION, THREE YEARS RUNNING.
DAMN ...!!
DAD IN HIS YOUTH

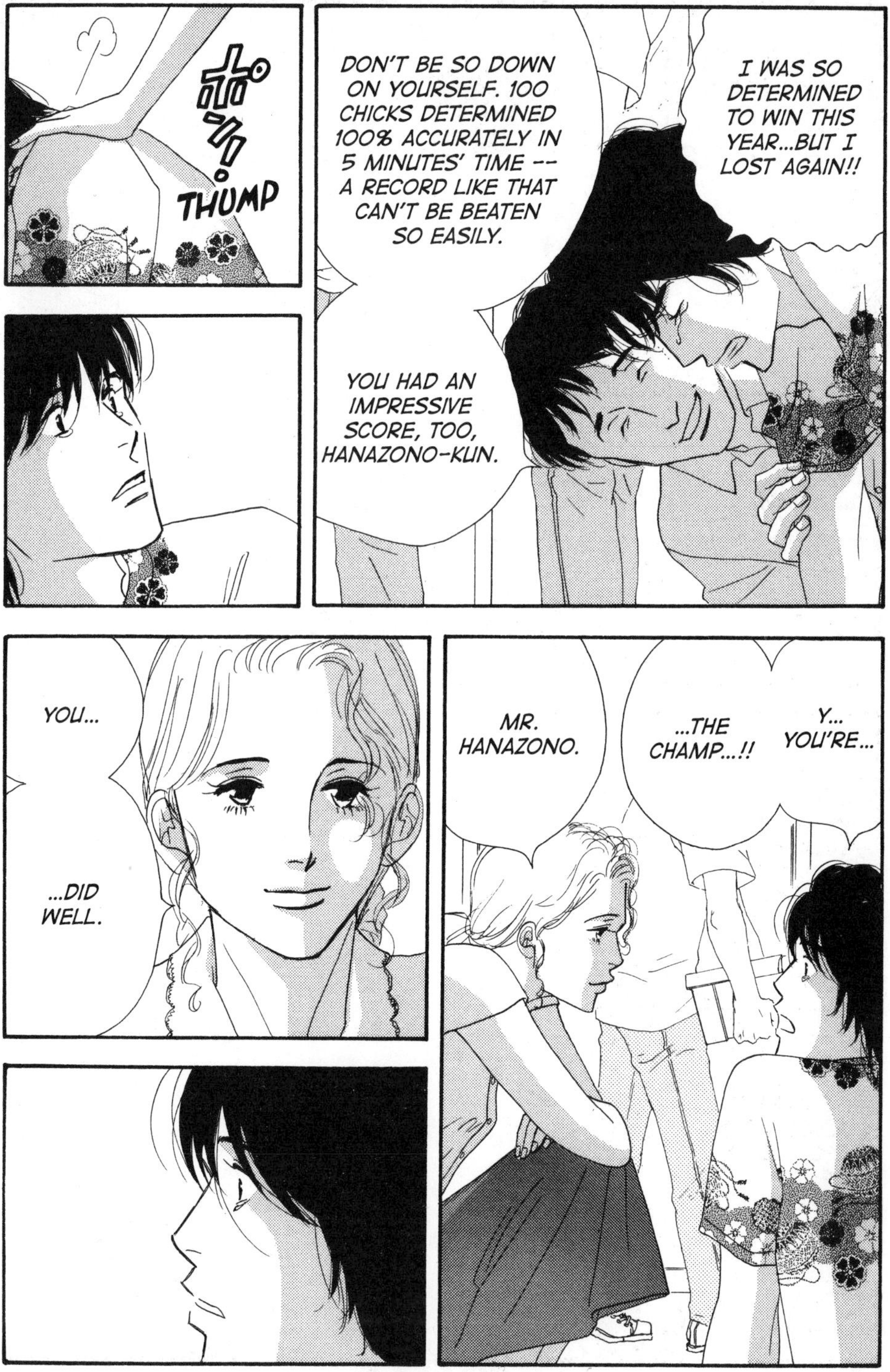
I WAS SO DETERMINED TO WIN THIS YEAR...BUT I LOST AGAIN!!
DON'T BE SO DOWN ON YOURSELF. 100 CHICKS DETERMINED 100% ACCURATELY IN 5 MINUTES' TIME -- A RECORD LIKE THAT CAN'T BE BEATEN SO EASILY.
YOU HAD AN IMPRESSIVE SCORE, TOO, HANAZONO-KUN.
ポッ!
THUMP
Y... YOU'RE...
...THE CHAMP...!!
MR. HANAZONO.
YOU...
...DID WELL.

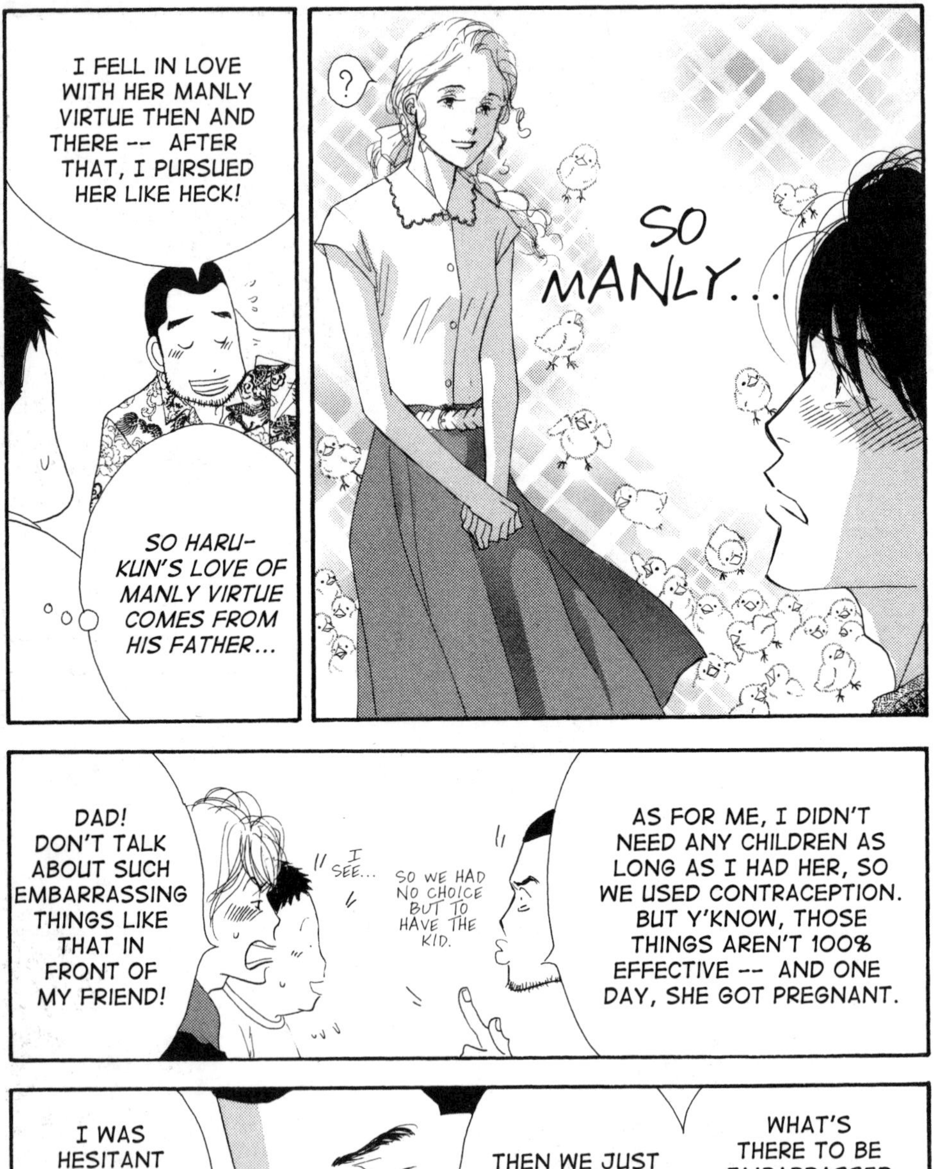
SO MANLY...
?
I FELL IN LOVE WITH HER MANLY VIRTUE THEN AND THERE -- AFTER THAT, I PURSUED HER LIKE HECK!
SO HARU-KUN'S LOVE OF MANLY VIRTUE COMES FROM HIS FATHER...
AS FOR ME, I DIDN'T NEED ANY CHILDREN AS LONG AS I HAD HER, SO WE USED CONTRACEPTION. BUT Y'KNOW, THOSE THINGS AREN'T 100% EFFECTIVE -- AND ONE DAY, SHE GOT PREGNANT.
SO WE HAD NO CHOICE BUT TO HAVE THE KID.
I SEE...
DAD! DON'T TALK ABOUT SUCH EMBARRASSING THINGS LIKE THAT IN FRONT OF MY FRIEND!
WHAT'S THERE TO BE EMBARRASSED ABOUT, MORON? ANYWAY, ONCE THE KID WAS BORN, IT WAS SO ADORABLE... DOUBLY SO BECAUSE IT WAS A GIRL...
THEN WE JUST DECIDED, "WHAT THE HECK," AND HAD A SECOND ONE...AND IT WAS JUST AS CUTE, ONLY THIS TIME IT TURNED OUT TO BE A BOY.
I WAS HESITANT ABOUT BEING TOO CLOYING BECAUSE OF THAT, BUT THEN -- AND I THINK YOU KNOW THIS ALREADY -- HE BECAME ILL...

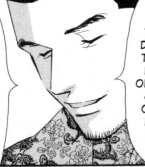

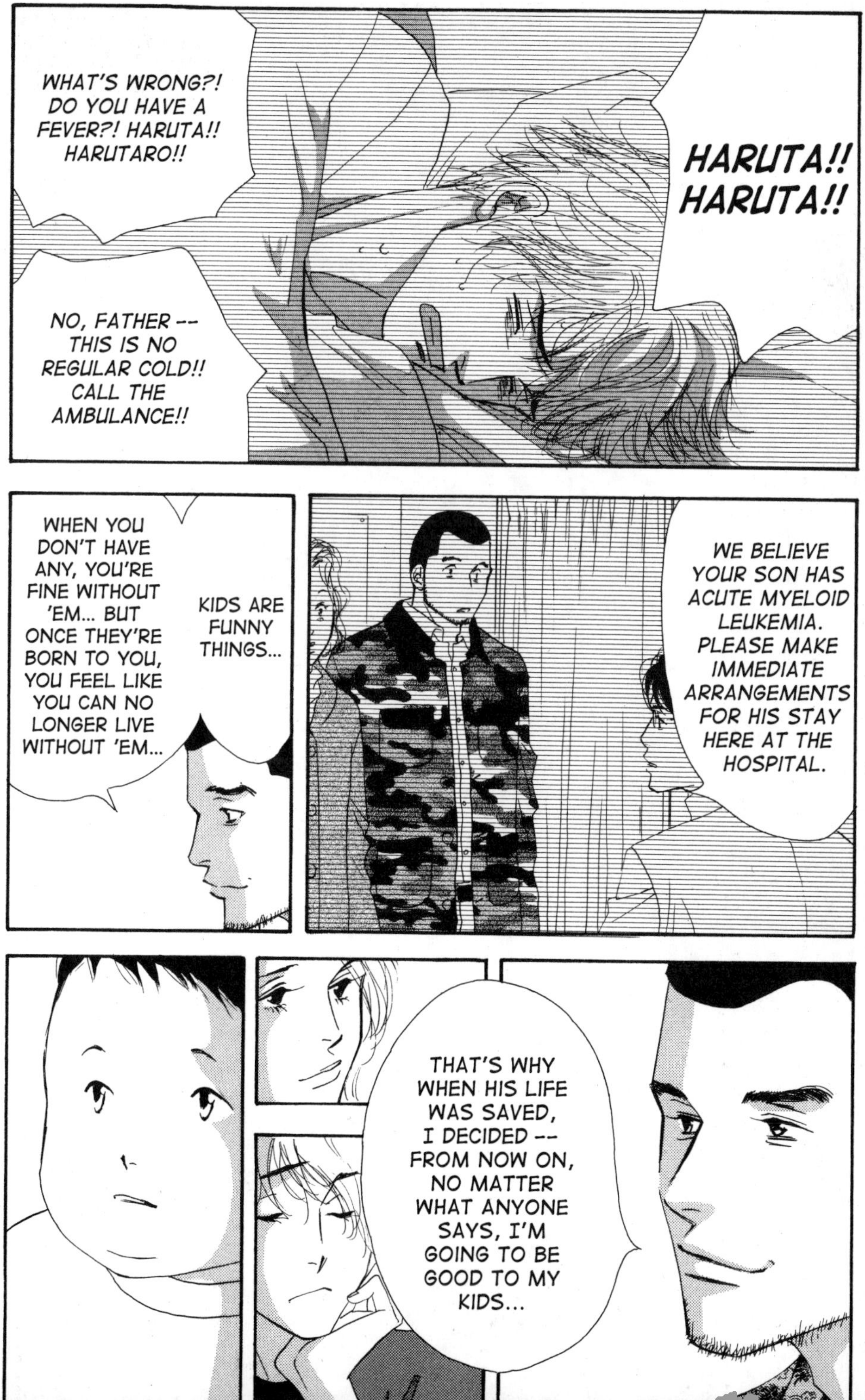
HARUTA!! HARUTA!!
WHAT'S WRONG?! DO YOU HAVE A FEVER?! HARUTA!! HARUTARO!!
NO, FATHER -- THIS IS NO REGULAR COLD!! CALL THE AMBULANCE!!
WE BELIEVE YOUR SON HAS ACUTE MYELOID LEUKEMIA. PLEASE MAKE IMMEDIATE ARRANGEMENTS FOR HIS STAY HERE AT THE HOSPITAL.
KIDS ARE FUNNY THINGS...
WHEN YOU DON'T HAVE ANY, YOU'RE FINE WITHOUT 'EM... BUT ONCE THEY'RE BORN TO YOU, YOU FEEL LIKE YOU CAN NO LONGER LIVE WITHOUT 'EM...
THAT'S WHY WHEN HIS LIFE WAS SAVED, I DECIDED -- FROM NOW ON, NO MATTER WHAT ANYONE SAYS, I'M GOING TO BE GOOD TO MY KIDS...

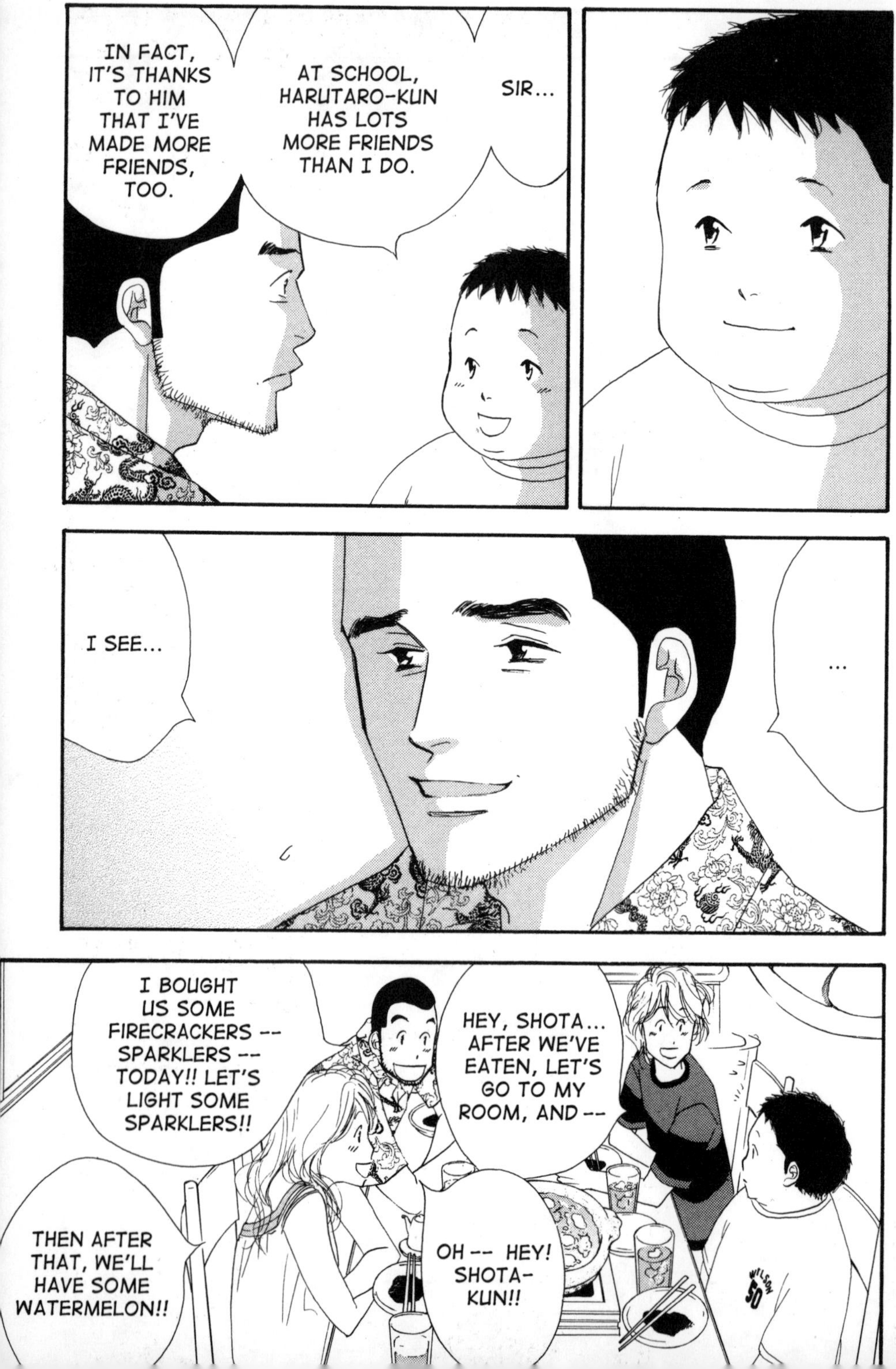
SIR...
AT SCHOOL, HARUTARO-KUN HAS LOTS MORE FRIENDS THAN I DO.
IN FACT, IT'S THANKS TO HIM THAT I'VE MADE MORE FRIENDS, TOO.
...
I SEE...
HEY, SHOTA... AFTER WE'VE EATEN, LET'S GO TO MY ROOM, AND --
I BOUGHT US SOME FIRECRACKERS -- SPARKLERS -- TODAY!! LET'S LIGHT SOME SPARKLERS!!
OH -- HEY! SHOTA-KUN!!
THEN AFTER THAT, WE'LL HAVE SOME WATERMELON!!
WILSON
50

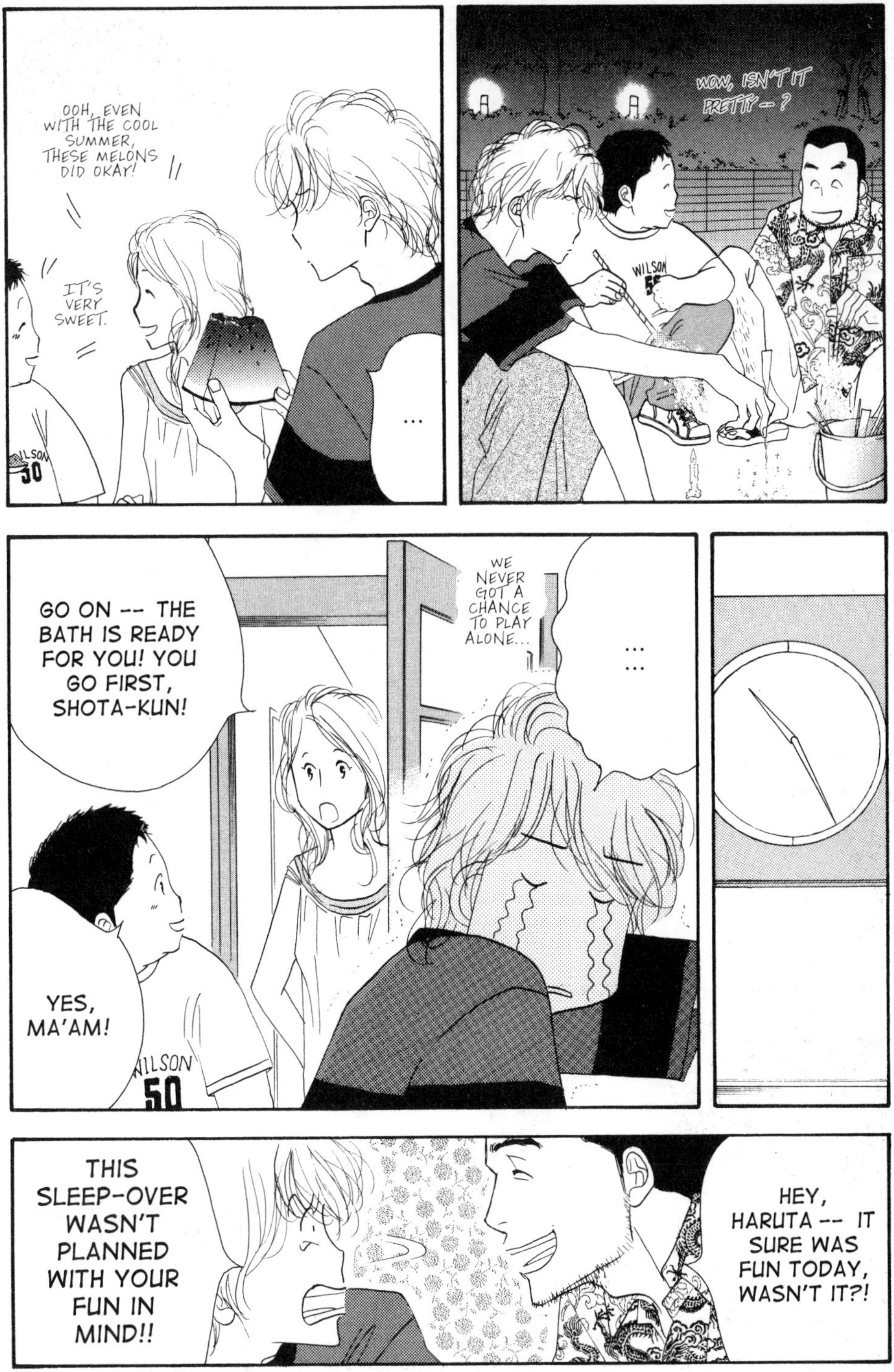
WOW, ISN'T IT PRETTY -- ?
OOH, EVEN WITH THE COOL SUMMER, THESE MELONS DID OKAY!
IT'S VERY SWEET.
...
WE NEVER GOT A CHANCE TO PLAY ALONE...
... ...
GO ON -- THE BATH IS READY FOR YOU! YOU GO FIRST, SHOTA-KUN!
YES, MA'AM!
HEY, HARUTA -- IT SURE WAS FUN TODAY, WASN'T IT?!
THIS SLEEP-OVER WASN'T PLANNED WITH YOUR FUN IN MIND!!

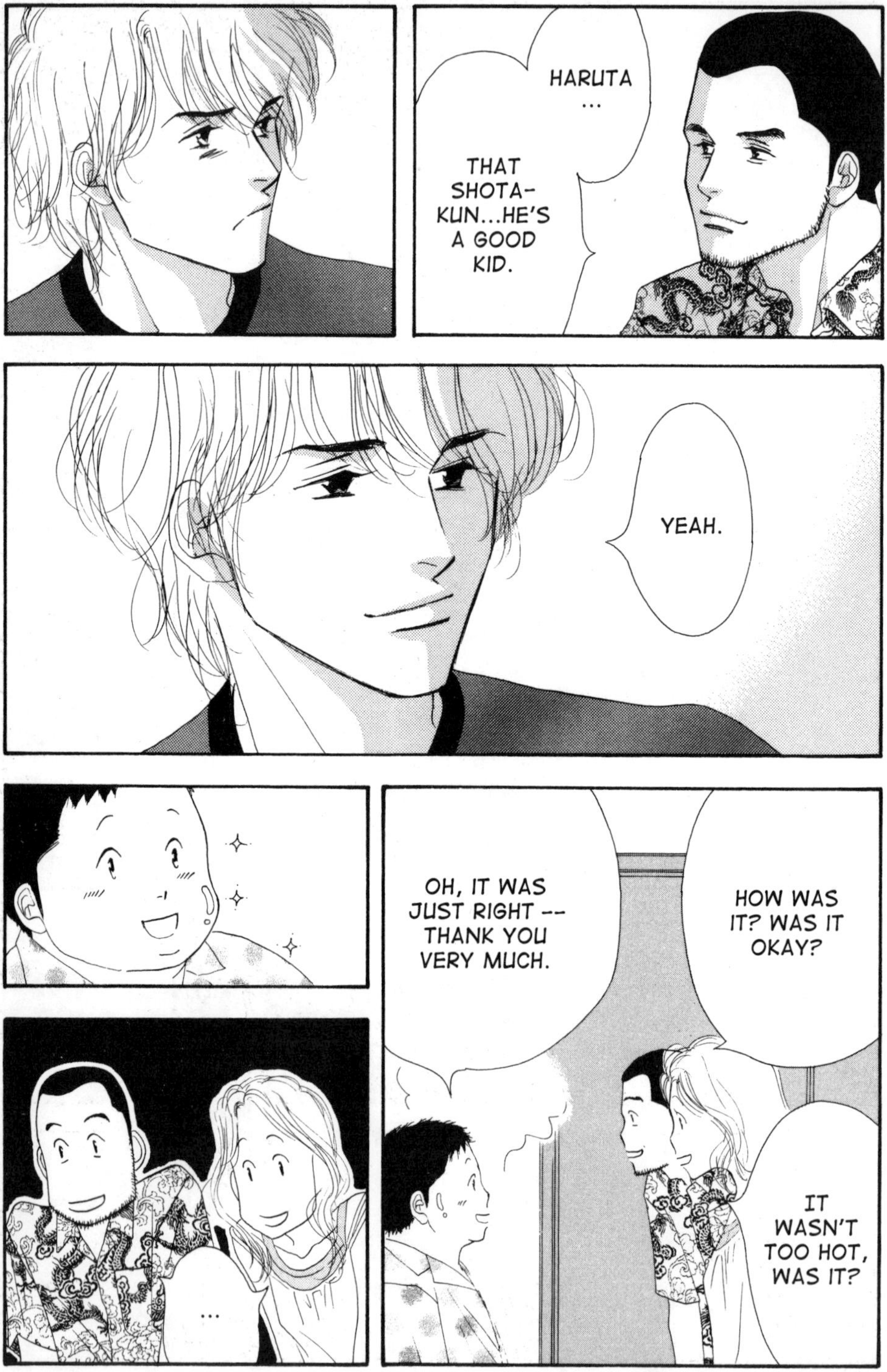
HARUTA
...
THAT SHOTA-KUN...HE'S A GOOD KID.
YEAH.
HOW WAS IT? WAS IT OKAY?
IT WASN'T TOO HOT, WAS IT?
OH, IT WAS JUST RIGHT -- THANK YOU VERY MUCH.
...

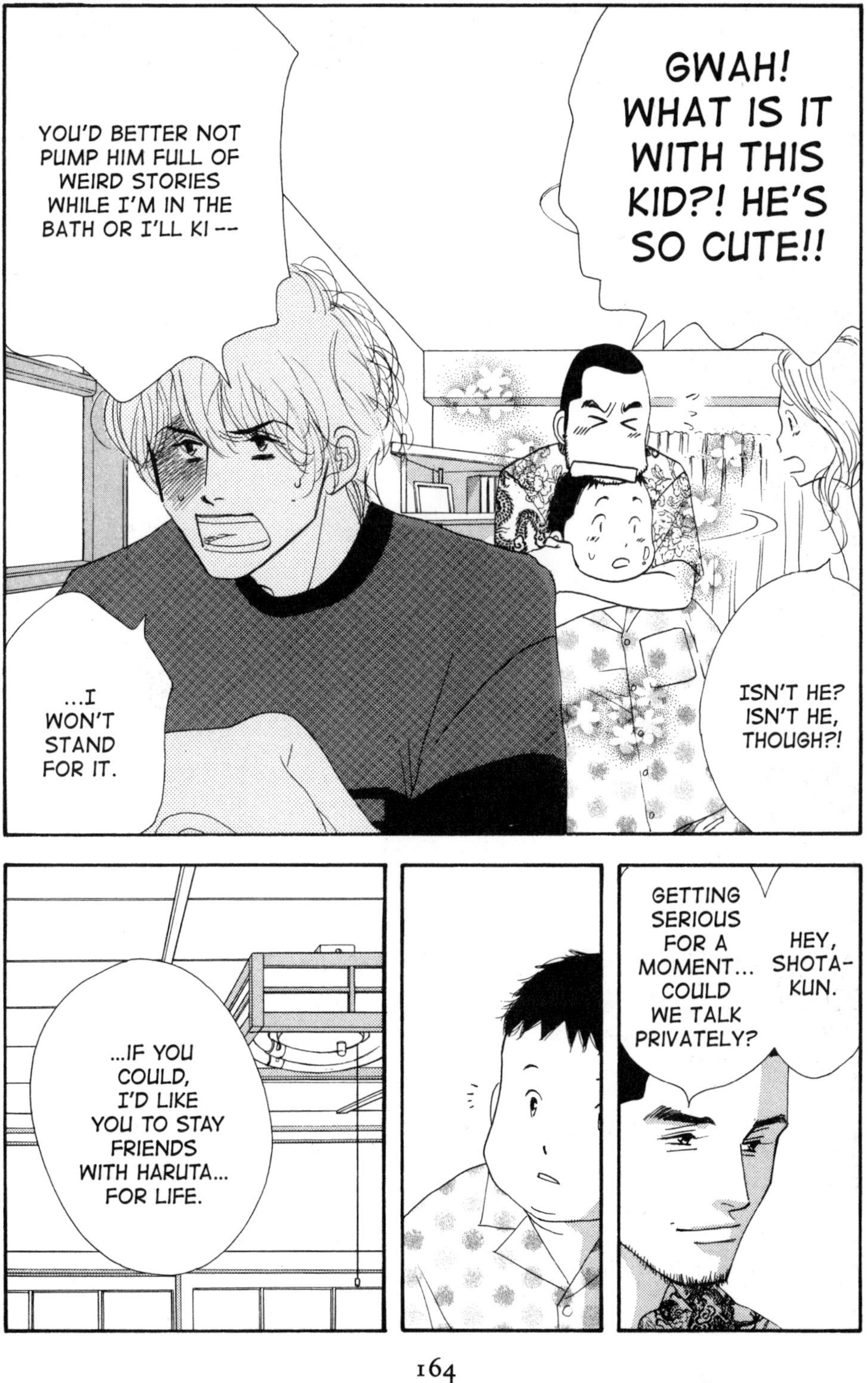
GWAH! WHAT IS IT WITH THIS KID?! HE'S SO CUTE!!
YOU'D BETTER NOT PUMP HIM FULL OF WEIRD STORIES WHILE I'M IN THE BATH OR I'LL KI --
ISN'T HE? ISN'T HE, THOUGH?!
...I WON'T STAND FOR IT.
HEY, SHOTA-KUN.
GETTING SERIOUS FOR A MOMENT... COULD WE TALK PRIVATELY?
...IF YOU COULD, I'D LIKE YOU TO STAY FRIENDS WITH HARUTA... FOR LIFE.

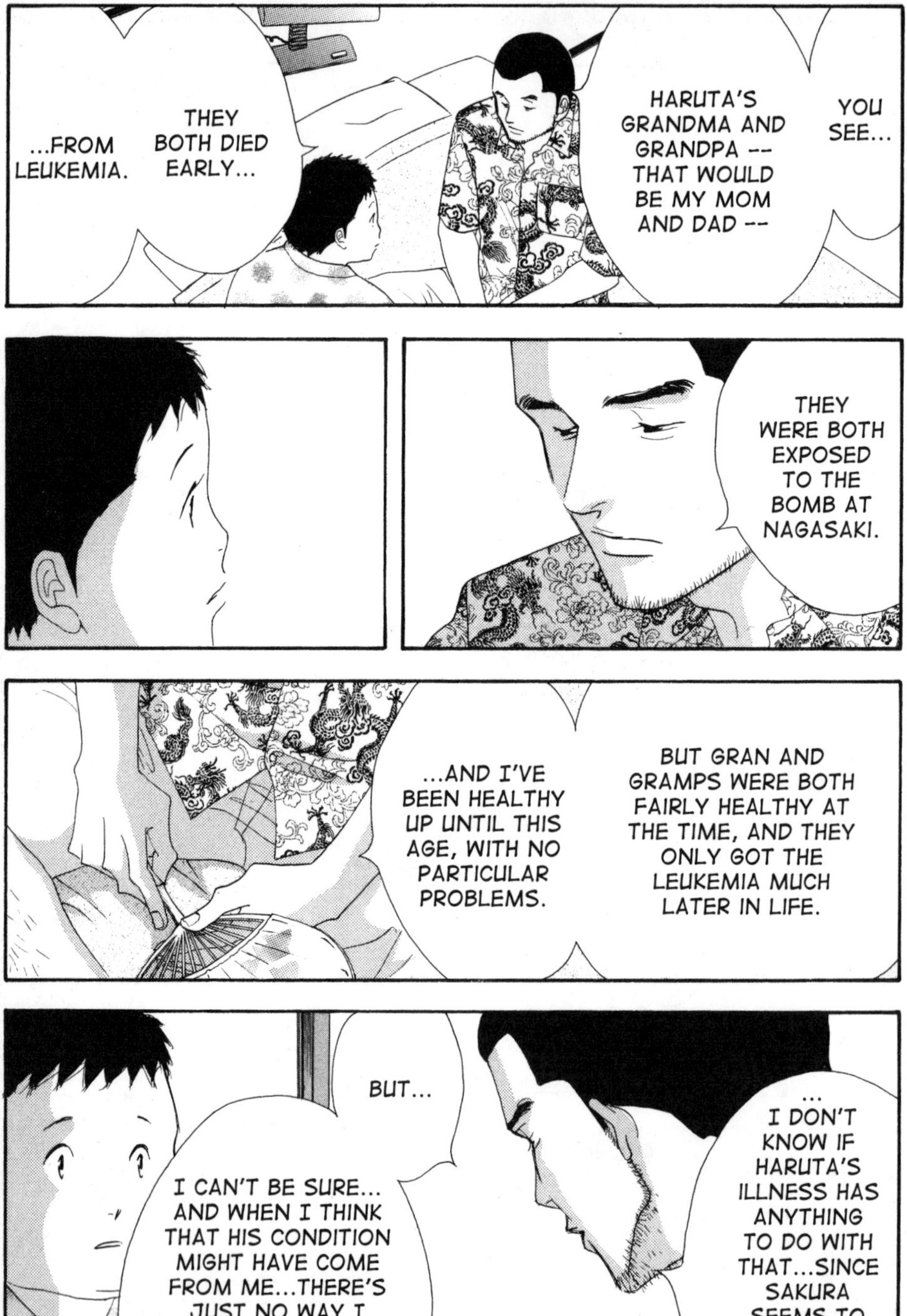
YOU SEE...
HARUTA'S GRANDMA AND GRANDPA -- THAT WOULD BE MY MOM AND DAD --
THEY BOTH DIED EARLY...
...FROM LEUKEMIA.
THEY WERE BOTH EXPOSED TO THE BOMB AT NAGASAKI.
BUT GRAN AND GRAMPS WERE BOTH FAIRLY HEALTHY AT THE TIME, AND THEY ONLY GOT THE LEUKEMIA MUCH LATER IN LIFE.
...AND I'VE BEEN HEALTHY UP UNTIL THIS AGE, WITH NO PARTICULAR PROBLEMS.
... I DON'T KNOW IF HARUTA'S ILLNESS HAS ANYTHING TO DO WITH THAT...SINCE SAKURA SEEMS TO HAVE TURNED OUT FINE...
BUT...
I CAN'T BE SURE... AND WHEN I THINK THAT HIS CONDITION MIGHT HAVE COME FROM ME...THERE'S JUST NO WAY I CAN MAKE IT UP TO THE LITTLE GUY.

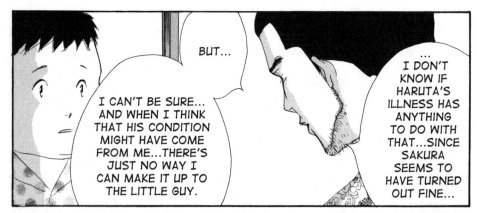

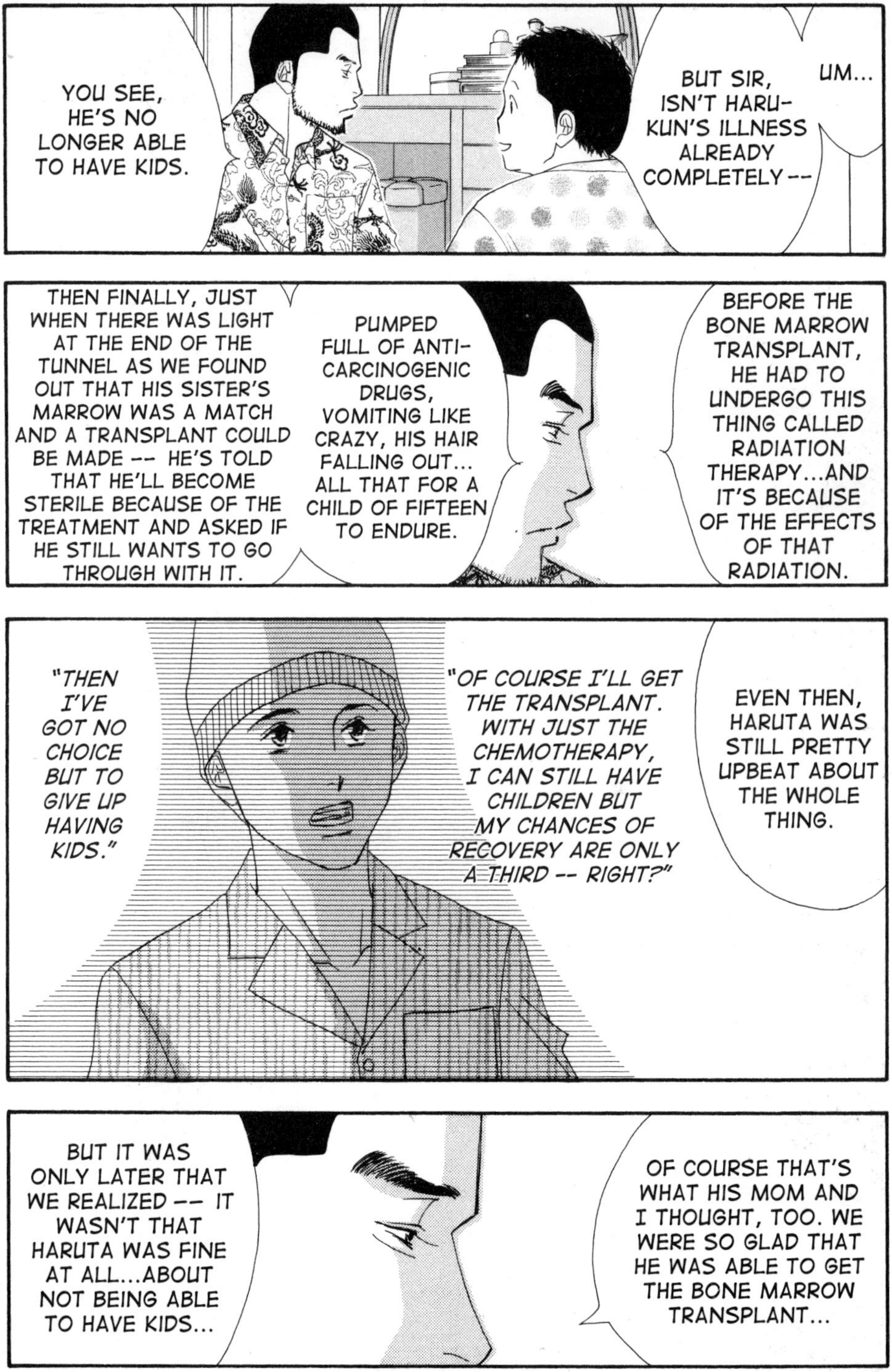
UM...
BUT SIR, ISN'T HARU-KUN'S ILLNESS ALREADY COMPLETELY --
YOU SEE, HE'S NO LONGER ABLE TO HAVE KIDS.
BEFORE THE BONE MARROW TRANSPLANT, HE HAD TO UNDERGO THIS THING CALLED RADIATION THERAPY...AND IT'S BECAUSE OF THE EFFECTS OF THAT RADIATION.
PUMPED FULL OF ANTI-CARCINOGENIC DRUGS, VOMITING LIKE CRAZY, HIS HAIR FALLING OUT... ALL THAT FOR A CHILD OF FIFTEEN TO ENDURE.
THEN FINALLY, JUST WHEN THERE WAS LIGHT AT THE END OF THE TUNNEL AS WE FOUND OUT THAT HIS SISTER'S MARROW WAS A MATCH AND A TRANSPLANT COULD BE MADE -- HE'S TOLD THAT HE'LL BECOME STERILE BECAUSE OF THE TREATMENT AND ASKED IF HE STILL WANTS TO GO THROUGH WITH IT.
EVEN THEN, HARUTA WAS STILL PRETTY UPBEAT ABOUT THE WHOLE THING.
"OF COURSE I'LL GET THE TRANSPLANT. WITH JUST THE CHEMOTHERAPY, I CAN STILL HAVE CHILDREN BUT MY CHANCES OF RECOVERY ARE ONLY A THIRD -- RIGHT?"
"THEN I'VE GOT NO CHOICE BUT TO GIVE UP HAVING KIDS."
OF COURSE THAT'S WHAT HIS MOM AND I THOUGHT, TOO. WE WERE SO GLAD THAT HE WAS ABLE TO GET THE BONE MARROW TRANSPLANT...
BUT IT WAS ONLY LATER THAT WE REALIZED -- IT WASN'T THAT HARUTA WAS FINE AT ALL...ABOUT NOT BEING ABLE TO HAVE KIDS...

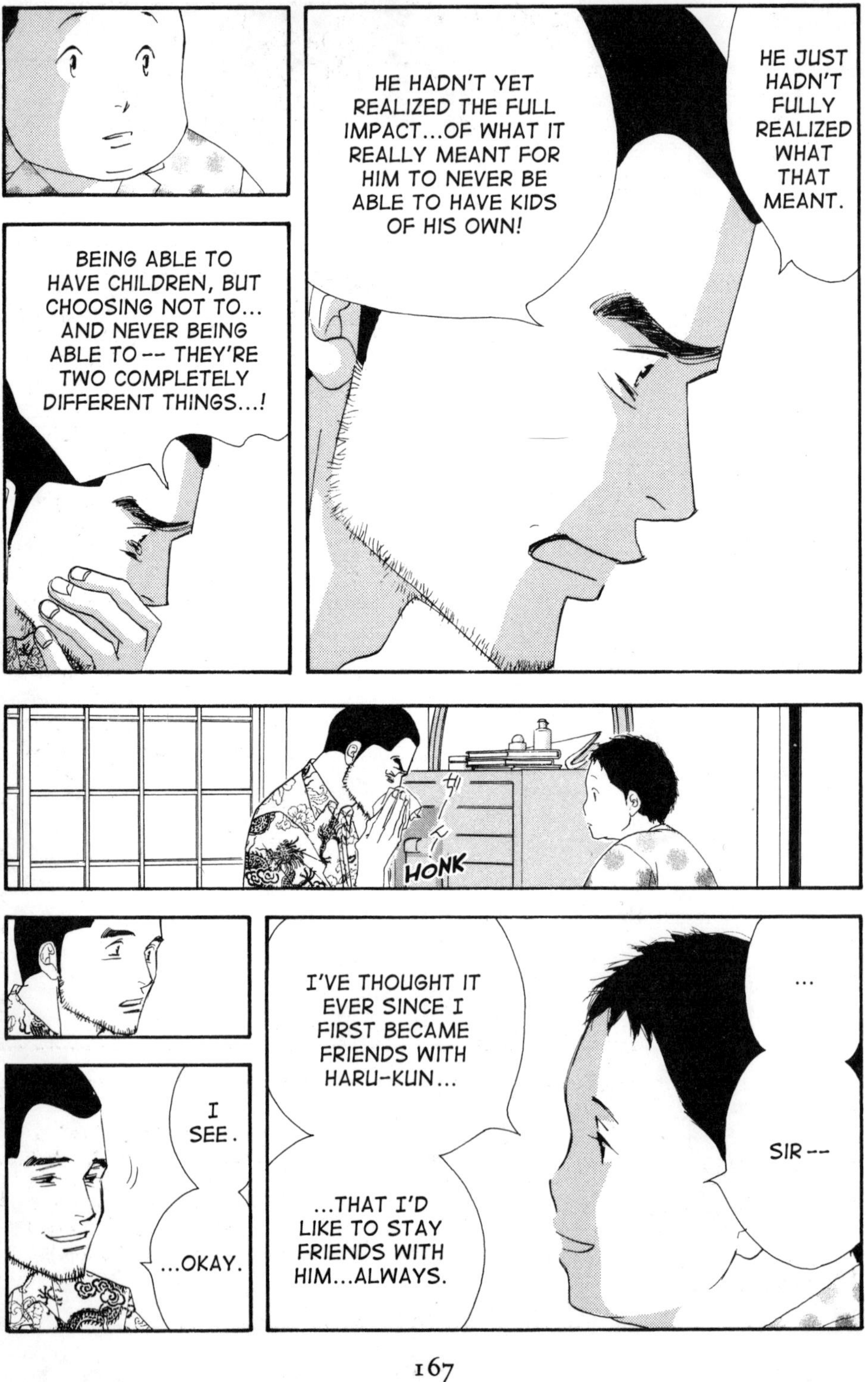
HE JUST HADN'T FULLY REALIZED WHAT THAT MEANT.
HE HADN'T YET REALIZED THE FULL IMPACT...OF WHAT IT REALLY MEANT FOR HIM TO NEVER BE ABLE TO HAVE KIDS OF HIS OWN!
BEING ABLE TO HAVE CHILDREN, BUT CHOOSING NOT TO... AND NEVER BEING ABLE TO-- THEY'RE TWO COMPLETELY DIFFERENT THINGS...!
HONK
...
SIR--
I'VE THOUGHT IT EVER SINCE I FIRST BECAME FRIENDS WITH HARU-KUN...
...THAT I'D LIKE TO STAY FRIENDS WITH HIM...ALWAYS.
I SEE.
...OKAY.

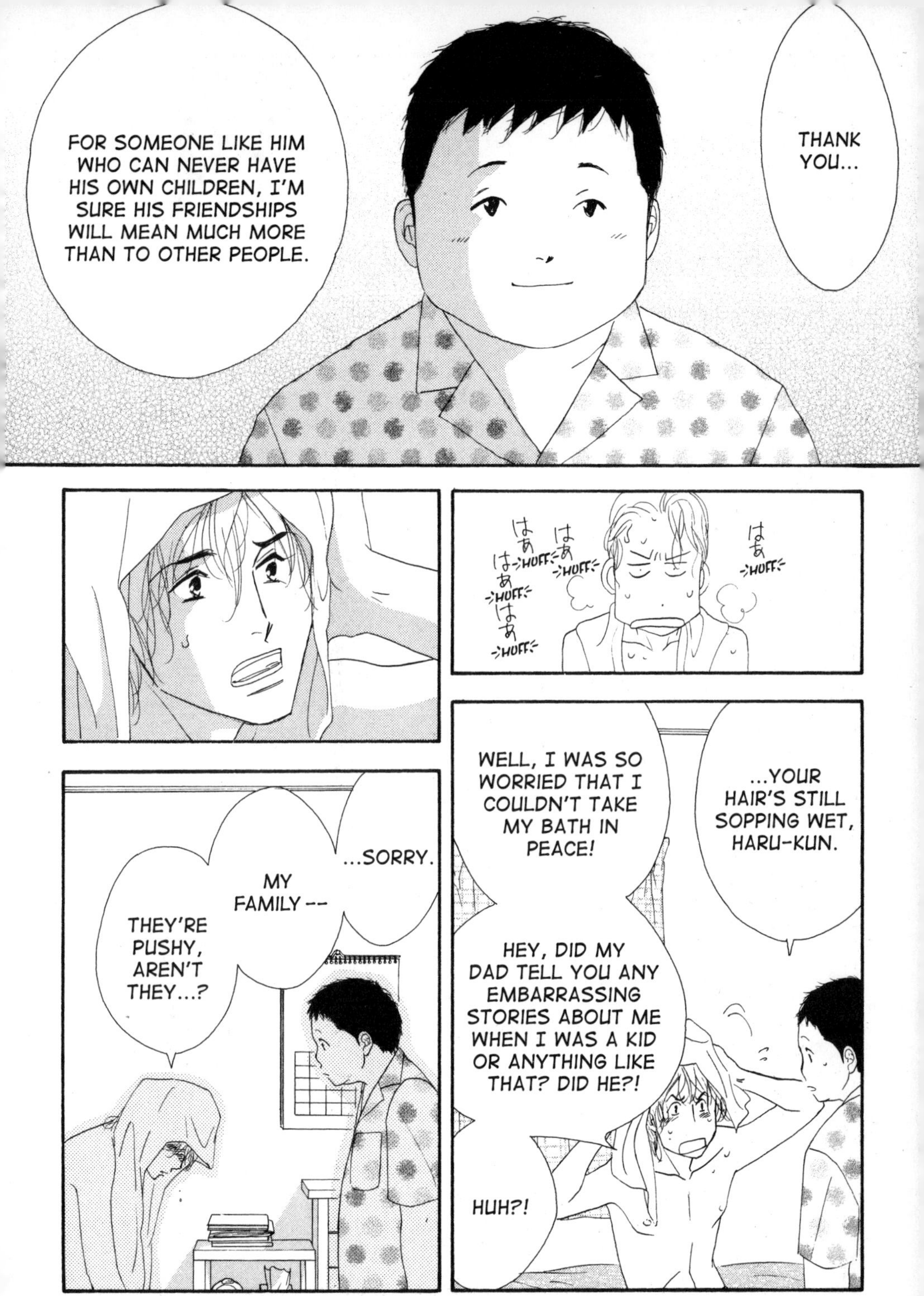
THANK YOU...
FOR SOMEONE LIKE HIM WHO CAN NEVER HAVE HIS OWN CHILDREN, I'M SURE HIS FRIENDSHIPS WILL MEAN MUCH MORE THAN TO OTHER PEOPLE.
はあ HUFF
はあ HUFF
はあ HUFF
はあ HUFF
はあ HUFF
...YOUR HAIR'S STILL SOPPING WET, HARU-KUN.
WELL, I WAS SO WORRIED THAT I COULDN'T TAKE MY BATH IN PEACE!
HEY, DID MY DAD TELL YOU ANY EMBARRASSING STORIES ABOUT ME WHEN I WAS A KID OR ANYTHING LIKE THAT? DID HE?!
HUH?!
...SORRY.
MY FAMILY --
THEY'RE PUSHY, AREN'T THEY...?

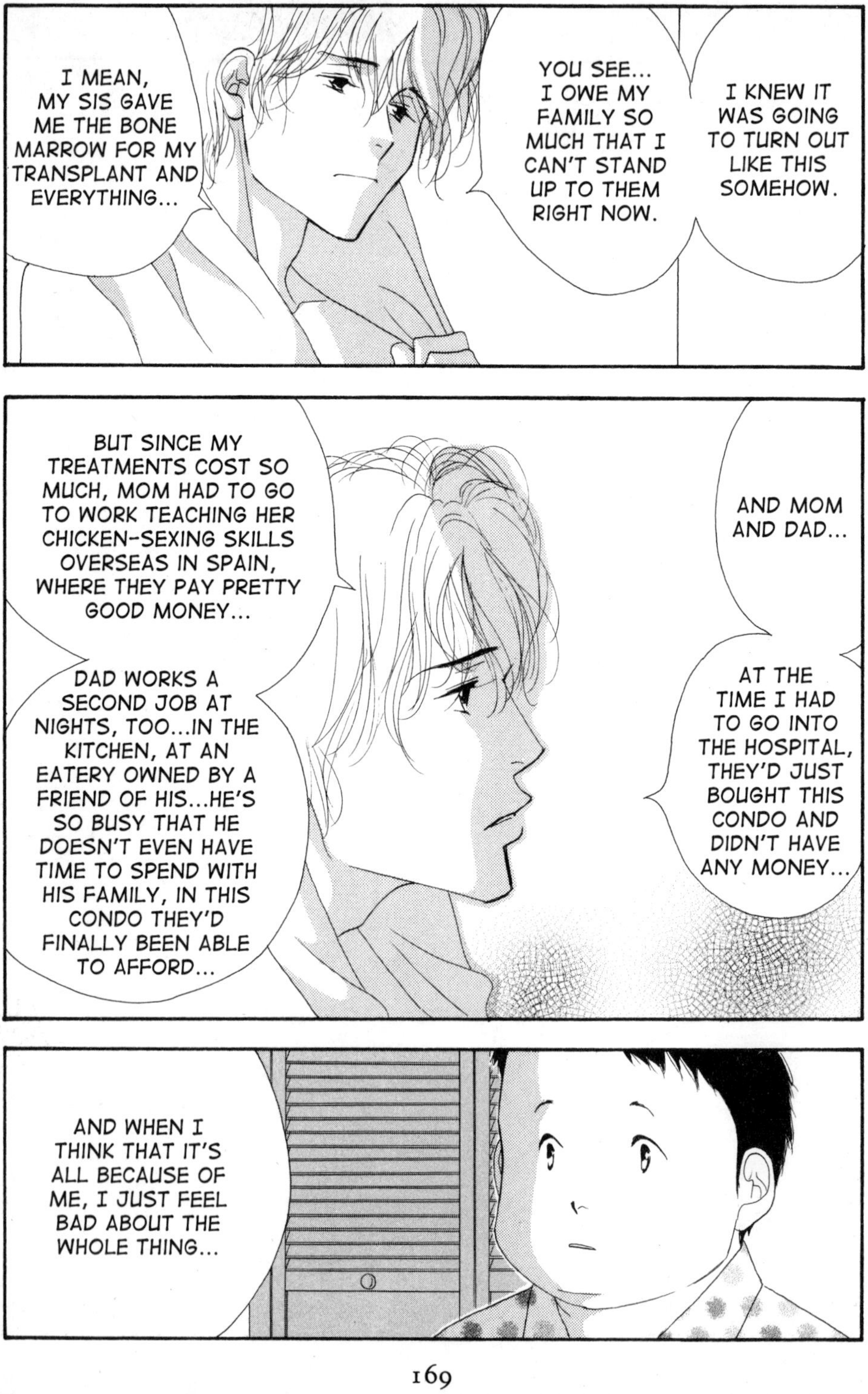
I KNEW IT WAS GOING TO TURN OUT LIKE THIS SOMEHOW.
YOU SEE... I OWE MY FAMILY SO MUCH THAT I CAN'T STAND UP TO THEM RIGHT NOW.
I MEAN, MY SIS GAVE ME THE BONE MARROW FOR MY TRANSPLANT AND EVERYTHING...
AND MOM AND DAD...
AT THE TIME I HAD TO GO INTO THE HOSPITAL, THEY'D JUST BOUGHT THIS CONDO AND DIDN'T HAVE ANY MONEY...
BUT SINCE MY TREATMENTS COST SO MUCH, MOM HAD TO GO TO WORK TEACHING HER CHICKEN-SEXING SKILLS OVERSEAS IN SPAIN, WHERE THEY PAY PRETTY GOOD MONEY...
DAD WORKS A SECOND JOB AT NIGHTS, TOO...IN THE KITCHEN, AT AN EATERY OWNED BY A FRIEND OF HIS...HE'S SO BUSY THAT HE DOESN'T EVEN HAVE TIME TO SPEND WITH HIS FAMILY, IN THIS CONDO THEY'D FINALLY BEEN ABLE TO AFFORD...
AND WHEN I THINK THAT IT'S ALL BECAUSE OF ME, I JUST FEEL BAD ABOUT THE WHOLE THING...

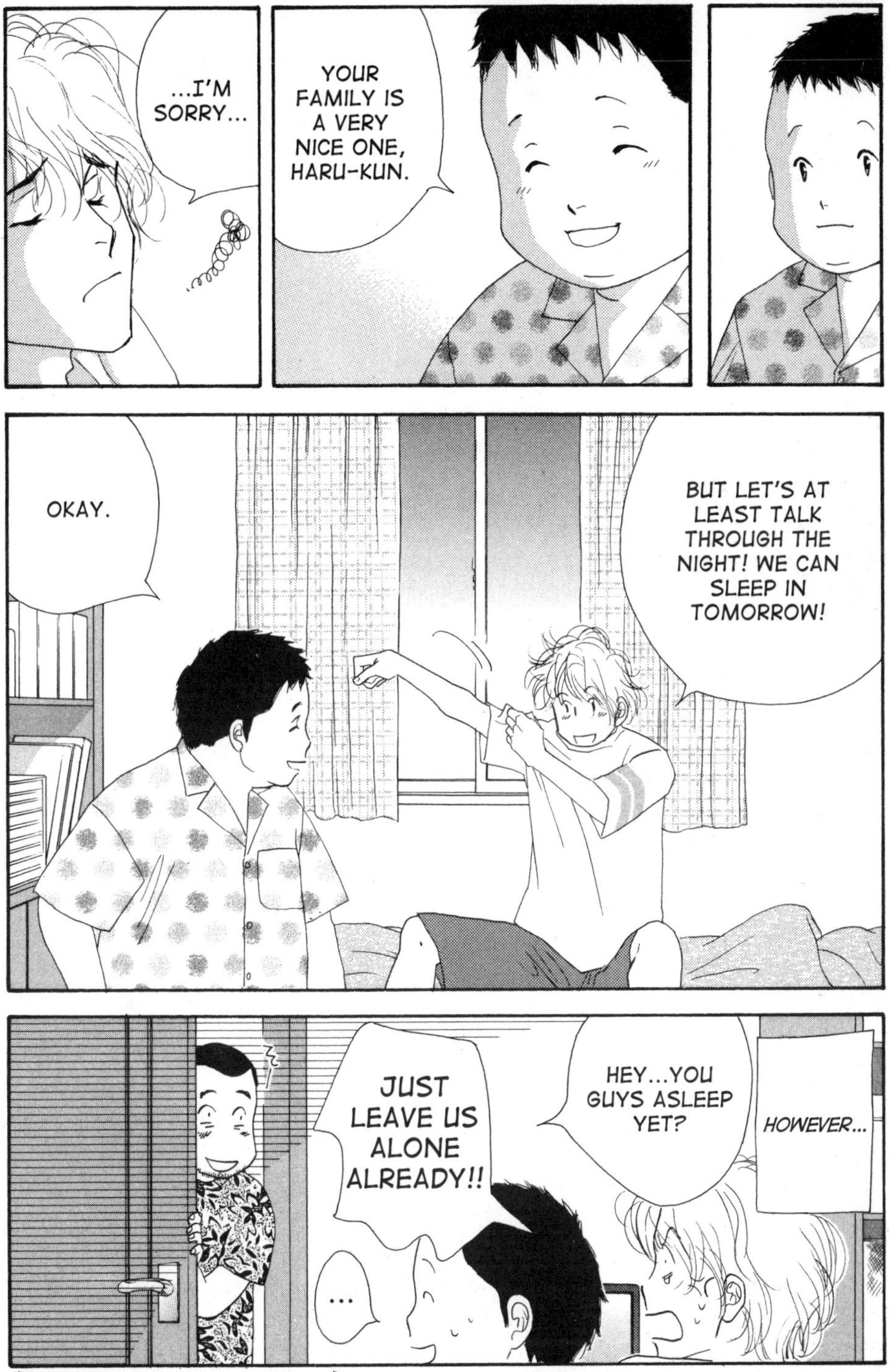
YOUR FAMILY IS A VERY NICE ONE, HARU-KUN.
...I'M SORRY...
BUT LET'S AT LEAST TALK THROUGH THE NIGHT! WE CAN SLEEP IN TOMORROW!
OKAY.
HOWEVER...
HEY...YOU GUYS ASLEEP YET?
JUST LEAVE US ALONE ALREADY!!
...

CONTINUED IN VOLUME 2

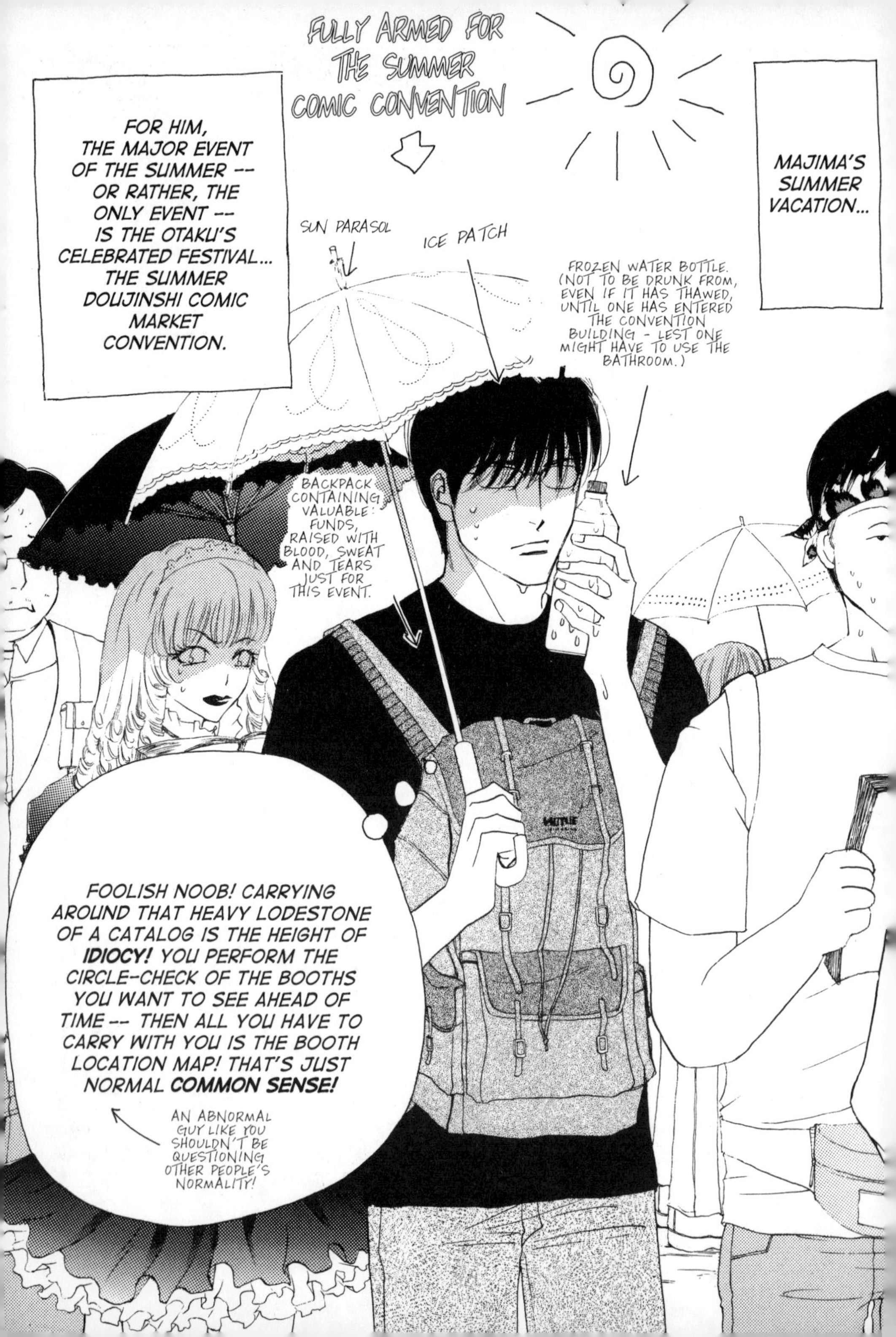
MAJIMA'S SUMMER VACATION...
FULLY ARMED FOR THE SUMMER COMIC CONVENTION
FOR HIM, THE MAJOR EVENT OF THE SUMMER -- OR RATHER, THE ONLY EVENT -- IS THE OTAKU'S CELEBRATED FESTIVAL... THE SUMMER DOUJINSHI COMIC MARKET CONVENTION.
FROZEN WATER BOTTLE. (NOT TO BE DRUNK FROM, EVEN IF IT HAS THAWED, UNTIL ONE HAS ENTERED THE CONVENTION BUILDING - LEST ONE MIGHT HAVE TO USE THE BATHROOM.)
ICE PATCH
SUN PARASOL
BACKPACK CONTAINING VALUABLE FUNDS, RAISED WITH BLOOD, SWEAT AND TEARS JUST FOR THIS EVENT.
FOOLISH NOOB! CARRYING AROUND THAT HEAVY LODESTONE OF A CATALOG IS THE HEIGHT OF IDIOCY! YOU PERFORM THE CIRCLE-CHECK OF THE BOOTHS YOU WANT TO SEE AHEAD OF TIME -- THEN ALL YOU HAVE TO CARRY WITH YOU IS THE BOOTH LOCATION MAP! THAT'S JUST NORMAL COMMON SENSE!
AN ABNORMAL GUY LIKE YOU SHOULDN'T BE QUESTIONING OTHER PEOPLE'S NORMALITY!

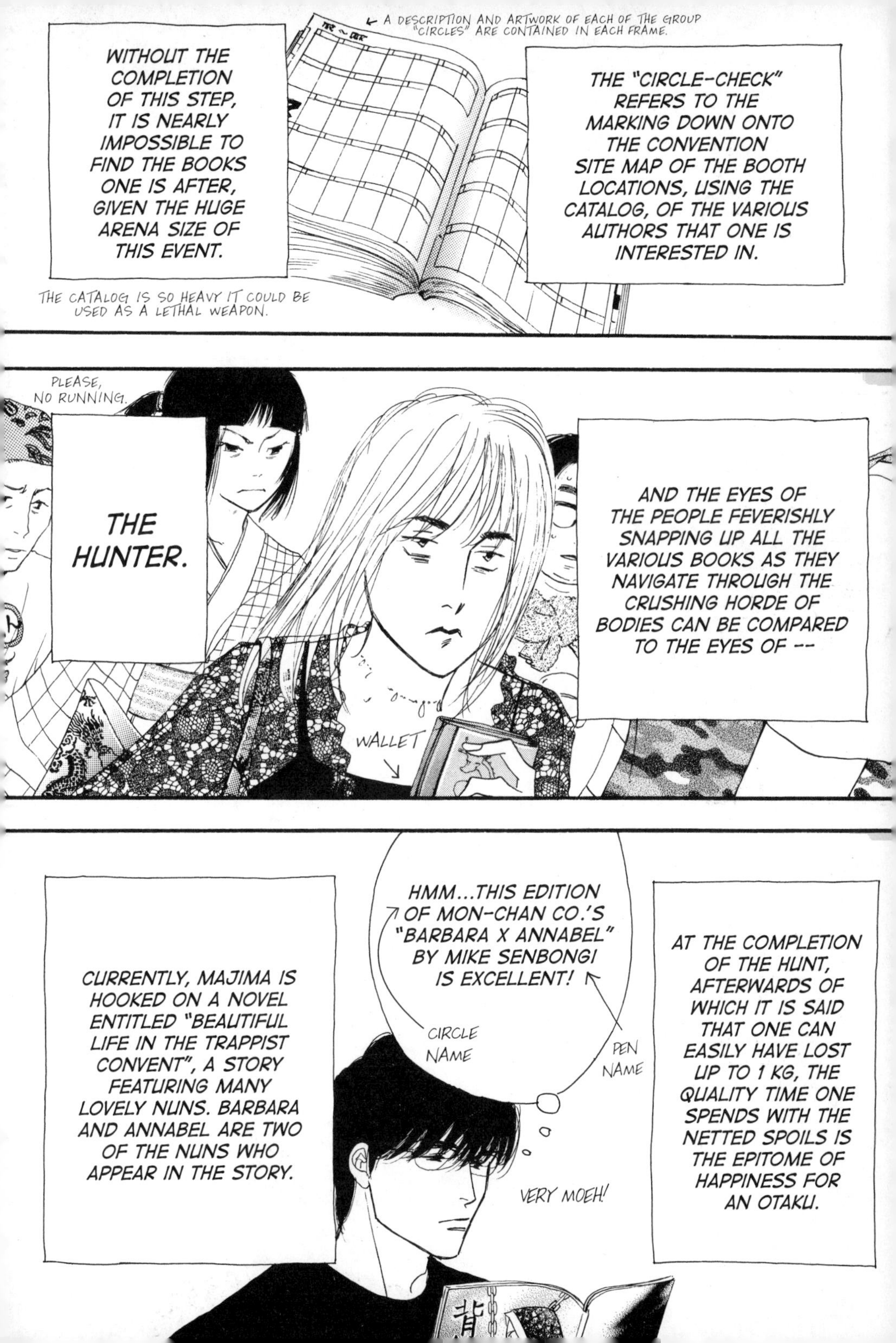

← A DESCRIPTION AND ARTWORK OF EACH OF THE GROUP "CIRCLES" ARE CONTAINED IN EACH FRAME.
THE "CIRCLE-CHECK" REFERS TO THE MARKING DOWN ONTO THE CONVENTION SITE MAP OF THE BOOTH LOCATIONS, USING THE CATALOG, OF THE VARIOUS AUTHORS THAT ONE IS INTERESTED IN.
WITHOUT THE COMPLETION OF THIS STEP, IT IS NEARLY IMPOSSIBLE TO FIND THE BOOKS ONE IS AFTER, GIVEN THE HUGE ARENA SIZE OF THIS EVENT.
THE CATALOG IS SO HEAVY IT COULD BE USED AS A LETHAL WEAPON.
AND THE EYES OF THE PEOPLE FEVERISHLY SNAPPING UP ALL THE VARIOUS BOOKS AS THEY NAVIGATE THROUGH THE CRUSHING HORDE OF BODIES CAN BE COMPARED TO THE EYES OF --
WALLET
THE HUNTER.
PLEASE, NO RUNNING.
AT THE COMPLETION OF THE HUNT, AFTERWARDS OF WHICH IT IS SAID THAT ONE CAN EASILY HAVE LOST UP TO 1 KG, THE QUALITY TIME ONE SPENDS WITH THE NETTED SPOILS IS THE EPITOME OF HAPPINESS FOR AN OTAKU.
HMM...THIS EDITION OF MON-CHAN CO.'S "BARBARA X ANNABEL" BY MIKE SENBONGI IS EXCELLENT!
CIRCLE NAME
PEN NAME
VERY MOEH!
CURRENTLY, MAJIMA IS HOOKED ON A NOVEL ENTITLED "BEAUTIFUL LIFE IN THE TRAPPIST CONVENT", A STORY FEATURING MANY LOVELY NUNS. BARBARA AND ANNABEL ARE TWO OF THE NUNS WHO APPEAR IN THE STORY.

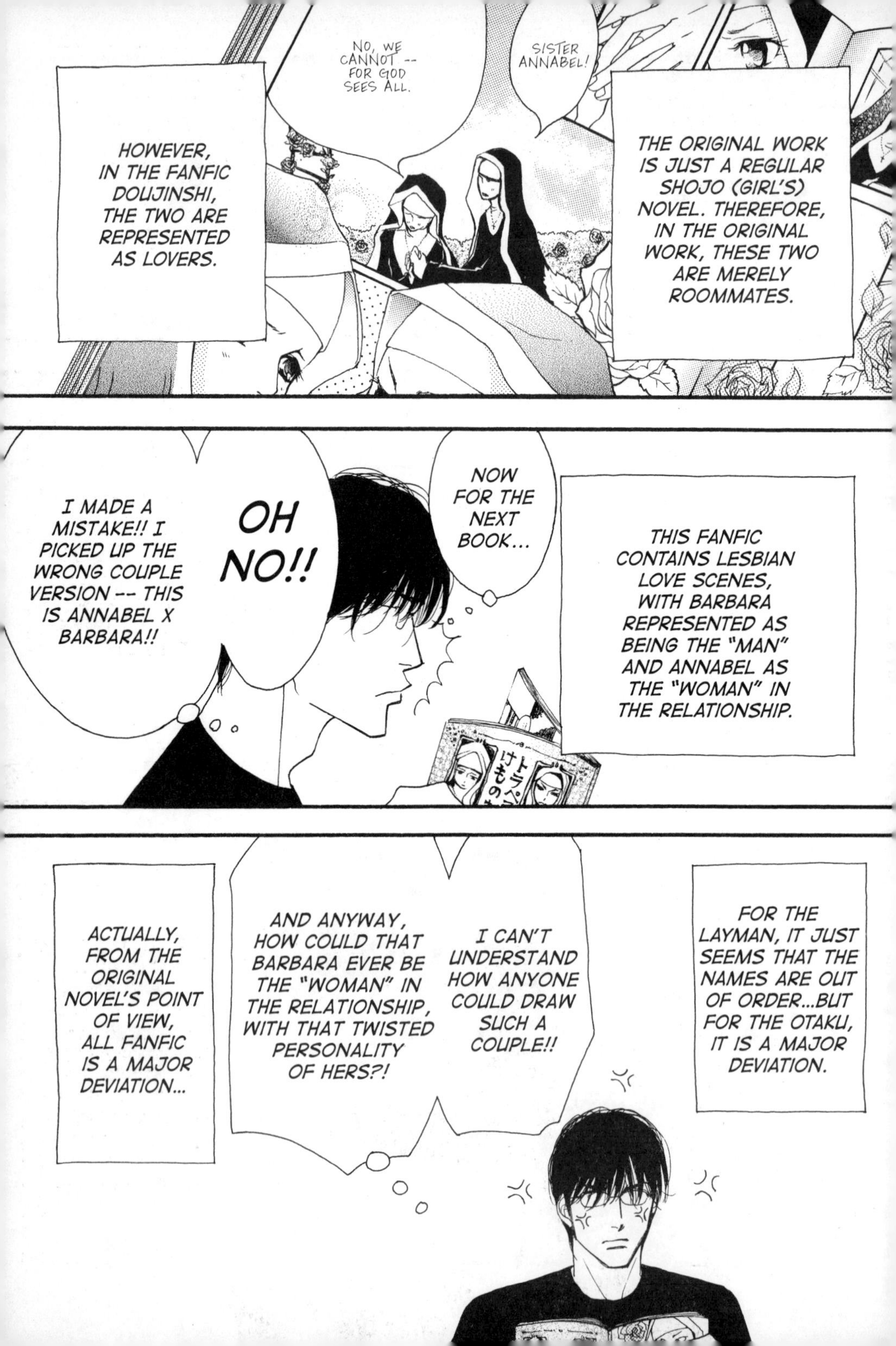
THE ORIGINAL WORK IS JUST A REGULAR SHOJO (GIRL'S) NOVEL. THEREFORE, IN THE ORIGINAL WORK, THESE TWO ARE MERELY ROOMMATES.
SISTER ANNABEL!
NO, WE CANNOT -- FOR GOD SEES ALL.
HOWEVER, IN THE FANFIC DOUJINSHI, THE TWO ARE REPRESENTED AS LOVERS.
THIS FANFIC CONTAINS LESBIAN LOVE SCENES, WITH BARBARA REPRESENTED AS BEING THE "MAN" AND ANNABEL AS THE "WOMAN" IN THE RELATIONSHIP.
NOW FOR THE NEXT BOOK...
OH NO!!
I MADE A MISTAKE!! I PICKED UP THE WRONG COUPLE VERSION -- THIS IS ANNABEL X BARBARA!!
FOR THE LAYMAN, IT JUST SEEMS THAT THE NAMES ARE OUT OF ORDER...BUT FOR THE OTAKU, IT IS A MAJOR DEVIATION.
I CAN'T UNDERSTAND HOW ANYONE COULD DRAW SUCH A COUPLE!!
AND ANYWAY, HOW COULD THAT BARBARA EVER BE THE "WOMAN" IN THE RELATIONSHIP, WITH THAT TWISTED PERSONALITY OF HERS?!
ACTUALLY, FROM THE ORIGINAL NOVEL'S POINT OF VIEW, ALL FANFIC IS A MAJOR DEVIATION...

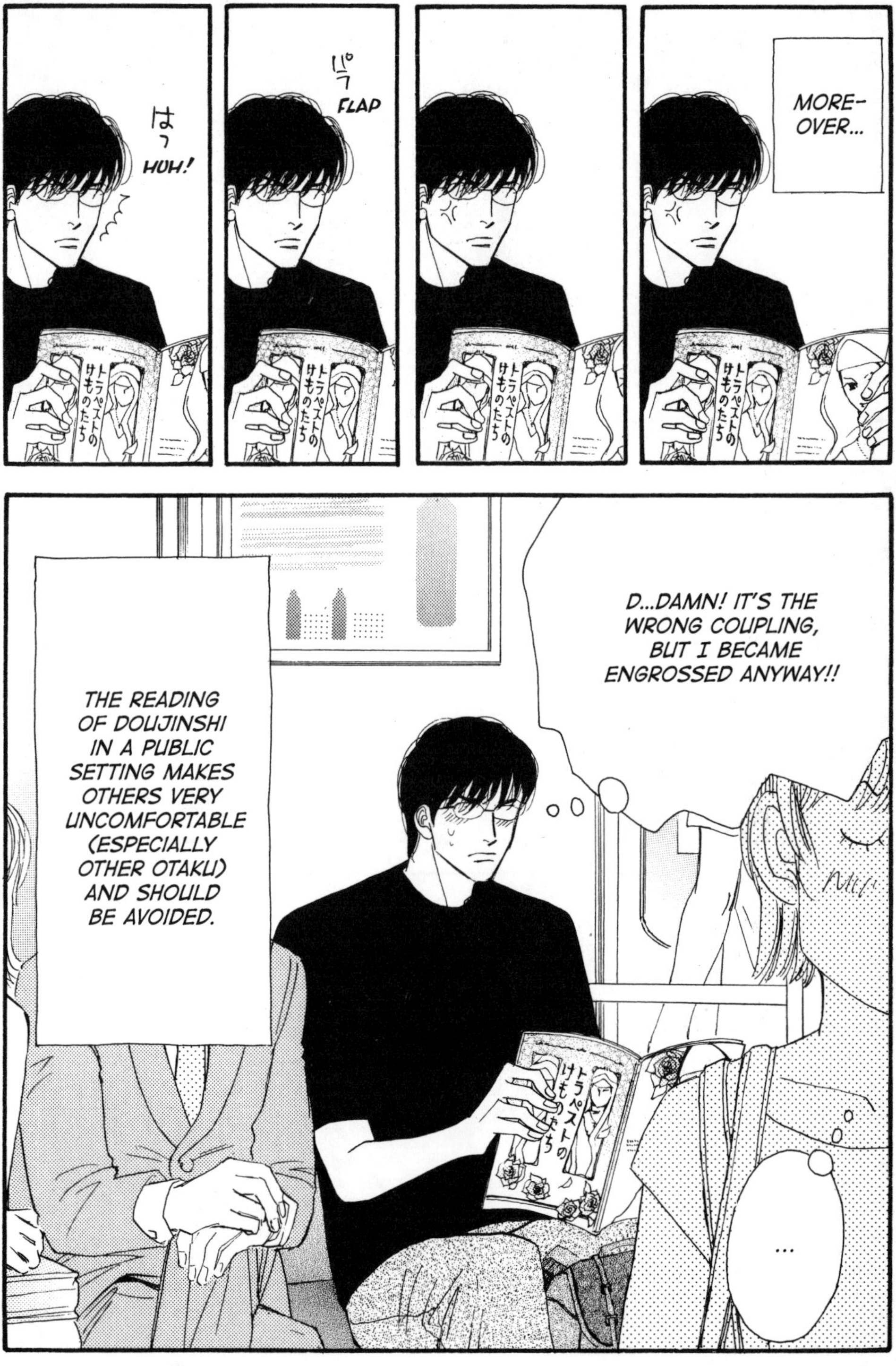
MORE-OVER...
パ
FLAP
はっ
HUH!
D...DAMN! IT'S THE WRONG COUPLING, BUT I BECAME ENGROSSED ANYWAY!!
THE READING OF DOUJINSHI IN A PUBLIC SETTING MAKES OTHERS VERY UNCOMFORTABLE (ESPECIALLY OTHER OTAKU) AND SHOULD BE AVOIDED.
トラペストのけものたち
...

THE Moon AND Sandals Vol. 1

月とサンダル

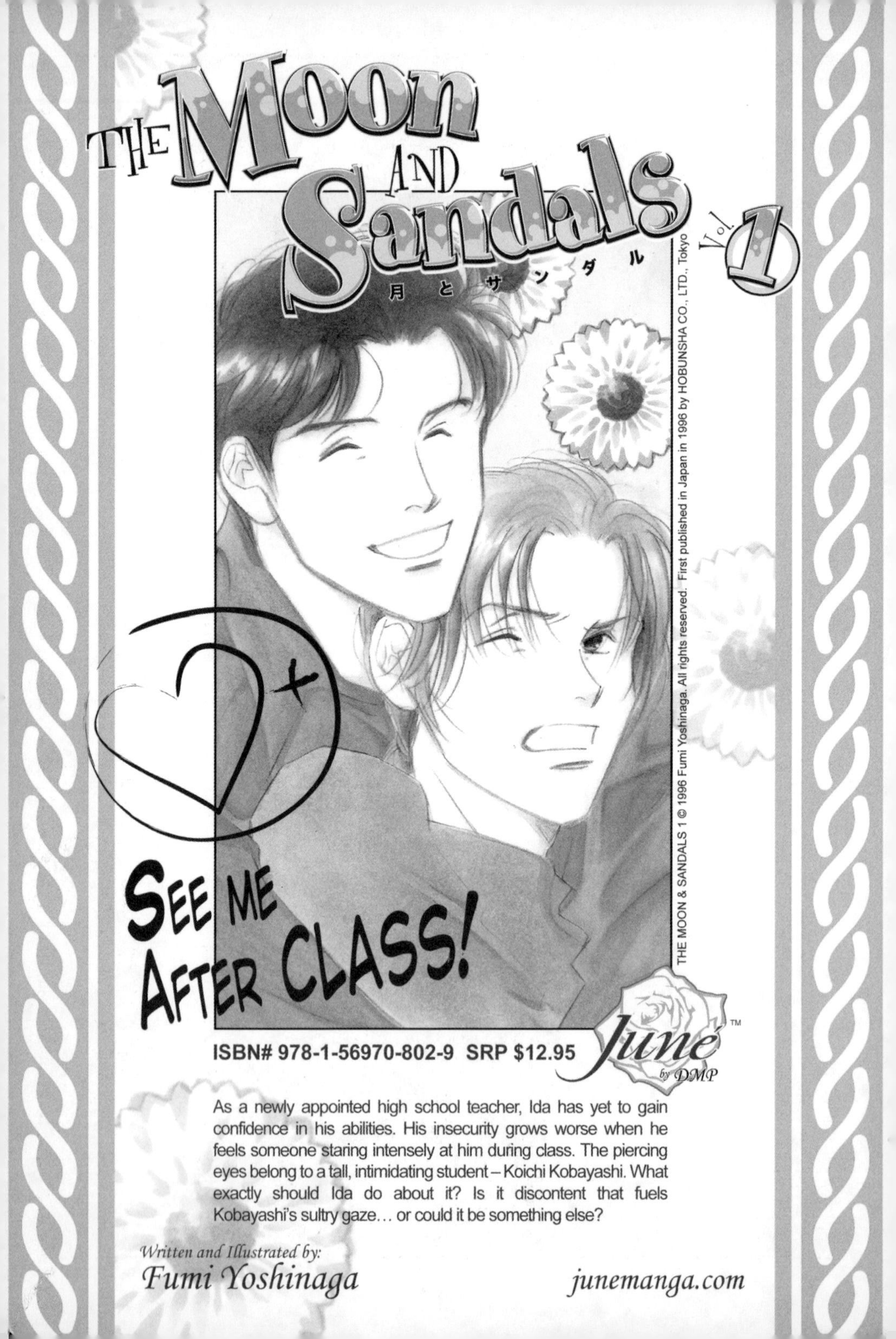
SEE ME AFTER CLASS!

ISBN# 978-1-56970-802-9 SRP $12.95

June™ by DMP

As a newly appointed high school teacher, Ida has yet to gain confidence in his abilities. His insecurity grows worse when he feels someone staring intensely at him during class. The piercing eyes belong to a tall, intimidating student – Koichi Kobayashi. What exactly should Ida do about it? Is it discontent that fuels Kobayashi's sultry gaze… or could it be something else?

Written and Illustrated by:
Fumi Yoshinaga

junemanga.com

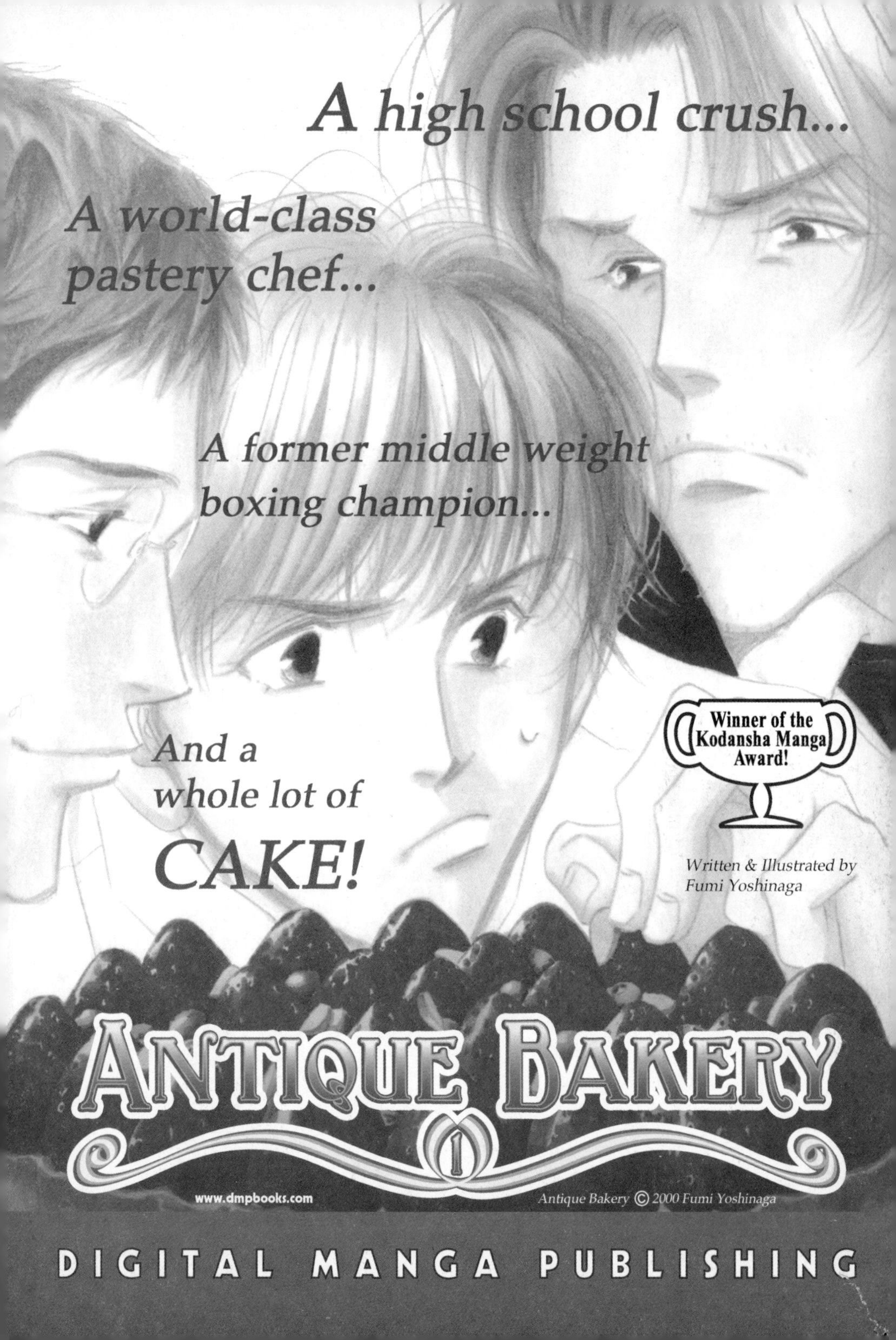

A high school crush...

A world-class
pastery chef...

A former middle weight
boxing champion...

And a
whole lot of
CAKE!

Winner of the
Kodansha Manga
Award!

Written & Illustrated by
Fumi Yoshinaga

ANTIQUE BAKERY
1

www.dmpbooks.com

Antique Bakery © 2000 Fumi Yoshinaga

DIGITAL MANGA PUBLISHING

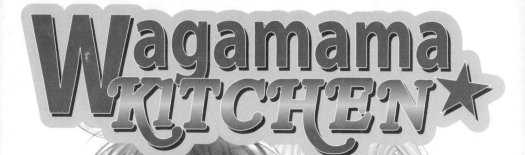

Wagamama KITCHEN ★

By Kaori Monchi

"Something's cooking in this kitchen!"

It takes the right ingredients...
to follow the recipe for wayward love.

ISBN# 978-1-56970-871-2 $12.95

WAGAMAMA KITCHEN © Kaori Monchi 2005.
Originally published in Japan in 2005 by BIBLOS Co., Ltd.

June™

junemanga.com

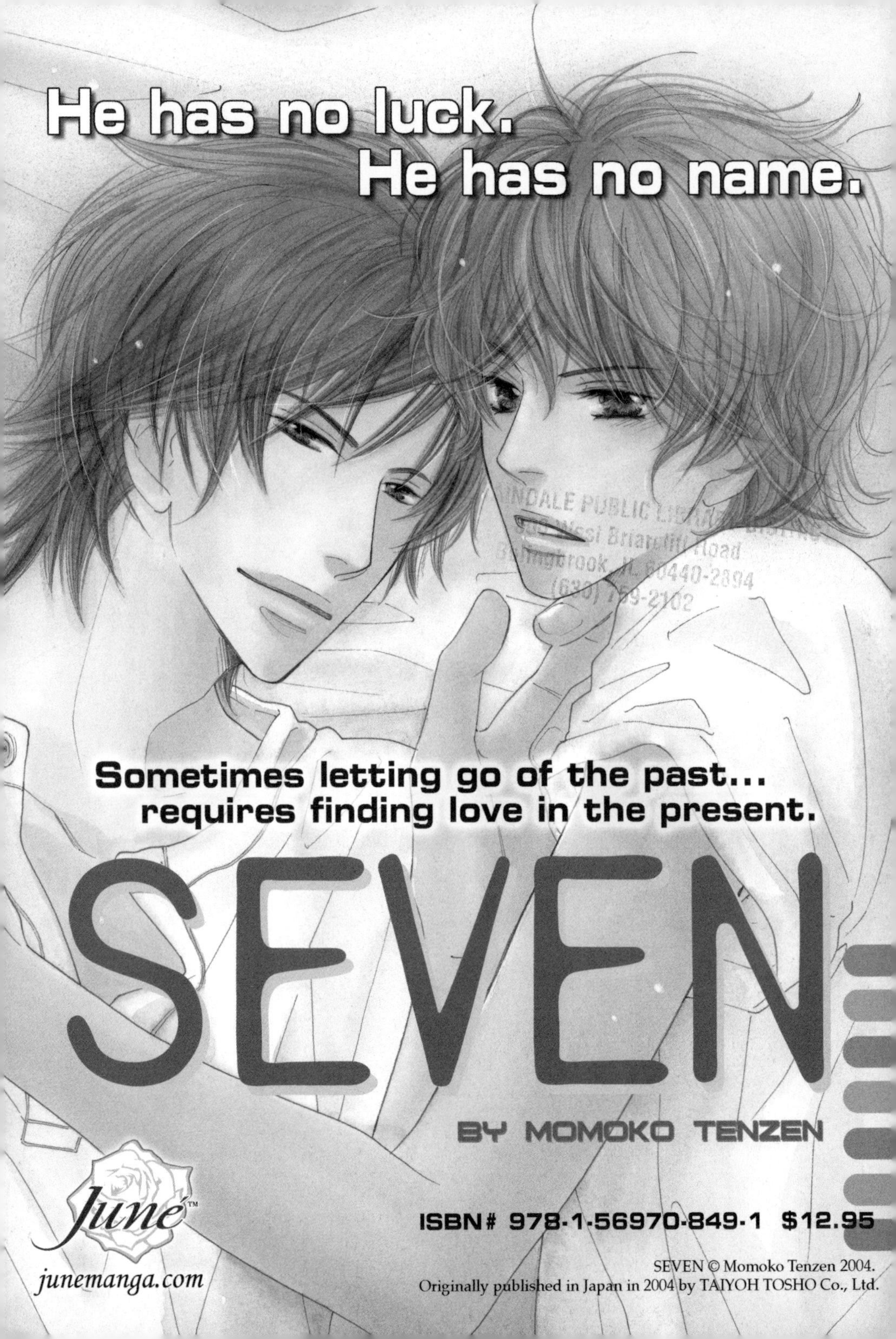
He has no luck.
He has no name.
Sometimes letting go of the past...
...requires finding love in the present.
SEVEN
BY MOMOKO TENZEN
June™
junemanga.com
ISBN# 978-1-56970-849-1 $12.95
SEVEN © Momoko Tenzen 2004.
Originally published in Japan in 2004 by TAIYOH TOSHO Co., Ltd.

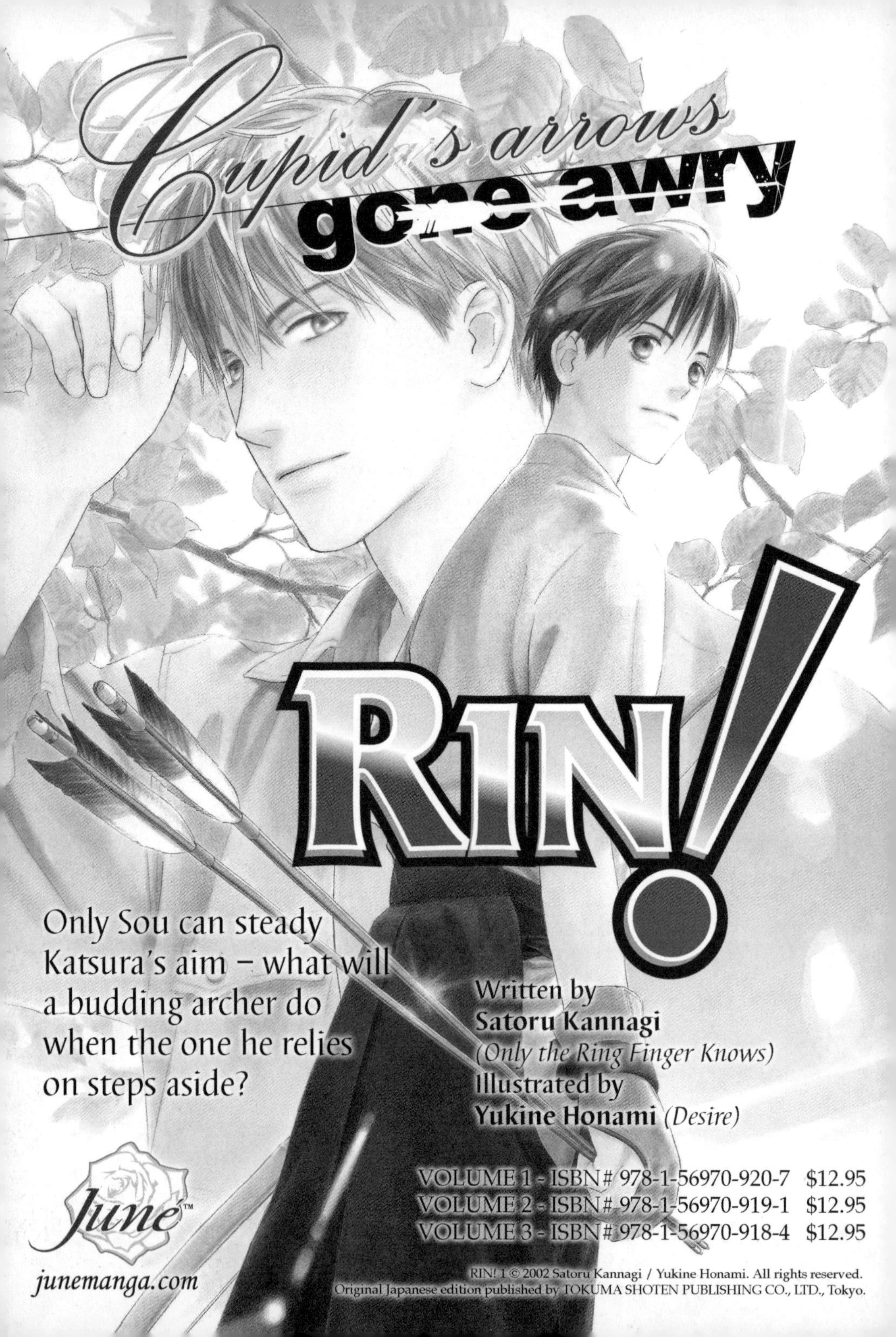

Cupid's arrows
gone awry

RIN!

Only Sou can steady
Katsura's aim – what will
a budding archer do
when the one he relies
on steps aside?

Written by
Satoru Kannagi
(*Only the Ring Finger Knows*)
Illustrated by
Yukine Honami (*Desire*)

VOLUME 1 - ISBN # 978-1-56970-920-7 $12.95
VOLUME 2 - ISBN # 978-1-56970-919-1 $12.95
VOLUME 3 - ISBN # 978-1-56970-918-4 $12.95

june™

junemanga.com

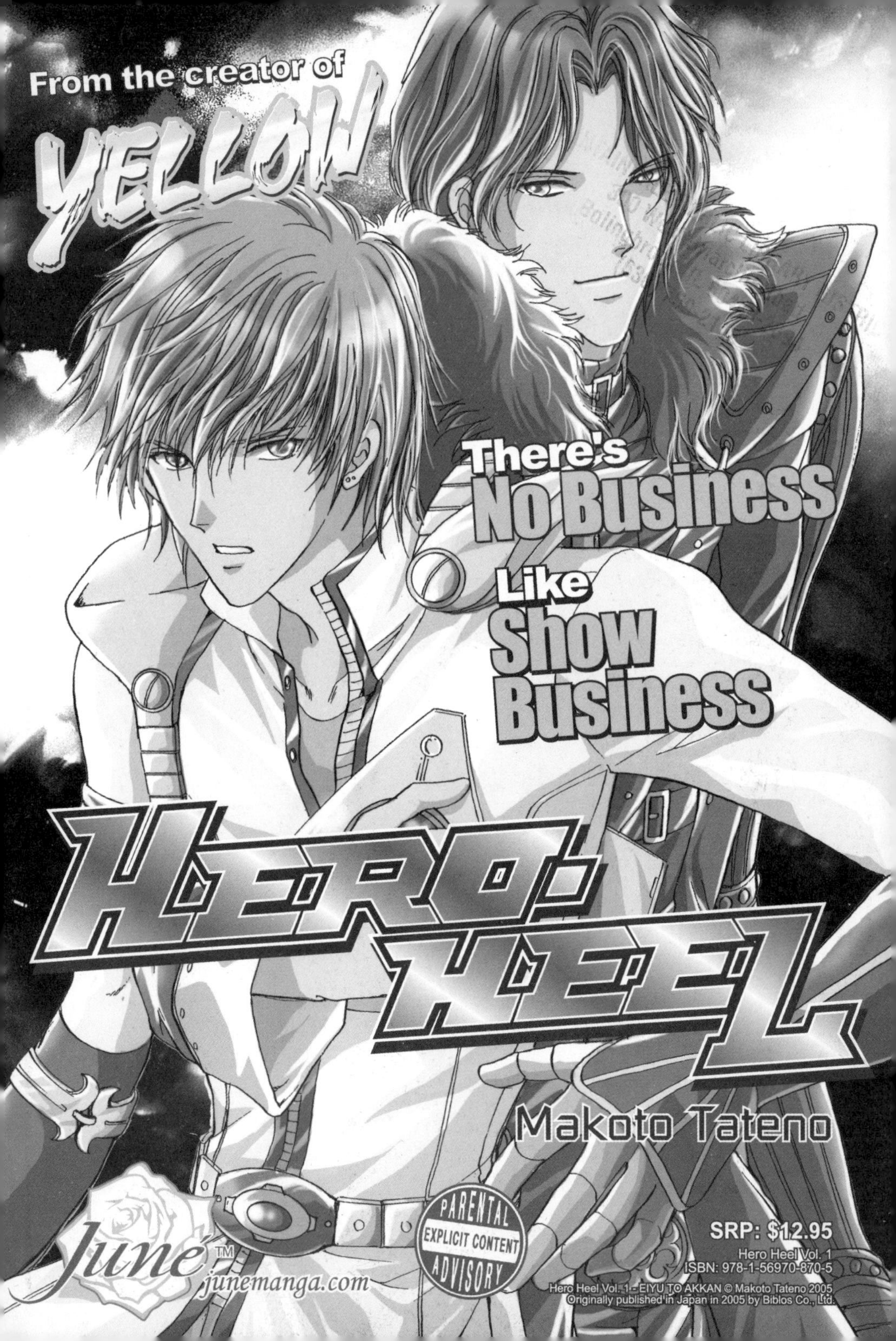
From the creator of
YELLOW
There's
No Business
Like
Show
Business
HERO HEEL
Makoto Tateno
PARENTAL
EXPLICIT CONTENT
ADVISORY
SRP: $12.95
Hero Heel Vol. 1
ISBN: 978-1-56970-870-5
Hero Heel Vol. 1 - EIYU TO AKKAN © Makoto Tateno 2005
Originally published in Japan in 2005 by Biblos Co., Ltd.
June™
junemanga.com

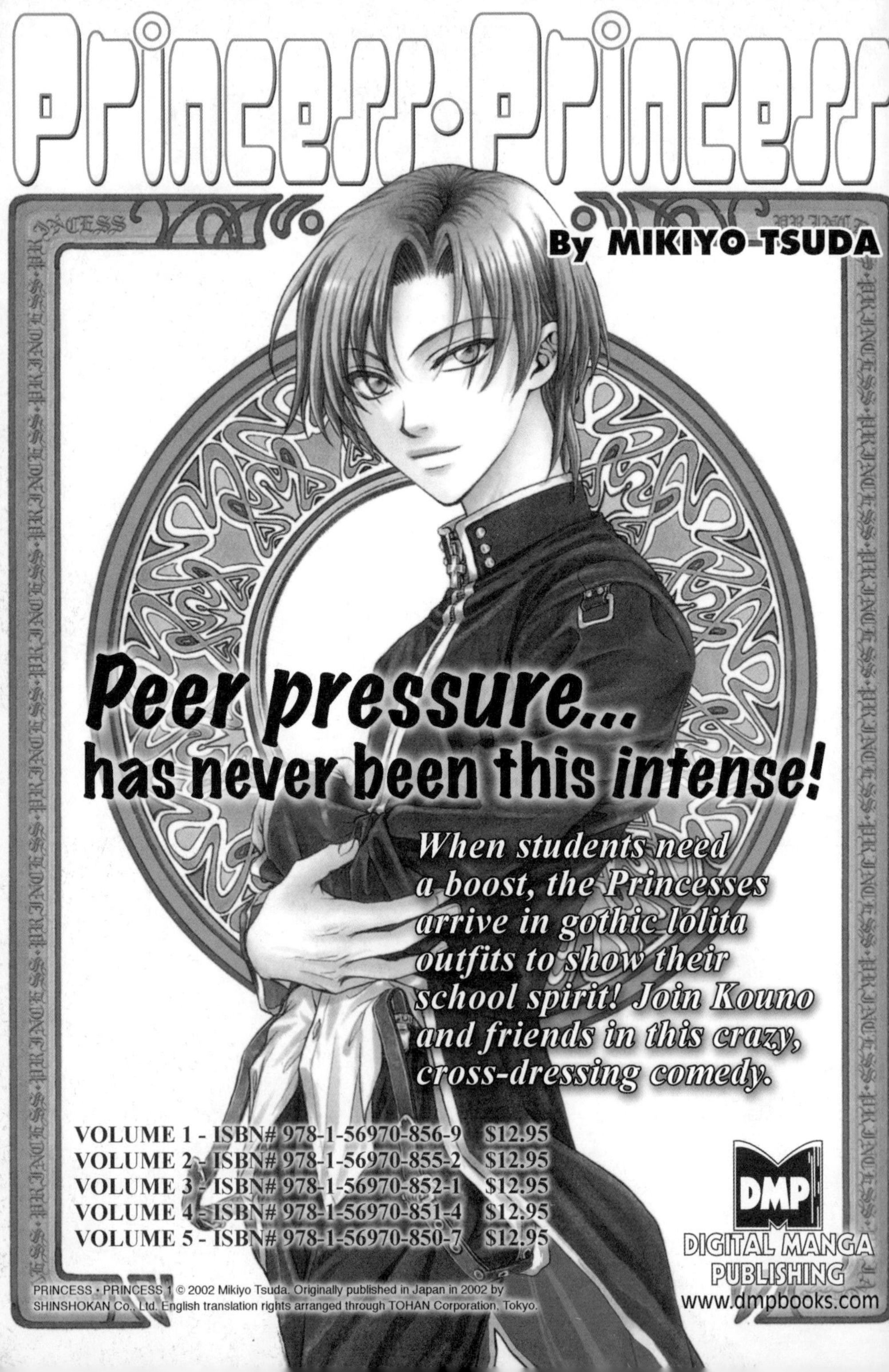
Princess·Princess
By MIKIYO TSUDA
Peer pressure... has never been this intense!
When students need a boost, the Princesses arrive in gothic lolita outfits to show their school spirit! Join Kouno and friends in this crazy, cross-dressing comedy.
VOLUME 1 - ISBN# 978-1-56970-856-9 $12.95
VOLUME 2 - ISBN# 978-1-56970-855-2 $12.95
VOLUME 3 - ISBN# 978-1-56970-852-1 $12.95
VOLUME 4 - ISBN# 978-1-56970-851-4 $12.95
VOLUME 5 - ISBN# 978-1-56970-850-7 $12.95
DMP
DIGITAL MANGA PUBLISHING
www.dmpbooks.com
PRINCESS • PRINCESS 1 © 2002 Mikiyo Tsuda. Originally published in Japan in 2002 by SHINSHOKAN Co., Ltd. English translation rights arranged through TOHAN Corporation, Tokyo.

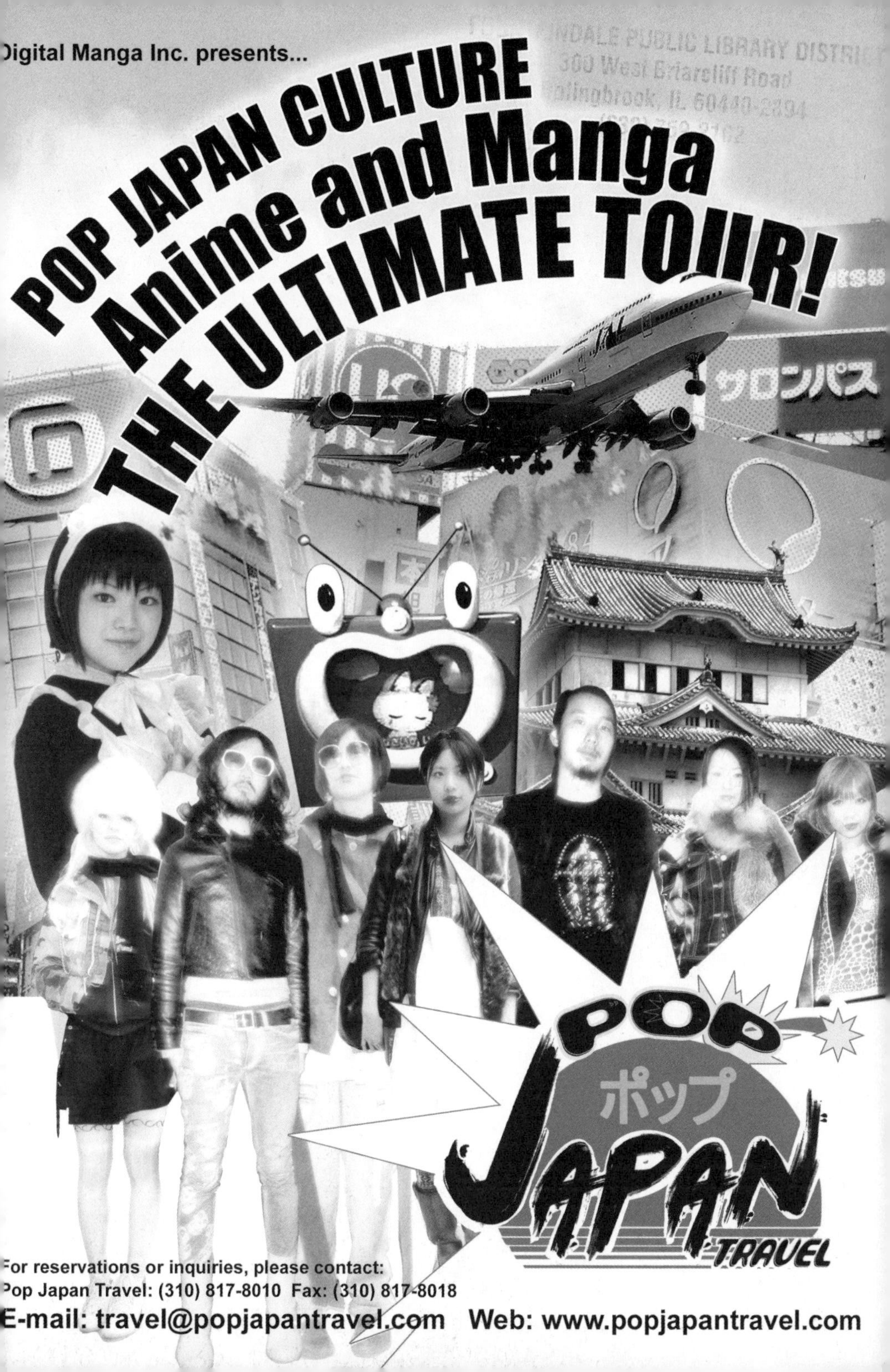
Digital Manga Inc. presents...
POP JAPAN CULTURE
Anime and Manga
THE ULTIMATE TOUR!
サロンパス
POP
ポップ
JAPAN
TRAVEL
For reservations or inquiries, please contact:
Pop Japan Travel: (310) 817-8010 Fax: (310) 817-8018
E-mail: travel@popjapantravel.com Web: www.popjapantravel.com

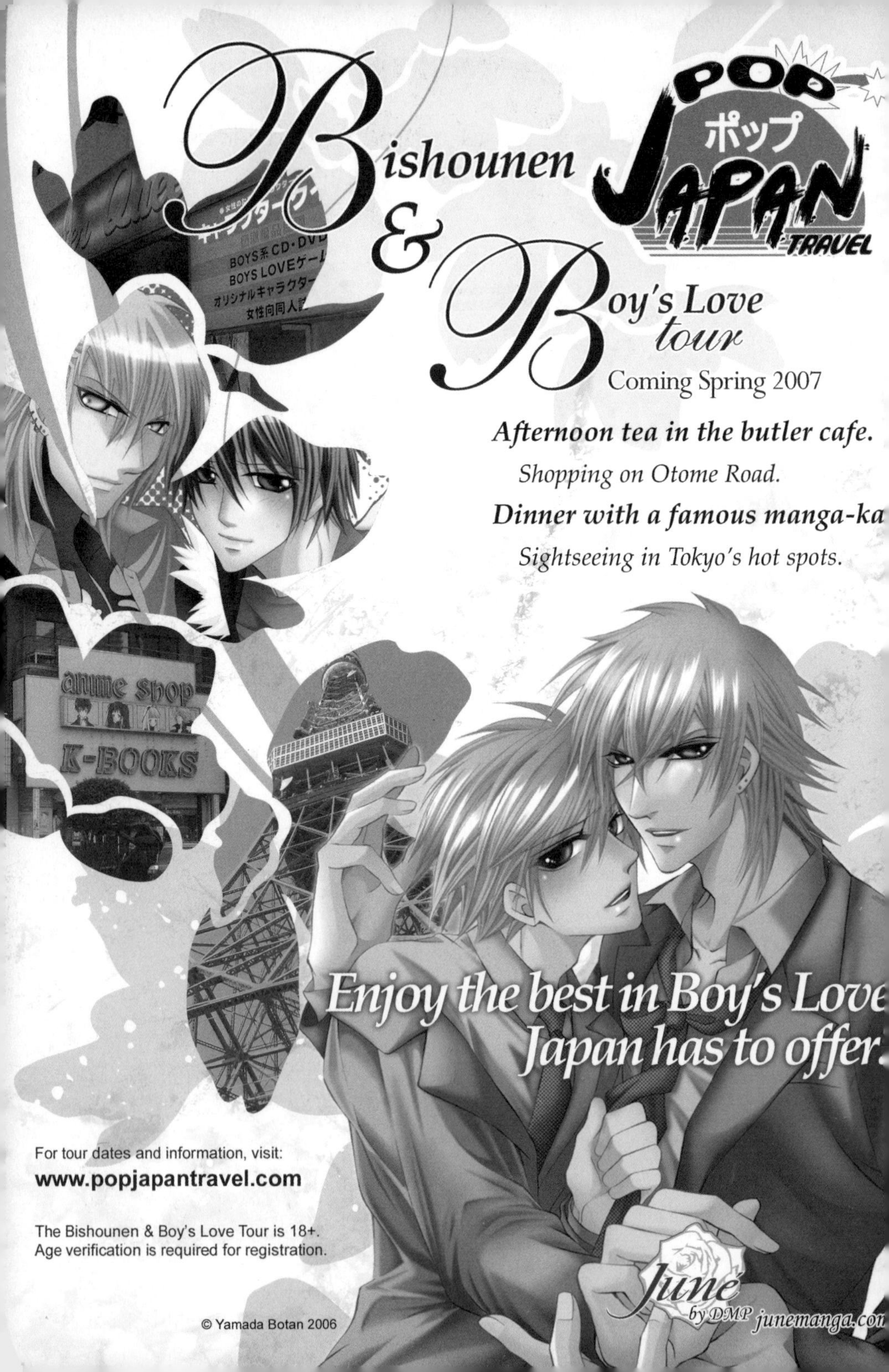
Bishounen
&
Boy's Love
tour
POP ポップ JAPAN TRAVEL
Coming Spring 2007
Afternoon tea in the butler cafe.
Shopping on Otome Road.
Dinner with a famous manga-ka
Sightseeing in Tokyo's hot spots.
anime shop
K-BOOKS
Enjoy the best in Boy's Love
Japan has to offer.
For tour dates and information, visit:
www.popjapantravel.com
The Bishounen & Boy's Love Tour is 18+.
Age verification is required for registration.
© Yamada Botan 2006
June by DMP junemanga.com

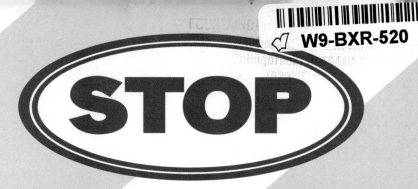

STOP

This is the back of the book! Start from the other side.

NATIVE MANGA readers read manga from *right to left*.

1
2
1
3
2
3
5
4
4
6
5
5
8
7
6

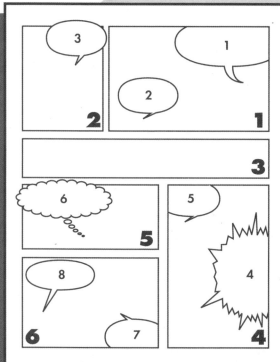

*If you run into our **Native Manga** logo on any of our books... you'll know that this manga is published in it's true original native Japanese right to left reading format, as it was intended. Turn to the other side of the book and start reading from right to left, top to bottom.*

Follow the diagram to see how its done.
Surf's Up!

NATIVE MANGA
READ RIGHT TO LEFT

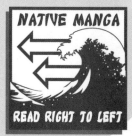